S0-AVB-704

YOUR PERSONAL HOROSCOPE 2014

JOSEPH
POLANSKY

YOUR PERSONAL HOROSCOPE 2014

Month-by-month forecast for every sign

The only one-volume horoscope you'll ever need

HARPER
element

HarperElement
An Imprint of HarperCollins*Publishers*
77–85 Fulham Palace Road,
Hammersmith, London W6 8JB

www.harpercollins.co.uk

and *HarperElement* are trademarks of
HarperCollins*Publishers* Ltd

Published by HarperElement 2013

1 3 5 7 9 10 8 6 4 2

© Star ★ Data, Inc. 2013

Star ★ Data assert the moral right to
be identified as the authors of this work

A catalogue record for this book is
available from the British Library

ISBN 978-0-00-747957-3

Printed and bound in Great Britain by
Clays Ltd, St Ives plc

MIX
Paper from
responsible sources
FSC˚ C007454

FSC™ is a non-profit international organisation established to promote
the responsible management of the world's forests. Products carrying the
FSC label are independently certified to assure consumers that they come
from forests that are managed to meet the social, economic and
ecological needs of present and future generations,
and other controlled sources.

Find out more about HarperCollins and the environment at
www.harpercollins.co.uk/green

The author is grateful to the people of STAR ★ DATA, who truly fathered this book and without whom it could not have been written.

Contents

Introduction

Welcome to the fascinating and intricate world of astrology!

For thousands of years the movements of the planets and other heavenly bodies have intrigued the best minds of every generation. Life holds no greater challenge or joy than this: knowledge of ourselves and the universe we live in. Astrology is one of the keys to this knowledge.

Your Personal Horoscope 2014 gives you the fruits of astrological wisdom. In addition to general guidance on your character and the basic trends of your life, it shows you how to take advantage of planetary influences so you can make the most of the year ahead.

The section on each sign includes a Personality Profile, a look at general trends for 2014, and in-depth month-by-month forecasts. The Glossary (page 5) explains some of the astrological terms you may be unfamiliar with.

One of the many helpful features of this book is the 'Best' and 'Most Stressful' days listed at the beginning of each monthly forecast. Read these sections to learn which days in each month will be good overall, good for money, and good for love. Mark them on your calendar – these will be your best days. Similarly, make a note of the days that will be most stressful for you. It is best to avoid booking important meetings or taking major decisions on these days, as well as on those days when important planets in your horoscope are retrograde (moving backwards through the zodiac).

The Major Trends section for your sign lists those days when your vitality is strong or weak, or when relationships with your co-workers or loved ones may need a bit more effort on your part. If you are going through a difficult time, take a look at the colour, metal, gem and scent listed in the 'At a Glance' section of your Personality Profile. Wearing a piece of jewellery that contains your metal and/or gem will strengthen your vitality, just as wearing clothes or decorating your room or office in the colour ruled by your sign, drinking teas made from the herbs ruled by your sign or wearing the scents associated with your sign will sustain you.

Another important virtue of this book is that it will help you to know not only yourself but those around you: your friends, co-workers, part-ners and/or children. Reading the Personality Profile and forecasts for their signs will provide you with an insight into their behaviour that you won't get anywhere else. You will know when to be more tolerant of them and when they are liable to be difficult or irritable.

In this edition we have included foot reflexology charts as part of the health section. So many health problems could perhaps be avoided or alleviated if we understood which organs were most vulnerable and what we could do to protect them. Though there are many natural and drug-free ways to strengthen vulnerable organs, these charts show a valid way to proceed. The vulnerable organs for the year ahead are clearly marked in the charts. It's very good to massage the whole foot on a regular basis, as the feet contain reflexes to the entire body. Try to pay special attention to the specific areas marked in the charts. If this is done diligently, health problems can be avoided. And even if they can't be completely avoided, their impact can be softened considerably.

I consider you – the reader – my personal client. By studying your Solar Horoscope I gain an awareness of what is going on in your life – what you are feeling and striving for and the challenges you face. I then do my best to address these concerns. Consider this book the next best thing to having your own personal astrologer!

It is my sincere hope that *Your Personal Horoscope 2014* will enhance the quality of your life, make things easier, illuminate the way forward, banish obscurities and make you more aware of your personal connec-tion to the universe. Understood properly and used wisely, astrology is a great guide to knowing yourself, the people around you and the events in your life – but remember that what you do with these insights – the final result – is up to you.

A Note on the 'New Zodiac'

Recently an article was published that postulated two things: the discovery of a new constellation – Ophiuchus – making a thirteenth constellation in the heavens and thus a thirteenth sign, and the statement that because the Earth has shifted relative to the constellations in the past few thousand years, all the signs have shifted backwards by one sign. This has caused much consternation, and I have received a stream of letters, emails and phone calls from people saying things like: 'I don't want to be a Taurus, I'm happy being a Gemini', 'What's my real sign?' or 'Now that I finally understand myself, I'm not who I think I am!'

All of this is 'much ado about nothing'. The article has some partial truth to it. Yes, in two thousand years the planets have shifted relative to the constellations in the heavens. This is old news. We know this and Hindu astrologers take this into account when casting charts. This shift doesn't affect Western astrologers in North America and Europe. We use what is called a 'tropical' zodiac. This zodiac has nothing to do with the constellations in the heavens. They have the same names, but that's about it. The tropical zodiac is based on the Earth's revolution around the Sun. Imagine the circle that this orbit makes, then divide this circle by twelve and you have our zodiac. The Spring Equinox is always 0 degrees (Aries), and the Autumn Equinox is always 180 degrees (Libra). At one time a few thousand years ago, these tropical signs coincided with the actual constellations; they were pretty much interchangeable, and it didn't matter what zodiac you used. But in the course of thousands of years the planets have shifted relative to these constellations. Here in the West it doesn't affect our practice one iota. You are still the sign you always were.

In North America and Europe there is a clear distinction between an astrological sign and a constellation in the heavens. This issue is more of a problem for Hindu astrologers. Their zodiac is based on the actual constellations – this is called the 'sidereal' zodiac. And Hindu astrologers have been accounting for this shift all the time. They keep close tabs on it. In two thousand years there is a shift of 23 degrees, and they subtract this from the Western calculations. So in their system many a Gemini would be a Taurus and this is true for all the signs. This is nothing new – it is all known and accounted for, so there is no bombshell here.

The so-called thirteenth constellation, Ophiuchus, is also not a problem for the Western astrologer. As we mentioned, our zodiac has nothing to do with the constellations. It could be more of a problem for the Hindus, but my feeling is that it's not a problem for them either. What these astronomers are calling a new constellation was probably considered a part of one of the existing constellations. I don't know this as a fact, but I presume it is so intuitively. I'm sure we will soon be getting articles by Hindu astrologers explaining this.

Glossary of Astrological Terms

Ascendant

We experience day and night because the Earth rotates on its axis once every 24 hours. It is because of this rotation that the Sun, Moon and planets seem to rise and set. The zodiac is a fixed belt (imaginary, but very real in spiritual terms) around the Earth. As the Earth rotates, the different signs of the zodiac seem to the observer to rise on the horizon. During a 24-hour period every sign of the zodiac will pass this horizon point at some time or another. The sign that is at the horizon point at any given time is called the Ascendant, or rising sign. The Ascendant is the sign denoting a person's self-image, body and self-concept – the personal ego, as opposed to the spiritual ego indicated by a person's Sun sign.

Aspects

Aspects are the angular relationships between planets, the way in which one planet stimulates or influences another. If a planet makes a harmonious aspect (connection) to another, it tends to stimulate that planet in a positive and helpful way. If, however, it makes a stressful aspect to another planet, this disrupts that planet's normal influence.

Astrological Qualities

There are three astrological qualities: *cardinal, fixed* and *mutable*. Each of the 12 signs of the zodiac falls into one of these three categories.

Cardinal Signs

Aries, Cancer, Libra and Capricorn

The cardinal quality is the active, initiating principle. Those born
under these four signs are good at starting new projects.

Fixed Signs

Taurus, Leo, Scorpio and Aquarius

Fixed qualities include stability, persistence, endurance and
perfectionism. People born under these four signs are good at
seeing things through.

Mutable Signs

Gemini, Virgo, Sagittarius and Pisces

Mutable qualities are adaptability, changeability and balance. Those
born under these four signs are creative, if not always practical.

Direct Motion

When the planets move forward through the zodiac – as they normally
do – they are said to be going 'direct'.

Grand Square

A Grand Square differs from a normal Square (usually two planets
separated by 90 degrees) in that four or more planets are involved.
When you look at the pattern in a chart you will see a whole and
complete square. This, though stressful, usually denotes a new manifestation in the life. There is much work and balancing involved in the
manifestation.

Grand Trine

A Grand Trine differs from a normal Trine (where two planets are 120 degrees apart) in that three or more planets are involved. When you look at this pattern in a chart, it takes the form of a complete triangle – a Grand Trine. Usually (but not always) it occurs in one of the four elements: Fire, Earth, Air or Water. Thus the particular element in which it occurs will be highlighted. A Grand Trine in Water is not the same as a Grand Trine in Air or Fire, etc. This is a very fortunate and happy aspect, and quite rare.

Houses

There are 12 signs of the zodiac and 12 houses of experience. The 12 signs are personality types and ways in which a given planet expresses itself; the 12 houses show 'where' in your life this expression takes place. Each house has a different area of interest. A house can become potent and important – a House of Power – in different ways: if it contains the Sun, the Moon or the 'ruler' of your chart; if it contains more than one planet; or if the ruler of that house is receiving unusual stimulation from other planets.

1st House
Personal Image and Sensual Delights

2nd House
Money/Finance

3rd House
Communication and Intellectual Interests

4th House
Home and Family

5th House
Children, Fun, Games, Creativity, Speculations and Love Affairs

6th House
Health and Work

7th House
Love, Marriage and Social Activities

8th House
Transformation and Regeneration

9th House
Religion, Foreign Travel, Higher Education and Philosophy

10th House
Career

11th House
Friends, Group Activities and Fondest Wishes

12th House
Spirituality

Karma

Karma is the law of cause and effect which governs all phenomena. We are all where we find ourselves because of karma – because of actions we have performed in the past. The universe is such a balanced instrument that any act immediately sets corrective forces into motion – karma.

Long-term Planets

The planets that take a long time to move through a sign show the long-term trends in a given area of life. They are important for forecasting the prolonged view of things. Because these planets stay in one sign for so long, there are periods in the year when the faster-moving (short-term) planets will join them, further activating and enhancing the importance of a given house.

Jupiter
stays in a sign for about 1 year

Saturn
2½ years

Uranus
7 years

Neptune
14 years

Pluto
15 to 30 years

Lunar

Relating to the Moon. See also 'Phases of the Moon', below.

Natal

Literally means 'birth'. In astrology this term is used to distinguish between planetary positions that occurred at the time of a person's birth (natal) and those that are current (transiting). For example, Natal Sun refers to where the Sun was when you were born; transiting Sun refers to where the Sun's position is currently at any given moment – which usually doesn't coincide with your birth, or Natal, Sun.

Out of Bounds

The planets move through the zodiac at various angles relative to the celestial equator (if you were to draw an imaginary extension of the Earth's equator out into the universe, you would have an illustration of this celestial equator). The Sun – being the most dominant and powerful influence in the Solar system – is the measure astrologers use as a standard. The Sun never goes more than approximately 23 degrees north or south of the celestial equator. At the winter solstice the Sun reaches its maximum southern angle of orbit (declination); at the summer solstice it reaches its maximum northern angle. Any time a planet exceeds this Solar boundary – and occasionally planets do – it is said to be 'out of bounds'. This means that the planet exceeds or trespasses into strange territory – beyond the limits allowed by the Sun, the Ruler of the Solar system. The planet in this condition becomes more emphasized and exceeds its authority, becoming an important influence in the forecast.

Phases of the Moon

After the full Moon, the Moon seems to shrink in size (as perceived from the Earth), gradually growing smaller until it is virtually invisible to the naked eye – at the time of the next new Moon. This is called the waning Moon phase, or the waning Moon.

After the new Moon, the Moon gradually gets bigger in size (as perceived from the Earth) until it reaches its maximum size at the time of the full Moon. This period is called the waxing Moon phase, or waxing Moon.

Retrogrades

The planets move around the Sun at different speeds. Mercury and Venus move much faster than the Earth, while Mars, Jupiter, Saturn, Uranus, Neptune and Pluto move more slowly. Thus there are times when, relative to the Earth, the planets appear to be going backwards. In reality they are always going forward, but relative to our vantage point on Earth they seem to go backwards through the zodiac for a period of time. This is called 'retrograde' motion and tends to weaken the normal influence of a given planet.

Short-term Planets

The fast-moving planets move so quickly through a sign that their effects are generally of a short-term nature. They reflect the immediate, day-to-day trends in a horoscope.

Moon
stays in a sign for only 2½ days

Mercury
20 to 30 days

Sun
30 days

Venus
approximately 1 month

Mars
approximately 2 months

T-square

A T-square differs from a Grand Square (see page 6) in that it is not a complete square. If you look at the pattern in a chart it appears as 'half a complete square', resembling the T-square tools used by architects and designers. If you cut a complete square in half, diagonally, you have a T-square. Many astrologers consider this more stressful than a Grand Square, as it creates tension that is difficult to resolve. T-squares bring learning experiences.

Transits

This term refers to the movements or motions of the planets at any given time. Astrologers use the word 'transit' to make the distinction between a birth, or Natal, planet (see 'Natal', page 9) and the planet's current movement in the heavens. For example, if at your birth Saturn was in the sign of Cancer in your 8th house, but is now moving through your 3rd house, it is said to be 'transiting' your 3rd house. Transits are one of the main tools with which astrologers forecast trends.

YOUR PERSONAL HOROSCOPE 2014

Aries

THE RAM

Birthdays from
21st March to
20th April

Personality Profile

ARIES AT A GLANCE

Element – Fire

Ruling Planet – Mars
  Career Planet – Saturn
  Love Planet – Venus
  Money Planet – Venus
  Planet of Fun, Entertainment, Creativity and Speculations – Sun
  Planet of Health and Work – Mercury
  Planet of Home and Family Life – Moon
  Planet of Spirituality – Neptune
  Planet of Travel, Education, Religion and Philosophy – Jupiter

Colours – carmine, red, scarlet

Colours that promote love, romance and social harmony – green, jade
  green

Colour that promotes earning power – green

Gem – amethyst

Metals – iron, steel

Scent – honeysuckle

Quality – cardinal (= activity)

Quality most needed for balance – caution

Strongest virtues – abundant physical energy, courage, honesty, independence, self-reliance

Deepest need – action

Characteristics to avoid – haste, impetuousness, over-aggression, rashness

Signs of greatest overall compatibility – Leo, Sagittarius

Signs of greatest overall incompatibility – Cancer, Libra, Capricorn

Sign most helpful to career – Capricorn

Sign most helpful for emotional support – Cancer

Sign most helpful financially – Taurus

Sign best for marriage and/or partnerships – Libra

Sign most helpful for creative projects – Leo

Best Sign to have fun with – Leo

Signs most helpful in spiritual matters – Sagittarius, Pisces

Best day of the week – Tuesday

Understanding an Aries

Aries is the activist *par excellence* of the zodiac. The Aries need for action is almost an addiction, and those who do not really understand the Aries personality would probably use this hard word to describe it. In reality 'action' is the essence of the Aries psychology – the more direct, blunt and to-the-point the action, the better. When you think about it, this is the ideal psychological makeup for the warrior, the pioneer, the athlete or the manager.

Aries likes to get things done, and in their passion and zeal often lose sight of the consequences for themselves and others. Yes, they often try to be diplomatic and tactful, but it is hard for them. When they do so they feel that they are being dishonest and phony. It is hard for them even to understand the mindset of the diplomat, the consensus builder, the front office executive. These people are involved in endless meetings, discussions, talks and negotiations – all of which seem a great waste of time when there is so much work to be done, so many real achievements to be gained. An Aries can understand, once it is explained, that talk and negotiations – the social graces – lead ultimately to better, more effective actions. The interesting thing is that an Aries is rarely malicious or spiteful – even when waging war. Aries people fight without hate for their opponents. To them it is all good-natured fun, a grand adventure, a game.

When confronted with a problem many people will say, 'Well, let's think about it, let's analyse the situation.' But not an Aries. An Aries will think, 'Something must be done. Let's get on with it.' Of course neither response is the total answer. Sometimes action is called for, sometimes cool thought. But an Aries tends to err on the side of action.

Action and thought are radically different principles. Physical activity is the use of brute force. Thinking and deliberating require one not to use force – to be still. It is not good for the athlete to be deliberating the next move; this will only slow down his or her reaction time. The athlete must act instinctively and instantly. This is how Aries people tend to behave in life. They are quick, instinctive decision-makers and their decisions tend to be translated into action almost immediately. When their intuition is sharp and well tuned, their actions are powerful and successful. When their intuition is off, their actions can be disastrous.

Do not think this will scare an Aries. Just as a good warrior knows that in the course of combat he or she might acquire a few wounds, so too does an Aries realize – somewhere deep down – that in the course of being true to yourself you might get embroiled in a disaster or two. It is all part of the game. An Aries feels strong enough to weather any storm.

There are many Aries people who are intellectual. They make powerful and creative thinkers. But even in this realm they tend to be pioneers – outspoken and blunt. These types of Aries tend to elevate (or sublimate) their desire for physical combat in favour of intellectual, mental combat. And they are indeed powerful.

In general, Aries people have a faith in themselves that others could learn from. This basic, rock-solid faith carries them through the most tumultuous situations of life. Their courage and self-confidence make them natural leaders. Their leadership is more by way of example than by actually controlling others.

Finance

Aries people often excel as builders or estate agents. Money in and of itself is not as important as are other things – action, adventure, sport, etc. They are motivated by the need to support and be well-thought-of by their partners. Money as a way of attaining pleasure is another important motivation. Aries function best in their own businesses or as managers of their own departments within a large business or corporation. The fewer orders they have to take from higher up, the better. They also function better out in the field rather than behind a desk.

Aries people are hard workers with a lot of endurance; they can earn large sums of money due to the strength of their sheer physical energy.

Venus is their money planet, which means that Aries need to develop more of the social graces in order to realize their full earning potential. Just getting the job done – which is what an Aries excels at – is not enough to create financial success. The co-operation of others needs to be attained. Customers, clients and co-workers need to be made to feel comfortable; many people need to be treated properly in order for success to happen. When Aries people develop these abilities – or hire someone to do this for them – their financial potential is unlimited.

Career and Public Image

One would think that a pioneering type would want to break with the social and political conventions of society. But this is not so with the Aries-born. They are pioneers within conventional limits, in the sense that they like to start their own businesses within an established industry.

Capricorn is on the 10th house (career) cusp of Aries' Solar horoscope. Saturn is the planet that rules their life's work and professional aspirations. This tells us some interesting things about the Aries character. First off, it shows that, in order for Aries people to reach their full career potential, they need to develop some qualities that are a bit alien to their basic nature: they need to become better administrators and organizers; they need to be able to handle details better and to take a long-range view of their projects and their careers in general. No one can beat an Aries when it comes to achieving short-range objectives, but a career is long term, built over time. You cannot take a 'quickie' approach to it.

Some Aries people find it difficult to stick with a project until the end. Since they get bored quickly and are in constant pursuit of new adventures, they prefer to pass an old project or task on to somebody else in order to start something new. Those Aries who learn how to put off the search for something new until the old is completed will achieve great success in their careers and professional lives.

In general, Aries people like society to judge them on their own merits, on their real and actual achievements. A reputation acquired by 'hype' feels false to them.

Love and Relationships

In marriage and partnerships Aries like those who are more passive, gentle, tactful and diplomatic – people who have the social grace and skills they sometimes lack. Our partners always represent a hidden part of ourselves – a self that we cannot express personally.

An Aries tends to go after what he or she likes aggressively. The tendency is to jump into relationships and marriages. This is especially true if Venus is in Aries as well as the Sun. If an Aries likes you, he or she will have a hard time taking no for an answer; many attempts will be made to sweep you off your feet.

Though Aries can be exasperating in relationships – especially if they are not understood by their partners – they are never consciously or wilfully cruel or malicious. It is just that they are so independent and sure of themselves that they find it almost impossible to see somebody else's viewpoint or position. This is why an Aries needs as a partner someone with lots of social graces.

On the plus side, an Aries is honest, someone you can lean on, someone with whom you will always know where you stand. What he or she lacks in diplomacy is made up for in integrity.

Home and Domestic Life

An Aries is of course the ruler at home – the Boss. The male will tend to delegate domestic matters to the female. The female Aries will want to rule the roost. Both tend to be handy round the house. Both like large families and both believe in the sanctity and importance of the family. An Aries is a good family person, although he or she does not especially like being at home a lot, preferring instead to be roaming about.

Considering that they are by nature so combative and wilful, Aries people can be surprisingly soft, gentle and even vulnerable with their children and partners. The sign of Cancer, ruled by the Moon, is on the cusp of their solar 4th house (home and family). When the Moon is well aspected – under favourable influences – in the birth chart, an Aries will be tender towards the family and want a family life that is nurturing and supportive. Aries likes to come home after a hard day on the battlefield of life to the understanding arms of their partner and the unconditional love and support of their family. An Aries feels that there is enough 'war' out in the world – and he or she enjoys participating in that. But when Aries comes home, comfort and nurturing are what's needed.

Horoscope for 2014

Major Trends

Life has been exciting – to say the least – since 2011 when Uranus entered your sign. Never a dull moment. It's been all about change, change, change and then more change after that. Life seemed hectic and frenetic. The unexpected always happened. On the surface this seemed like a 'craziness', but underneath there was a deep spiritual agenda happening. You were (and are) being liberated, released from all kinds of attachments and bondages. You wake up one morning and discover that there are no longer any obstructions to following the path of your dreams. These obstructions have been blasted away – sometimes in dramatic fashion – and the path is clear. These trends are continuing in 2014. In previous years it was the 'early' Aries, those born early on in the sign, who felt this the most, but now even those of you born later in the sign will feel it. This is a time to embrace change, to make it your friend, to be calm in the midst of it. Beyond the drama there is an open road to your dreams. You are in a cycle where it is important to express your personal freedom.

Neptune, the most spiritual of all the planets, moved into Pisces, your 12th house of spirituality, in February 2012. This initiated a great and powerful spiritual influence generally, but especially upon you, Aries. You are becoming more spiritual. Your spiritual understanding is increasing by leaps and bounds. And much of the change going on in your life has to do with the spiritual changes happening deep within you – unseen and unnoticed by the world. This transit will be in effect for another 12 or so years. There's more on this later.

Pluto has been in Capricorn, your 10th house of career, for many years now and will be there for many more years. A cosmic detox is going on in your career – both in your actual career and in your attitudes towards it. Many of you are rethinking your career path and perhaps even changing it. Even if you do stick with the present career, it will be with a whole new attitude. Again, there's more on this later.

The year ahead looks prosperous and basically happy – the latter part of the year, from July 16 onwards, more than the early part of the year. Benevolent Jupiter will move into Leo on July 16th and start making fabulous aspects to your Sun. This brings prosperity, good fortune in speculations, enhanced creativity and just more 'joy of life'. Aries of childbearing age were more fertile last year and the trend continues in 2014.

Your most important areas of interest this year will be the body, the image and personal pleasure; home and family (until July 16); fun, children and creativity (from July 16 onwards); love, romance and social activities (until July 26); sex, personal transformation and reinvention, occult studies, reincarnation and life after death (until December 24); career; and spirituality.

Your paths of greatest fulfilment in the year ahead will be home and family (until July 16); children, fun and creativity (from July 16 onwards); sex, personal transformation and reinvention, occult studies, reincarnation and life after death (until February 19); and love, romance and social activities (from February 19 onwards).

Health

(Please note that this is an astrological perspective on health and not a medical one. In days of yore there was no difference, both of these perspectives were identical. But in these times there could be quite a difference. For a medical perspective, please consult your doctor or health practitioner.)

The years 2011 and 2012 were very challenging healthwise. If you got through those years, you'll get through the year ahead with flying colours. Since 2011 we note a steady, gradual improvement in health and energy. Though challenging, 2012 was better than 2011; 2013 was better than 2012; and 2014 will be better than 2013.

Though health is improving it still needs watching for the first half of the year, until July 16. Three long-term planets will be in stressful aspect with you. On July 16 Jupiter will move from a stressful aspect to a harmonious one, and on July 26 Mars will move out of his stressful aspect. You should feel a big positive difference in your overall vitality from July 16 onwards.

With your 6th house of health basically empty for most of the year (only the short-term planets will move through there) the danger is that you won't pay enough attention here. And you should. You will have to force yourself to pay attention to your health – to follow good health regimes – even though you don't feel like it.

Uranus has been in your sign since 2011. This often indicates experimentation with the physical body – a tendency to test its limits. Basically this is a good urge. Our bodies are capable of much more than we think and we only learn about this through testing it. But these experiments should be done in mindful and conscious ways, otherwise there could be a tendency to indulge in daredevil kinds of stunts and this can lead to injury. Testing is best done through regimes such as yoga or martial arts, which are basically disciplined and safe ways.

The most important thing for the first half of the year is to maintain high energy levels. When energy is high – when the auric field is strong – the body resists disease. It is basically immune to microbes and destructive kinds of bacteria. But let the auric field weaken for whatever reason and the body becomes more vulnerable to these sorts of things. The auric field is the spiritual equivalent of the physical immune system. Weakness in the auric field, in overall energy, has other consequences

Reflexology

Try to massage the whole foot on a regular basis, but pay extra attention to the points highlighted on the chart. When you massage, be aware of 'sore spots', as these need special attention. It's also a good idea to massage the ankles and the top of the feet.

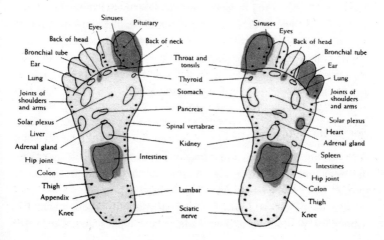

too. The vision, the hearing, the reflexes become a tad slower than normal. They are not up to standard and this can lead to accidents. So, rest when tired. Don't burn the candle at both ends. Work rhythmically and alternate activities. Wear the colours, gems and aromas of your sign (see the Personality Profile at the beginning of this sign). Have regular massages or reflexology treatments. This will enhance your energy in subtle ways. It might also be advisable to take weekends (or longer holidays) at a health spa – depending on your finances.

Health can also be enhanced through regular scalp and facial massage. The head and face is one of your vulnerable areas. When you massage the head and face you not only strengthen those areas but the whole body as well. There are reflexes there that go to the whole body. Also enhance the health by paying more attention to the lungs, arms, shoulders and small intestine. Arms and shoulders should be regularly massaged. Tension tends to collect in the shoulders and needs to be released. The heart is also more vulnerable this year. The reflexes to the heart are shown in the chart. Avoid worry and anxiety – the main spiritual root causes of heart problems.

Mercury, your health planet, is fast moving. During the course of the year he will move through all the signs and houses of your Horoscope, as our regular readers know. Thus there are many short-term trends in health that are best dealt with later in the monthly reports.

Mercury goes retrograde three times this year – from February 6 to February 28; June 7 to July 2; and from October 4 to October 25. These are not times to make drastic changes to your health regime or to make important health decisions. These are times for study and review.

Favourable numbers for health and healing are 1, 3, 6, 8 and 9. If you are exercising or making affirmations do them in sets of 1, 3, 6, 8 and 9 – you will get more out of your exercises.

Home and Family

Your 4th house of home and family is a house of power this year, so there is a great focus here now. With Jupiter in your 4th house since June 26 2013 it is a happy area of life.

Many of you moved in the past year. If you didn't then, it can still happen this year. As our regular readers know, Jupiter moving through the 4th house does not always indicate a 'literal' move but an 'as if' move. Sometimes people buy additional homes or properties. Sometimes they buy expensive items for the home, or renovate or enlarge the existing home. The effect is 'as if' a move has occurred. The home is enlarged and more comfortable than it was before.

Since Jupiter is the ruler of your 9th house of travel, many of you are moving or thinking of moving to foreign countries or faraway places in your own country. Or, as we mentioned, are acquiring properties in these kinds of places.

The family circle gets enlarged under this kind of aspect. Generally this happens through birth or marriage, but it often also happens through meeting people who are 'like family' – who are emotionally supportive. They play the role of 'family' in your life. In many cases the 'like' family can be more supportive and helpful than the actual biological family.

As we mentioned earlier, this aspect indicates heightened fertility for those Aries who are of childbearing age. This will be the case all year – even when Jupiter leaves the 4th house and enters the 5th on July 16. The focus then will shift from family as a whole to a focus on children.

Jupiter in the 4th house shows that the family as a whole is prospering and more supportive this year. When people are prosperous and optimistic it is only natural that they will increase their support. They are much more generous this year. If you need a favour from them – especially from a parent figure – this is the year to ask for it.

Children (or children figures in your life) become more prosperous after July 16. I have noticed that it doesn't matter what age they are. Even infants and toddlers prosper under this aspect – they receive expensive kinds of items or a parent or grandparent sets up a fund for them behind the scenes.

Jupiter is the planet of religion and higher education. Thus I can see many of you holding religious services in the home – perhaps classes too. The family as a whole seems more religious. Moreover, many of you will be adding a library to the home or expanding your present one. The home is a place of study as much as a home.

Finance and Career

The year ahead will be prosperous. Things will start slowly, but as the year progresses, and especially in the latter half, prosperity will increase.

Your 2nd house of finance is not a house of power this year, so finances are not a major focus. And perhaps this is the major weakness. You might not be giving them the attention they deserve. You can be too distracted by family, home, personal freedom or the desire for personal pleasure. If finances are troubling you, the solution might be to give the area more attention. Force yourself.

With Uranus in your own sign you are in the mood for new ventures, new start ups. You are an experimenter with almost everything in your life, including finance. You tend to be a risk-taker by nature, and these days even more so. And when you hit the big time, it will be BIG. Failures however – and there will be a few – can also be big. Risk taking – speculations – are much better during the latter half of the year – after July 16 – than before.

Venus is your financial planet. Regular readers assuredly know that Venus is a fast-moving planet. During the year she will move through all the signs and houses of the chart. Thus there will be many short-term financial trends, all depending on where Venus is and the aspects she receives. These are best dealt with in the monthly reports.

With Venus as your financial planet your social skills (and, Aries, you need to develop these more) are a huge factor in earnings. It's not so much your innate ability and merit, though these are important – it's the likeability factor, people skills, the ability to get on with others that are important. When Aries develop these qualities, there's no stopping them. The sky is the limit.

In the Personality Profile (page 15) we discuss the best financial areas for Aries. These should be reviewed this year.

Your spouse, partner or current love is having financial challenges. He or she feels squeezed. Perhaps some new expense or financial burden has been placed on them. They just need to reorganize things, shift things around here and there, and work to get financially healthier. If they do, they will find that they have all the resources they need. They have been making very dramatic financial changes in the past two years and there is more to come. But after this year, their finances should stabilize.

If you are involved with estates or tax issues, be patient. Only time will resolve things. Borrowing – accessing outside money – is more challenging this year. Again patience and persistence will win the day.

Your favourable financial numbers are 2, 3, 7 and 9.

Though money is not that big a deal, career is very important. What I like here is that you have a great single-minded focus, an intense drive to succeed. This tends to success. We get what we focus on. The only problem here is that you might be too career driven – too fanatic about it. This leads to conflict, strife and perhaps to making some dangerous enemies. There is sort of a 'tunnel vision' when it comes to the career and it can make you unaware of whose toes or turf is being stepped on.

Pluto in the career house indicates that there is great change and transformation happening in your company and industry; deep and fundamental change. The rules can be so changed that it is 'as if' you have embarked on a completely different career. Often Pluto brings 'near-death' experiences in the career. But always keep in mind that after death or near-death experiences comes resurrection and renewal. This is a cosmic law.

Bosses, parents and authority figures in your life are having surgery or near-death kinds of experiences too. The company you work for can be having a near-death experience as well.

Love and Social Life

Your 7th house of love, romance and social activities is a house of power until July 26. Thus there is great focus here. Focus tends to bring success.

However, love is complicated this year. You've recently come through some very stressful love years in 2011 and 2012, perhaps even trau-matic years. Many of you divorced. Relationships that survived those years will probably last forever. Although 2013 was a little easier in the love department, it was nothing special.

If you are just coming out of a divorce, you need some quiet time. There is no need to jump into a new relationship too quickly – though perhaps you want to. Uranus in your sign is not especially good for marriage or committed relationships. Uranus craves personal freedom. Too much personal freedom doesn't go well with a committed relationship, which by definition is a 'limitation' of freedom. Those involved romantically with Aries need to understand this. Give them as much space as possible so long as it isn't destructive.

You are very socially active until July 26. You tend to be aggressive and go after what you want. You are creating the social life that you want. You are popular and well liked and you go out of your way for others. This is good. But will this lead to marriage? Unlikely.

Love affairs, though, are very favourable this year – especially after July 16. However, these are more in the nature of entertainment than serious love. My advice is to enjoy them for what they are without projecting too many expectations on to them.

Those working on their first or second marriages are not likely to marry this year. They will date and have fun, but most likely will not marry. Those working on their third marriage, however, will have a serious love opportunity in the latter half of the year. September looks especially good for that.

With Venus, a fast-moving planet, as your love planet there will be many short-term trends in love that are better discussed in the monthly reports.

Parents or parent figures who are unattached have good romantic opportunities this year. It will be a good social year for them. Children of marriageable age have strong love opportunities in September. Those already married are having their marriages tested this year (this has been going on for a few years now). Single siblings (or sibling figures in the life) are not likely to marry this year. Married siblings (or sibling figures) will have their marriages tested late in the year – after December 24. Grandchildren of marriageable age are having a 'status quo' kind of year. Those who are married will tend to stay married; singles will tend to stay single.

Your favourable numbers for love are 3, 7 and 11.

Self-improvement

The planet Neptune is always radiating a refining, elevating, spiritual-izing kind of force. But now that Neptune is in his own sign and house – Pisces and your 12th house – his power is greatly magnified. You are feeling this. Many of the things that appealed to you in the past have lost their appeal. Many of the things that you considered important are not that important any more. A new and more powerful energy is coming into you. If you are already on the spiritual path you are making greater progress now. You are having dramatic spiritual experiences and revelations. Your spiritual faculties – soul faculties – are opening up and becoming stronger. Those of you who are spiritual practitioners are much busier and more in demand than ever before. More and more people are interested in your work.

Those not yet on the spiritual path will most likely enter onto it this year or in future years. Neptune will be in Pisces for the next 11 or so years. The Cosmos has its way of bringing you into the fold. In some cases people have vivid Technicolor dreams that are real but don't make sense to the rational mind. In some cases there is this vague feeling of dissatisfaction that pervades the worldly life. Though the person attains the things or goals that were thought to make them happy, they find that they are not happy. They have a feeling of disil-lusionment. Sometimes a problem child brings them into the fold. They are forced to examine things more deeply, to study things to find answers. Sometimes tragedy does it. It is different for each person.

When Neptune – the ruler of the highest heaven – is active, the things of this world seem tawdry and cheap – pale imitations of what is possible and doable – which is the cause for the inner dissatisfaction that many experience. Let this feeling be seen as a call to deeper and higher knowledge and not as an excuse to overindulge in alcohol or drugs.

Synchronistic experiences will increase these days. Those on the spiritual path will understand them completely, while those not on the path will scratch their heads. You'll think of someone and they call you. You'll feel your phone buzz in your pocket only you don't have your phone in your pocket, but when you get home you'll see that someone messaged you at the exact time that you felt the buzz!

Saturn is still in your 8th house of transformation and regeneration for practically all of the year ahead (until December 24). This shows a need to re-order the sex life and the use of the sexual energies. Better less sex but quality sex than many mediocre experiences.

Month-by-month Forecasts

January

Best Days Overall: 7, 8, 17, 18, 26, 27
Most Stressful Days Overall: 1, 2, 14, 15, 22, 23, 28, 29
Best Days for Love: 1, 2, 9, 10, 19, 20, 22, 23, 28, 29
Best Days for Money: 1, 2, 5, 6, 9, 10, 14, 15, 19, 20, 24, 25, 28, 29
Best Days for Career: 1, 2, 5, 6, 14, 15, 24, 25, 28, 29

January promises to be a hectic, fast paced but successful month. Last month you entered a yearly career peak and it is still underway in the month ahead. You are in the noon time of your year. This is a time to act on your career dreams and goals – to act in a physical kind of way. Plans made during the night time of your year are now ready to be implemented. Eighty per cent of the planets are moving forward this month, which is another indication of a fast paced, active kind of month.

Family is important to you – Jupiter has been in your 4th house of home and family for many months and will be there for many more months – but this is a time when you can (and should) shift your attention to your career and worldly goals. This is the best way to serve your family right now.

The main challenge this month is health. Hyperactivity can be overdone. Yes, act and succeed, but try to schedule more rest periods into your days, and perhaps a massage or two. Your health planet, Mercury, is 'out of bounds' from the 1st to the 8th. This indicates that you are going outside the norm in your health regime and your approach to health. It seems necessary. You need something new. When it comes to health you are 'thinking outside the box'. This is true in your work as well. The demands of the job take you outside your normal boundaries.

This month enhance the health (until the 11th) by giving more attention to the spine, knees, teeth, bones, skin and overall skeletal alignment. Regular back and knee massage will be good, and give the knees
more support when exercising. A visit to the chiropractor or osteopath
is a good idea. After the 11th give more attention to the ankles and
calves. These should be massaged regularly, and support the ankles
more when you exercise.

Job seekers also need to 'go out of bounds' in their search for work,
although they seem successful this month.

Venus, your love planet, is retrograde all month. And though you
are active socially – and seem very popular – love needs time and
thought. Avoid important love decisions one way or the other. The
same holds true in finance. Do more homework and avoid major
purchases or investments right now. Review the financial life and see
where improvements can be made. With Venus retrograde, your
thinking on love and finance might not be realistic right now. Get
more facts.

February

Best Days Overall: 3, 4, 13, 14, 22, 23
Most Stressful Days Overall: 10, 11, 12, 18, 19, 24, 25
Best Days for Love: 5, 6, 7, 16, 17, 18, 19, 24, 25
Best Days for Money: 1, 2, 5, 6, 7, 10, 11, 12, 16, 17, 20, 21, 24,
    25, 28
Best Days for Career: 2, 11, 12, 21, 24, 25, 28

Venus, your love and financial planet, started to move forward on
January 31. This is good news for both love and finance. There is more
mental clarity on these issues and your decisions should be better.

There's more good news. Your health is much improved over last
month. You still need to be watchful, but overall energy is better than
last month. (The improvement began on January 20.) Continue to
enhance the health by giving more attention to the ankles and calves
as we have mentioned. The feet are important from the 1st to the 13th.
Mercury goes retrograde from the 6th to the end of the month, so avoid
making drastic changes to the health regime or diet during this period.

Study things more carefully, and avoid making major health decisions too. Time will show what needs to be done.

Like last month, love and money are high on your agenda. This is another positive. You are focused here, the desire is there, and, this is 90 per cent of the battle. We get what we focus on.

In finance money seems to come from the career – perhaps you have a pay rise or a promotion. You have the financial favour of those in authority in your life, and your good professional reputation aids the bottom line. Good relations with the government seem important. Money can come from government payments or the favour of government officials. Venus, your financial planet, in the sign of Capricorn is also a positive. It shows sound financial judgement and a good practical sense. You are taking a long-term perspective on wealth and seem willing to engage in disciplined savings and investment regimes. If one takes a long-term view, avoiding short cuts, wealth is just inevitable over time. The main problems are impatience and lack of stamina.

This calculating approach is wonderful for finance, but not so wonderful for love. You can appear cold without meaning too. You will need to work harder to project love and warmth to others. You seem more practical in love. You are attracted to people of high status and position – people who can help you careerwise. Some of you might look at love as just another career choice this month. This is temporary, but this is how you feel at the moment.

Your career is still very strong, and 80 per cent of the planets are above the horizon this month. You can advance your career through social means, through attending or hosting the right parties or gatherings. The 'likeability' factor is important in the career. It's not just about actual achievement.

March

Best Days Overall: 3, 4, 12, 13, 22, 23, 30, 31
Most Stressful Days Overall: 10, 11, 17, 18, 24, 25
Best Days for Love: 7, 17, 18, 26, 27
Best Days for Money: 1, 2, 5, 6, 7, 10, 11, 17, 18, 19, 20, 26, 27, 28, 29
Best Days for Career: 1, 2, 10, 11, 19, 20, 24, 25, 28, 29

The Eastern sector of the Horoscope – your favourite sector – has been dominant since the beginning of the year. You have been in a cycle of personal independence. You have the power and the energy to make the changes that you need to make, to create the conditions that you want in your life. And you should. This month (and next month too) you are in a period of maximum independence. Other people are always important, but less so these days. Pursue your personal happiness (so long as it isn't destructive to others) and let the world adapt to you.

Health and energy are much improved this month. If there have been any health problems there should be good news on that front. You can enhance your health even further by giving more attention to the ankles and calves (until the 17th) and to the feet after that date. Spiritual healing methods become powerful from the 17th onwards. You respond well to these things.

Mars, the ruler of your Horoscope, is in retrograde motion the whole month. You have the power to create conditions to suit you but perhaps lack clarity of what you really want. This is a time to attain this clarity.

Venus has been in Capricorn, your 10th house, since the beginning of the year. So, as we mentioned, you have been practical in love, and perhaps a bit hard headed – perhaps a bit cold and calculating. But this is about to change. On March 6 Venus enters Aquarius and changes the energy of your love life. Power and position become less important, while friendship becomes more important. You want to be friends with the beloved as well as lovers. Singles will find love opportunities through groups, group activities and organizations. The online world also seems a source of romantic opportunity. Existing love relationships become more harmonious after the 6th as well.

Venus will activate a previous eclipse point from the 17th to the 19th. This can make your partner or current love more temperamental. More patience is needed. This transit also affects finances. Perhaps there is a short-term disturbance or upheaval. A change needs to be made.

Overall finances are good this month. The online world seems to provide financial opportunity as well as love opportunity. Most likely you are spending on high-tech equipment and software, and the investment is good. Your technological abilities are important in finance. Friends and groups are also helpful in finance.

Mars will activate a past eclipse point from the 11th to the 18th. Avoid risk taking and daredevil-type activities during this period.

April

Best Days Overall: 8, 9, 10, 18, 19, 26, 27
Most Stressful Days Overall: 6, 7, 13, 14, 15, 20, 21
Best Days for Love: 4, 5, 6, 13, 14, 15, 16, 17, 24, 25
Best Days for Money: 1, 2, 4, 5, 6, 7, 16, 17, 24, 25, 29, 30
Best Days for Career: 6, 7, 16, 17, 20, 21, 24, 25

The main headline this month is the two eclipses that are happening. This ensures change and volatility. Generally we are not comfortable with this while they happen, but the end result tends to be good.

The Lunar Eclipse of the 15th occurs in your 7th house of love and marriage and will test your love life and partnerships. This is when the dirty laundry comes out and needs to be dealt with. Your spouse, partner or current love is likely to be more temperamental, and often with good reason; there are dramas happening in their lives. Family members are also more temperamental. Be more patient with them. If there are flaws in your home, now is when you find out and can make any corrections needed.

The Solar Eclipse of the 29th occurs in your money house. This brings financial changes. Since you seem prosperous this month these changes might indicate a need to adjust your thinking in a more positive way. Perhaps you have been too conservative or too pessimistic about things. Speculations, though, should be avoided during this eclipse period. Children and children figures in your life need to be kept out of harm's way. Let them spend more quiet time at home. There are personal dramas happening with them.

You are still independent these days and can have things your way – the problem is that you're not sure what your way really is! Mars is still retrograde.

Venus in Pisces in your 12th house is very nice for love. Venus is in her most 'exalted' position, and the love energy is capable of its highest expression. Your social magnetism is unusually strong, and love is tender and idealistic. Singles can find love opportunities in spiritual-type settings from the 6th onwards – at the yoga retreat, the meditation seminar, the prayer meeting or at spiritual lectures, and at charity events as well. Spiritual compatibility is now an issue in love. Everything else can be right, but if that is not OK there will be problems. You and your beloved need to be on the same page spiritually – sharing similar spiritual ideals and practices. You need a relationship which enables you to grow spiritually (and where you can help your partner in this regard as well). This seems to be happening this month – an important romantic meeting is indicated between the 10th to the 13th.

Finances should also be good this month. The financial intuition is excellent – especially from the 10th to the 13th. Pay attention to your dream life or to messages from psychics, gurus, ministers and other spiritual channels. You will find that it is good to go deeper into the spiritual dimensions of wealth.

Job seekers have excellent opportunities from the 7th onwards.

May

Best Days Overall: 6, 7, 15, 16, 24, 25
Most Stressful Days Overall: 3, 4, 5, 11, 12, 17, 18, 31
Best Days for Love: 6, 11, 12, 13, 14, 24, 25
Best Days for Money: 3, 4, 5, 6, 13, 14, 21, 22, 26, 27, 31
Best Days for Career: 3, 4, 5, 13, 14, 17, 18, 21, 22, 31

The upper half of your Horoscope has been strong all year thus far. In fact it will be strong for the entire year ahead. You will always have at least four planets above the horizon. But last month, on the 7th, the planetary power started to shift from the upper half to the lower half of your Horoscope. On May 3 the lower half becomes stronger than the upper half for the first time this year. Your career is still important, but you can start shifting more attention to your family and to your emotional needs.

Astrology is all about the study of cycles. Things that are right and proper at one stage of a cycle are inappropriate at another stage. It's not so much the nature of an action, but WHEN the action is happening. Dreaming, visualizing and setting goals were not so appropriate – until now. You were in period for overt, physical action. Now inward reflection becomes appropriate.

Love seems very happy this month. On the 3rd Venus crosses your Ascendant and moves into your 1st house. This indicates that love is pursuing you. (Up till now, you have been the instigator.) Though you are still active socially – perhaps more than you need to be – love will find you as you go about your daily affairs. Love also seems more harmonious. Venus (the beloved) and Mars (you) are in 'mutual reception' from the 3rd onwards. Each is a guest in the house of the other. This shows good co-operation between you and the beloved. It shows 'mutual devotion'.

Aries tend to be 'love at first sight' people. This has been especially true this year, and this month the tendency is stronger still. All we can say is 'look before you leap'.

You also seem in harmony with the 'money people' in your life. They are supportive of you and you of them.

Venus moving into your 1st house shows that money is seeking you – money and financial opportunity. There is not much that you need to do. You are spending on yourself, on clothing, personal accessories and on your image. Personal appearance seems unusually important in finance this month so these expenditures seem like a good investment.

Last month, on the 20th, you entered a yearly financial peak and this is continuing during this month as well.

Mars is opposite Uranus for the latter part of the month. Avoid daredevil stunts or risk-taking activities.

June

Best Days Overall: 2, 3, 12, 13, 20, 21, 29, 30
Most Stressful Days Overall: 1, 7, 8, 14, 15, 27, 28
Best Days for Love: 5, 6, 7, 8, 14, 15, 23, 24
Best Days for Money: 1, 5, 6, 10, 11, 14, 15, 18, 19, 22, 23, 24, 27, 28
Best Days for Career: 1, 9, 10, 14, 15, 18, 19, 27, 28

Health has been reasonable the past few months, but on June 21 you need to start paying more attention here. Your energy levels are not up to their usual standard. Things that you have always done with no problem might not be that easy during this period. You should do your best to maintain high energy levels. You can enhance your health by paying more attention to the diet until the 18th, and to the lungs, arms, shoulders and respiratory system after then. Regular shoulder massage is always good for you but especially after the 18th. Emotional harmony is especially important until the 18th, and women should give more attention to the breasts until then too.

Your health planet, Mercury, goes retrograde on the 7th, so avoid making major health decisions or changes then. This is a time for study and review. The health of family members seems a concern until the 18th.

This month and next month, the lower half of your Horoscope will be at its maximum strength for the year. Thus, as we mentioned, give more attention now to the family and to your emotional well-being. The two planets involved with your career – Saturn and Pluto – are both retrograde this month, which is another reason to shift attention away from the career.

Retrograde activity is increased this month – 40 per cent of the planets are moving backwards from the 9th onwards. This is the maximum limit for the year – we never go above 40 per cent this year. The pace of life slows down. Though you like a fast-paced lifestyle, this is perhaps good. You need to slow down – especially after the 21st.

On May 29, Venus moved into your money house, which is a good signal for wealth. She will be there until the 23rd. Venus in Taurus – in her own sign and house – is stronger than usual. This indicates that your earning power is strong, and your financial judgement is sound and practical. This tends to prosperity. Venus will activate an eclipse point (the Solar Eclipse of April 29) on the 5th and 6th. This brings some financial disturbance and change – perhaps an unexpected expense. But this is short lived. Make the changes that need to be made. You know what they are. When the dust settles, prosperity resumes. Be more patient with the beloved on the 5th and 6th as well. He or she needs to stay out of harm's way and to avoid risky kinds of activities.

Love is very practical this month, especially until the 23rd. Wealth is a turn on and singles are attracted to 'money people' – the good provider – the one who can help attain financial goals. Material gifts are alluring. This is how you show love and this is how you feel loved. When Venus moves into Gemini on the 23rd the attitude will change. Mental compatibility – ease of communication – becomes important, and money becomes less important.

July

Best Days Overall: 1, 9, 10, 17, 18, 27, 28
Most Stressful Days Overall: 4, 5, 6, 11, 12, 24, 25
Best Days for Love: 4, 5, 6, 13, 14, 24
Best Days for Money: 4, 5, 6, 7, 8, 11, 12, 16, 17, 19, 20, 21, 24, 25, 27
Best Days for Career: 7, 8, 11, 12, 15, 16, 24, 25

There has been a Grand Square in the heavens (at varying degrees of exactness) all year thus far, and it is still strong for most of this month. You have been working hard. You have been involved in some major project – very delicate and very complicated. It will be finalized by the end of the month and you will be able to breathe easier.

Jupiter makes a major move out of your 4th house and into your 5th house of fun and creativity on the 17th, and will be there for the rest of the year ahead. You've worked hard, now it is time for some R&R, time to have some fun. On the 22nd the Sun will move into your 5th house as well and you enter a powerful yearly personal pleasure peak.

In the meantime continue to watch your health. Don't shirk your duties or responsibilities but schedule more rest periods into your day. Make sure you distinguish between real duties and false ones. Much of what we consider 'responsibility' is not real; it is merely things foisted on us.

You can enhance your health by giving more attention to the lungs, arms, shoulders and respiratory system until the 13th and to the stomach after that. (Women should pay more attention to the breasts after the 13th.) Emotional harmony is important these days as most of the planets are below the horizon, but this month it is a health issue.

Depression, anger and discord are the first symptoms of disease. These things can happen – they seem unavoidable on the human level – but don't stay in these states. Get back into harmony as quickly as you can.

By the 22nd you should see a remarkable increase in health and energy. Mars, Jupiter and the Sun will have moved away from their stressful aspects and should be starting to make harmonious ones. You feel like a load of lead has been lifted off your shoulders.

Mars's move into Scorpio and your 8th house of regeneration increases the libido. Whatever your age or stage in life, your libido is stronger than usual, and July is a more sexually active kind of month from the 18th onwards.

Finances are good this month, but not as important as they have been in previous months. Venus, your financial planet is in your 3rd house until the 18th, which indicates that financial opportunity can be found in your neighbourhood and with neighbours and siblings (or sibling figures). It shows earning through retailing, trading, buying and selling. Good marketing – good PR – is important in earnings. On the 18th your financial planet will move into Cancer, your 4th house. This indicates good family support. (Indeed, family support seems good for the past year.) Family connections also seem important in finance. You are spending more on the home and family but can earn from there as well.

August

Best Days Overall: 5, 6, 13, 14, 23, 24
Most Stressful Days Overall: 1, 2, 8, 20, 21, 22, 28, 29
Best Days for Love: 1, 2, 3, 4, 12, 13, 23, 24, 28, 29
Best Days for Money: 3, 4, 5, 12, 13, 14, 16, 17, 23, 24
Best Days for Career: 3, 4, 7, 8, 11, 12, 20, 21, 22, 30, 31

Though this is a basically happy month – your 5th house of fun is full of planets and you are still in the midst of a yearly personal pleasure peak – there are a few bumps on the road. Technically there are no eclipses this month. But because many planets are reactivating the eclipse points of April, it is 'as if' the month is filled with 'mini-eclipses'. Things not dealt with at the time of the actual eclipses are being dealt with now. Happily, with much fire in the Horoscope and mostly harmonious aspects, you have the energy to deal with these things.

The Sun transits an eclipse point (in Square aspect) on the 1st and 2nd of the month. Thus children can be more temperamental. They should avoid risky kinds of activities. Sometimes this transit brings power blackouts. You are basically lucky in speculations this month, but it's probably wise to avoid them on the 1st and 2nd.

Mercury transits this same eclipse point (the Solar Eclipse of April 29) on the 5th and 6th. Be more careful driving. Communications can be unpredictable and equipment is more prone to malfunction. There can be disturbances at the job. Sometimes there are health scares – but health is basically good.

Mars transits this point from the 10th to the 14th, affecting you more personally. Avoid risk taking, confrontations, rush and haste. Spend more quiet time near home.

Venus transits this point from the 18th to the 20th. This can bring short-term financial upheavals and testing times in love. Be more patient with the beloved during this period. Finances and love are actually very good this period but they are more stressful than usual – and good things can be just as stressful as bad things. Finally, Jupiter transits this point from the 24th to the 31st. Avoid gratuitous foreign travel. Many of you will be travelling this month, but try to schedule your trips around this time.

Aries loves adventure, and risk is fundamental to every adventure. Thus this month, with all its ups and downs, is probably exciting and enjoyable for you. There's never a dull moment.

Last month the planetary power shifted from the East to the West – from the sector of independence to the sector of relationships and other people. Thus personal independence is lessened. This is a cycle for developing social skills and not for personal initiative. There is nothing wrong with personal initiative and nothing wrong with consensus. It is all a matter of what stage of the cycle you're in. Now your goals are more easily attained through the co-operation of others, not through purely personal effort.

September

Best Days Overall: 2, 3, 10, 11, 19, 20, 29, 30
Most Stressful Days Overall: 4, 5, 17, 18, 24, 25
Best Days for Love: 2, 3, 12, 13, 23, 24, 25
Best Days for Money: 1, 2, 3, 10, 11, 12, 13, 19, 20, 23, 29, 30
Best Days for Career: 4, 5, 8, 9, 17, 18, 27, 28

This month the planetary power shifts once again from the bottom half of your Horoscope to the top half. Dawn is breaking in your year. It is sunrise; time to get up, let go of the dream world and make your goals happen by physical means – the methods of the day. If you have used the past few months to good effect, if you have visualized your goals, the actions needed to achieve them should proceed naturally and harmoniously. They will happen as a sort of 'side effect' to your inner work of visualization and planning.

During this month and the next the planetary power is in the maximum Western position. This means your social life becomes hyperactive (you begin a yearly social peak on the 23rd) and cultivating the social graces becomes more important. Personal skills and initiative are always important but now the 'likeability' factor is important too. Changing conditions arbitrarily is more difficult now, so adapt to them as best you can. A new cycle of independence will begin in late December and it will be easier to make any necessary changes then.

Your health becomes more delicate after the 23rd. The important thing is to watch your energy levels. High energy is the number one defence against disease. A strong aura will repel any microbe. But if the aura weakens – which can easily happen after the 23rd – then problems can occur. You can enhance your health by paying attention to the kidneys and hips until the 28th, and to the colon, bladder and sexual organs after then. Health is a major focus until the 23rd and this is good. Your focus should build strength for afterwards.

Love is good this month. With Uranus in your 1st house for many years to come marriage is probably not advisable, but the opportunities will be there. Venus, your love planet, moves very fast this month through three signs and houses of your Horoscope. This indicates social confidence. You are on the move, covering a lot of ground, making much progress. Until September 5 love is not very serious – just amusement and entertainment. From the 5th to the end of the month Venus will be in Virgo in your 6th house of health and work. This indicates that romantic opportunities happen at work or with co-workers. It can also happen as you pursue your health goals – at your doctor's surgery or at the health spa. You could be attracted to healers and health practitioners too. Children (or children figures) of the appropriate age also have strong romantic opportunities towards the end of the month.

Finances are also good this month. You have financial confidence and make quick progress. Until the 5th you need to beware of over-spending, but afterwards your financial judgement is sound. From the 5th onwards money comes from work – the old-fashioned way. Job seekers have good fortune this month too.

October

   Best Days Overall: 7, 8, 16, 17, 18, 26, 27
   Most Stressful Days Overall: 1, 2, 14, 15, 21, 22, 23, 28, 29
   Best Days for Love: 3, 12, 13, 21, 22, 23
   Best Days for Money: 3, 7, 8, 9, 10, 12, 13, 17, 18, 22, 23, 26, 27
   Best Days for Career: 1, 2, 5, 6, 14, 15, 24, 25, 28, 29

There is a tumultuous but successful month ahead. Many changes are happening both in your personal life and in the world at large. Two eclipses this month practically ensure this.

The Lunar Eclipse of October 8 occurs in your own sign and affects Uranus and Pluto. It is a strong one. Make sure you take it nice and easy during this period. The Cosmos will show you, in language you understand, when the eclipse period is beginning, and you can lay low during that period. This eclipse occurs in your 1st house so it brings a redefinition of your personality and concept of yourself. You will upgrade them. You will start (and this is a six-month process) to present a new image to the world. Generally this brings wardrobe changes, changes of hair style, a new look. If you haven't been careful in dietary matters it can bring a detox of the body. You need to take it easy until the 23rd anyway, but especially during the eclipse period.

This eclipse will test friendships and will bring life-changing kinds of dramas to the lives of friends. There will be shake-ups and upheavals in professional organizations that you are involved with. There can be encounters with death (most likely on the psychological level) as well. There can be dramas in the family and in the home. Be more patient with family members at this time.

The Solar Eclipse of October 23 occurs right on the cusp of your 8th house of transformation. Again this can indicate encounters with death (although not necessarily literal, physical death). Children (and children figures in your life) should be kept out of harm's way. They don't need to be involved in risky kinds of activities. Speculations are also best avoided during this period. Friends will have their marriages tested, and your spouse, partner or current love could have a financial crisis that requires dramatic financial changes.

Eclipses are not punishments. They are merely the Cosmos's way of clearing obstructions and blockages. The changes that happen tend to be good in the long term, but while they happen they can be uncomfortable.

The career focus should be continued. On the 26th Mars will cross your Mid-heaven and enter your 10th house. This is an important transit that indicates career success. You are on top – above everyone in your world – calling the shots. You are respected and honoured and your achievements are appreciated. You are working hard, but you are succeeding.

Mars is 'out of bounds' all month. This shows that you are moving outside your normal circles. You are exploring new ventures and new methods. This seems to help the career.

Health still needs watching until the 23rd. Review our discussion of it last month. It will be good to spend more time at the health spa or to schedule some regular massages.

November

Best Days Overall: 4, 5, 13, 14, 22, 23
Most Stressful Days Overall: 10, 11, 18, 19, 25, 26
Best Days for Love: 2, 3, 11, 12, 18, 19, 22, 23
Best Days for Money: 2, 3, 4, 5, 6, 7, 11, 12, 14, 22, 23
Best Days for Career: 3, 11, 12, 21, 25, 26, 30

The view from the top has its good points. You are strong, effective and in charge. You are seen as successful. You have honour and respect. But there are some downsides to all of this too. You are more of a target for competitors, associates and those under you. You are like a lightning rod. This needs to be handled 'just so'. Do your best to avoid confrontations, especially from the 8th to the 16th. Avoid risk-taking activities then too, and drive more carefully.

Your 8th house is very strong this month (it was strong last month too) and Mars is travelling with Pluto. Therefore surgery might be recommended to you. This doesn't mean that you have to have it – it is always good to get a second opinion. Also there will be more confrontations with death – not literal, personal death but psychological confrontations. Perhaps you have some 'close call', something that could have caused death or serious injury. Those things make a person think and review their lives. Life here on Earth is short and fragile. It can end at any time. We need to be about our true purposes.

These same aspects indicate the power of detox regimes. You respond well to them.

Technically there are no eclipses this month, but many planets are activating eclipse points now – thus it is 'as if' there is a re-experience of the eclipse. Uranus will camp out very near an eclipse point all month. This indicates dramas in the lives of friends and the testing of friendships. Children or children figures in your life are having their relationships tested.

The Sun re-activates an eclipse point on the 6th and 7th. This affects the children or children figures in your life and they have dramas. It will be best to avoid speculations during this period too.

Mercury transits this same eclipse point (the Lunar Eclipse of October 8) from the 8th to the 10th. Communications can be challenging;

communication equipment might not work as it should. There is drama at the workplace and instability with employees. Mars, the ruler of your Horoscope – and a very important planet for you – re-activates this point on the 15th and 16th and we have already discussed this.

Your spouse, partner or current love has been financially squeezed during the past year, but this month their finances are much improved. He or she is in the midst of a yearly financial peak until the 22nd.

December

Best Days Overall: 1, 2, 10, 11, 20, 21, 28, 29
Most Stressful Days Overall: 8, 9, 15, 16, 22, 23
Best Days for Love: 1, 2, 12, 13, 15, 16, 21, 22, 30, 31
Best Days for Money: 1, 2, 3, 4, 10, 11, 12, 13, 20, 21, 22, 28, 29, 30, 31
Best Days for Career: 8, 9, 19, 22, 23, 28

Your overall health and energy began improving in July. Jupiter and Mars moved away from their long-term stressful aspects with you. This month – on the 24th – Saturn is going to move into harmonious aspect with you. Health is still delicate from the 22nd onwards, but nowhere near as delicate as it was in July and October. The stress is mostly coming from short-term planets. If you got through July and October you'll breeze through December. You can enhance your health further by giving more attention to the liver and thighs until the 17th, and to the spine, knees, teeth, bones, skin and overall skeletal alignment afterwards. Liver detox and thigh massage is powerful until the 17th, while back and knee massage is powerful after then.

The main headline this month is the career. On the 22nd you enter another one of your yearly career peaks. Your 10th house is very powerful all month, with 60 per cent of the planets either there or moving through there this month. It will be a month of continued career success and advancement. There is a 'cosmic conspiracy' to bring you success and elevation. It is quite OK to let go of home and family issues now and focus on the career.

Mars will re-activate an eclipse point from the 4th to the 7th. Avoid risk-taking activities, drive more carefully and avoid rush and haste then. On the 5th Mars will move out of your 10th house and into the 11th house of friends. This has been a delicate area of late and you seem to be more devoted to your friends; you want to be there for them.

Love seems happy this month. Until the 10th love opportunities happen in religious or educational settings, in foreign countries or with foreigners. Love is passionate and fiery – just the way you like it. On the 10th Venus will cross the Mid-heaven and enter your 10th house. This indicates love opportunities as you pursue your career goals and with people who are involved in your career. Often this indicates love opportunities occurring with bosses and superiors – people above you in status. In general you are mixing with the high and mighty – you have both their social and financial favour.

Children or children figures in your life have wonderful job opportunities this month. But their relationships are still being tested.

On the 22nd the planetary power shifts back to the Eastern sector of the chart. Personal independence is now much stronger. It is easier to change or create conditions as you want them to be. So now, and for the next six or so months, is the time to do it.

With your career planet in your 9th house from the 24th onwards, there will be more business travel happening. You will feel it more next year, but it is in effect now. This willingness to travel enhances your career.

Taurus

THE BULL

Birthdays from
21st April to
20th May

Personality Profile

TAURUS AT A GLANCE

Element – Earth

Ruling Planet – Venus
  Career Planet – Uranus
  Love Planet – Pluto
  Money Planet – Mercury
  Planet of Health and Work – Venus
  Planet of Home and Family Life – Sun
  Planet of Spirituality – Mars
  Planet of Travel, Education, Religion and Philosophy – Saturn

Colours – earth tones, green, orange, yellow

Colours that promote love, romance and social harmony – red-violet, violet

Colours that promote earning power – yellow, yellow-orange

Gems – coral, emerald

Metal – copper

Scents – bitter almond, rose, vanilla, violet

Quality – fixed (= stability)

Quality most needed for balance – flexibility

Strongest virtues – endurance, loyalty, patience, stability,
    a harmonious disposition

Deepest needs – comfort, material ease, wealth

Characteristics to avoid – rigidity, stubbornness, tendency to be overly
    possessive and materialistic

Signs of greatest overall compatibility – Virgo, Capricorn

Signs of greatest overall incompatibility – Leo, Scorpio, Aquarius

Sign most helpful to career – Aquarius

Sign most helpful for emotional support – Leo

Sign most helpful financially – Gemini

Sign best for marriage and/or partnerships – Scorpio

Sign most helpful for creative projects – Virgo

Best Sign to have fun with – Virgo

Signs most helpful in spiritual matters – Aries, Capricorn

Best day of the week – Friday

Understanding a Taurus

Taurus is the most earthy of all the Earth signs. If you understand that Earth is more than just a physical element, that it is a psychological attitude as well, you will get a better understanding of the Taurus personality.

A Taurus has all the power of action that an Aries has. But Taurus is not satisfied with action for its own sake. Their actions must be productive, practical and wealth-producing. If Taurus cannot see a practical value in an action they will not bother taking it.

Taurus' forte lies in their power to make real their own or other people's ideas. They are generally not very inventive but they can take another's invention and perfect it, making it more practical and useful. The same is true for all projects. Taurus is not especially keen on starting new projects, but once they get involved they bring things to completion. Taurus carries everything through. They are finishers and will go the distance, so long as no unavoidable calamity intervenes.

Many people find Taurus too stubborn, conservative, fixed and immovable. This is understandable, because Taurus dislikes change – in the environment or in their routine. They even dislike changing their minds! On the other hand, this is their virtue. It is not good for a wheel's axle to waver. The axle must be fixed, stable and unmovable. Taurus is the axle of society and the heavens. Without their stability and so-called stubbornness, the wheels of the world (and especially the wheels of commerce) would not turn.

Taurus loves routine. A routine, if it is good, has many virtues. It is a fixed – and, ideally, perfect – way of taking care of things. Mistakes can happen when spontaneity comes into the equation, and mistakes cause discomfort and uneasiness – something almost unacceptable to a Taurus. Meddling with Taurus' comfort and security is a sure way to irritate and anger them.

While an Aries loves speed, a Taurus likes things slow. They are slow thinkers – but do not make the mistake of assuming they lack intelligence. On the contrary, Taurus people are very intelligent. It is just that they like to chew on ideas, to deliberate and weigh them up.

Only after due deliberation is an idea accepted or a decision taken. Taurus is slow to anger – but once aroused, take care!

Finance

Taurus is very money-conscious. Wealth is more important to them than to many other signs. Wealth to a Taurus means comfort and security. Wealth means stability. Where some zodiac signs feel that they are spiritually rich if they have ideas, talents or skills, Taurus only feels wealth when they can see and touch it. Taurus' way of thinking is, 'What good is a talent if it has not been translated into a home, furniture, car and holidays?'

These are all reasons why Taurus excels in estate agency and agricultural industries. Usually a Taurus will end up owning land. They love to feel their connection to the Earth. Material wealth began with agriculture, the tilling of the soil. Owning a piece of land was humanity's earliest form of wealth: Taurus still feels that primeval connection.

It is in the pursuit of wealth that Taurus develops intellectual and communication ability. Also, in this pursuit Taurus is forced to develop some flexibility. It is in the quest for wealth that they learn the practical value of the intellect and come to admire it. If it were not for the search for wealth and material things, Taurus people might not try to reach a higher intellect.

Some Taurus people are 'born lucky' – the type who win any gamble or speculation. This luck is due to other factors in their horoscope; it is not part of their essential nature. By nature they are not gamblers. They are hard workers and like to earn what they get. Taurus' innate conservatism makes them abhor unnecessary risks in finance and in other areas of their lives.

Career and Public Image

Being essentially down-to-earth people, simple and uncomplicated, Taurus tends to look up to those who are original, unconventional and inventive. Taurus people like their bosses to be creative and original – since they themselves are content to perfect their superiors' brainwaves. They admire people who have a wider social or political consciousness and they feel that someday (when they have all the comfort and security they need) they too would like to be involved in these big issues.

In business affairs Taurus can be very shrewd – and that makes them valuable to their employers. They are never lazy; they enjoy working and getting good results. Taurus does not like taking unnecessary risks and they do well in positions of authority, which makes them good managers and supervisors. Their managerial skills are reinforced by their natural talents for organization and handling details, their patience and thoroughness. As mentioned, through their connection with the earth, Taurus people also do well in farming and agriculture.

In general a Taurus will choose money and earning power over public esteem and prestige. A position that pays more – though it has less prestige – is preferred to a position with a lot of prestige but lower earnings. Many other signs do not feel this way, but a Taurus does, especially if there is nothing in his or her personal birth chart that modifies this. Taurus will pursue glory and prestige only if it can be shown that these things have a direct and immediate impact on their wallet.

Love and Relationships

In love, the Taurus-born likes to have and to hold. They are the marrying kind. They like commitment and they like the terms of a relationship to be clearly defined. More importantly, Taurus likes to be faithful to one lover, and they expect that lover to reciprocate this fidelity. When this doesn't happen, their whole world comes crashing down. When they are in love Taurus people are loyal, but they are also very possessive. They are capable of great fits of jealousy if they are hurt in love.

Taurus is satisfied with the simple things in a relationship. If you are involved romantically with a Taurus there is no need for lavish entertainments and constant courtship. Give them enough love, food and comfortable shelter and they will be quite content to stay home and enjoy your company. They will be loyal to you for life. Make a Taurus feel comfortable and – above all – secure in the relationship, and you will rarely have a problem.

In love, Taurus can sometimes make the mistake of trying to control their partners, which can cause great pain on both sides. The reasoning behind their actions is basically simple: Taurus people feel a sense of ownership over their partners and will want to make changes that will increase their own general comfort and security. This attitude is OK when it comes to inanimate, material things – but is dangerous when applied to people. Taurus needs to be careful and attentive to this possible trait within themselves.

Home and Domestic Life

Home and family are vitally important to Taurus. They like children. They also like a comfortable and perhaps glamorous home – something they can show off. They tend to buy heavy, ponderous furniture – usually of the best quality. This is because Taurus likes a feeling of substance in their environment. Their house is not only their home but their place of creativity and entertainment. The Taurus' home tends to be truly their castle. If they could choose, Taurus people would prefer living in the countryside to being city-dwellers. If they cannot do so during their working lives, many Taurus individuals like to holiday in or even retire to the country, away from the city and closer to the land.

At home a Taurus is like a country squire – lord (or lady) of the manor. They love to entertain lavishly, to make others feel secure in their home and to encourage others to derive the same sense of satisfaction as they do from it. If you are invited for dinner at the home of a Taurus you can expect the best food and best entertainment. Be prepared for a tour of the house and expect to see your Taurus friend exhibit a lot of pride and satisfaction in his or her possessions.

Taurus people like children but they are usually strict with them. The reason for this is they tend to treat their children – as they do most things in life – as their possessions. The positive side to this is that their children will be well cared for and well supervised. They will get every material thing they need to grow up properly. On the down side, Taurus can get too repressive with their children. If a child dares to upset the daily routine – which Taurus loves to follow – he or she will have a problem with a Taurus parent.

Horoscope for 2014

Major Trends

The past few years have been prosperous ones, and now you seem at a place of satiation. The fruits of wealth and prosperity are free time – time for mental and intellectual development and for spiritual growth. This is happening in the year ahead. The opportunities are there but it is up to you to take them.

The love and social life have been marred by instability and stress. Love relationships – and even business partnerships – have been severely tested. This trend continues in the year ahead, but by now, though, you are probably handling it better. More on this later.

Taurus is a down-to-earth, practical sign. Their spirituality tends to be of the 'earth' – practical. Spirituality means being a good provider to your family, being a good husband or wife, a good parent, etc. But now that Uranus is in your 12th house for many years to come we see an expansion of the spiritual life. Spirituality is good for its own sake, regardless of its practical consequences. Spiritual attitudes and practices are undergoing major and dramatic change. And with Neptune now in your 11th house of friends you are attracting more spiritual-type friends, and this is a factor here too.

Pluto, the planet of transformation and renewal, has been in your 9th house of religion, philosophy and higher education for some years now and will be there for many more years. Thus your religious and philosophical beliefs – your world view – is getting detoxed and purified. This is part and parcel of the spiritual growth that we are seeing. Letting go – or even modifying – deeply held beliefs is not easy. Sometimes dramatic methods must be used and the Cosmos is supplying whatever it takes.

Your most important interests in the year ahead – and you have many – are communication and intellectual interests (until July 16); home and family (from July 16 onwards); health (until July 26); love, romance and social activities; religion, philosophy, higher education and foreign travel; friends, groups and group activities; and spirituality.

Your paths of greatest fulfilment in the year ahead are communication and intellectual interests (until July 16); home and family (from July 16 onwards); and health and work (until July 26).

Health

(Please note that this is an astrological perspective on health and not a medical one. In days of yore there was no difference, both of these perspectives were identical. But in these times there could be quite a difference. For a medical perspective, please consult your doctor or health practitioner.)

Your 6th house of health is strong this year until July 26, so health is an important focus. This I consider a positive for your health. You are not likely to allow little things to develop into big things. You are willing to put in the time and effort needed to maintain good health.

Your health is basically good, but it does need watching. The main problem (and you had this last year too) is Saturn's stressful alignment

Reflexology

Try to massage the whole foot on a regular basis, but pay extra attention to the points highlighted on the chart. When you massage, be aware of 'sore spots', as these need special attention. It's also a good idea to massage the ankles and the top of the feet.

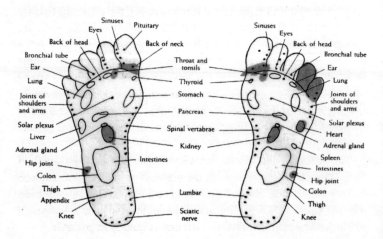

with your Sun. This year, Jupiter also comes into stressful alignment with you after July 16. These things of themselves are not enough to cause disease, but they do affect your overall energy. If you allow yourself to get overtired the spiritual immune system – the auric field – weakens and you become vulnerable to all sorts of 'invasions'. Also, spiritually speaking, we see the body as 'a dynamic energy system' and not just a 'thing' or 'chemical factory'. It obeys the laws of energy. When the energy field changes – for good or ill – there are corresponding changes in the body.

Jupiter and Saturn by themselves are not enough to cause disease. But there will be periods in the year when the short-term planets 'gang up' with them and these are the times to be especially careful – make sure you get a lot of rest. This year these periods will be from January 20 to February 18; July 23 to August 23; and October 23 to November 21.

Health can be enhanced by giving more attention to the following areas: the heart (avoid worry and anxiety, the spiritual root causes of heart problems); the kidneys and hips (the hips should be regularly massaged); the head, face and scalp (this is important until July 26 and regular scalp and face massage will be very powerful during this period); the neck and throat (always a vulnerable area for Taurus, regular neck massage is always beneficial and should be a part of your health regime as tension tends to collect in the neck and needs to be released); and the adrenals (avoid fear and anger, the emotions that are the root causes of adrenal problems). The reflexes to these areas are shown in the chart.

Mars spends an unusual amount of time in your 6th house – almost seven months. (His usual transit is a month and a half to two months.) Thus the muscles need to be 'toned' and in shape. If a muscle weakens, the spine and skeletal alignment goes out of whack and other problems develop from that. Regular physical exercise seems important until July 26.

With Venus as your health planet love issues play a role in health. If there are problems or discord in the marriage or the current relationship, or with friends, physical health can be affected. This area has been stressed for the past few years and is no doubt a factor in any physical problems. The solution: restore harmony as quickly as possible.

Venus is a fast-moving planet. She moves through your entire Horoscope in any given year. Thus there are many short-term trends in health that are best dealt with in the monthly reports.

Home and Family

Your 4th house of home and family will become powerful from July 16 onwards, as Jupiter moves into it and stays there for the rest of the year. This is a wonderful transit and bodes well for happiness in this area of life this year.

Often this transit indicates a move – a happy move – to larger and more expansive quarters. But as our regular readers know by now, it is not always a literal move that happens. Often people buy additional homes or expand and enlarge the present one. Or they buy expensive items for the home, which makes things more comfortable and satisfying. The effect is 'as if' they have moved.

Jupiter in the 4th house is a great career aspect for your spouse, partner or current love. There is success for them this year, and happy career opportunities.

Jupiter in this aspect also indicates good family support, financially and in other ways. It shows that the family circle will expand in the coming year. Generally this happens through birth or marriage, but not always. Often one meets people who are 'like' family – who play that kind of a role in your life. Often these people are more supportive than even your biological family.

Psychological growth in the year ahead is also indicated by Jupiter's transit through the 4th house. Your understanding of your personal moods and the moods of others is enlarged. Those of you involved in therapy, either as patient or practitioner, should have good experiences here.

Taurus people of childbearing age start to become more fertile than usual under this transit. And this transit indicates the prosperity of the family as a whole – and especially of one of the parent figures in your life. If you are a woman it shows the prosperity and generosity of the father figure. If you are a man it shows the same thing for the mother figure.

Moods will tend to be optimistic from July 16 onwards. And when one understands how the spiritual law works, the mood, the feeling of optimism always precedes the tangible event. Thus happy financial and other events are likely.

If the parents or parent figures are married, their relationship gets even better after July 16. If however they are unattached, there is strong romantic opportunity for them – perhaps even a marriage. Moves are not advisable for them this year, however. Better to wait. The same is true for children or children figures in your life. Siblings or sibling figures are prospering this year, probably travelling, but domestically it is a 'status quo' kind of year. They seem basically content with their present home and situation.

Parents or parent figures need to take better care of the heart. Surgery could be recommended to them, but they should get a second opinion. They seem pre-disposed to see surgery as a solution and are perhaps too quick to jump into it.

Finance and Career

As we mentioned earlier, you're coming out of a period of prosperity. Financial goals are probably fulfilled. With your money house basically empty this year, you have no need to pay special attention here or to make important financial changes. It will be a 'status quo' kind of financial year – there will be no disasters, but nothing especially positive either.

Jupiter is moving through your 3rd house of communication until July 16. This indicates a new car and new communication equipment – and of high quality. It also shows the prosperity of siblings and sibling figures. If you have investments (and what Taurus doesn't?) you are earning more income from them. Perhaps the companies whose stock you own raise their dividends, or the bank raises its interest rate. This transit is especially good for those of you involved in sales, marketing, advertising and promotion. It shows success in these endeavours. It is also wonderful for those of you who teach or write. Ideas are a form of wealth, and this is a year where you understand this more clearly.

The 3rd house rules buying, selling, retailing and trading and these endeavours also seem prosperous.

Real estate is a naturally good field for Taurus: you have a natural instinct for things of the Earth. This year it seems especially favoured

– particularly residential real estate. Until July 16 Jupiter will be in the sign of Cancer, which rules residential real estate, and after that date Jupiter moves into your 4th house – the house that rules residential real estate.

Mercury is your financial planet. And as our regular readers know, he is a fast-moving planet. In the course of the year he will move through all the signs and houses of your chart. Thus there will be many short-term trends in finance depending on where Mercury is and the aspects he receives. These are best covered in the monthly reports.

Your spouse, partner or current love seems prosperous, especially during the first half of the year. Later on though – towards the end of the year – he or she will need to consolidate and re-organize.

Your favourable financial numbers this year are 1, 3, 6, 8 and 9.

Though your 10th house of career is basically empty this year – only short-term planets will move through there – career does seem successful and important. Four long-term planets are above the horizon of the Horoscope. This means that there will always be 40 per cent of the planets above the horizon. This denotes ambition and interest. Thus there is great career drive – great desire – and this tends to success. Furthermore, when Jupiter moves into Leo on July 16 he will start making fabulous aspects to your career planet, Uranus. This denotes career elevation. If you work for others it shows pay rises and promotions. If you own your own business, your status in your industry or profession is elevated. Your achievements receive more recognition. September and early October seem especially powerful careerwise. I can see outside investors investing in your career.

High-tech expertise is important careerwise. It is worth spending on the latest and best. It is also important that you be original in your approach and in what you do. Never copy, never imitate. Follow your innate genius and originality.

With your career planet Uranus in the spiritual 12th house since 2012, you are idealistic about your career. It is not enough for you to merely make money or achieve fame. The career has to be truly helpful to people, has to be in line with your own ideals. It is good to be involved in charities and altruistic causes as well. These activities will enhance your outward career.

The dream life, psychics, ministers, gurus and other spiritual channels will all provide important information regarding your career.

Love and Social Life

The 7th house is a house of power this year, just like last year. It is an area of great focus and deservedly so. As we mentioned, this has been a problem area for a few years. The love life is highly unstable. Marriages and relationships have been seriously tested since 2011, and many have not survived this testing.

In many cases these break-ups have been blessings in disguise. Taureans are not known for 'letting go'. They are havers and holders, conservative and traditional. They like the status quo even if it is not the best that they can have. They have to be 'hit on the head' (in the vernacular) in order to let go. And, basically, this is what has happened to you over the past few years. You needed real drama to let go.

The Cosmos wants the best for you. And if the current relationship is not up to standard it will go by the wayside. Friendships and business partnerships have also been tested, and this trend will continue in the year ahead. As we mentioned, relationships that have survived the past few years (and that survive the year ahead) will survive anything. And this too is part of the divine agenda. Only basically sound relationships can survive this kind of testing. In many cases the relationship or friendship was tested because of dramas and life-changing events in the partners' personal lives. It might not have had anything to do with the actual relationship. Still, this is the Cosmos's way of saying, 'Good though this is, I have something better for you.'

For singles (and those working towards their first marriage) it is probably not advisable to marry just yet. If you meet someone eligible allow love to grow and develop as it will. There's no rush. Those in or working on their second marriage are having their relationships tested as well. The unattached who are working towards their second marriage have marriage opportunities, but the stability of it is in question. Again, there's no need to rush to tie the knot. Those working towards a third marriage, however, have excellent romantic and marriage opportunities. This was the case during the latter half of last year and for the early part of 2014. This relationship seems spiritual.

Singles seem more attracted to older, more established people. They gravitate to corporate types – people of high status and prestige. The danger here is of entering a relationship of convenience rather than of real love. Romantic opportunities will happen in foreign countries, with foreigners, and in religious or educational-type settings.

In general Taureans need to work harder to express love and warmth to others. On some subconscious level, you are coming over as cold and distant to others. You may not be aware of this, but this energy is coming out. You are naturally loving – Venus rules your sign – but you need to work harder to express it these days.

Self-improvement

Like last year, the main challenges in the year ahead are in the social sphere – the love life. Love problems can be a spiritual minefield. The actual difficulty is only the tip of the iceberg. Love problems tend to ignite problems in other areas of life – self-esteem, self-worth, health (especially in your case) and finance. Discord in love can create spiritual problems too, as the flow of spiritual power gets blocked. The Cosmos is giving you a 'crash course' in learning how to handle these things.

When a romantic relationship or business partnership goes sour there is going to be a certain amount of negativity. This is a given. But you can decide whether you want to take the path of maximum negativity or that of minimum negativity. All too often I have seen many choose the former. Thus something essentially simple gets magnified and prolonged and becomes much more painful than it needs to be. Then people wonder why they end up ill or in hospital. They don't see the connection.

Eckhard Tolle correctly points out that there is a difference between 'pain' and 'suffering'. Pain is the organism's response to something negative. You cut your finger; you feel a stab of pain. This is natural. Suffering is of the mind. The cut finger becomes a tale of woe – 'bad things are always happening to me', 'I'm being punished by God because I'm a bad person', 'I'm just unlucky', etc., etc., etc. Now you have suffering – mental and emotional anguish. And now there is a disconnection from the spiritual source. The cut finger, something basically minor, becomes a major thing. This is true in love as well.

These subsidiary issues that come up – the mental anguish – can be useful to someone on the spiritual path. It shows the content of the unconscious – the impurities there – and thus you can clear them. Forgiveness is a very important skill to learn in love and relationships. But for forgiveness to be effective, it needs to be 'real' and not 'strategic'. It has to be genuine and from the heart. Forgiveness will be easier when you understand that we forgive the person and not the actions. The hurtful actions were wrong and we don't try to whitewash them. We don't do violence to the intellect or judgement. The person is another story. He or she was acting from a certain conditioning and mind set and thus couldn't help doing what was done. If we were in this person's shoes we might have acted in the same way. When we understand what was behind the actions, forgiveness comes naturally and easily.

Month-by-month Forecasts

January

Best Days Overall: 1, 2, 9, 10, 19, 20, 28, 29
Most Stressful Days Overall: 3, 4, 17, 18, 24, 25, 30, 31
Best Days for Love: 1, 2, 9, 10, 19, 20, 24, 25, 28, 29
Best Days for Money: 1, 2, 5, 6, 10, 11, 12, 13, 14, 15, 22, 23, 24, 25, 30, 31
Best Days for Career: 3, 4, 7, 8, 17, 18, 26, 27, 30, 31

You begin your year with 70 and sometimes 80 per cent of the planets above the horizon, and on the 20th you will enter one of your yearly career peaks. So, this is the focus this month. Not only is it safe to let go of home and family issues, but the family seems to actually support your career goals. You have their blessing.

There are two ways that we achieve things: the inner way (meditation, visualization, conscious directed dreaming), and the outer way – through objective physical activity. Both are important at different times. Now you are in a cycle for the latter. Take the physical actions needed to achieve your career goals. This is a successful month.

The planetary momentum is overwhelmingly forward this month. Eighty per cent of the planets are moving forwards so you should see fast progress towards your goals. However, one of the two retrograde planets is Venus – the ruler of your Horoscope. Perhaps you feel you lack direction, are aimless and not sure of your personal goals. This is quite OK. The Cosmos is telling you to acquire mental clarity in this area. This is a great time to reflect on present conditions – your body, your image, your personal circumstances – and to see what changes can be made to improve things. The time for implementing these things will come shortly, but the important thing is to decide what you want.

Job seekers should exercise caution this month. Don't jump at the first job offered. Study things more. Things are not what they seem.

Health is excellent until the 20th. After that you need to rest and relax more. Keep the energy levels high and focus on the essentials. You can enhance the health further by giving attention to the areas mentioned in the yearly report and by looking after the spine, knees, teeth, bones, skin and overall skeletal alignment. Back and knee massages will be powerful, and regular visits to a chiropractor or osteopath will also be good. Spiritual healing techniques will also be powerful. With your health planet Venus retrograde all month, avoid making drastic changes to the diet or health regime. Study things more.

Finances seem excellent this month. Until the 11th Mercury, your financial planet, is in the 9th house – a fortunate house. Earnings are increased. Foreigners seem important financially, and foreign investments or interaction with foreign countries also bring profits. On the 11th Mercury crosses the Mid-heaven and enters your 10th house. This is a powerful financial period too. Money comes from your good professional reputation and from parent figures, elders, bosses and authority figures. If you need financial favours from the government this is a good time to ask – they seem favourably disposed.

February

Best Days Overall: 5, 6, 7, 15, 16, 17, 24, 25
Most Stressful Days Overall: 13, 14, 20, 21, 26, 27
Best Days for Love: 5, 6, 7, 15, 16, 17, 20, 21, 24, 25
Best Days for Money: 1, 2, 8, 9, 10, 11, 12, 19, 20, 21, 26, 27, 28
Best Days for Career: 3, 4, 13, 14, 22, 23, 26, 27

Venus, your ruling planet, started to move forward on January 31 and she will be travelling forward for the rest of the year ahead. Hopefully you have achieved clarity on what needs to be changed in your personal life and now, as the planets start shifting to the East (this trend will gather strength next month), you have the power to make the necessary changes. You are entering a period of personal independence and can have things your way. Other people and their opinions are always important, but if they don't go along with you, go it alone.

You are in a yearly career peak until the 18th, so outward success is happening. Pay rises and promotions could have happened last month, but if not, they can still happen in the month ahead and even next month.

Mercury, your financial planet, goes retrograde on the 6th, so try to wrap up important purchases or investments before then. From the 6th to the end of the month it is good to review your financial life and see where improvements can be made. It is not a time for implementing your ideas – that will come next month – but for resolving doubts and planning improvements.

Health still needs watching until the 18th. Review our discussion of this last month – the trends are still in effect. On the 18th your health and energy will start to improve.

Love is still being tested, but less severely than usual this month. Venus has been travelling with Pluto, your love planet, and is more or less conjunct to Pluto all month. Thus the love life is a bit easier. A foreign trip or worshiping together as a couple can improve things. Singles could have met a special someone late last month. It could happen early this month as well. But marriage is not on the cards right now.

The Sun conjuncts with Neptune from February 22 to the 24th; this will activate your dream life – and the dream life of family members too. Spiritual understanding – spiritual revelation – will help you solve family issues. Be more patient with family members from the 9th to the 12th – they are apt to be more grumpy than usual. This is a short-term issue.

A parent or parent figure prospers on the 28th.

Your 11th house of friendship becomes powerful from the 18th onwards, heralding a social, but not necessarily romantic, period. A good time to be involved with groups, group activities and organizations.

March

Best Days Overall: 5, 6, 15, 16, 24, 25
Most Stressful Days Overall: 12, 13, 19, 20, 26, 27
Best Days for Love: 5, 6, 7, 15, 16, 17, 18, 19, 20, 24, 25, 26, 27
Best Days for Money: 1, 2, 7, 8, 10, 11, 19, 20, 28, 29
Best Days for Career: 3, 4, 12, 13, 22, 23, 26, 27, 30, 31

Last month the Water element was very strong in the Horoscope, with 40 and sometimes 50 per cent of the planets in water signs. We have the same situation in the month ahead. This much water enhances sensitivity, which has its good points: people will be more in touch with their feelings and share feelings more freely. Emotional intimacy becomes easier. On the other hand there can be much hyper-sensitivity. Little things, body language or voice tone, can set others off. So be more aware of this.

On the 6th (and you might feel this even earlier) Venus crosses the Mid-heaven and enters your 10th career house. She will be in your 10th house all month, bringing a mini career peak. The aspect indicates that you are on top of everyone in your world (or are trying to be). You are number one and will not accept a lesser position, however prestigious. It indicates elevation, honour and respect. You are seen as successful by others. Your personal appearance is a big factor here too.

Your financial planet is now travelling forwards. Hopefully you have clarified your financial goals and made plans for improvements, as now you can set these plans into motion. Mercury will be in your 10th house until the 17th. This shows earnings from the career (pay rises, your good professional reputation) and from the favour of parents, parent figures, bosses and elders. They are helping your financial goals and are supportive of them.

After the 17th, earnings come from social connections, from friends and from involvement with groups and organizations. Money can be earned in the online world as well. Mercury will be in the sign of Pisces from the 17th onwards. This indicates good financial intuition, and your intuition will be especially good from the 21st to the 23rd as Mercury conjuncts Neptune. There is a spiritual dimension to supply and providence which you will learn more about from the 17th onwards.

Love is still being tested and is quite volatile. This volatility increases on the new Moon of the 30th. Relationships don't have to break up, but they will require a lot more effort to keep going. This same new Moon boosts the career.

Health is much improved over last month. In addition to what we mentioned in the yearly report, give more attention to the ankles and calves to enhance the health. Avoid risk-taking activities from the 17th to the 19th. There is some disturbance at work then too.

This is a spiritual kind of month. The Sun is in spiritual Pisces until the 20th, and after that it moves into your spiritual 12th house. This is a powerful time for meditation and spiritual studies, and it is also good for charitable kinds of activities.

April

Best Days Overall: 1, 2, 11, 12, 20, 21, 29, 30
Most Stressful Days Overall: 8, 9, 10, 16, 17, 22, 23
Best Days for Love: 1, 2, 4, 5, 6, 11, 12, 16, 17, 20, 21, 24, 25, 29, 30
Best Days for Money: 3, 4, 5, 6, 7, 8, 16, 17, 18, 19, 24, 25, 29, 30
Best Days for Career: 9, 10, 18, 19, 22, 23, 26, 27

The planetary power is now approaching its maximum Eastern position – the period of maximum personal independence. You don't need others as much as usual. You can achieve things – make changes – on your own initiative. This is a good month to make those changes you've been planning – we have two eclipses and change is in the air.

There is career success and opportunity on the 1st and 2nd.

The Lunar Eclipse of the 15th occurs in your 6th house of health and work. This can bring health scares and long term, dramatic changes to the health regime. The workplace is unstable as well. Lunar eclipses tend to affect communications – equipment and your ability to communicate. This one is no different. The good news here is that Venus travels with Neptune from the 10th to the 13th and you are receiving spiritual guidance – either in dreams or through spiritual channels or psychics – as to how to handle things. Be more careful driving this period. Cars tend to act up during this kind of eclipse as well.

The Solar Eclipse of the 29th has a much stronger effect on you. It occurs in your own sign and in your 1st house. Take it nice and easy during this period. It indicates a redefinition of your personality and self-concept, which will be a six-month process. You will change the way you think about yourself and the way that you want others to see you. It's always a good idea to redefine yourself every now and then – to upgrade your self-concept – but now the eclipse forces the issue. Generally this redefinition, this image change, involves wardrobe changes as well. In your Horoscope every Solar Eclipse affects the home and the family. The Sun is your family planet. So there are dramas at home with family members or with a parent or parent figure. The emotional life is also more volatile, sometimes with disturbing dreams. If there are flaws in the home now is when you find out about them and have opportunity to correct things.

There are important financial changes happening this month – not necessarily eclipse related. Your financial planet travels with Uranus from the 13th to the 15th. This brings sudden, unexpected financial increase. A parent, parent figure or boss is generous with you – perhaps the government as well. Sometimes this aspect shows an unexpected expense too.

Love is a little easier than last month, but not much. Your love planet, Pluto, goes retrograde on the 14th so avoid making major decisions after that date. Rather, it is a time to review and attain clarity on the subject.

May

Best Days Overall: 8, 9, 10, 17, 18, 26, 27
Most Stressful Days Overall: 5, 6, 13, 14, 19, 20
Best Days for Love: 6, 8, 9, 13, 14, 17, 18, 24, 25, 26, 27
Best Days for Money: 1, 2, 3, 4, 5, 11, 12, 13, 14, 19, 20, 21, 22, 28, 29, 30, 31
Best Days for Career: 6, 7, 15, 16, 19, 20, 24, 25

Some of you had birthdays in the past month, while many others have one coming up in this one. There is much more to a birthday than merely opening presents and attending parties. There's nothing wrong with these things, but these customs arose from something deeper. There is a sacredness about a birthday. It is an actual celestial event. The Sun returns to its original position at the time of your birth and begins a new cycle for the year. It is your 'personal new year'. The old is over with and you're making a new beginning. Life is full of new beginnings if we but knew it. Take time to reflect on the past year. Correct past mistakes and set new goals for the year ahead. Start your new year with a clean slate.

Most of the planets are still above the horizon, and so career and outer activities are still paramount. But this is about to change. By the end of the month – on the 29th – the lower half of the Horoscope will be stronger than the upper half (for the first time this year). The Sun is setting in your year; it is time to finish up the activities of the day and prepare for the activities of the night. In the meantime enjoy the career success that is happening – especially on the 14th and 15th. By then the goals of the previous career cycle will more or less be attained (and if not completely attained then there has been progress in their achievement) and you will start preparing for the next cycle of career activity in about six months' time.

On April 20 you entered one of your yearly personal pleasure peaks. And this is going on for the month ahead. Now it's good to focus on the body and image and get them into shape. It's also good for pampering the body and enjoying the sensual delights. Self-esteem and self-confidence are at their strongest for the year. Perhaps a given relationship is troubling, but you are still attractive to the opposite sex.

Love is better than it has been for a while (and next month it will be even better). Marriage at this time is still not advisable, however.

Your financial planet moved into your sign on April 23 and will be there until May 7. This is wonderful financially. Money and financial opportunity seek you out. Financial windfalls happen. You earn on your own terms, with honour. You feel rich and look rich (each according to their status and stage in life). On the 21st the Sun will join Mercury in your money house and you enter a yearly financial peak. The month ahead is prosperous indeed – Taurus heaven.

Mercury goes 'out of bounds' on the 12th and stays that way for the rest of the month. This shows that you are exploring new paths to wealth, going outside your usual boundaries, going outside the box, breaking with old limitations. This might horrify family members or a parent figure, but it works.

June

Best Days Overall: 5, 6, 14, 15, 22, 23
Most Stressful Days Overall: 2, 3, 9, 10, 16, 17, 29, 30
Best Days for Love: 5, 6, 9, 10, 14, 15, 22, 23, 24
Best Days for Money: 1, 9, 10, 11, 17, 18, 19, 24, 25, 26, 27, 28
Best Days for Career: 2, 3, 12, 13, 16, 17, 20, 21, 29, 30

You are still well into a yearly financial peak and you have a prosperous month ahead. Your financial planet is still 'out of bounds' until the 5th, and your forays into the unknown seem to work out. Mercury goes retrograde on the 7th. This will not stop your earnings, it will not stop the prosperity, but it slows it down a bit. It is time to review your finances and make plans for improvements. But first mental clarity is needed. Doubts need to be resolved. If you're planning major purchases of expensive items or major investments, it will be best to wrap these things up before the 7th. If you must do these things after that date (circumstances sometimes force us), do your homework well and take steps to protect yourself. Check the return policy at the shop. Financial thinking is often unrealistic under a retrograde aspect and you need to protect yourself against mistakes. Financial delays can happen, but the overall prosperity remains intact.

Personal appearance is very important financially after the 23rd. Good to invest in this.

Love is relatively good this month. Everything in life is relative. Venus in your sign adds beauty to the image. You dress well and look good. You are attractive to the opposite sex. Venus makes beautiful aspects to the love planet, Pluto, from the 8th to the 12th. Singles will meet interesting prospects. With Pluto still retrograde, allow love to develop as it will without pushing it. Just be yourself. There's no need to make important love decisions now. You are still a seeker of 'clarity' in your love life. If there is one thing that Taurus can't deal with it is instability – and this is the situation in love these days. There are cosmic lessons to be learned here.

This is a good period for buying clothing and personal accessories – until the 23rd. You have a good instinct for this. Your taste is impeccable.

Health is good, as it was last month too. You can enhance it further through neck massage (always important for you) and arm and shoulder massage (from the 23rd onwards). Mind–body healing methods are powerful after the 23rd.

Venus, the ruler of your Horoscope, re-activates the Solar Eclipse of April 29 on the 5th and 6th. Take it easy and avoid taking risks. Children (or children figures) should also take it easy.

Mars opposes Uranus from the 22nd to the 26th – a very dynamic aspect. Avoid confrontations and drive more carefully. There can be short-term upheavals in your career and with those involved in your career – especially parents, parent figures, bosses and authority figures. They should avoid risk taking too. Your intuition needs to be verified more then too, rather than just acted upon.

July

Best Days Overall: 2, 3, 11, 12, 19, 20, 21, 29, 30, 31
Most Stressful Days Overall: 1, 7, 8, 13, 14, 27, 28
Best Days for Love: 2, 3, 4, 5, 6, 7, 8, 11, 12, 13, 14, 19, 20, 24, 29, 30
Best Days for Money: 5, 6, 7, 8, 13, 14, 16, 17, 22, 23, 24, 25, 27
Best Days for Career: 1, 9, 10, 13, 14, 17, 18, 27, 28

There are some interesting phenomena this month. While the short-term planets are reaching their nadir (the lowest point in your Horoscope), and technically you are near the midnight hour of your year, Mars's move into Scorpio on the 18th makes the upper half of the Horoscope just as strong as the lower half. Not so easy now to get a 'good night's rest' and work by the methods of night! It's as if you are being woken up to deal with outer affairs. Your challenge this month will be to handle your career AND your home, family and emotional needs. Handle career demands by all means, but make sure you rest whenever possible. Constantly being on the go is never advisable, but sometimes it can't be helped.

Jupiter makes a major move this month – on the 17th – from Cancer into Leo, from your 3rd house to the 4th. He will be there for the rest of the year ahead and well into next year. This often indicates moves or renovations of the home. The home life is basically happy and there is good family support. Some family members, perhaps a parent or parent figure, can be having dramatic experiences – surgery or encounters with death – but these are just bumps on the road. Family support is still strong in the year ahead.

Mars moves into your 7th house of love on the 18th. This complicates an already tricky love situation. If you're not careful conflicts can escalate. There will most likely be negativity here, but it is up to you to minimize or maximize it – and it is best to minimize negativity where possible. Mars is your spiritual planet. Thus the message here is to surrender the love life to a Higher Power and let that handle things. When this is done sincerely, peace enters the situation.

Finances are still very good. They are perhaps not as active as last month, but they are still good. Your financial planet starts moving forward on the 2nd and your financial judgement is back to its normally good standard. The money house remains powerful until the 18th. This indicates a strong focus on finance, and we get what we focus on. Sales, marketing, advertising and good PR are always important for you on a financial level, but this month more so than usual. The financial planet is in the sign of Gemini until the 13th and then moves into your 3rd house of communication, and the above activities come under the domain of Gemini and the 3rd house. Trading is also a good source of income this month.

The 3rd house of communication and intellectual interests is very powerful this month. Thus it is a good period to catch up on all those letters, calls, emails and texts that you owe. It's also very good for taking courses in subjects that interest you – good for reading and studying. Students have a successful month.

August

Best Days Overall: 8, 16, 17, 25, 26, 27
Most Stressful Days Overall: 3, 4, 10, 23, 24, 30, 31
Best Days for Love: 3, 4, 12, 13, 23, 24, 30, 31
Best Days for Money: 5, 6, 13, 14, 15, 18, 19, 23, 24, 25, 26
Best Days for Career: 5, 6, 9, 10, 13, 14, 23, 24

Like last month you are delicately balancing between home and career. Both are demanding much attention. Both have to be handled properly. Normally at this time of the year you would be letting go of the career and focusing on the home and family. You would be gathering the forces for the next career push. But this year it's not happening. Many exciting and happy career developments are occurring this month. It is like being woken up in the middle of the night by someone saying 'get to the office, you've been promoted'. You are happy and will probably get up, but you've lost a night's sleep. There is a price tag attached to this. The good news is that the family seems understanding and supportive of your career goals. Career progress could be behind a coming move.

Health needs more attention this month. A lot of planets are in stressful alignment with you. Do whatever needs to be done, but try to schedule more rest periods into your day. It might be good to invest in massages and spend some free time at the health spa. It will also be good to enhance your health in the ways mentioned in the yearly report. You can add to this by giving more attention to the stomach and diet until the 12th and to the heart afterwards. Women should give more attention to the breasts this month. Venus, your health planet, spends the month in the sign of Cancer until the 12th and in the 4th house from the 12th onwards. Emotional harmony and equilibrium (which come under the domain of Cancer and the 4th house) are thus ultra important to health. Keep your harmony at all cost.

This is a tumultuous kind of month with many shocks and surprises (many of them good, but good things can be as stressful, and time consuming, as bad things). This month the Solar Eclipse point of April 29 is getting re-activated by many planets. It is 'as if' we are having many 'mini-eclipses' – replays of the previous eclipse. The main re-activation for you is Venus's transit from the 18th to the 20th. A nice easy schedule is called for (as far as you can manage). Mercury's transit on the 5th and 6th affects finances and children, but this is a short-term disturbance. It follows a nice financial windfall during the 1st to the 3rd.

Family support is good all year, but especially from the 1st to the 3rd. Family connections are helpful this month too. Real estate seems like an interesting investment. On the 15th Mercury moves into Virgo and the financial aspects get much easier. There is luck in speculations and from work – both bring profits. This is a period for 'happy money' – money that is earned in happy ways. (Working can sometimes be fun too.) You are spending on fun kinds of activities, and are generally enjoying your wealth.

Love. What can we say here? Try not to make things worse than they need to be. Things should improve after the 23rd.

September

Best Days Overall: 4, 5, 12, 13, 22, 23
Most Stressful Days Overall: 6, 7, 19, 20, 27, 28
Best Days for Love: 2, 3, 4, 5, 12, 13, 22, 23, 27, 28
Best Days for Money: 1, 2, 3, 4, 10, 11, 12, 13, 14, 15, 19, 20, 21, 28, 29, 30
Best Days for Career: 2, 3, 6, 7, 10, 11, 19, 20, 29, 30

Health and energy started to improve on August 23 and the trend will continue this month. On the 14th Mars will move away from his stressful aspect to you. A lot of the negative pressure from the short-term planets is gone. If there have been health problems you should hear some good news this month. Enhance the health in the ways mentioned in the yearly report. Until the 5th pay attention to the heart; from the 5th onwards give more attention to the small intestine (diet is important then). With your health planet Venus spending the month in Leo and then your 5th house, the Horoscope is saying that happiness – fun and joy – are powerful healing forces this month. If you feel under the weather, do something that is fun. Keep the belly laughs going, and avoid depression like the plague.

There is great focus on health this month. Many planets are in Virgo (the sign of health) and your 6th house (the house that rules health). This is good news. You are on the case. You're not letting little things develop into bigger problems.

This power in Virgo and the 6th house is also good news for job seekers. There is good fortune and many job opportunities.

Last month the planetary power made an important shift from East to West. At least 70 per cent (and sometimes 80 per cent) of the planets are now in the Western sector. Your cycle of personal independence is over for now. It will be much more difficult to change conditions and circumstances now. (It can be done, but with great, great effort.) It is best now to adapt to situations and make note of what displeases you. Then, when your cycle of personal independence returns, you can make these changes. For now you are living with the conditions that you yourself created, experiencing the karma, good or bad. You've had six months of developing your personal initiative and now the Cosmos is calling on you to hone and develop your social skills. It has its own ways of doing this, which are different for each person. Taureans in general have good social skills, but there is always room for improvement.

On August 23, as the Sun moved into your 5th house of fun and creativity, you entered another yearly personal pleasure peak. This continues until the 23rd of this month. A party period. Personal creativity will be stronger than usual too, and your ability to relate to children is enhanced. After the 23rd you enter a more serious, work-oriented period. This is a good time to do those menial, detailed, boring tasks that everyone tends to put off – your accounts, balancing the cheque book, filing, etc.

October

Best Days Overall: 1, 2, 9, 10, 19, 20, 28, 29
Most Stressful Days Overall: 3, 4, 16, 17, 18, 24, 25, 31
Best Days for Love: 1, 2, 3, 9, 10, 12, 13, 19, 20, 22, 23, 24, 25, 28, 29
Best Days for Money: 5, 6, 7, 8, 12, 13, 17, 18, 22, 23, 26, 27, 31
Best Days for Career: 3, 4, 7, 8, 16, 17, 18, 26, 27, 31

When Mars left your 7th house on the 14th of last month, love should have become a bit easier. Power struggles in love are never fun. But two eclipses this month will further test your relationship – as if you didn't have enough of this already! Relationships that have survived the testing of the past two years will probably survive anything, but less perfect relationships will most likely founder. Taureans don't like change, even if the change is ultimately good. They have a tendency to 'hang on' to things and sometimes the Cosmos has to use drastic measures to pry them loose. No one 'hangs in there' like a Taurus.

Two eclipses – one on the 8th and one on the 23rd – are the main headlines for the month.

The Lunar Eclipse on the 8th is relatively benign to you, but it won't hurt to reduce your schedule anyway. It occurs in your 12th house of spirituality, signalling long-term changes in your spiritual practice, teachers and teachings. (Your spiritual planet, Mars, is 'out of bounds' all month, suggesting that you are going outside your normal boundaries in your spiritual practice – taking a less beaten path.) There are shake-ups and upheavals in spiritual organizations or charities that you are involved with. Every Lunar Eclipse will test your car and communication equipment and affects communication in general, and this one is no exception. Therefore it is a good idea to drive more defensively during this period too. This eclipse occurs exactly on Uranus, your career planet, indicating that important career changes are happening now. Even if you stay in the same career or job, the 'rules of the game' seem changed. There are dramatic events in the lives of parents, parent figures and bosses too. This eclipse also 'sideswipes' Pluto, your love planet, leading to more testing of a current relationship. Partnerships and friendships will also get tested.

The Solar Eclipse of the 23rd has a stronger effect on you, so take it nice and easy and avoid (where possible) stressful or risky activities. If you can, reschedule such activities for another time. The eclipse occurs in your 7th house of love and marriage. So, as we mentioned, a current relationship, a partnership gets tested once again. Every Solar Eclipse affects the home and family and this one is no different. Family members are apt to be more temperamental. Dramas happen with a parent or parent figure.

Health needs watching from the 23rd onwards. As always, the first line of defence is the maintenance of high energy levels. Thus rest and relax more. If you can, schedule in some massages or some time in a health spa; that would be wonderful. Enhance health in the ways mentioned in the yearly report, but in addition give more attention to the kidneys and hips until the 23rd, and to the colon, bladder and sexual organs afterwards. Detox regimes will be powerful from the 23rd onwards.

November

Best Days Overall: 6, 7, 15, 16, 17, 25, 26
Most Stressful Days Overall: 13, 14, 20, 21, 27, 28
Best Days for Love: 2, 3, 6, 7, 11, 12, 15, 16, 17, 20, 21, 22, 23, 25, 26
Best Days for Money: 1, 4, 5, 8, 9, 10, 11, 14, 20, 21, 23
Best Days for Career: 4, 5, 13, 14, 22, 23, 27, 28

Love, as we mentioned, is being severely tested, but there is some good news here too. On the 23rd of last month you entered a yearly social peak, and this continues until November 22. There is a stronger focus on love and this focus – this drive – enables you to handle all the various challenges that arise. A given relationship might be problematic, but the overall love life is good – very active now. Marriage is still unlikely and still not advisable, but you can enjoy the ample social opportunities that are happening for what they are.

You have been personally more popular since October 23rd. You are going out of your way for others. You are there for your friends. You are more aggressive in love, going after what you want.

Health is still delicate until the 22nd. Review our discussion of this last month. You can enhance the health in the ways mentioned last month, but after the 17th give more attention to the liver and thighs. Regular thigh massage will be good. Health and energy will be much improved after the 22nd.

Finances are a bit more challenging this month. Mercury, your financial planet, is far away from his natural home, wandering in a far country. He is not as strong as he could be. Generally Taurus is most comfortable when focused on his or her own financial interests. But this month the Cosmos calls you to focus on the financial interests of others – to even consider them ahead of your own. As you help others to prosper, your own prosperity naturally happens. Also this kind of thinking will make any proposals you want to make much easier to sell.

The eclipses of last month are still being felt. Uranus, your career planet, is camping out on an eclipse point all month. Therefore career changes are afoot. There are dramatic changes in your company and industry and dramas in the lives of parents, parent figures and bosses.

Mars travels with Pluto from the 8th to the 12th and squares Uranus from the 12th to the 14th – a very dynamic transit. It further reinforces the career changes that we mentioned above. It also indicates a time to drive more carefully and avoid risky kinds of activities. (This applies to parents or parent figures as well.)

Mercury's re-activation of an eclipse point from the 8th to the 10th creates a short-term financial disturbance. Try not to make it worse than it needs to be. It will pass.

December

Best Days Overall: 3, 4, 13, 14, 22, 23, 30, 31
Most Stressful Days Overall: 10, 11, 18, 19, 24, 25
Best Days for Love: 1, 2, 3, 4, 12, 13, 14, 18, 19, 21, 22, 23, 30, 31
Best Days for Money: 1, 2, 5, 6, 10, 11, 20, 21, 22, 28, 29, 30, 31
Best Days for Career: 1, 2, 10, 11, 20, 21, 24, 25, 28, 29

Love is still unstable this month but there is much improvement happening. On the 24th Saturn will leave your 7th house. He has done his job. You have weeded out the good relationships from the mediocre ones. Your relationship has undergone the worst of the testing and your social life has been placed in right order. Along with this your love planet, Pluto, receives much positive stimulation after the 9th. In fact we could say that you are entering, from the 9th onwards, another yearly social peak.

Uranus is still camped out on the Lunar Eclipse point of October 8. So there is much career change happening. Much of this is good. The changes seem beneficial to you, although perhaps not pleasant. Between 80 and 90 per cent of the planets are above the horizon. The cosmic power is in the upper half of the Horoscope. Ambitions are powerful. There is much career progress and success happening. Mars crosses the Mid-heaven and enters your 10th career house on the 5th. The demands of your career are therefore strong and you are fending off competitors and rivals. You can enhance your career (and your public image) by getting involved in charity work or altruistic causes.

The planetary momentum is overwhelmingly forward at this time. At least 80 per cent (and sometimes 90 per cent) of the planets are in forward motion. So there is rapid progress towards your goals.

Love may have been problematic but the sex life doesn't seem to have suffered. Your 8th house of regeneration has been powerful since November 22 and remains powerful until the 22nd of this month. Whatever your age or stage in life, your libido is stronger than usual.

Taureans are big 'acquirers'. They love to possess things and tend to hold on to their acquisitions. But during this period up to the 22nd it might be good to take stock and get rid of what you don't need or don't use. Give it to charity or sell it. Clear the decks. There's nothing wrong with 'getting', but there are times to let go too. One does not always breathe in; you have to exhale too.

The spiritual law about possessions, as I understand it, is this – you are entitled to anything that you can use and enjoy. You may pray for these things and the Cosmos will grant them. The Cosmos wants you to have them. It doesn't matter how expensive they are. They will come to you, lawfully and legitimately. But things that you can't use or enjoy are merely burdens on you – not real wealth – just headaches. These should be let go of.

Gemini

Ⅱ

THE TWINS

Birthdays from
21st May to
20th June

Personality Profile

GEMINI AT A GLANCE

Element – Air

Ruling Planet – Mercury
  Career Planet – Neptune
  Love Planet – Jupiter
  Money Planet – Moon
  Planet of Health and Work – Pluto
  Planet of Home and Family Life – Mercury

Colours – blue, yellow, yellow-orange

Colour that promotes love, romance and social harmony – sky blue

Colours that promote earning power – grey, silver

Gems – agate, aquamarine

Metal – quicksilver

Scents – lavender, lilac, lily of the valley, storax

Quality – mutable (= flexibility)

Quality most needed for balance – thought that is deep rather than superficial

Strongest virtues – great communication skills, quickness and agility of thought, ability to learn quickly

Deepest need – communication

Characteristics to avoid – gossiping, hurting others with harsh speech, superficiality, using words to mislead or misinform

Signs of greatest overall compatibility – Libra, Aquarius

Signs of greatest overall incompatibility – Virgo, Sagittarius, Pisces

Sign most helpful to career – Pisces

Sign most helpful for emotional support – Virgo

Sign most helpful financially – Cancer

Sign best for marriage and/or partnerships – Sagittarius

Sign most helpful for creative projects – Libra

Best Sign to have fun with – Libra

Signs most helpful in spiritual matters – Taurus, Aquarius

Best day of the week – Wednesday

Understanding a Gemini

Gemini is to society what the nervous system is to the body. It does not introduce any new information but is a vital transmitter of impulses from the senses to the brain and vice versa. The nervous system does not judge or weigh these impulses – it only conveys information. And it does so perfectly.

This analogy should give you an indication of a Gemini's role in society. Geminis are the communicators and conveyors of information. To Geminis the truth or falsehood of information is irrelevant, they only transmit what they see, hear or read about. Thus they are capable of spreading the most outrageous rumours as well as conveying truth and light. Geminis sometimes tend to be unscrupulous in their communications and can do both great good or great evil with their power. This is why the sign of Gemini is symbolized by twins: Geminis have a dual nature.

Their ability to convey a message – to communicate with such ease – makes Geminis ideal teachers, writers and media and marketing people. This is helped by the fact that Mercury, the ruling planet of Gemini, also rules these activities.

Geminis have the gift of the gab. And what a gift this is! They can make conversation about anything, anywhere, at any time. There is almost nothing that is more fun to Geminis than a good conversation – especially if they can learn something new as well. They love to learn and they love to teach. To deprive a Gemini of conversation, or of books and magazines, is cruel and unusual punishment.

Geminis are almost always excellent students and take well to education. Their minds are generally stocked with all kinds of information, trivia, anecdotes, stories, news items, rarities, facts and statistics. Thus they can support any intellectual position that they care to take. They are awesome debaters and, if involved in politics, make good orators. Geminis are so verbally smooth that even if they do not know what they are talking about, they can make you think that they do. They will always dazzle you with their brilliance.

Finance

Geminis tend to be more concerned with the wealth of learning and ideas than with actual material wealth. As mentioned, they excel in professions that involve writing, teaching, sales and journalism – and not all of these professions pay very well. But to sacrifice intellectual needs merely for money is unthinkable to a Gemini. Geminis strive to combine the two. Cancer is on Gemini's solar 2nd house (of money) cusp, which indicates that Geminis can earn extra income (in a harmonious and natural way) from investments in residential property, restaurants and hotels. Given their verbal skills, Geminis love to bargain and negotiate in any situation, and especially when it has to do with money.

The Moon rules Gemini's 2nd solar house. The Moon is not only the fastest-moving planet in the zodiac but actually moves through every sign and house every 28 days. No other heavenly body matches the Moon for swiftness or the ability to change quickly. An analysis of the Moon – and lunar phenomena in general – describes Gemini's financial attitudes very well. Geminis are financially versatile and flexible; they can earn money in many different ways. Their financial attitudes and needs seem to change daily. Their feelings about money change also: sometimes they are very enthusiastic about it, at other times they could not care less.

For a Gemini, financial goals and money are often seen only as means of supporting a family; these things have little meaning otherwise.

The Moon, as Gemini's money planet, has another important message for Gemini financially: in order for Geminis to realize their financial potential they need to develop more of an understanding of the emotional side of life. They need to combine their awesome powers of logic with an understanding of human psychology. Feelings have their own logic; Geminis need to learn this and apply it to financial matters.

Career and Public Image

Geminis know that they have been given the gift of communication for a reason, that it is a power that can achieve great good or cause unthinkable distress. They long to put this power at the service of the highest and most transcendental truths. This is their primary goal, to communicate the eternal verities and prove them logically. They look up to people who can transcend the intellect – to poets, artists, musicians and mystics. They may be awed by stories of religious saints and martyrs. A Gemini's highest achievement is to teach the truth, whether it is scientific, inspirational or historical. Those who can transcend the intellect are Gemini's natural superiors – and a Gemini realizes this.

The sign of Pisces is in Gemini's solar 10th house of career. Neptune, the planet of spirituality and altruism, is Gemini's career planet. If Geminis are to realize their highest career potential they need to develop their transcendental – their spiritual and altruistic – side. They need to understand the larger cosmic picture, the vast flow of human evolution – where it came from and where it is heading. Only then can a Gemini's intellectual powers take their true position and he or she can become the 'messenger of the gods'. Geminis need to cultivate a facility for 'inspiration', which is something that does not originate in the intellect but which comes through the intellect. This will further enrich and empower a Gemini's mind.

Love and Relationships

Geminis bring their natural garrulousness and brilliance into their love life and social life as well. A good talk or a verbal joust is an interesting prelude to romance. Their only problem in love is that their intellect is too cool and passionless to incite ardour in others. Emotions sometimes disturb them, and their partners tend to complain about this. If you are in love with a Gemini you must understand why this is so. Geminis avoid deep passions because these would interfere with their ability to think and communicate. If they are cool towards you, understand that this is their nature.

Nevertheless, Geminis must understand that it is one thing to talk about love and another actually to love – to feel it and radiate it. Talking about love glibly will get them nowhere. They need to feel it and act on it. Love is not of the intellect but of the heart. If you want to know how a Gemini feels about love you should not listen to what he or she says, but rather, observe what he or she does. Geminis can be quite generous to those they love.

Geminis like their partners to be refined, well educated and well travelled. If their partners are more wealthy than they, that is all the better. If you are in love with a Gemini you had better be a good listener as well.

The ideal relationship for the Gemini is a relationship of the mind. They enjoy the physical and emotional aspects, of course, but if the intellectual communion is not there they will suffer.

Home and Domestic Life

At home the Gemini can be uncharacteristically neat and meticulous. They tend to want their children and partner to live up to their idealistic standards. When these standards are not met they moan and criticize. However, Geminis are good family people and like to serve their families in practical and useful ways.

The Gemini home is comfortable and pleasant. They like to invite people over and they make great hosts. Geminis are also good at repairs and improvements around the house – all fuelled by their need to stay active and occupied with something they like to do. Geminis have many hobbies and interests that keep them busy when they are home alone.

Geminis understand and get along well with their children, mainly because they are very youthful people themselves. As great communicators, Geminis know how to explain things to children; in this way they gain their children's love and respect. Geminis also encourage children to be creative and talkative, just like they are.

Horoscope for 2014

Major Trends

You have been in a cycle of prosperity since June of 2012 and it continues in the year ahead – especially during the first half of the year. More on this later on.

Pluto has been in your 8th house for some years now and will be there for many more years. This shows that you are dealing with death and death issues. Perhaps you have had some 'near death' kinds of experiences or experienced the loss of a loved one. Understanding death is perhaps just as important as understanding life, and this is the cosmic agenda here.

Neptune made an important and long-term move in 2012. He moved from your 9th house into your 10th house of career. This is bringing a new sense of idealistic fervour to your career. It is not enough for you to merely make money and be successful in the worldly sense. Your career has to have some spiritual meaning; it has to involve the spiritual good of humanity as a whole. There's more on this later.

Uranus has been in your 11th house of friends since 2011. Thus there is great ferment happening here. Friendships are being tested and many are going by the wayside. By the time Uranus is finished with you, you will be in an entirely new circle of friends.

Health is basically good, but there have been a few scares in recent years and perhaps surgery as well. This area is still unstable in the year ahead. More details later.

Jupiter will move into your 3rd house of communication and intellectual interests on July 16. You are always a gifted communicator, but now your gifts become more enhanced and perhaps more recognized. Your already sharp mind becomes even sharper.

There is foreign travel in your chart after July 16, and next year too.

Your major areas of interest in the coming year are finance (until July 16); communication and intellectual interests (from July 16 onwards); fun, creativity and children (until July 26); health and work (almost all year, until December 24); sex, personal transformation, personal reinvention, death, death issues, and life after death; career; and friends, groups, group activities and online activities.

Your paths of greatest fulfilment this year will be finance (until July 16); communication and intellectual interests (from July 16 onwards); health and work (until February 19); and fun, creativity and children (from February 19 onwards).

Health

(Please note that this is an astrological perspective on health and not a medical one. In days of yore there was no difference, both of these perspectives were identical. But in these times there could be quite a difference. For a medical perspective, please consult your doctor or health practitioner.)

Health and vitality are basically good this year. There is only one long-term planet in stressful alignment with you – Neptune. The rest are either in harmonious aspect or leaving you alone. It is true that some of you might be needing surgery, and if this is the case, it seems successful. You recover well. Basic fundamental vitality is very important in recovering from surgery and you have this.

Your 6th house of health is powerful this year, and thus there is much focus and attention on it. With Pluto as your health planet, you have a predisposition to surgery – a tendency to see it as a 'quick fix' to health problems. But keep in mind that Pluto also rules detox. In many cases detoxification will often do more good than surgery, although the process is much slower. Get a second opinion if you are considering surgery.

Good though the health is, you can make it even better. Pay more attention to the following areas – the vulnerable areas in the year ahead: the colon, bladder and sexual organs. These are always an issue for you. The colon needs to be clean and clear of all toxic build-ups (colonic irrigation might be a good idea). Safe sex and sexual moderation is also important. The spine, knees, teeth, bones, skin and overall skeletal alignment are also very important this year – and for many years to come. Regular back massage will be good. Knees should also be massaged and given more support when exercising. Regular visits to a chiropractor or osteopath are a good idea; the spine needs to be kept in right alignment. (Yoga, Pilates, the Alexander Technique or the Feldenkrais Method are excellent therapies for the spine.) The gall bladder is also vulnerable this year, and back massage will help the gall bladder as well as the back. There are reflexes along the spine that go to all the organs of the body.

If more attention is paid to these areas, many problems can be prevented. And even if they can't be totally prevented, they can be lessened to a great extent.

Your health planet Pluto is in the sign of Capricorn, which rules the spine, knees, teeth, bones, skin and overall skeletal alignment – hence their importance in your overall health. Saturn, the planet that rules these areas, is in your 6th house of health – reinforcing what we say here.

In the past few years we have seen a lot of dramatic changes to the health regime, and this continues in the year ahead. These changes will basically be good. Favourable numbers for health are 8, 11, 13 and 20. If you can somehow incorporate these into your health regime it

Reflexology

Try to massage the whole foot on a regular basis, but pay extra attention to the points highlighted on the chart. When you massage, be aware of 'sore spots', as these need special attention. It's also a good idea to massage the ankles and the top of the feet.

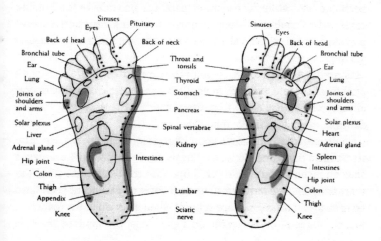

would be helpful. If you are saying affirmations or doing exercises, then do them in sets of 8, 11, 13 or 20. Creative Geminis will find other ways to use these numbers.

Home and Family

Home and family are always important to you. Mercury, the ruler of your Horoscope, is also the ruler of your 4th house of home and family. This shows how close this area is to your heart. It also shows a special bond between you and one of the parents or parent figures in your life – a special closeness, a feeling that you are 'one flesh'. (Your personal Horoscope cast for your exact time of birth could modify this.)

This year though, home and family seems fairly neutral: your 4th house is basically empty. Only short-term planets will move through there, and their effects will be temporary. Thus the Cosmos gives you free will in this area. You have the freedom to make of this what you will – the Cosmos neither pushes you one way nor another. But with lack of interest, the tendency is towards the status quo. We generally don't make changes unless we are 'pushed' by circumstances. I also read this as satisfaction with the way things are. No need to make dramatic changes.

A parent or parent figure seems to have moved in recent years, but this year there are no moves seen. In fact, moves don't even seem advisable for a while. A parent or parent figure may be undergoing surgery. This could have happened in recent years too, but the aspect is in effect in the year ahead as well. One of the parent figures is under-going great spiritual transformation. The body is being refined and sensitized. Alcohol and drugs should be avoided.

Siblings or sibling figures in your life enter a cycle of prosperity on July 16. They travel more than usual and live the 'high life'. Moves, however, are not advisable this year.

Children of the appropriate age might not move, but they seem to be investing in the home. Serious renovations are likely. Their marriages or relationships seem highly unstable though. Grandchildren of the appropriate age are having a status quo home and domestic year. Love and possible marriage is happening for them later on in the year.

Finance and Career

As we mentioned, you have been in a prosperity cycle since 2012. Wealth and financial opportunities increase, and assets you own increase in value. You are catching the lucky financial breaks.

Jupiter, your love planet, is in your money house until July 16. This indicates business partnerships or joint ventures. This was the case last year and the trend is still very much in effect for the first half of 2014. This transit also shows the importance of the social dimension in earnings. Who you know – your social connections – is just as important as how much you have. Financial statements are wonderful tools, but in your case they would be inaccurate. They would not show your hidden assets – your wealthy friends and the financial support of friends.

A lot of your socializing this year seems business related. There's more on this later.

Jupiter generically rules publishing, travel and higher education. Many Geminis are writers, so it looks as if this is a good year to have your work published (as it was last year too). I also like these fields as investments – publishers, private collages and the travel business.

Investments in foreign countries or in foreign companies also seem profitable this year. You are doing more business-related travel as well.

Pluto has been in your 8th house of transformation for some years now. The ruler of your 8th house, Saturn, is in 'mutual reception' with Pluto, which indicates wonderful co-operation between the two planets. Each is a guest in the other's house. Thus there is good access to outside money. Your line of credit should increase this year. Your ability to obtain or pay down debt (depending on your need) is good. If you have good ideas it seems easy to attract outside investment to your projects. Also, you will have opportunities to invest in troubled or even bankrupt properties or companies and turn them around.

It is said that the only major difference between a poor person and a rich person is that the rich person has easy access to outside money. Business runs on credit. Rarely is personal money used. So this easy access to credit that you have is another signal of financial success. The only caveat here is that credit should be used and not abused. And you are in a cycle where you are learning the difference between constructive and destructive debt.

On July 16 Jupiter will leave your money house. I read this as you having mostly attained your financial goals (we never fully attain them as there is always more, more to do and more to be had – but there is a sense of satiation). Instead you will start turning your attention to your true love and true gift – communication and intellectual interests. On the financial level, Jupiter's move from the 2nd to the 3rd house of communication shows increased income from savings and investments. This generally comes through increased dividend or interest income.

The Moon is your financial planet. As regular readers know, she is the fastest of all the planets. Where fast-moving Mercury will move through all your signs and houses in a year, the Moon does this every month. Month after month. Thus there are many short-term trends in finance that are best covered in the monthly reports.

Your favourable financial numbers are 2, 4, 7 and 9.

Love and Social Life

The years 2012 and 2013 were exceptionally strong in terms of your love and social life. Many of you married or got involved in relationships that were 'like' a marriage. Some of you met people you would consider marrying – people who were 'marriage material'. The 7th house of love and marriage is not a house of power this year, and I read this as a basic satisfaction with things as they are. There is no need for dramatic changes. Married couples will tend to stay married and singles will tend to stay single.

In 2013 the aspects were favourable for business-type partnerships and joint ventures – this too is a form of marriage but on the economic level. This can still happen in 2014 as well.

With Jupiter as your love planet you have a natural affinity with wealthy, jet-setting types of people – and this year even more so than usual. Jupiter spends the first half of the year in your money house. Wealth is definitely a romantic turn-on.

However, wealth alone is not enough. Jupiter in the sign of Cancer shows that the beloved must have strong family values. Emotional intimacy – emotional sharing and nurturing – is very important in love, perhaps just as important as the physical aspects. There is such a thing as 'emotional sex'. The sexual act has to happen emotionally as well as physically.

Like last year you show love in material ways – though giving financial support and material gifts. And this is how you feel loved as well. Until July 16 the still-unattached Gemini finds love opportunities as he or she pursues financial goals, and perhaps with people who are involved in his or her finances. Love attitudes start to change after July 16 as the love planet moves into Leo, your 3rd house. The mental connection becomes important in love. Communication is always important to you but now it becomes a love issue. There is a need for mental compatibility, a need to fall in love with the mind as well as the body. Ease of communication is a romantic turn-on. Speech is a form of foreplay. The mind is an erogenous zone.

When Jupiter moves into Leo, love opportunities will happen within the neighbourhood and perhaps with neighbours. Love is close to home. Love opportunities also happen in educational-type settings – at school or school functions, at lectures or seminars, in the library or at the magazine rack at your local newsagent. These are good venues as the sharing of mental interests is a good first step in love – a good first connection.

The Horoscope not only shows the needs in love but the way problems in a relationship get resolved. Until July 16 a nice gift will assuage bruised feelings and restore harmony. After July 16, this will change. It might be wise to read the same book (together as a couple) or attend lectures or take courses together. This will create harmony on the mental level, which is necessary now.

Your favourable numbers for love are 4, 9, 10 and 14.

Self-improvement

Saturn has been in your 6th house of health since October 2012, and will remain there for almost the whole year ahead. Aside from the physical aspects of health, which we have discussed, this indicates changes in attitude. It shows a need to avoid 'quickie' health fixes – things that only give temporary relief – and a focus on long-term cure and prevention. Generally this involves lifestyle adjustments. Also it shows a need – and an ability – to undertake disciplined, rigorous daily health regimes. This is a positive for your health. However, this transit can also make a person ultra conservative in health matters, unwilling to try new and perhaps beneficial therapies. Just because something is new doesn't mean that it is bad. Do your homework.

Neptune, as we mentioned, is now in your 10th house of career for the long term – for the next 12 or so years. This brings idealism to the career, as we said. In many cases it indicates a career in a non-profit or charitable organization. Perhaps the pay is not what you would like, but there will be great personal satisfaction – something that money can't buy. In other cases this indicates a spiritual type of career – ministry, the psychic or astrological field, spiritual channelling, music, poetry or the fine arts. Any calling that involves the 'flow' of spiritual inspiration would appeal to you. Anyone who has experienced this flow can testify that it is euphoric. One is 'high' without drugs or alcohol, and many of you are going to experience this in the coming years. It is a high that has nothing to do with any physical or material thing or event. It is something internal.

For many of you this shows that your true mission (as opposed to your outer career or work) is your spiritual practice, your spiritual growth. Though these practices seem solitary and subtle (nothing overt seems to happen) they are nevertheless very powerful. First they change your internal condition on a personal level. This in turn affects the internal condition of family members and those you come in contact with. Then the waves spread out to the community, the city, the country and the world.

Many people think that world changes happen in the White House, Wall Street, Brussels or in Parliament. The truth is that it is spiritual breakthroughs made by solitary practitioners – away from the crowds, flashing cameras and hoopla – that change the world. The activities of the politicians and rulers are merely the end result of changes that were made by individuals meditating alone.

So these activities are a valid career path from the spiritual perspective of things.

Many of you are questioning what to do with your lives – what path to pursue. With Neptune in your 10th house there will be much revelation on this subject. Take notice of your dreams. Astrologers, psychics, ministers, priests – these kinds of people – have important guidance on these issues.

Month-by-month Forecasts

January

Best Days Overall: 3, 4, 12, 13, 22, 23, 30, 31
Most Stressful Days Overall: 5, 6, 19, 20, 26, 27
Best Days for Love: 1, 2, 5, 6, 9, 10, 14, 15, 19, 20, 24, 25, 26, 27, 28, 29
Best Days for Money: 1, 2, 5, 6, 9, 10, 14, 15, 21, 22, 24, 25, 30, 31
Best Days for Career: 5, 6, 14, 24

You begin your year with the planetary power mostly in the upper half of the Horoscope, with at least 60 per cent and sometimes 70 per cent of the planets in the top hemisphere. You are in the late morning of your year – a time to be physically active and to pursue your goals in a physical kind of way, by the methods of day. It is safe and advisable to let go of family and emotional issues for a while and focus on your career and outer objectives. For the next few months, you are in a cycle of career success.

The planetary power is also mostly in the West – the social sector. Personal independence is not yet what it should be or will be. It is more difficult to change conditions and circumstances, so rather adapt to them as best you can. Take note of what displeases you and when the cycle of personal independence comes – and it will – you can make the appropriate changes. They will happen easily and naturally then. For now, cultivate your social skills. Your way might not be the best way at this time. Consult with others, take advice, and work for consensus and co-operation.

Finances, overall, will be wonderful in the year ahead. You will see substantial increases in earnings and in your overall net worth. If your financial goals are stratospheric, you might not see the complete attainment of them, but you will make good progress towards them.

This should also be considered success. Finances look good in the month ahead too. With the Moon as your financial planet, the new Moon and full Moon are especially powerful financial days. This month we have two new Moons (generally there is only one) – this is like the Cosmos throwing you a bonus payday. The two new Moons are on the 1st and the 30th. The full Moon (also a powerful financial day) will be on the 16th (and will occur in your money house to boot). In general earning power will be strongest when the Moon waxes (grows larger) – this will be from the 1st to the 16th and on the 30th and 31st.

You have some good financial days when the Moon is waning too, but they won't be as good as the good financial days when the Moon is waxing.

Love is more complicated this month. The love planet, Jupiter, is retrograde all month, so there is a feeling of being 'directionless' in love and in a current relationship. This is a time for reviewing the love life, not for decision making. Short-term stressful transits to Jupiter can give you a false impression of the state of a current relationship and to your love prospects in general. Review, get the facts, and allow love to develop as it will. Love will improve after the 20th.

Health is basically good this month. You can enhance it further in the ways mentioned in the yearly report.

February

Best Days Overall: 8, 9, 18, 19, 26, 27
Most Stressful Days Overall: 1, 2, 15, 16, 17, 22, 23, 28
Best Days for Love: 1, 2, 5, 6, 7, 10, 11, 16, 17, 20, 21, 22, 23, 24, 25, 28
Best Days for Money: 1, 2, 8, 9, 10, 11, 12, 20, 21, 28
Best Days for Career: 1, 2, 10, 20, 28

What the Cosmos gave last month it takes away this month. This month there are NO new Moons – also highly unusual. Overall prosperity is still intact however. Jupiter is still occupying your money house. Earnings are accruing but not as much as last month. The full Moon of the 14th will be a powerful financial day – also the waxing Moon period from the 1st to the 14th.

Your 9th house of religion, travel and learning was strong last month and remains so until the 18th. Thus foreign lands call to you. Travel is in the air. Opportunities will come. This is also an excellent period for students – they should do well in their studies. The interest and passion for learning is there and this is 90 per cent of success. Those of you of a religious bent will have religious and philosophical break-throughs. This is a good period for the study of sacred literature.

On the 18th you enter one of your yearly career peaks, although you will feel the effects of this before that date. Mercury, the ruler of your Horoscope, crosses the Mid-heaven and enters the 10th house on the 1st. He will basically 'camp out' – make what is called a 'station' – right on Neptune, your career planet, until the 13th. This shows career success and elevation. You are on top for a while, in charge, above everyone in your world. However, Mercury will go retrograde on the 6th and you will start to back away from this. Perhaps it is not what you thought it would be. You seem unsure as to whether you want this. Mercury will be retrograde until the 28th and it will be good to review your personal and career aspirations now. In spite of Mercury's retro-grade, you will have career success. Next month might be better, but this month is OK.

It is still good to focus on the career and to let family issues go for a while. With Mercury retrograde there's not much to be done to solve family problems – only time will solve them.

Mercury's station on Neptune is not only a good career aspect but a highly spiritual one too. The dream life will be more active – and perhaps prophetic. ESP (extra-sensory perception) faculties will be enhanced. Spiritual breakthroughs are likely. When these things happen it is most joyous – these breakthroughs tend to be 'game changers'.

Overall, health is basically good. However, after the 18th you enter a short-term vulnerable period. Compared to other periods of the year, it is 'less easy', so schedule in more rest periods then. Refuse to allow yourself to get overtired. Regular readers know that high energy levels are the 1st line of defence against illness. Enhance the health in the ways mentioned in the yearly report.

March

Best Days Overall: 7, 8, 17, 18, 26, 27
Most Stressful Days Overall: 1, 2, 15, 16, 22, 23, 28, 29
Best Days for Love: 1, 2, 7, 10, 11, 17, 18, 19, 20, 22, 23, 26, 27, 28, 29
Best Days for Money: 1, 2, 10, 11, 19, 20, 21, 22, 28, 29, 30, 31
Best Days for Career: 1, 2, 10, 19, 28, 29

Health will still need attention until the 20th of this month. Success (which you are having) can be as stressful as failure (although a lot more fun). Review our discussion of this last month. Health and energy will rebound after the 20th.

Though overall energy could be better, many nice things are happening for you. You are still in the midst of a yearly career peak until the 20th. Mercury crosses the Mid-heaven on the 17th and again enters your 10th house of career. This shows you are once again appreciated, honoured and respected. Personal appearance is a big factor in your career from the 17th onwards, so pay attention here. Mercury will travel with Neptune, your career planet, from the 17th to the 19th – this too brings career elevation and opportunity. (It is a repeat of what we saw last month, only now Mercury is moving forward.)

Mercury moving forward indicates more self-confidence and self-esteem.

Love was reasonable last month – especially after the 18th – but Jupiter's retrograde motion was complicating things. This month, on the 6th, Jupiter will start moving forward. A current relationship will also move forward. There is more social confidence. Mercury will make beautiful aspects to the love planet from the 17th onwards, but especially from the 24th to the 27th. Singles or those unattached will have a romantic connection then. Existing relationships should be more romantic than usual as well. Business partnerships can also happen.

Singles find opportunities for love as they pursue their career and financial goals or with people involved in these areas. Wealth is a turn-on in love – this has been the case since last year.

What the cosmos took away last month it now gives in the month ahead. Once again we have two New Moons – you get an extra pay day.

These New Moons happen on the 1st and the 30th. The Full Moon – also a nice pay day – happens on the 16th. In general earning power will be stronger from the 1st to the 16th and on the 30th and 31st – as the Moon waxes. Partnerships and joint ventures should be explored too.

Venus re-activates a previous eclipse point from the 21st to the 23rd. Children or children figures in your life should slim down their schedule over this period. This time can bring spiritual changes as well.

Mars will activate an eclipse point from the 11th to the 18th. Computer equipment could play up and its replacement or repair might be needed. Friends should drive more carefully and avoid confrontations.

April

Best Days Overall: 3, 4, 5, 13, 14, 15, 22, 23
Most Stressful Days Overall: 11, 12, 18, 19, 24, 25
Best Days for Love: 4, 5, 6, 7, 16, 17, 18, 19, 24, 25
Best Days for Money: 6, 7, 9, 10, 16, 17, 19, 20, 24, 25, 29, 30
Best Days for Career: 6, 7, 16, 17, 24, 25

Last month on the 17th the planetary power started to shift from the West to the East. This month, on the 6th, the shift is established. The Eastern sector of personal independence is now dominant in the Horoscope. People skills are wonderful but now it is time to assert yourself more and to follow your personal path of bliss. Hopefully you've made a note of the changes that you need to make to create conditions to suit you, as now is the time (and for the next five or so months) to make those changes. This is a time to please yourself. Your way is best for you. So long as others are not being hurt you should please yourself. The Cosmos wants you to be happy.

We have two eclipses this month, which ensures that this is a month of dramatic change. Things or projects that are not in line with the cosmic plan get blasted away. Things in line with the plan are generally left alone.

The Lunar Eclipse of the 15th occurs in your 5th house of fun and creativity, and it can test a love affair (although not a marriage or committed relationship). It brings change and dramas in the lives of children or children figures. If you are of childbearing age it often indicates a pregnancy. Friendships also get tested. This eclipse happens right on Mars. Dramas are happening in friends' lives and perhaps their current relationships get tested. If you are involved in leisure activities keep them safe and risk-free. Every Lunar Eclipse brings financial change and adjustment for you and this one is no different. It is good that twice a year you get a chance to make any necessary changes and upgrades.

The Solar Eclipse of the 29th occurs in your 12th house of spirituality. This signals long-term spiritual change. It won't happen overnight, but is a six-month process. Those not on a spiritual path might embark on one. Those already on that path will make important changes, perhaps in their teachers or practice. Spiritual attitudes will get tested by 'life facts'. Every Solar Eclipse affects siblings (or sibling figures in your life), neighbours and your neighbourhood. So there are dramas here. Sometimes major construction is begun in your neighbourhood and travel is inconvenient for a few months. Cars and communication equipment will get tested. Drive more carefully during this period.

Health is basically good, but it won't hurt to take things easy during the eclipse periods.

Those of you involved in the arts will have special inspiration from the 10th to the 18th. Singles will have opportunities for romance with spiritual types – artists, musicians, poets, yogis: these kinds of people.

May

Best Days Overall: 1, 2, 11, 12, 19, 20, 28, 29
Most Stressful Days Overall: 8, 9, 10, 15, 16, 21, 22
Best Days for Love: 3, 4, 5, 6, 13, 14, 15, 16, 21, 22, 24, 25, 31
Best Days for Money: 3, 4, 5, 8, 9, 10, 13, 14, 17, 18, 21, 22, 28, 29, 31
Best Days for Career: 3, 4, 13, 14, 21, 22, 31

You entered a very spiritual period on the 20th of last month and this continues until the 21st of this. It would be normal to crave more solitude – more quiet time – now (nothing is wrong with you!). It is a very good period for spiritual studies and practice, and for getting more involved with charities and causes that you believe in. This spiritual period is good in other ways too. Your birthday is coming up this month or next, and your birthday (really your 'Solar Return') is your personal new year. You are closing out an old year and beginning a new cycle. So it is the perfect time to review the past year and see what has been accomplished or not accomplished. What could have been done better? What mistakes were made? Do you feel regrets? The correction of past mistakes was called 'atonement' in the old religious language. That's all atonement is. We confess and correct. Once this is done, set your goals for the year ahead. This way you start your new year with a clean slate.

On the 21st, as the Sun enters your own sign, you begin one of your yearly personal pleasure peaks. This is a time for pampering the body, allowing it to enjoy its pleasures. The Sun's entry into your own sign is wonderful for health and energy. Health should be good. You exude more life and this is reflected in your personal appearance. You have more of that 'It' quality – personal charisma and magnetism. You have increased self-confidence and self-esteem too. Generally this is good for love because you become more attractive to the opposite sex. But love needs more than just physical attraction to work. The love life will be much better next month.

Be more patient with elders, parents and parent figures and bosses on the 11th, 28th and 29th. If you need favours from them, try at a different time.

Mercury moves speedily this month, which shows that you are active and covering a lot of territory. This also shows good self-esteem and confidence. Mercury is also 'out of bounds' from the 12th onwards, so you are going way out of your normal environment during this period. You are taking the less travelled road in your search for happiness.

Career is still important but it is beginning to wind down. The planets are starting to shift to the lower half of the Horoscope. It doesn't fully happen this month, but they're getting ready to move and by next month the shift will be established. This month you are in a twilight period. You're dividing your attention between home and career.

Finances are good this month, but next month will be even better.

June

Best Days Overall: 7, 8, 16, 17, 24, 25, 26
Most Stressful Days Overall: 5, 6, 12, 13, 18, 19
Best Days for Love: 1, 5, 6, 10, 11, 12, 13, 14, 15, 18, 19, 23, 24, 27, 28
Best Days for Money: 1, 7, 8, 10, 11, 16, 17, 18, 19, 27, 28
Best Days for Career: 1, 9, 10, 18, 19, 27, 28

On the 23rd the lower half of the Horoscope becomes dominant. It is time to shift attention from the career and outer goals and focus on the family and your emotional well-being. The next five or six months are for gathering the forces for the next career push. It is like getting a good night's sleep. You seem inactive but mighty processes are happening in this inactivity. The deeper mind is building in the patterns for the next day.

During last month and this, the planets are in their maximum Eastern position for the year. Thus you are in your period of greatest personal independence. Change what should be changed and create your life according to your specs. It's all up to you now. The world will adapt to you.

This is basically a happy month. Career goals have more or less been attained. And if not completely attained, much progress has been made towards them. Health is still excellent. You look even better than you did last month, for now Venus is entering your sign on the 23rd. This gives a sense of style and beauty to the image. You have grace. The mind is sharp and clear. On the 21st you enter a yearly financial peak – a period of prosperity. Earnings and net worth will increase. Love is also good. Venus in your sign makes you more attractive to the opposite sex. Jupiter, your love planet, is starting to receive positive stimulation.

The only real problem is Mercury's retrograde from the 7th onwards. This detracts somewhat from your confidence and self-esteem. These are still good, but not as strong as they could be. Also, this month we have the maximum of retrograde activity for the year – 40 per cent of the planets are moving backwards from the 9th onwards. (We won't exceed this percentage again this year.) So the pace of life is slower and things get done more slowly. Patience. Patience. Patience.

Geminis are not especially fertile this year (of course your personal Horoscope cast just for you could modify this), but as Venus enters your 1st house from the 23rd onwards there is a window of enhanced fertility.

Finances are excellent from the 21st onwards as we have mentioned, but you have nice paydays on the full Moon of the 13th and the new Moon of the 27th. Earning power will also be strong from the 1st to the 13th and from the 27th onwards – as the Moon is waxing.

July

Best Days Overall: 4, 5, 6, 13, 14, 22, 23
Most Stressful Days Overall: 2, 3, 9, 10, 15, 16, 29, 30, 31
Best Days for Love: 4, 5, 6, 7, 8, 9, 10, 13, 14, 16, 17, 24, 27
Best Days for Money: 7, 8, 15, 16, 17, 24, 25, 27
Best Days for Career: 7, 8, 15, 16, 24, 25

Finance is the main headline of the month ahead. You are well into a yearly financial peak which continues until July 22. Your 2nd money house is easily the most powerful in the Horoscope – half the planets are either there or moving through there this month. This is a lot of financial power. Earnings should be unusually strong. You seem to do the same things that you always do, yet you prosper. People suddenly want what you have to offer. You have a golden financial touch.

By the 22nd your short-term financial goals should have been achieved and you now have the freedom to pursue your first love: intellectual development – studying, reading and general mental expansion.

Jupiter makes a major move from the money house into your 3rd house of communication on the 17th. He will be there for the rest of the year ahead and well into next year. On the purely mundane level this indicates a new high end car and new communication equipment coming to you. Never mind 'how' – the Cosmos will arrange things. (It is likely this month, but could also happen over the next six months.)

The Sun will join Jupiter in the 3rd house on the 22nd. This is Gemini heaven. All kinds of new books and information will come to you. You are always in a mood for study and learning but now even more so. This is an excellent period for students. Writers, teachers, sales and marketing people should have a banner month too. Your skills are greatly enhanced.

This month (and for the year ahead) you get a taste of what Gemini is really all about – a messenger-spokesperson of the gods.

Health is excellent and you can enhance it further in the ways mentioned in the yearly report.

Jupiter's move from Cancer to Leo signals a shift in the love life and your love attitudes. Wealth is less important to you now (probably because you have achieved most of your financial goals). Instead you are interested in intellectual and mental compatibility. You want someone who is easy to talk to, someone who listens well, someone you can share ideas with. You want to fall in love with their mind as much as their body. You also want someone who can show you a good time – a fun person, a happy person. The venue of romance is also changing. Romantic opportunities happen in the neighbourhood and perhaps with neighbours, in educational settings – in lectures and seminars – and perhaps at the library.

August

Best Days Overall: 1, 2, 10, 18, 19, 28, 29
Most Stressful Days Overall: 5, 6, 11, 12, 25, 26, 27
Best Days for Love: 3, 4, 5, 6, 12, 13, 14, 23, 24
Best Days for Money: 5, 6, 13, 14, 20, 21, 22, 23, 24, 25
Best Days for Career: 3, 4, 11, 12, 20, 21, 30, 31

You are now approaching the midnight hour of your year. Outer activity is lessened but dynamic inner activity is happening. Career is much less important these days (though last month brought success and opportunity from the 17th to the 20th). It is time to recharge the batteries, to deal with the home and family, and to get the emotional life in order. This is the time to shore up the psychological foundations for future career success. Work on your career by the methods of night – through visualizing where you want to be; controlled dreaming. Actions will grow out of this visualization in due course in a very natural way. Your career planet Neptune has been retrograde for some months now. Thus it is safe to let go of the career (relatively speaking) and focus on the home and family.

This is a month for inner psychological progress rather than outer progress, although one is related to the other. Inner progress leads to outer progress and outer progress leads to inner progress. It is just a matter of understanding your place in the cycle.

You are still very much in Gemini heaven until August 23. Read, study, take courses and build up your knowledge base. Writing will go very well this month, and sales and marketing people will enjoy success.

You are still in a period of personal independence but this is soon to end. If there are still personal changes to make, now is the time to do so. Later on it will be more difficult.

Love is good this month. A very happy romantic meeting happens between the 1st and the 3rd. If you are already in a relationship, this can indicate a happy social opportunity.

Health needs more attention after the 23rd.

There are no eclipses this month, but because many planets are activating eclipse points from previous events it will feel as if eclipses are happening. There will be many sudden and dramatic happenings. The Sun transits an eclipse point on the 1st and 2nd. Be more careful driving. Communications can be disrupted. On the 5th and 6th Mercury will transit this point, which means you should make sure you have a nice easy, relaxed schedule during this period. Jupiter will transit this point from the 24th to the 31st. This tends to bring dramas in love. Be more patient with the beloved during this period.

September

Best Days Overall: 6, 7, 14, 15, 24, 25
Most Stressful Days Overall: 2, 3, 8, 9, 22, 23, 29, 30
Best Days for Love: 1, 2, 3, 10, 11, 12, 13, 19, 20, 23, 29, 30
Best Days for Money: 1, 2, 3, 4, 5, 10, 11, 12, 13, 17, 18, 19, 20, 23, 24, 29, 30
Best Days for Career: 8, 9, 16, 17, 26, 27

The planetary power shifts this month from the East to the West. On the 5th, as Venus moves to the West, the Western, social sector of the Horoscope starts to dominate. Your period of personal independence is over with. Now, for the rest of the year, you will have to live with what you have managed to create, for good or bad. If your creations have been amiss, you will experience the discomfort of the mistakes and see how you can correct them later on down the road. This is called 'paying karma'. It is not as dramatic as it sounds. Creations have consequences and until we experience the consequences we don't really understand what we have created. These are not punishments, only learning experiences. Now and for the rest of the year ahead you are being called on to develop your social skills once again. It is more difficult to act arbitrarily. You need others to help achieve your goals. Likeability is perhaps as important now as your personal skills.

Your 4th house of home and family became powerful on the 23rd of last month and is powerful until the 23rd of the month ahead. Geminis are mental people. No one can verbalize feelings better than a Gemini. But to actually feel – to experience a real feeling directly – this is another story. It is another universe, an alien universe. Yet this is what is happening this month. The world of feeling has its own kind of logic and this is what you are experiencing this month.

Health has been delicate since the 23rd of last month. There's nothing seriously wrong with you, but this not your best month for health. Your energy levels are not up to their normal standard and this can make a pre-existing condition seem worse, or make you vulnerable to opportunistic infections. Thus rest and relax more. Do your best to maintain high energy levels. Get massages or spend more time in a health spa. You can also enhance your health in the ways mentioned in the yearly report.

Finances are not such a big deal these days, ever since Jupiter left your money house. I read this as a positive. You are more or less satisfied with the status quo. Earning power will be strongest from the 1st to the 8th and from the 24th to the 30th – as the Moon waxes. The full Moon of the 8th and the new Moon of the 24th are nice paydays.

Love is reasonable this month. Nothing special is happening here, but there are no disasters either. You should see improvement in this area after the 14th.

October

Best Days Overall: 3, 4, 12, 13, 21, 22, 23, 31
Most Stressful Days Overall: 5, 6, 19, 20, 26, 27
Best Days for Love: 3, 7, 8, 12, 13, 17, 18, 22, 23, 26, 27
Best Days for Money: 3, 4, 7, 8, 12, 13, 14, 15, 17, 18, 22, 23, 26, 27
Best Days for Career: 5, 6, 14, 23, 24

On September 23 you entered another of your yearly personal pleasure peaks, which will continue until the 23rd of this month. This makes this a party kind of month, a month for fun and leisure activities. Though the month ahead is tumultuous for the world (we have two eclipses) you still manage to have fun. If we can enjoy ourselves in the midst of all kinds of crises, we have attained something great.

The Lunar Eclipse on the 8th occurs in your 11th house. This indicates a testing of friendships. Generally this happens because of dramas in friends' personal lives, and is not necessarily due to the relationship itself. But if the relationship is fundamentally flawed it can break up now. This eclipse occurs very near Uranus, the ruler of your 9th house of religion, travel and learning. Unnecessary travel abroad is best avoided now. This also shows that your religious and philosophical beliefs are getting tested (a six-month process) and many of these will be changed. Often an eclipse here produces a 'crisis of faith'. Pluto, your health and work planet, also gets sideswiped by this eclipse. Thus there can be disturbances at the job or workplace, and perhaps job changes. There are changes in the overall health regime too (this is also a six-month process). Every Lunar Eclipse brings financial change and this one is no different. Generally we don't make needed changes unless there is crisis – and this is the purpose of the crisis.

The Solar Eclipse of the 23rd occurs right on the cusp of the 6th house of health and work. Again this shows disturbances at the job or workplace and perhaps job changes. These changes can be with your present company or with another one. It also indicates changes in the health regime and diet. Sometimes it brings health scares. Since your health is basically good, these will be nothing more than scares. If necessary, get second opinions. Communications tend to be interrupted during a Solar Eclipse and this one is no different. Cars and communication equipment get tested.

Notwithstanding the eclipse of the 23rd, health is basically good this month, and you can enhance it further in the ways mentioned in the yearly report.

Job seekers should have good fortune from the 23rd onwards. Your 6th house becomes very powerful. You are in the mood for work and are focused on it, and this is 90 per cent of the battle. Prospective employers pick up on this.

Mars spends most of the month in the 7th house of love. You seem more aggressive in love and in social matters this period, more willing to push things. Avoid power struggles in love. This is the main danger now.

Earning power this month is strongest from the 1st to the 8th and from the 23rd onwards – as the Moon is waxing.

November

Best Days Overall: 8, 9, 18, 19, 27, 28
Most Stressful Days Overall: 2, 3, 15, 16, 17, 22, 23, 29, 30
Best Days for Love: 2, 3, 4, 5, 11, 12, 14, 22, 23
Best Days for Money: 2, 3, 4, 5, 10, 11, 12, 14, 21, 22, 23
Best Days for Career: 2, 3, 10, 11, 20, 29, 30

The planetary power makes an important shift this month, from the lower to the upper half of your Horoscope. It begins to happen on the 22nd, and gets even stronger on the 28th. It is morning in your year. It is time to get up and work by the methods of day, time to be focused on your outer life – your career and outer goals. If you have prepared for this using the methods of night for the past six months, the actions you take will be natural and spontaneous. You will just be 'following through' on your previous inner work. You can start to let go of home and family issues (though they will always be important to you) and give more attention to the career. Your career planet starts to move forward on the 16th so your career judgement is much better now.

The month ahead is still excellent for job seekers. There are many happy job opportunities out there. The problem is not 'getting a job' but in choosing from many possibilities.

Those already in jobs are more successful at work and more productive. Superiors are taking note. This period is also good for doing the boring, detailed tasks that need to be done periodically, such as your accounts, filing, etc.

Health is good until the 22nd but after then it becomes more delicate. Overall your health is basically good, but energy levels are not up to their usual standards. Be sure to get enough sleep. More massages might also be a good idea. Enhance your health in the ways mentioned in the yearly report.

On the 22nd you enter a yearly love and social peak. The social life gets very active. Also, the planets will be making very nice aspects to Jupiter, your love planet. He will be part of a Grand Trine in fire from the 17th onwards. If you are single you are likely to meet a special someone now. Those already in relationships will have more harmony within that relationship. Many of you might decide to marry during this period.

Friendships are still delicate, so be more patient with your friends. There is much ferment and change happening in trade or professional organizations you're involved with. Computers and high-tech equipment seem temperamental now, and cars and communication equipment are more temperamental than normal between the 17th and the 19th.

Your finances are more or less satisfactory. Earning power is strongest from the 1st to the 6th and from the 22nd to the 30th as the Moon waxes. There are nice paydays on the 6th and 22nd.

December

Best Days Overall: 5, 6, 15, 16, 24, 25
Most Stressful Days Overall: 13, 14, 20, 21, 26, 27
Best Days for Love: 1, 2, 10, 11, 12, 13, 20, 21, 22, 28, 29, 30, 31
Best Days for Money: 1, 2, 8, 9, 10, 11, 20, 21, 28, 29, 30, 31
Best Days for Career: 8, 18, 26, 27

You end your year pretty much as you began it (though you are undoubtedly richer and wiser). The planetary power is focused in the West and in the upper half of the Horoscope. The focus is on the career and the social life. You are honing your people skills now. Your way is most likely not the best way, so get input from others. Achieve your goals through consensus and co-operation. Your personal skills are always important but these days the 'likeability' factor is perhaps just as important. If there are conditions that are uncomfortable, adapt and adjust to them as best you can. The time for you to make changes will come in the next few months.

Health still needs watching until the 22nd. Rest and relax more and enhance the health in the ways mentioned in the yearly report. Now that Saturn is moving into Sagittarius (on the 24th), health and energy is going to be more of an issue for the next two years. You are only feeling the beginnings of this transit, especially those of you born early in the sign of Gemini (from May 21–23).

The love life is still excellent. You are still in the midst of a yearly love and social peak, and Jupiter is still receiving positive aspects. But Jupiter will go into retrograde motion on the 8th and if you're planning a marriage or party, try to schedule it before then. Saturn's move into Sagittarius on the 24th will impact on the love life as well. You've expanded your social life a lot these past few years, but now Saturn will test these things – will separate the wheat from the chaff. You will feel this more next year, but the beginnings of it are happening now.

Your 8th house of transformation and regeneration becomes power-ful from the 22nd onwards – in fact unusually powerful. Sixty per cent of the planets are either there or moving through there this month. This indicates a sexually active kind of month. Whatever your age or stage in life, your libido is stronger than usual. It is also a month for dealing with death and issues around death. Probably you will attend more funerals and memorial services than usual. It is time to get a deeper understanding of this area of life. When we understand death we will understand life and live differently.

This is a very good month to take stock and get rid of possessions that you no longer need or use. With Gemini there is a plethora of 'intellectual' possessions – books, magazines, flyers, pamphlets. It's good to get rid of the clutter now. Ideas and concepts – the content of the mind – should also be cleansed; 90 per cent of it is not valid. It could be interesting, but not really useful.

Your spouse, partner or current love is in a yearly financial peak and is probably more generous with you. You have nice paydays on the 6th and 21st. Earning power will be strongest from the 1st to the 6th and from the 21st to the 31st.

Cancer

THE CRAB

Birthdays from
21st June to
20th July

Personality Profile

CANCER AT A GLANCE

Element – Water

Ruling Planet – Moon
   Career Planet – Mars
   Love Planet – Saturn
   Money Planet – Sun
   Planet of Fun and Games – Pluto
   Planet of Good Fortune – Neptune
   Planet of Health and Work – Jupiter
   Planet of Home and Family Life – Venus
   Planet of Spirituality – Mercury

Colours – blue, puce, silver

Colours that promote love, romance and social harmony – black, indigo

Colours that promote earning power – gold, orange

Gems – moonstone, pearl

Metal – silver

Scents – jasmine, sandalwood

Quality – cardinal (= activity)

Quality most needed for balance – mood control

Strongest virtues – emotional sensitivity, tenacity, the urge to nurture

Deepest need – a harmonious home and family life

Characteristics to avoid – over-sensitivity, negative moods

Signs of greatest overall compatibility – Scorpio, Pisces

Signs of greatest overall incompatibility – Aries, Libra, Capricorn

Sign most helpful to career – Aries

Sign most helpful for emotional support – Libra

Sign most helpful financially – Leo

Sign best for marriage and/or partnerships – Capricorn

Sign most helpful for creative projects – Scorpio

Best Sign to have fun with – Scorpio

Signs most helpful in spiritual matters – Gemini, Pisces

Best day of the week – Monday

Understanding a Cancer

In the sign of Cancer the heavens are developing the feeling side of things. This is what a true Cancerian is all about – feelings. Where Aries will tend to err on the side of action, Taurus on the side of inaction and Gemini on the side of thought, Cancer will tend to err on the side of feeling.

Cancerians tend to mistrust logic. Perhaps rightfully so. For them it is not enough for an argument or a project to be logical – it must feel right as well. If it does not feel right a Cancerian will reject it or chafe against it. The phrase 'follow your heart' could have been coined by a Cancerian, because it describes exactly the Cancerian attitude to life.

The power to feel is a more direct – more immediate – method of knowing than thinking is. Thinking is indirect. Thinking about a thing never touches the thing itself. Feeling is a faculty that touches directly the thing or issue in question. We actually experience it. Emotional feeling is almost like another sense which humans possess – a psychic sense. Since the realities that we come in contact with during our lifetime are often painful and even destructive, it is not surprising that the Cancerian chooses to erect barriers – a shell – to protect his or her vulnerable, sensitive nature. To a Cancerian this is only common sense.

If Cancerians are in the presence of people they do not know, or find themselves in a hostile environment, up goes the shell and they feel protected. Other people often complain about this, but one must question these people's motives. Why does this shell disturb them? Is it perhaps because they would like to sting, and feel frustrated that they cannot? If your intentions are honourable and you are patient, have no fear. The shell will open up and you will be accepted as part of the Cancerian's circle of family and friends.

Thought-processes are generally analytic and dissociating. In order to think clearly we must make distinctions, comparisons and the like. But feeling is unifying and integrative.

To think clearly about something you have to distance yourself from it. To feel something you must get close to it. Once a Cancerian has accepted you as a friend he or she will hang on to you. You have to be really bad to lose the friendship of a Cancerian. If you are related to Cancerians they will never let you go no matter what you do. They will always try to maintain some kind of connection even in the most extreme circumstances.

Finance

The Cancer-born has a deep sense of what other people feel about things and why they feel as they do. This faculty is a great asset in the workplace and in the business world. Of course it is also indispensable in raising a family and building a home, but it also has its uses in business. Cancerians often attain great wealth in a family business. Even if the business is not a family operation, they will treat it as one. If the Cancerian works for somebody else, then the boss is the parental figure and the co-workers are brothers and sisters. If a Cancerian is the boss, then all the workers are his or her children. Cancerians like the feeling of being providers for others. They enjoy knowing that others derive their sustenance because of what they do. It is another form of nurturing.

With Leo on their solar 2nd house (of money) cusp, Cancerians are often lucky speculators, especially with residential property or hotels and restaurants. Resort hotels and nightclubs are also profitable for the Cancerian. Waterside properties allure them. Though they are basically conventional people, they sometimes like to earn their livelihood in glamorous ways.

The Sun, Cancer's money planet, represents an important financial message: in financial matters Cancerians need to be less moody, more stable and fixed. They cannot allow their moods – which are here today and gone tomorrow – to get in the way of their business lives. They need to develop their self-esteem and feelings of self-worth if they are to realize their greatest financial potential.

Career and Public Image

Aries rules the 10th solar house (of career) cusp of Cancer, which indicates that Cancerians long to start their own business, to be more active publicly and politically and to be more independent. Family responsibilities and a fear of hurting other people's feelings – or getting hurt themselves – often inhibit them from attaining these goals. However, this is what they want and long to do.

Cancerians like their bosses and leaders to act freely and to be a bit self-willed. They can deal with that in a superior. They expect their leaders to be fierce on their behalf. When the Cancerian is in the position of boss or superior he or she behaves very much like a 'warlord'. Of course the wars they wage are not egocentric but in defence of those under their care. If they lack some of this fighting instinct – independence and pioneering spirit – Cancerians will have extreme difficulty in attaining their highest career goals. They will be hampered in their attempts to lead others.

Since they are so parental, Cancerians like to work with children and make great educators and teachers.

Love and Relationships

Like Taurus, Cancer likes committed relationships. Cancerians function best when the relationship is clearly defined and everyone knows his or her role. When they marry it is usually for life. They are extremely loyal to their beloved. But there is a deep little secret that most Cancerians will never admit to: commitment or partnership is really a chore and a duty to them. They enter into it because they know of no other way to create the family that they desire. Union is just a way – a means to an end – rather than an end in itself. The family is the ultimate end for them.

If you are in love with a Cancerian you must tread lightly on his or her feelings. It will take you a good deal of time to realize how deep and sensitive Cancerians can be. The smallest negativity upsets them. Your tone of voice, your irritation, a look in your eye or an expression on your face can cause great distress for the Cancerian. Your slightest gesture is registered by them and reacted to. This can be hard to get used to, but stick by your love – Cancerians make great partners once you learn how to deal with them. Your Cancerian lover will react not so much to what you say but to the way you are actually feeling at the moment.

Home and Domestic Life

This is where Cancerians really excel. The home environment and the family are their personal works of art. They strive to make things of beauty that will outlast them. Very often they succeed.

Cancerians feel very close to their family, their relatives and especially their mothers. These bonds last throughout their lives and mature as they grow older. They are very fond of those members of their family who become successful, and they are also quite attached to family heirlooms and mementos. Cancerians also love children and like to provide them with all the things they need and want. With their nurturing, feeling nature, Cancerians make very good parents – especially the Cancerian woman, who is the mother *par excellence* of the zodiac.

As a parent the Cancerian's attitude is 'my children right or wrong'. Unconditional devotion is the order of the day. No matter what a family member does, the Cancerian will eventually forgive him or her, because 'you are, after all, family'. The preservation of the institution – the tradition – of the family is one of the Cancerian's main reasons for living. They have many lessons to teach others about this.

Being so family-orientated, the Cancerian's home is always clean, orderly and comfortable. They like old-fashioned furnishings but they also like to have all the modern comforts. Cancerians love to have family and friends over, to organize parties and to entertain at home – they make great hosts.

Horoscope for 2014

Major Trends

The year 2011 was extremely challenging; 2012 was challenging as well but less so. In 2013, however, things began to get easier. It's as if you have come through a long dark tunnel and now you are in the light. Health is much improved over the previous few years but it still needs attention. There's more on this later.

In spite of all the challenges you've been facing, many nice things are happening. In 2013 – on June 26 – Jupiter entered your own sign of

Cancer, beginning a multi-year prosperity cycle for you. This prosperity cycle is in full swing in 2014.

For the first seven months of 2014 (until July 26) there is a Grand Square pattern in the heavens that affects you very strongly. You seem involved in some large, major undertaking. Something big. Something larger than life. Perhaps you are founding a business or some institution. Perhaps you are intimately involved in this on behalf of others. These things are exciting but delicate and stressful. However, with Jupiter in your own sign it looks successful.

The love situation was good in 2013 and seems good in 2014 as well. Many of you met a special someone and many of you got involved in a relationship that was 'like' a marriage. The romantic opportunities were there and this continues. More details later.

Uranus has been in your 10th house of career since 2011. This has meant there has been much career change and instability happening. These changes are not just personal, but affect your industry, your profession and the company you work for too. The good news is that the career is very exciting – glamorous even. There's never a dull moment. Anything can happen at any time. It keeps the adrenaline flowing. This trend continues in the year ahead.

Your most important areas of interest this year are the body, image and personal pleasure (until July 16); finance (after July 16); home and family (until July 26); children, fun and creativity; love, romance and social activities; religion, philosophy, higher education and foreign travel; and career.

Your paths of greatest fulfilment this year are the body, image and personal pleasure (until July 16); finance (from July 16 onwards); children, fun and creativity (until February 19); and home and family (from February 19 onwards).

Health

(Please note that this is an astrological perspective on health and not a medical one. In days of yore there was no difference, both of these perspectives were identical. But in these times there could be quite a difference. For a medical perspective, please consult your doctor or health practitioner.)

Your 6th house of health is not a house of power this year. (It only becomes powerful on December 24 – for six days out of the whole year.) Generally I read this as a positive for health, but this year I'm not so sure. The Grand Square pattern that we mentioned earlier is in effect until July 26. These things tend to be stressful – they are energy drainers. Most likely you will be working very hard – perhaps overworking. So, the empty 6th house, in this context, could be showing that you are so involved with your project (or projects) that you are not paying attention to your health. There could be a price to pay for this later on. (Indeed, Saturn's move into your 6th house at the end of the year shows a need to pay attention.)

As our regular readers know, the most important thing is to maintain high energy levels. To rest when tired. But with your hectic schedule this year, this will be a challenge; the demands on you are great. If you focus on essentials and let the 'small stuff' go, you should be able to handle your workload and maintain your health. Tough decisions have to be made, and not everyone will be happy with them. It might

Reflexology

Try to massage the whole foot on a regular basis, but pay extra attention to the points highlighted on the chart. When you massage, be aware of 'sore spots', as these need special attention. It's also a good idea to massage the ankles and the top of the feet.

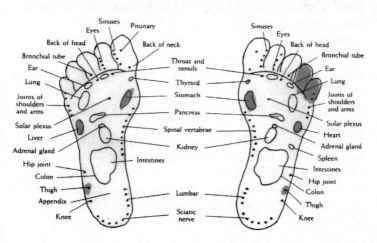

be advisable to spend some leisure time at a health spa or schedule regular massages into your diary. This will add energy.

There is much you can do to improve the health and prevent problems from developing. As we mentioned, the most important is to maintain overall high energy levels. Next, you can give special focus to the heart, the stomach and breasts, and the liver and thighs, using the chart shown.

Avoid worry and anxiety, the spiritual root causes of heart problems. If there is something positive that can be done about a situation, take the positive action. If nothing can as yet be done, how does worrying help? File it on the shelf for future action and refuse to worry. Meditation is a big help here.

The stomach and breasts are always important areas for you. Watch the diet, and eat slowly and prayerfully. Elevate the act of eating from mere animal appetite into something sublime – an act of worship. This will change the energy of the food and your body. Make sure you massage the thighs regularly, too.

These are the areas that are most vulnerable in the year ahead. Giving them extra energy – keeping them fit – will tend to prevent problems from developing. And even if they can't be totally prevented, problems can be minimized to a great extent.

Jupiter will be in your sign until July 16. This is basically a happy aspect, but there is a down side. It can lead to over-indulgence – too much of the good life – and there is a price to pay for this later on. Your weight will need watching, and Cancerians of childbearing age will be more fertile than usual.

It's difficult enough having three long-term planets in stressful alignment with you. But there will be periods in the year when other, short-term planets join in the stress. These are more vulnerable periods and you need to make sure you get more rest and massages or health treatments. These periods will be from January 1 to January 20 and March 21 to April 19. September 23 to October 23 is also a delicate period, but less so than the previous two. We will discuss this in the monthly reports as well.

Home and Family

Home and family is always important to you Cancer, but this year – especially during the first half – even more so than usual. Mars will spend more than six months in your 4th house, which is highly unusual. Generally he only spends a month and a half to two months in a sign.

Mars in your family house has many readings and interpretations. Generally this shows that construction or major repairs are going on the home. Tempers can be flaring with family members, and there may be conflicts in the family. Maintaining your temper will be a challenge.

While Mars is in your 4th house he will be opposite Uranus and in square aspect to Pluto (in different degrees of exactitude). This suggests a need to make the home safer. Smoke detectors and alarms should be kept in good working order, and the house should be checked for toxic elements (paint, furnishings, etc.) or negative geo-pathological fields. (There are dowsers who specialize in this kind of work.) Dangerous implements should be kept out of the reach of children. In fact, if you are renovating – and many of you are – safety issues should be a focus.

Mars is your career planet. The obvious message here is that your home and family are your real career these days, regardless of your actual job or profession. This aspect indicates that you are working more from home. A home-based business could be interesting this year. The home seems as much a place of business as a home.

Parents or parent figures in your life are having surgery or near-death kinds of experiences this year. Moves could happen for them as well, which seem happy. Perhaps they buy additional homes.

The family situation in general seems unstable, and thus your complete focus is called for. There are many crises and dramas this year and you need to be on the case.

Personal moves are not indicated; renovations are more likely. Children or children figures in your life are likely to move after July 16, and the moves seem fortunate. Siblings or sibling figures are better off staying put and making better use of the space that they have. Grandchildren (or those who play this role in your life) have a quiet domestic year.

Venus, your family planet, is very fast moving. She will move through all the signs and houses of your Horoscope in any given year. Thus there are many short-term trends with family that are best covered in the monthly reports.

There is a Lunar Eclipse in your 4th house on April 15, which affects you and your family strongly. Do your best to keep your family out of harm's way. Let them spend more quiet time at home during that period.

Finance and Career

It has been many years since finance has been a major issue for you. Oh, you earned your living but the passion was not there. Things are starting to change. As we mentioned earlier, you entered a cycle of prosperity in 2013, and this year it gets even stronger.

Until July 16, Jupiter is in your own sign – in your 1st house. This is a wonderful transit in general – it tends to happiness and success – but also wonderful for finances. We may have written about this last year, but it is still in effect now. It indicates you leading the life-style of a 'rich' person. (Of course this is a relative thing. Most of you won't be living like millionaires, but you will be living in accordance with your own concepts of the 'high life'.) You will eat in the good restaurants, travel, and enjoy the pleasures of the senses. Sensual fantasies get fulfilled these days – each according to their own stand-ard. How much money one has in the bank or earns is never the issue with this transit – one lives 'as if' one were rich. One lives on a higher standard. And, interestingly enough, the money to cover this happens.

You feel richer and more optimistic. You dress more expensively. This is powerful money magic. You attract, by this means, wealth opportunities and a richer class of people around you.

Jupiter is the ruler of your 6th house of health and work. Thus happy job opportunities are coming to you. This was true last year too. You have probably landed a nice job by now, but if not, the aspects are still good in the year ahead. Like last year, there's not much you need to do to achieve this – no need to pore over classified ad sections in the paper or online. The job will find you.

Those of you who employ others will attract just the right employee(s) with little stress or effort.

Jupiter in your own sign tends to what the world calls 'good luck'. So, it might be advisable to invest harmless sums on the lottery or other kind of speculations. But only do so when intuition dictates. This should never be an automatic kind of thing.

On July 16 Jupiter enters your money house and stays there for the rest of the year and well into next year. This is a classic indicator of prosperity. Assets you own will increase in value. You might find things in your attic or basement that turn out to be worth much more than you thought. A stock you own rockets in value. Happy job opportunities continue to come.

Though you are 'lucky' this year, Jupiter in the money house indicates money from work – money that is earned. (Jupiter is your work planet.) I read this as your 'work' creates good luck as a side effect. Luck might enhance your earnings, but it is work that produces the bulk of it.

When Jupiter enters your money house he will start to make very nice aspects to Uranus, the ruler of your 8th house of transformation. This often indicates an inheritance – though hopefully no one has to actually die. You can be named in someone's will or be appointed as their executor or to some other kind of function in a will. The aspect can show a nice tax refund. Sometimes it indicates paying more taxes than usual, which is also a prosperity signal. Higher taxes are generally related to higher income. It shows ease in paying down debt or taking on new debt – according to your need. Your ability to attract outside money – either through borrowing or investment – is enhanced. It also shows the prosperity of the spouse, partner or current love. He or she will be more generous with you.

There will be periods in the year when prosperity is stronger or weaker – this will depend on the Sun's position and the aspects he makes with other planets, as the Sun is your money planet. These are best covered in the monthly reports. However, generally money is not a problem this year.

Your favourable financial numbers are 5, 6, 8 and 19.

There is much career change and instability this year, as we have mentioned. It will be important to stay up to date on all the latest technology. Your high-tech expertise is very important. Canceriens have a natural flair for residential real estate, the food business, restaurants, hotels and family businesses – and this year even more so than usual.

Love and Social Life

You have been in a good love cycle ever since June 26 last year, and the trend continues in the year ahead. Jupiter's entry into your own sign was an excellent aspect for love. He started to make beautiful aspects to your love planet, Saturn. In fact, your love planet has been part of Grand Trine in Water since that time. This is still the case for the first part of 2014.

If you have not yet found that special someone, it is likely to happen in the year ahead. Many of you have already found him or her. While literal marriage might not have happened, many of you are in relationships that are 'like' marriage. Marriage is merely a 'legalism'; the Horoscope shows the 'actuality'.

Saturn, your love planet, and Pluto (the occupant of your 7th house of marriage) are in 'mutual reception' for almost all the year ahead. This means that each is a 'guest' in the sign and house ruled by the other, and shows great co-operation between the two planets. (This was so all of last year too.) Pluto is the ruler of your 5th house of love affairs, fun and creativity. Thus your marriage or current relationship is more fun, more 'honeymoonish' this year. It shows that singles have options – they can opt for love affair-type relationships or committed relationships. Both seem equally available.

Romantic and social opportunities happen in the usual kinds of places this year, at parties, resorts, places of entertainment, at the theatre or cinema – places of this nature. This year love is about fun. You are attracted to the person who can show you a good time. And the sexual magnetism and chemistry seem unusually important.

With this kind of chart there would be a tendency to place too much stock on the sexual chemistry. No one denies its importance, but by itself this is not enough to produce a happy, long term relationship. Other factors should be taken into account and you might not be doing that. This can lead to pain later on down the road. Even the best of sexual chemistries have a life-span of about a year. Once that abates you have a real person to deal with. You had these same tendencies last year too.

Towards the end of the year, after December 24 there will be a change in the love attitudes. Sexual chemistry will still be important – Pluto will still be in your 7th house – but you will also want someone who serves your interests.

This year you seem attracted by corporate types – traditional types. Perhaps people older and more established than yourself. You have this tendency by birth, but these days the tendency is even stronger.

The year ahead seems sexually active. Aside from what we mentioned, Jupiter will be making powerful aspects to the ruler of your 8th house from July 16 onwards. Whatever your age or stage in life, your libido is stronger than usual.

Your favourable numbers for love are 3, 10, 15 and 21.

Self-improvement

With Uranus in your career house now and for many years to come you are likely to be bored with 'same old, same old' kinds of careers. You need a career that offers a lot of variety and change, where assignments change periodically. Often this favours a 'freelance' kind of career. But if you can get this variety within your present career path, it would be good. Also it seems important to be original in your career path. Don't even attempt to copy what others are doing – it won't work for you. Your innate originality should be explored.

Neptune has been in your 9th house since February 2012. Thus your religious ideas, your personal philosophy of life, your world view is becoming more spiritualized. You are able (and this ability will increase in future years) to interpret personal and world events from a more spiritual perspective, to see them as outcomes of Higher Forces. This will change many other aspects of your life and improve your psychological reactions to things. This year and in coming years I see religious paths that are more mystical and experiential. The dry study of scripture or robotic repetition of prayers is not for you. Every religion has its mystical tradition and this is what you should seek out now. This will bring more fulfilment and satisfaction.

Saturn has been in your 5th house of children since October 2012. Thus the Cosmos is bringing this area into right order. Disciplining children or children figures in your life is a high art form. It needs to be done 'just so'. Too much (and this seems the tendency these days) and you stifle the child and instil fear into him or her – development can be stunted. Too little, and you have chaos – and this too is harmful to the child. If a behavioural problem could have been dealt with at a young age and, later on, the child commits some crime or heinous act – the karma will be yours as much as the child's. Children need freedom, it is true. But the freedom has to be within limits. Certain lines cannot be crossed. Destructive behaviour should be punished swiftly – not in anger but firmly. This right balance of freedom and limits is the main lesson to learn in the year ahead.

Month-by-month Forecasts

January

Best Days Overall: 5, 6, 14, 15, 24, 25
Most Stressful Days Overall: 1, 2, 7, 8, 22, 23, 28, 29
Best Days for Love: 1, 2, 5, 6, 9, 10, 14, 15, 19, 20, 24, 25, 28, 29
Best Days for Money: 1, 2, 5, 6, 9, 10, 14, 15, 17, 18, 21, 22, 24, 25, 30, 31
Best Days for Career: 3, 4, 7, 8, 12, 13, 22, 23, 30, 31

You begin your year in the midst of a yearly love and social peak. Romance is going very well. The social life is hyperactive. Those of you currently in a relationship could easily decide to marry during this period (this decision could have been made last month too). Those of you who are unattached are likely to meet good prospects. Love is in the air now. The only problem in love is the retrograde of Venus all month. So don't rush into marriage too quickly. And perhaps it is better to schedule a wedding for later in the year.

The planetary power is mostly in the West now. Over 70 per cent of the planets are in the Western, social sector of your Horoscope. This means this is a period for developing your people skills and for cultivating the grace and favour of others. Your personal concerns are not that important right now. Cultivate good relationships. If there are conditions in your life that irk you, make a mental note of them but adapt to them as best you can. The time will come (and it's not that far off) when the appropriate changes can be made.

Last month the planetary power shifted from the lower half of the Horoscope to the upper half. Home and family is always important to you, but now you can serve them best by succeeding in your 'external', public life.

Health is basically good but you are not in one of your best health periods right now – especially before the 20th. Make sure to get enough rest. Enhance the health in the ways mentioned in the yearly report. Your health planet Jupiter is retrograde this month, so avoid making drastic changes to the diet or exercise regime. This is a time for studying these things, not for taking action. Health and energy will improve dramatically after the 20th.

Job seekers have good opportunities this month (and for many months in the future) but don't be too quick to jump into anything. Get the facts first. Ask questions. Resolve any doubts.

This month finances are excellent. Your financial planet transits previous eclipse points from the 14th to the 17th and on the 30th and 31st. These can bring temporary financial disturbances and you will have to make changes and adjustments. But these changes will be good. These are bumps on the road and not long-term problems.

There are some family dramas from the 1st to the 7th. Be patient with family members then as they are apt to be more temperamental than usual. Handle the drama and keep focusing on your career.

February

Best Days Overall: 1, 2, 10, 11, 12, 20, 21, 28
Most Stressful Days Overall: 3, 4, 18, 19, 24, 25
Best Days for Love: 2, 5, 6, 7, 11, 12, 16, 17, 21, 24, 25, 28
Best Days for Money: 1, 2, 8, 9, 10, 11, 12, 13, 14, 20, 21, 28
Best Days for Career: 3, 4, 8, 9, 18, 19, 26, 27

The planetary momentum is overwhelmingly forward this month. Until the 6th 90 per cent of the planets are moving forward, and even after the 6th it is 80 per cent. If you are releasing a new product or starting a new venture this is a good month to do it. (The 1st to the 6th seem best – the Moon will be waxing.) In general, things get done faster than usual.

Things seem to be going well with you. We have had a Grand Trine in the Water element since last month, and Water is your natural element. On the 18th, as the Sun enters Pisces, the power in the Water element will be even stronger. This is very comfortable for you. People are more sensitive to other people's feelings, and it is easier to share your feelings with others.

Love is going very well. You are not as socially active as last month, but the love life is good. Venus will be moving forward this month and your love planet receives very beautiful aspects. If any of you are still unattached this is a good month to meet someone special. Those in existing relationships have more harmony in their relationship.

The spouse, partner or current love entered a yearly financial peak last month on the 20th. He or she is still in this in the month ahead. In general prosperity is excellent for this person and he or she is likely to be more generous with you. With your financial planet in the 8th house until the 18th, you prosper by prospering others. You need to think about the financial interests of others and help them achieve their goals. As you do this your own prosperity will happen very naturally. Moreover, understanding the true financial interest of another will help you sell any proposals better.

Travel has been indicated in your chart for many months. But after the 18th, as the Sun enters your 9th house, this tendency is even stronger. Foreign travel is not only fun in itself, but seems to help the bottom line too. There is business travel happening after the 18th. There are financial opportunities in foreign lands and with foreigners.

Health is much improved over the last month. With Jupiter in your own sign, the only problem is too much of a good thing – too much high life – too much good food and drink. You need to watch your weight.

Job seekers have good fortune on the 28th. But again, more study and research is necessary.

March

Best Days Overall: 1, 2, 10, 11, 19, 20, 28, 29
Most Stressful Days Overall: 3, 4, 17, 18, 24, 25, 30, 31
Best Days for Love: 1, 2, 7, 10, 11, 17, 18, 19, 20, 24, 25, 26, 27, 28, 29
Best Days for Money: 1, 2, 10, 11, 12, 13, 19, 20, 21, 22, 28, 29, 30, 31
Best Days for Career: 3, 4, 7, 8, 17, 18, 26, 27, 30, 31

You've been working hard so far this year and you seem involved in some big and complicated project. This trend continues in the month ahead. Health has been good so far, but after the 20th you will need to pay more attention to this area. Do what needs to be done in your life – you won't be able to avoid some things, but let go of things of lesser importance. Enhance the health in the ways mentioned in the yearly report. Overwork seems the main danger.

The month ahead is hectic, but successful. On the 20th you enter a yearly career peak. Home and family is always important and always a focus for you, but you can serve your family best by succeeding in the outer world.

Finances look good – a prosperous month. Until the 20th, your financial planet is in the 9th house. This is generally a fortunate position and shows financial expansion – expanded earnings, high goals. Financial opportunity happens in foreign lands and perhaps with foreigners. Business travel is also indicated. Your financial intuition is exceptional. On the 20th the financial planet crosses the Mid-heaven and enters the 10th house. This shows a strong focus on money and earnings. These are very important to you, and we get what we focus on. But this also indicates the financial favour of the authority figures in your life – parents, parent figures, elders and bosses. It often shows pay rises. Your good professional reputation is rewarded on the financial level. Often this transit shows money from the government, either directly or indirectly.

Love seems very happy these days. Existing relationships are harmonious and singles have no problem finding romance. The only complication is the retrograde of Saturn on the 2nd. You and your current love lack direction in your relationship. You are sort of 'treading water'. There's nothing to worry about; it just needs to be understood. The love planet will be retrograde for many more months. It doesn't stop love or romance, but it does slow things down a bit. This is a time for achieving more clarity on your social goals. It is also a good time to review the love life and see where improvements can be made.

Take a nice easy schedule around the new Moon of the 30th. It is a prosperous new Moon for the spouse, partner or current love.

Pay attention to the dream life on the 21st and 31st. Your dreams seem very significant. And be more patient with family members from the 17th to the 19th. They seem more temperamental.

April

Best Days Overall: 6, 7, 16, 17, 24, 25
Most Stressful Days Overall: 13, 14, 15, 20, 21, 26, 27
Best Days for Love: 4, 5, 6, 7, 16, 17, 20, 21, 24, 25
Best Days for Money: 6, 7, 8, 9, 10, 16, 17, 19, 20, 24, 25, 29, 30
Best Days for Career: 3, 4, 5, 13, 14, 15, 22, 23, 26, 27

The planets are slowly shifting from the West to the Eastern sector of your Horoscope. The shift will be established next month, but you're beginning to feel it now. Personal independence is growing stronger day by day. Every day you have more power to change things that you don't like and create conditions as you desire them to be. Hopefully, over the past few months you've made a note of what needs to be changed. Now you can start doing it.

Independence doesn't mean riding rough shod over others. It just means that we need not rely on them for our personal happiness. So long as you're not destructive to others you should (and can) have things your way.

You are still in the midst of your yearly career peak. So keep your focus on the outer career goals. Success is still happening.

Health still needs attention until the 20th. There's nothing seriously wrong with you, but this is not your best health period. Overall your energy is not what you are used to, thus pre-existing conditions seem to get worse (for a time). Lower energy levels can make you vulnerable to opportunistic infections, so be sure to rest and relax more. Enhance the health in the ways mentioned in the yearly report. Health will improve dramatically after the 20th.

There are two eclipses this month. The Lunar Eclipse of the 15th occurs in your 4th house and impacts on Mars, the career planet. Every Lunar Eclipse affects you strongly as the Moon is ruler of your Horoscope. So relax your schedule during this period. The eclipse brings dramas at home with family members and with parents and parent figures. Be more patient with family members this period. Career changes are happening too – but they seem good.

The Solar Eclipse of the 29th occurs in your 10th house and affects finances (every Solar Eclipse impacts on finances). The financial life is basically good right now, but it probably needs 'tweaking' and the eclipse forces you to make the necessary changes. Parents and parent figures are affected here too.

A sudden windfall happens on the 1st and 2nd – sometimes this comes disguised as a sudden expense, which leads to the windfall.

In spite of the retrograde of your love planet Saturn, love is wonderful. It is romantic and tender. Venus moves into Pisces on the 6th and starts to make wonderful aspects to Saturn. Between the 23rd and 26th seems an exceptionally good period for love. But there is no rush; take things nice and easy.

May

Best Days Overall: 3, 4, 5, 13, 14, 21, 22, 31
Most Stressful Days Overall: 11, 12, 17, 18, 24, 25
Best Days for Love: 3, 4, 5, 6, 13, 14, 17, 18, 21, 22, 24, 25, 31
Best Days for Money: 3, 4, 5, 6, 7, 8, 9, 10, 13, 14, 17, 18, 21, 22, 28, 29, 31
Best Days for Career: 1, 2, 11, 12, 19, 20, 24, 25, 29, 30

The shift of the planetary power to the East is firmly established from the 3rd onwards. It is time to have life on your terms, so long as it isn't destructive. If others don't go along with your plans, you have the power to go it alone. Now is the time to explore your own personal happiness and to develop your personal initiative.

Overall the love life is very good, but this month, until the 21st at least, it seems more complicated. There could be financial disagreements with the beloved and perhaps differences of opinion on other subjects too. This is all short term. By the 21st these things are resolved and the love life is again harmonious.

Mars is positioned more or less opposite to Uranus all month. This indicates that the home needs to be made safer. Parents or parent figures need to avoid risky, strenuous activities. There are some upheavals in the career – perhaps in your industry or corporate hierarchy. The rules of the game are changed.

Finances are good; May is basically a prosperous month. Until the 21st the social dimension is important in finance (like last month). Friends and social connections play a large and positive role. Technology is important too and it will be good to stay up-to-date with the latest developments. You are probably spending money on these things. Good to be involved with groups, trade or professional organizations too. On the 21st your financial planet moves into your spiritual 12th house. Your financial intuition should be good and should be relied upon. This is a period where you go deeper into the spiritual dimensions of wealth. You are more charitable this period too. Involvement with spiritual organizations and spiritual-type people enhances the bottom line.

Health is good this month. You can enhance it even further in the ways mentioned in the yearly report.

Venus travels with Uranus on the 14th and 15th. Be more patient with friends and family members then. They are apt to be more temperamental. Children and children figures in your life are apt to be more rebellious.

Dreams and intuitions need more verification on the 11th before they are acted upon.

Authority figures – bosses, parents and parent figures – are financially supportive on the 30th and 31st.

June

Best Days Overall: 1, 9, 10, 18, 19, 27, 28
Most Stressful Days Overall: 7, 8, 14, 15, 20, 21
Best Days for Love: 1, 5, 6, 9, 10, 14, 15, 18, 19, 23, 24, 27, 28
Best Days for Money: 1, 2, 3, 7, 8, 10, 11, 16, 17, 18, 19, 27, 28, 29, 30
Best Days for Career: 7, 8, 16, 17, 20, 21, 25, 26

You have a happy and prosperous month ahead. The only problem is the high percentage of retrograde planets – 40 per cent after the 9th. This won't stop good things from happening, but it will slow things down a bit.

When you have a lot of planets moving backwards at once, the Cosmos is calling you to perfection in all that you do. Shortcuts are to be avoided (they are illusions). Being perfect in all the details will slow you down, but the slow way is the fastest way now. Mistakes will come back to bite you and you'll just have to re-do the work or spend time straightening things out.

Your 12th house of spirituality became powerful on the 21st of last month and remains so until the 21st of this month. So you are in a strong spiritual period. There are spiritual breakthroughs happening for those who are interested, and it is a very good period for meditation and spiritual studies. Very good for artists, poets and musicians too – as there is more inspiration happening. Spiritual studies will help the financial life too, in interior kinds of ways.

On the 21st the Sun crosses the Ascendant and enters your 1st house. This brings financial increase and opportunity. Earning power is much stronger than usual. You spend on yourself. You look wealthy to others. You adopt the image of wealth, which in turn brings greater financial opportunity to you. This transit is also wonderful for the personal appearance and image, and for the health too. You look good. You have more star quality than usual. The body shines. You enter one of your yearly personal pleasure periods. (You have in fact been in a personal pleasure period for almost a year, but now it becomes even stronger.) The desires of the body are fulfilled very well.

Job seekers have good fortune this month. However, there are disturbances at the workplace from the 21st to the 26th. If you employ others there is instability with employees during that period.

Love is good all month, but especially after the 21st. There are opportunities for business partnerships and joint ventures to happen then.

Once again you seem involved in some big and complicated project, but it seems successful. Also you have all the energy you need to deal with it.

Parents and parent figures in your life need to drive more carefully and avoid risky kinds of activities this month, especially from the 22nd to the 26th. There are career changes indicated then too.

July

Best Days Overall: 7, 8, 15, 16, 24, 25
Most Stressful Days Overall: 4, 5, 6, 11, 12, 17, 18
Best Days for Love: 4, 5, 6, 7, 8, 11, 12, 13, 14, 15, 16, 24, 25
Best Days for Money: 1, 7, 8, 15, 16, 17, 27, 28
Best Days for Career: 4, 5, 6, 13, 14, 17, 18, 24, 25

The Water element has been strong all year, but especially last month and this. Last month at least 40 per cent (and sometimes 50 per cent) of the planets were in Water signs. This month (until the 22nd) the percentage is even higher – 60 per cent and sometimes more. On a world level this shows more rain and humid weather. But personally it is very good for you. You are in an 'era of good feeling'. You are most powerful when your mood is right. (This is so for everyone, but especially so for you.) In the right mood you can conquer the world; in a wrong mood, nothing much happens.

Power in Water has metaphysical implications for those of you involved in prayer and meditation. A successful prayer happens when one enters the 'feeling' of 'it is done'. When there is much water, it is much easier to enter this feeling than at other times.

You are still in one of your yearly personal pleasure peaks until the 22nd. By all means enjoy all the pleasures of the body, but there's no need to over-indulge.

Venus crosses the Ascendant and enters your 1st house on the 18th. You are attracted to high-tech equipment or gadgetry. You look good. You dress elegantly and have natural sense of style. You have been spending on yourself since last month, but now is a good time to buy clothing and accessories if you need them. You have a natural grace during this period. You attract the opposite sex. Love will be happy this month, with the love planet receiving beautiful planetary aspects all month. Furthermore, Saturn will start moving forward on the 20th. Current relationships get clarified and start to move forward too. Social confidence improves as well.

You are more or less having life on your terms now. This is a time – perhaps the best time of the year – to create conditions as you desire them to be.

The Sun travels with Jupiter from the 24th to the 27th. This indicates a nice payday happening. It also brings a happy job opportunity. The new Moon of the 26th seems an especially lucrative time.

Jupiter makes a major move out of your sign and into Leo on the 17th. Prosperity has been strong this year so far, and is about to get even stronger. This planetary move affects your job goals. Up to now personal satisfaction and comfort were important job-wise, now it is strictly about pay. If the pay is good, you will feel personally satisfied.

Your health needs also shift. Now more attention needs to be paid to the heart.

August

Best Days Overall: 3, 4, 11, 12, 20, 21, 22, 30, 31
Most Stressful Days Overall: 1, 2, 8, 13, 14, 28, 29
Best Days for Love: 3, 4, 7, 8, 11, 12, 13, 20, 21, 22, 23, 24, 30, 31
Best Days for Money: 5, 6, 13, 14, 23, 24, 25
Best Days for Career: 3, 4, 11, 12, 13, 14, 20, 21, 30, 31

On July 23 the Sun joined Jupiter in your money house and you entered one of your yearly financial peaks. Indeed, this financial peak should be a lot stronger than those of previous years. There is much luck in the financial realm now. But your work will create the good luck. The money that comes to you now is happy money – money earned in happy ways. You are spending more on leisure activities too. You are enjoying your wealth, and not everyone can say this.

This month the planetary power shifts from the upper to the lower half of your Horoscope. Uranus began to retrograde on the 22nd of last month, in your 10th House of Career. This is a very clear message. Career issues will only be resolved by time. Now it is good to shift your attention to the home, family and your emotional well-being. Your career is still important to you, but not as much as it was. Now is the time to work on your career goals by interior methods – through meditation, visualization, prayer and goal-setting. This too is work, but not of the physical kind. Try to enter the 'feeling state' of what you want to achieve. Imagine that you have already achieved that goal. Feel it deeply. Then let go. Repeat as needed. Now it is important to find and function from your personal point of emotional harmony. Up until now it was all about 'doing good'; now it is about 'feeling good'.

You entered a yearly financial peak last month and this month it is even stronger. Almost half the planets are in or moving through your money house. This is a lot of financial power, signalling a prosperous month ahead. You have a lot of help from all sorts of sources – the job, the family, parents or parent figures, bosses and siblings (or sibling figures). The financial intuition is also very good – especially until the 15th.

Love is more problematic this month but there is no major crisis, more like short-term disagreements or conflicts. Your spouse, partner or current love needs to be more cautious in financial matters as the financial planet is retrograde.

Health is good now. It is even improved over that of last month as Mars is now making harmonious aspects to you.

There are some bumps on the road ahead, but nothing that you can't handle. Many planets are re-activating earlier eclipse points this month and this tends to create 'mini disturbances'. The Sun's transit over an eclipse point on the 1st and 2nd signals financial changes, but overall finances (as we mentioned) are wonderful. Mercury's transit over the same eclipse point on the 5th and 6th shows a need to drive more carefully and be more careful in communications, while Venus's transit between the 18th and the 20th shows a need for more patience with family members.

Mars's transit from the 10th to the 14th indicates career changes and dramas with a parent or parent figure.

September

Best Days Overall: 8, 9, 17, 18, 27, 28
Most Stressful Days Overall: 4, 5, 10, 11, 24, 25
Best Days for Love: 2, 3, 4, 5, 8, 9, 12, 13, 17, 18, 23, 27, 28
Best Days for Money: 1, 2, 3, 4, 5, 10, 11, 12, 13, 19, 20, 23, 24, 29, 30
Best Days for Career: 1, 8, 9, 10, 11, 19, 29, 30

Wealth is a wonderful thing and everyone should have it. But it is not an end in itself. One of the privileges of wealth is free time – time to read, study and pursue intellectual interests and passions. And this is what you have right now. It began on the 23rd of last month and continues until the 23rd of this. This is a time to explore the pleasures of the mind, the pleasures of learning and mental expansion. It is a pleasure all too foreign to many people. It is wonderful to curl up with a good book and just enter the writer's world. It is a form of astral travel. We come back from our trip changed in subtle ways – and if the writer is good we are changed in good ways. This is a month for this kind of thing, and to take courses in subjects that interest you, or attend lectures or seminars. The mind is sharper than usual and absorbs information better.

On the 23rd you enter Cancerien heaven. The 4th house of home and family becomes powerful. The Cosmos impels you to do what you most love. This marks the midnight hour of your year. Outer activity is lessened, but there is much dynamic inner activity happening. The 4th house is the house of endings and beginnings. The old day is over – it has died – and the new day begins. Midnight, the 4th house, is when the new day technically begins. It is not yet visible but it has begun. So you are digesting the past career year and now the psyche, the deeper mind, will prepare the ground for the coming day (your coming year). This is a period for psychological progress and psychological breakthroughs. You already have a strong understanding of these things, but now you go deeper into them.

Health needs more attention from the 23rd onwards. Overall your health is very good, but this is a more vulnerable period in your year. Try to rest and relax more. Midnight is for sleeping. You can enhance your health in the ways mentioned in the yearly report.

Finances are good this month. Until the 23rd there is luck in speculations. Sales, marketing and good use of the media are important this month. The word needs to get out about your product or service. There is money to be made in trading – buying and selling. After the 23rd the Sun, your financial planet, moves into your 4th house. You will probably spend more on the family and home, but you can also earn from them too. Family and family connections will play a big role in finance during this period. You have good family support and good support from a parent or parent figure.

Love is much improved over last month.

October

Best Days Overall: 5, 6, 14, 15, 24, 25
Most Stressful Days Overall: 1, 2, 7, 8, 21, 22, 23, 28, 29
Best Days for Love: 1, 2, 3, 5, 6, 12, 13, 14, 15, 22, 23, 24, 25, 28, 29
Best Days for Money: 3, 4, 7, 8, 12, 13, 16, 17, 18, 22, 23, 26, 27
Best Days for Career: 7, 8, 17, 18, 28

Last month the planetary power shifted from the independent East to the Western sector of 'Others'. This is a major psychological shift for you. Your period of personal independence, having things your own way, and creating your own conditions is over with. Now it is time to live with the consequences, good or bad, of what you have created. If you have created well, the next six months should be pleasant. You will have 'good karma'. If you made mistakes, you learn about them, experience the consequences, and have an opportunity to correct them when the next cycle of personal independence comes. In the meantime adapt to current conditions as best you can. The Cosmos once again calls you to develop your people skills. Your advances come through other people now.

Two eclipses this month show a turbulent month for the world at large. It is an active, hectic kind of month.

The Lunar Eclipse of the 8th occurs in your 10th house and has a strong effect on you. Take a nice, easy, relaxed schedule over that period. (Actually you should be taking it easy until the 23rd anyway, but especially during this eclipse period – a few days before and after.) Every Lunar Eclipse brings a redefinition of the image and personality – a re-definition of the self-concept. And this one is no different. But there are also career changes. Perhaps you will pursue the same career but in a different way. Perhaps you will even change your career. There are shake-ups in your industry and in the hierarchy of your company. Sometimes new policies come down and the rules of the career game change. There are family dramas and dramas with a parent or parent figure in your life. (They too should reduce their schedules at this time.) This eclipse impacts on Uranus, so your spouse, partner or current love is making dramatic financial changes. Children are also impacted by this eclipse and make dramatic personal changes too.

The Solar Eclipse of the 23rd occurs right on the cusp of the 5th house. So again children are affected. They should be kept out of harm's way and take it nice and easy. Every Solar Eclipse brings financial changes – changes in thinking and strategy. Often this happens due to some disturbance or financial crisis, but once the changes are made the crisis resolves itself and the finances should be better than before. This eclipse can bring surgery or near-death kinds of experiences for a parent or parent figure, although not necessarily literal physical death.

Health needs watching until the 23rd. Be sure to get enough rest. Enhance the health in the ways mentioned in the yearly report; it will improve from the 23rd onwards.

November

Best Days Overall: 2, 3, 10, 11, 20, 21, 29, 30
Most Stressful Days Overall: 4, 5, 18, 19, 25, 26
Best Days for Love: 2, 3, 11, 12, 21, 22, 23, 25, 26, 30
Best Days for Money: 2, 3, 4, 5, 10, 11, 12, 13, 14, 21, 22, 23
Best Days for Career: 4, 5, 6, 7, 15, 16, 17, 25, 26

Overall prosperity is still very much intact and will continue well into next year. But until the 22nd there are some temporary bumps on the road. If these are handled properly prosperity should increase even further. The financial planet re-activates an eclipse point on the 6th and the 7th. This can bring some financial disturbance – an unexpected expense or obligation. This generally leads to a positive change. The Sun travels with Saturn from the 17th to the 19th. This creates a feeling of 'tightness' – lack. Again, if you shift things around, tweak a little here or there, you will have the resources that you need. Your financial planet is in Scorpio until the 22nd. Scorpio is about 'cutting back' – eliminating waste and duplication. You should take a surgeon's approach to this and cut away, remove, only those things which are unnecessary. (It's a good idea to go through your possessions too, and sell or give to charity the things that you don't use or need.) Cutting waste is as much a part of prosperity as increasing earnings. On the 22nd the Sun enters Sagittarius, which is a very positive signal for prosperity. Financial confidence is good. You spend more freely but also earn a lot more. The financial goals are very high.

This is a very good month for job seekers. Until the 22nd there are challenges here, either at the present job, or in finding a job – depending on your situation. But after the 22nd things improve and there are multiple happy job opportunities, either at your present company or with another one.

Health is excellent this month. You have the energy of ten people. This by itself enlarges your outlook on life and what you can and cannot achieve. With energy the world is your oyster, without it even the smallest thing becomes a chore.

Love also looks very happy. Singles are meeting romantic partners. With so much power in the Water element until the 22nd, you have much charisma. You are attracting the opposite sex. Those already involved in relationships deepen them.

Uranus is very near an eclipse point all month. This indicates major and dramatic financial changes for your spouse, partner or current love. It also shows that you are dealing with death and death issues this month – perhaps attending funerals or memorial services.

The Fire element becomes dominant from the 22nd onwards. This is generally an 'upbeat' kind of energy. Events move quickly. Progress is rapid. (Retrograde activity is lessened this month as well. After the 16th 90 per cent of the planets are moving forward and this reinforces what we are saying.)

December

Best Days Overall: 8, 9, 18, 19, 26, 27
Most Stressful Days Overall: 1, 2, 15, 16, 22, 23, 28, 29
Best Days for Love: 1, 2, 8, 9, 12, 13, 19, 21, 22, 23, 28, 30, 31
Best Days for Money: 1, 2, 10, 11, 20, 21, 28, 29, 30, 31
Best Days for Career: 1, 2, 3, 4, 15, 16, 24, 25, 28, 29

The planetary power is now in its maximum Western position this month. It is a social month. It's time to take a vacation from yourself and your personal interests and focus more on others. Self-interest is basically a good thing, but sometimes it gets overdone. The periodic shifting of the planets from one sector to the other is the Cosmos's way to keep the balance. The happiness of others is another form of self-interest and enhances our own interests. These are the lessons of the month ahead. It is not a time to try to change uncomfortable conditions now. Instead, adapt to them as best you can. The time for change and personal creation will come in the next few months.

On the 22nd, as the Sun moves into your 7th house, you enter a yearly love and social peak. Love sparkles now. On the 24th your love planet, Saturn, makes one of his rare (once every two and a half years) moves out of Scorpio and into Sagittarius, out of your 5th house and into the 6th. This signals a long-term shift in your love attitudes and needs. For the past two and a half years sexual magnetism was the main attraction in love. This will continue to be important, but now other things also come to the fore. You want someone who will not only give you pleasure but will 'do' for you too – who will serve your interests. This is how you feel loved and this is how you show love. There will be a greater attraction to health practitioners, co-workers and those involved in your health. Playboys or playgirls will be of less interest. The venue of romance will also start to change – a long-term trend. Romantic opportunities will happen at work, the health spa, gym or doctor's surgery as you pursue your health and work goals.

Health needs more attention after the 22nd. Overall health is still good, but there is a short-term 'blip' caused by the short-term planets. As always, make sure you get enough rest. Don't allow yourself to get overtired. Don't burn the candle at both ends.

You are still in an overall trend of prosperity and the month ahead seems prosperous too. Until the 22nd the Sun is in Sagittarius, signalling high financial goals and financial confidence. This tends to prosperity. However the problem here can be too much of a good thing and this transit can lead to over-spending. On the 22nd this issue is resolved as the financial planet moves into conservative Capricorn. Your financial judgement will be sound and you will look at wealth in a long-term way. This period is very good for setting up investment and savings plans, for setting up wealth for the future. Over the long term, if one follows the rules, wealth is just inevitable. The problem is that this approach is 'boring' to many people. Many like to see quick results and this often gets them into trouble. But now, after the 22nd, you are in this frame of mind.

Leo

♌

THE LION

Birthdays from
21st July to
21st August

Personality Profile

LEO AT A GLANCE

Element – Fire

Ruling Planet – Sun
  Career Planet – Venus
  Love Planet – Uranus
  Money Planet – Mercury
  Planet of Health and Work – Saturn
  Planet of Home and Family Life – Pluto

Colours – gold, orange, red

Colours that promote love, romance and social harmony – black, indigo, ultramarine blue

Colours that promote earning power – yellow, yellow-orange

Gems – amber, chrysolite, yellow diamond

Metal – gold

Scents – bergamot, frankincense, musk, neroli

Quality – fixed (= stability)

Quality most needed for balance – humility

Strongest virtues – leadership ability, self-esteem and confidence, generosity, creativity, love of joy

Deepest needs – fun, elation, the need to shine

Characteristics to avoid – arrogance, vanity, bossiness

Signs of greatest overall compatibility – Aries, Sagittarius

Signs of greatest overall incompatibility – Taurus, Scorpio, Aquarius

Sign most helpful to career – Taurus

Sign most helpful for emotional support – Scorpio

Sign most helpful financially – Virgo

Sign best for marriage and/or partnerships – Aquarius

Sign most helpful for creative projects – Sagittarius

Best Sign to have fun with – Sagittarius

Signs most helpful in spiritual matters – Aries, Cancer

Best day of the week – Sunday

Understanding a Leo

When you think of Leo, think of royalty – then you'll get the idea of what the Leo character is all about and why Leos are the way they are. It is true that, for various reasons, some Leo-born do not always express this quality – but even if not they should like to do so.

A monarch rules not by example (as does Aries) nor by consensus (as do Capricorn and Aquarius) but by personal will. Will is law. Personal taste becomes the style that is imitated by all subjects. A monarch is somehow larger than life. This is how a Leo desires to be.

When you dispute the personal will of a Leo it is serious business. He or she takes it as a personal affront, an insult. Leos will let you know that their will carries authority and that to disobey is demeaning and disrespectful.

A Leo is king (or queen) of his or her personal domain. Subordinates, friends and family are the loyal and trusted subjects. Leos rule with benevolent grace and in the best interests of others. They have a powerful presence; indeed, they are powerful people. They seem to attract attention in any social gathering. They stand out because they are stars in their domain. Leos feel that, like the Sun, they are made to shine and rule. Leos feel that they were born to special privilege and royal prerogatives – and most of them attain this status, at least to some degree.

The Sun is the ruler of this sign, and when you think of sunshine it is very difficult to feel unhealthy or depressed. Somehow the light of the Sun is the very antithesis of illness and apathy. Leos love life. They also love to have fun; they love drama, music, the theatre and amusements of all sorts. These are the things that give joy to life. If – even in their best interests – you try to deprive Leos of their pleasures, good food, drink and entertainment, you run the serious risk of depriving them of the will to live. To them life without joy is no life at all.

Leos epitomize humanity's will to power. But power in and of itself – regardless of what some people say – is neither good nor evil. Only when power is abused does it become evil. Without power even good things cannot come to pass. Leos realize this and are uniquely qualified to wield power. Of all the signs, they do it most naturally. Capricorn, the other power sign of the zodiac, is a better manager and administrator than Leo – much better. But Leo outshines Capricorn in personal grace and presence. Leo loves power, whereas Capricorn assumes power out of a sense of duty.

Finance

Leos are great leaders but not necessarily good managers. They are better at handling the overall picture than the nitty-gritty details of business. If they have good managers working for them they can become exceptional executives. They have vision and a lot of creativity.

Leos love wealth for the pleasures it can bring. They love an opulent lifestyle, pomp and glamour. Even when they are not wealthy they live as if they are. This is why many fall into debt, from which it is sometimes difficult to emerge.

Leos, like Pisceans, are generous to a fault. Very often they want to acquire wealth solely so that they can help others economically. Wealth to Leo buys services and managerial ability. It creates jobs for others and improves the general well-being of those around them. Therefore – to a Leo – wealth is good. Wealth is to be enjoyed to the fullest. Money is not to be left to gather dust in a mouldy bank vault but to be enjoyed, spread around, used. So Leos can be quite reckless in their spending.

With the sign of Virgo on Leo's 2nd house (of money) cusp, Leo needs to develop some of Virgo's traits of analysis, discrimination and purity when it comes to money matters. They must learn to be more careful with the details of finance (or to hire people to do this for them). They have to be more cost-conscious in their spending habits. Generally, they need to manage their money better. Leos tend to chafe under financial constraints, yet these constraints can help Leos to reach their highest financial potential.

Leos like it when their friends and family know that they can depend on them for financial support. They do not mind – and even enjoy – lending money, but they are careful that they are not taken advantage of. From their 'regal throne' Leos like to bestow gifts upon their family and friends and then enjoy the good feelings these gifts bring to everybody. Leos love financial speculations and – when the celestial influences are right – are often lucky.

Career and Public Image

Leos like to be perceived as wealthy, for in today's world wealth often equals power. When they attain wealth they love having a large house with lots of land and animals.

At their jobs Leos excel in positions of authority and power. They are good at making decisions – on a grand level – but they prefer to leave the details to others. Leos are well respected by their colleagues and subordinates, mainly because they have a knack for understanding and relating to those around them. Leos usually strive for the top positions even if they have to start at the bottom and work hard to get there. As might be expected of such a charismatic sign, Leos are always trying to improve their work situation. They do so in order to have a better chance of advancing to the top.

On the other hand, Leos do not like to be bossed around or told what to do. Perhaps this is why they aspire so for the top – where they can be the decision-makers and need not take orders from others.

Leos never doubt their success and focus all their attention and efforts on achieving it. Another great Leo characteristic is that – just like good monarchs – they do not attempt to abuse the power or success they achieve. If they do so this is not wilful or intentional. Usually they like to share their wealth and try to make everyone around them join in their success.

Leos are – and like to be perceived as – hard-working, well-established individuals. It is definitely true that they are capable of hard work and often manage great things. But do not forget that, deep down inside, Leos really are fun-lovers.

Love and Relationships

Generally, Leos are not the marrying kind. To them relationships are good while they are pleasurable. When the relationship ceases to be pleasurable a true Leo will want out. They always want to have the freedom to leave. That is why Leos excel at love affairs rather than commitment. Once married, however, Leo is faithful – even if some Leos have a tendency to marry more than once in their lifetime. If you are in love with a Leo, just show him or her a good time – travel, go to casinos and clubs, the theatre and discos. Wine and dine your Leo love – it is expensive but worth it and you will have fun.

Leos generally have an active love life and are demonstrative in their affections. They love to be with other optimistic and fun-loving types like themselves, but wind up settling with someone more serious, intellectual and unconventional. The partner of a Leo tends to be more political and socially conscious than he or she is, and more libertarian. When you marry a Leo, mastering the freedom-loving tendencies of your partner will definitely become a life-long challenge – and be careful that Leo does not master you.

Aquarius sits on Leo's 7th house (of love) cusp. Thus if Leos want to realize their highest love and social potential they need to develop a more egalitarian, Aquarian perspective on others. This is not easy for Leo, for 'the king' finds his equals only among other 'kings'. But perhaps this is the solution to Leo's social challenge – to be 'a king among kings'. It is all right to be regal, but recognize the nobility in others.

Home and Domestic Life

Although Leos are great entertainers and love having people over, sometimes this is all show. Only very few close friends will get to see the real side of a Leo's day-to-day life. To a Leo the home is a place of comfort, recreation and transformation; a secret, private retreat – a castle. Leos like to spend money, show off a bit, entertain and have fun. They enjoy the latest furnishings, clothes and gadgets – all things fit for kings.

Leos are fiercely loyal to their family and, of course, expect the same from them. They love their children almost to a fault; they have to be careful not to spoil them too much. They also must try to avoid attempting to make individual family members over in their own image. Leos should keep in mind that others also have the need to be their own people. That is why Leos have to be extra careful about being over-bossy or over-domineering in the home.

Horoscope for 2014

Major Trends

Jupiter has been in your 12th house of spirituality since June 26 2013 and he will be there until July 16 of this year. Thus you are in a period of deep and profound spiritual growth and internal development. Growth and development that is not visible (as yet) to others but happening nonetheless. This period is a period for spiritual-type revelations. And when these happen (and they are happening) it is most joyous; your whole perspective on life changes. And this, eventually, will bring positive change to the visible, outer life.

When Jupiter enters your own sign on July 16, you enter a cycle of prosperity which you will experience for the next few years – well into 2016. More on this later.

Be patient on the love front. The year starts off slowly in this department but will end with a bang. There is serious love in the air from July 16 onwards. In the meantime, you're getting inwardly prepared for it. There's more on this later.

Uranus has been in your 9th house of religion, travel and learning since 2011, indicating that your religious and philosophical beliefs are getting tested. There are big changes going on here. Changes in personal philosophy and religion always lead to changes in the rest of the affairs of life as events are interpreted differently. Also, many binding, deeply entrenched beliefs are being blasted away.

Since October 2012 Saturn has been making stressful aspects to you and this is still the situation for almost all the year ahead. Overall energy needs watching, but your health is basically good. Health will improve at the end of the year when Saturn moves away from his stressful aspect. More details later.

Your most important areas of interest in the coming year are the body, image and personal pleasure (after July 16); home and family; health and work; sex, personal transformation, taxes, debt, estates, occult studies; religion, philosophy, higher education and foreign travel; and spirituality (until July 16).

Your paths of greatest fulfilment this year are spirituality (until July 16); the body, image and personal pleasure (from July 16 onwards);

home and family (until February 19); and communication and intellectual interests (from February 19 onwards).

Health

(Please note that this is an astrological perspective on health and not a medical one. In days of yore there was no difference, both of these perspectives were identical. But in these times there could be quite a difference. For a medical perspective, please consult your doctor or health practitioner.)

Your 6th house of health is a house of power this year and this has been the case for many years now. This year I read it as a good thing. With Saturn your health planet in stressful aspect to you, you need to be focused more here.

Saturn's aspect alone is not enough to cause disease. However, when the short-term planets join in the stressful aspects, things can happen if one is not careful. This year those vulnerable periods are

Reflexology

Try to massage the whole foot on a regular basis, but pay extra attention to the points highlighted on the chart. When you massage, be aware of 'sore spots', as these need special attention. It's also a good idea to massage the ankles and the top of the feet.

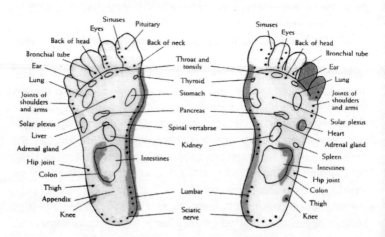

from January 20 to February 18, April 20 to May 20 and October 23 to November 21. Be sure to get plenty of rest during these periods, and it might be a good idea to schedule massages, reflexology or acupuncture treatments at these times – and also perhaps to spend time in a health spa or clinic.

Saturn's stressful aspect tends to weaken the overall energy. It's as if we try to drive a car with the handbrake on. The car moves forward, but slowly and more fuel is used. You use more energy just to do your normal activities – never mind extra things. So, your energy levels need to be maintained. This, as our regular readers know, is the most important thing. Rest when tired. Focus on the really important things in life and let the lesser things go. Alternate your activities and work smoothly.

Specific attention should be given to the heart. This is always important for you but this year more so than normal. The reflex to the heart is shown on the chart. Do your best to avoid worry and anxiety, the two emotions that are the root causes of heart problems. If positive steps can be taken about a situation, take them. If not, don't worry – enjoy your life. Worry does nothing for you.

The spine, knees, teeth, bones, skin and overall skeletal alignment are also always important for you. Regular back massage is powerful, and the knees should also be massaged and given more support when exercising. If you're out in the sun use a good sun screen. Yoga, Pilates, Alexander Technique and the Feldenkrais Method are excellent therapies for the spine and regular visits to a chiropractor or osteopath might be a good idea as well.

The gall bladder is another area to pay attention to this year, and the colon, bladder and sexual organs have been important since 2002 when Pluto entered your 6th house of health. Safe sex and sexual moderation are important these days. You seem more sexually active this year so this advice is important. Indulge but don't over indulge.

With your health planet in the sign of Scorpio, which rules detoxification and Pluto, the planet that rules detoxification, in your 6th house, you respond beautifully to these kinds of regimes. Sometimes this aspect shows a tendency to surgery, but detoxing will often have the same effect (although it takes longer).

Your health planet, Saturn, is in your 4th house of home and family almost all year, only leaving on December 24. Thus family relationships need to be kept in harmony. If there are problems here, it can impact on your physical health. Your emotions and moods need to be kept positive and constructive. Avoid depression like the plague. Happily Leos rarely stay depressed for too long.

Leo in general is a fertile sign, but this year, for those of childbearing age, even more so than usual – especially after July 16.

Favourable numbers for health are 3, 10, 15 and 21.

Home and Family

Your 4th house has been powerful ever since October 2012 when Saturn, a long-term planet, entered this house. It remains powerful for almost the whole year ahead too, so this is an area of focus.

There is a need now to reorganize the home and domestic life – to put things into a right order. The Cosmos impels this by applying pressure. Perhaps there are new family responsibilities to be handled. Perhaps the health of a family member fails and responsibility falls on you. Perhaps the home feels cramped but you can't move (nor is it advisable this year), and so you are forced to make better use of the space that you have. The fact is that you DO have enough space; you just need to rearrange things a bit.

Family responsibilities can seem overwhelming these days, but this is only 'appearance'. If you reorganize things you will find that everything can be handled.

Though your year ahead seems personally happy – especially after July 16 – family life doesn't seem that happy. It seems a burden, a chore, a drag. You (and perhaps family members as well) don't feel safe in expressing your real feelings, and perhaps these are being repressed.

Creating happiness in the home can be done – in fact it must be done – but it will take conscious effort. Every day try to do something that makes things happier. Perhaps a new picture on the wall, perhaps some knick-knack that makes you smile; perhaps a kindness – a kind word or deed – to a family member (and especially to a parent or parent figures). These little things – if practised persistently – will have a cumulative effect.

Saturn is your health planet. His position in the 4th house shows that you are working to make the home a healthier place, in various ways. This can be through removing unhealthy kinds of furniture or substances from the home, or removing impurities in the air or water. In many cases this will manifest as buying health gadgets for the home, or installing gym, exercise equipment, saunas or whirlpools. If you had your way the home would be as much a health spa as a home.

Saturn is your planet of work as well. Thus though you may work for a company, you are taking more work home. Many of you will install home offices this year. (These things could have happened last year too.)

A parent or parent figure seems depressed. Self-esteem and self-confidence are not what they should be. He or she feels their age and seems pessimistic about life and themselves. They need some of your Leo good cheer. Perhaps their health is not what it should be either. Interestingly though, they seem very successful in their careers. Overwork could be a problem for them.

Finance and Career

As with love, the year starts off slowly. Nothing special seems to be happening on the financial front. There are no disasters, but nothing out of the ordinary on the positive side either. But as the year progresses the financial life (and life in general) gets better and better. Meanwhile, you're in preparation for this. Good things – big things – can never happen without adequate preparation. Indeed, the preparatory phases are often longer and require more work than the actual events that happen. We see this in many areas of life. A show that you enjoyed perhaps lasted an hour or two, but the preparation for it could have taken years. So it is with you. Last year and the early half of this year is about preparing for affluence and success – being psychologically ready. When this affluence manifests physically and tangibly, you will be able to handle it.

Jupiter's transit into anyone's sign is always happy and positive. But with you the positivity will be even greater, for Jupiter is the ruler of your 5th house of fun, creativity and speculations – one of the most beneficent of houses. Jupiter is behaving like a 'mega Jupiter'. He brings personal pleasure, the fulfilment of sensual desires, the pleasures of the body, optimism and what the world calls 'good luck'.

Leo's tend to be speculators. I'd wager that if one walked through a casino and randomly checked birthdays, one would find a disproportionate percentage of Leos. (And if you went into things more deeply and actually checked people's Horoscopes, you would see the sign of Leo and planets in the 5th house featuring very prominently.) However, I'd suggest that you hold off a bit on this until after July 16 when Jupiter enters your sign. Speculations will be more cost effective, more favourable then.

Jupiter doesn't only bring money. He brings an increase in lifestyle. Regardless of how much a person actually has, he or she lives 'as if' they had a lot of money. They live above their normal standards.

This will be a fun kind of year from July 16 onwards. A party kind of year.

Jupiter will bring foreign travel too, and almost a 'jet set' kind of lifestyle (each according to their notions of 'jet set'). This travel doesn't seem related to business. It is more about fun – pleasure travel.

Many Leos (also a disproportionate percentage) are in the entertainment business, either performing or on the business side of the industry. This will be a good year for these activities. Industries involving children will also be profitable and there will be many happy opportunities here. Personal creativity will increase and will be more marketable.

Mercury, your financial planet, moves very quickly. During the year he will move through all the signs and houses of your Horoscope and will receive all kinds of different aspects. He even moves backwards (in retrograde motion) three times a year. Thus there are many short-term financial trends that are best covered in the monthly reports.

Your favourable financial numbers are 1, 3, 6, 8 and 9.

Love and Social Life

Your 7th house of love and marriage is not a house of power this year. So marriage is not likely. Next year – 2015 – seems much better for marriage than this year. However, there is nothing indicating against marriage either. It's a free-will decision.

As we mentioned above, the love life starts off slowly in 2014. The first half of the year is just so-so – nothing special one way or the other.

As the year progresses however – and especially after July 16 – the love life improves dramatically.

As with finance, there is a need for patience early in the year. 'Patience,' says Isidore Friedman 'is merely the conscious knowledge of what is actually happening.' If it takes three hours to bake a cake, we must allow the three hours. You are being prepared for serious love. Allow the preparations to happen. Good preparation is 95 per cent of success in any venture – including love. A certain degree of spiritual, interior growth is necessary and this is what is happening now.

The wait seems worth it. Jupiter will start to make fabulous aspects to your love planet Uranus from July 16 onwards. It would be a mistake to jump into a serious relationship early in the year from a sense of 'settling' or 'compromise'. What you really want is on its way.

The relationship seems very happy – honeymoonish. It has the hallmarks of a love affair but will develop into something more serious. This person is certainly 'marriage material'.

Your love planet has been in Aries since March 2011. You are by nature a 'love at first sight' kind of person, but now even more so than normal. Your tendency is to jump into serious relationships too prematurely. Enjoy your love, but let it develop naturally. Many will want to jump the gun and marry this year, but as we mentioned, next year seems better for that.

Many of the trends that we have written about in past years are still in effect now. Uranus is a very slow-moving planet. You are attracted to 'unconventional' kinds of people – the computer whiz, the astrologer or astronomer, the rebel, the professor or minister. Foreigners are unusually alluring these days, and foreign trips (which are happening this year) can lead to love.

Love happens in foreign countries and in religious and educational-type settings – at university or religious services. You gravitate to highly educated, refined and perhaps religious people. You have the aspects of someone who falls in love with the professor or pastor. You gravitate to people you can learn from, who expand your mental and philosophical horizons.

Physical chemistry is always important to you, but these days philosophical and religious compatibility is perhaps just as important. You need to be on the 'same page' in your world view – in your view of what life is all about. Problems here will sink even the best of physical chemistries.

Married couples will be having more fun in their relationships. You and the beloved will be indulging in travel and fun kinds of activities. The marriage seems very happy. Scheduling a second honeymoon – after July 16 – seems like a good idea.

Love seems happy whether you are in or working on your first, second or fourth marriage. Those in or working on their third marriage have a status quo kind of year.

Favourable numbers for love are 0, 2, 11 and 17.

Self-improvement

As we have mentioned, spirituality was important last year and is still important during the first half of 2014. Jupiter moving through your 12th house shows that this is both an enjoyable and successful area of life.

Leos are extraordinarily creative people in general. But this year your creativity is being inspired from the spirit and a whole new (and better) level of creativity is happening for you. Just be open and accept it. The path of creativity is a valid spiritual path this year. There's nothing wrong with the standard methods – attending your place of worship, attending lectures, meditating or doing yoga. But it seems to me that you will get more spiritual advancement from allowing your creativity to flow. It is not only enjoyable – the creative flow is euphoric – but educational as well. The same laws that go into creating a song, paint-ing or sculpture are what the Supreme Creator uses to create universe and galaxies. By imitating (even to a small degree) the Creator we get insight into these Laws.

The Creator is always engaged in the creation of beauty, always releasing more joy into the world. It is a non-stop eternal process. And if we are open, the Creator will use us for these activities. We become channels.

This is a year where supernatural experiences become normal and natural – especially for those of you on a spiritual path. For those not on such a path there will be many 'head scratching' moments – how did that happen? How could I have dreamed of you before I even met you? How did I know that you would call before you called? How did I know to see that film where the hero speaks exactly what I needed to hear?

The invisible world (the origin and source of all visible things) is calling to you – letting you know that it is around. It has many wonders to reveal to you. If it is allowed to operate without interference it will transform this drab, dreary, earthly experience into something magical and miraculous.

Neptune is now in your 8th house of transformation and regeneration, and will be there for the next 12 or so years. Your sex life is being elevated and spiritualized these days. Leos are highly sexual people by nature. But the Horoscope is saying that it isn't more and more sex that you need, but a better and higher quality of sex. The sexual act needs to be elevated from mere animal appetite into something sublime and holy – an act of worship. This will not only make the act more enjoyable but will improve the health. It will be less taxing on the sexual organs, which are vulnerable this year. As time goes on you will be exploring deeper into the spiritual dimensions of sex. For those on the Eastern path it indicates Kundalini Yoga or Tantra. For those on the Western Path, the methods of hermetic science and Kabbala. Dion Fortune's *The Esoteric Philosophy of Love and Marriage* is an excellent book to read on this subject.

Month-by-month Forecasts

January

Best Days Overall: 7, 8, 17, 18, 26, 27
Most Stressful Days Overall: 3, 4, 9, 10, 24, 25, 30, 31
Best Days for Love: 1, 2, 3, 4, 7, 8, 9, 10, 17, 18, 19, 20, 26, 27, 28, 29, 30, 31
Best Days for Money: 1, 2, 5, 6, 10, 11, 14, 15, 19, 20, 22, 23, 24, 25, 30, 31
Best Days for Career: 1, 2, 9, 10, 19, 20, 28, 29

The king is in exile this month. The Sun, the ruler of your Horoscope, is far, far from home – far from his natural habitat and the sign of Leo.

And this is how you feel. With at least 70 per cent (and sometimes 80 per cent) of the planets in the Western sector – including the Sun – the focus is on other people and not yourself. It is as if the king is on a 'listening tour', seeing what the needs and concerns are for other people – the people in his or her kingdom. This kind of information is vital for any ruler. Others come first these days. Your own concerns can wait. You will have ample time to deal with those things later on when the planets shift to the East. The good news here is that you seem more popular than usual. You are there for the beloved and for your friends. On the 20th you enter a yearly love and social peak. The social life seems active and happy.

This month the planetary power shifts from the lower to the upper half of your Horoscope. It is morning in your year, time to wake and focus on your career and outer goals. Dreaming and visualizing were fine for the past six months, but now it is time to make those dreams happen by physical means – by the methods of day. There is no need to rush into any rash action though – the cycle is just beginning – but you're getting prepared. Also, with your career planet Venus retrograde all month, you need to achieve mental clarity on your career goals and objectives.

Until January 20 your 6th house of health is very strong, so you are focused on health and health issues. This is good. The health regimes you put in place before the 20th will stand you in good stead afterwards when your health becomes more delicate. Make sure you get enough rest after the 20th. Enhance the health in the ways mentioned in the yearly report.

The Sun will re-activate previous eclipse points from the 14th to the 17th and on the 30th and 31st. Avoid risky, stressful kinds of activities during those periods; there's no need for any daredevil stunts.

Your financial planet Mercury transits eclipse points from the 8th to the 11th and on the 18th and 19th. This can create financial disturbances. Sometimes this manifests as an unexpected bill or some apparent financial loss. Things are not what they seem, however, and the disturbances are only temporary. The purpose is to goad you into making some necessary financial changes.

In general finance is good this month. Until the 11th Mercury is in Capricorn, indicating sound, stable financial judgement. Money is earned the old fashioned way – through work. Speculation (a favourite Leo activity) is not so advisable then. On the 11th Mercury will move into Aquarius, your 7th house. This shows the importance of the social dimension in finance. Your financial good happens through others. Your social grace, your ability to get on with others, is crucial in your finances now. Friends seem supportive.

February

Best Days Overall: 3, 4, 13, 14, 22, 23
Most Stressful Days Overall: 5, 6, 7, 20, 21, 26, 27
Best Days for Love: 3, 4, 5, 6, 7, 13, 14, 16, 17, 22, 23, 24, 25, 26, 27
Best Days for Money: 1, 2, 10, 11, 12, 15, 16, 17, 19, 20, 21, 26, 27, 28
Best Days for Career: 5, 6, 7, 16, 17, 24, 25

The planetary power is still mostly in the West and you are still in a yearly love and social peak. Adapt to conditions as best you can. This is not a time for creating new conditions to suit you. This will happen later on. Review our discussion of this from last month.

Your financial planet, Mercury, goes retrograde on the 6th and will be retrograde for the rest of the month. Try to wrap up major purchases or investments before that date. After the 6th, it will be a good time to review your finances and see where improvements can be made. Then when Mercury goes forward next month you can put your plans into effect. Mercury's retrograde will not stop earnings, only slow things down a bit. Be especially careful of how you communicate about money matters (in business, with banks, brokerages, etc.). Don't take things for granted. Take the extra time to ensure that they got your message and that you got theirs. This will save a lot of aggravation later on. Mercury retrograde tends to increase the number of glitches that happen, but generally they don't tend to be too serious; they are more annoying than the cause of serious damage. A financial disagreement with a family member or parent or parent figure between the 18th to the 20th is merely inconvenient – miscommunication is most likely at the root of it.

Health still needs watching until the 18th. The most important thing is to get enough rest. High energy levels are your main defence against disease. Enhance your health in the ways mentioned in the yearly report, and after the 18th you should feel a dramatic improvement in health and overall energy.

Job seekers have good fortune after the 18th.

The sexuality of Leo is legendary, and after the 18th it is further amplified. Your 8th house of regeneration becomes very powerful. This must be understood in terms of a person's age and stage in life. The sexuality of an 80-year-old will not be that of a 20-year-old, but it will be greater than usual. A happy sexual opportunity comes from the 22nd to the 24th.

Power in the 8th house is about much more than just sex, though this is part of it. It is about 'resurrection' and transformation. You have a special ability in these areas now. Many of you are involved in these kinds of projects – personal transformation, personal renewal, giving birth to the person that you want to be – and these projects go well during this time.

Detox regimes will go well too (and especially from the 22nd to the 24th), and it is a very good period for weight loss regimes as well. However, try to avoid confrontations and drive more carefully now too.

This power in the 8th house shows that your spouse, partner or current love is prospering this month – he or she is in a yearly financial peak now.

March

Best Days Overall: 3, 4, 12, 13, 22, 23, 30, 31
Most Stressful Days Overall: 5, 6, 19, 20, 26, 27
Best Days for Love: 3, 4, 7, 12, 13, 17, 18, 22, 23, 26, 27, 30, 31
Best Days for Money: 1, 2, 7, 8, 10, 11, 15, 16, 19, 20, 28, 29
Best Days for Career: 5, 6, 7, 17, 18, 26, 27

Most of the planets are above the horizon of your chart, in the upper half of the Horoscope and Venus, your career planet, is moving forward. So you can safely let go of home and family concerns and focus on your career. With Venus moving forward there should be clarity in your objectives and this is 90 per cent of the battle. Career judgement is good now.

The month ahead seems prosperous. The Sun is making beautiful aspects to Jupiter on the 1st and 2nd (as indeed it did on February 28) and this shows overall luck and good fortune. There is luck in speculations too. Mercury, the financial planet, starts to move forward on the 1st, which is another good sign. Financial judgement is sound and there is more confidence. The social dimension of finance is still very important, until the 17th. Social contacts (and your overall likeability) boost the bottom line. There are good opportunities for partnerships and joint ventures. Until March 20 your focus should be on the prosperity of others, and it's important to understand this when making a presentation or proposal. There is a karmic law involved with this too – as you prosper others, your own prosperity will also happen, perhaps not immediately but it will happen. These efforts on behalf of others are like money deposited in a spiritual savings account collecting interest. You will be able to draw on this when in need.

The financial planet will be in the 8th house from the 17th onwards and this reinforces what we said about regeneration above. It also shows a need to take stock of the finances, the expenses, the duplications, the waste, and eliminate them as far as possible. Grow by pruning the dead wood. Now is the time. There are areas in your financial life that need 'resurrection and renewal' and this will happen as you eliminate waste. This also indicates that you will have opportunities to invest in or buy up troubled properties or companies and turn them around. Mercury in the mystical sign of Pisces shows good financial intuition. This is especially so from the 21st to the 23rd as Mercury travels with Neptune. Pay attention to the dream life then: there are financial messages contained in it for you.

The sex life has been more active since February 18, but, as everyone knows, sex and love are two different things. This month there is more romance in the air. The new Moon of the 30th makes it happen. An already existing relationship should get stronger, while the unattached will meet promising prospects.

Health is good this month.

April

Best Days Overall: 8, 9, 10, 18, 19, 26, 27
Most Stressful Days Overall: 1, 2, 16, 17, 22, 23, 29, 30
Best Days for Love: 4, 5, 6, 9, 10, 16, 17, 18, 19, 22, 23, 24, 25, 26, 27
Best Days for Money: 6, 7, 8, 11, 12, 16, 17, 18, 19, 24, 25, 29, 30
Best Days for Career: 1, 2, 4, 5, 6, 16, 17, 24, 25, 29, 30

This is an active, tumultuous but highly successful month. Career is one of the main headlines this month. You are entering a yearly career peak on the 20th. You are reaching for the heights and attaining them. These things generally don't come easy so you can expect a few bumps on the road. A Solar Eclipse on the 29th occurs in your 10th house and shakes up your career and the corporate hierarchy – perhaps even your industry.

However, this month you seem in your rightful place – above everyone in your world, in charge and calling the shots. Your personal appearance and charisma seem very important in your career these days.

The other main headlines this month are two eclipses. These shake things up in the world at large. When barriers to progress need to be broken, eclipses tend to bring this about – often in dramatic kinds of ways.

The Lunar Eclipse of the 15th occurs in your 3rd house and its affects are relatively mild on you. Being in your 3rd house it impacts on your car and communication equipment. This often brings communication challenges – adventures at the post office, with emails and texts. There are dramatic events in the lives of siblings and sibling figures in your life, with neighbours and in your neighbourhood. Mars is affected by this eclipse, so foreign travel is not so advisable during this period. If you must travel, try to reschedule your journey around this time. Every Lunar Eclipse affects your spiritual life and brings changes – in practice, teachers and perhaps teachings. This one is no different. It also brings shake-ups in charities or spiritual organizations that you are involved with.

The Solar Eclipse of the 29th has a much stronger impact on you, so take a nice, easy, relaxed schedule during it. (You need to rest more from the 20th onwards anyway, but especially around this eclipse period.) Those of you who were born from July 31 to August 2 are going to feel the impact of this eclipse much more strongly than other Leos. Big changes are happening for you over the next six months. This eclipse, as we mentioned, affects the career, the corporate hierarchy and your industry. Big changes are going on. The rules of the game get altered. New policies come into effect. Dramatic events happen in the lives of bosses, elders, parents or parent figures. Every Solar Eclipse affects your image and self-concept. It is wonderful that, twice a year, you get a chance to upgrade this area of your life.

Health is more delicate from the 20th onwards, so make sure you get plenty of rest. If you feel under the weather a good night's sleep might do you more good than a visit to the doctor. Enhance your health in the ways mentioned in the yearly report.

May

Best Days Overall: 6, 7, 15, 16, 24, 25
Most Stressful Days Overall: 13, 14, 19, 20, 26, 27
Best Days for Love: 6, 7, 13, 14, 15, 16, 19, 20, 24, 25
Best Days for Money: 3, 4, 5, 8, 9, 10, 11, 12, 13, 14, 19, 20, 21, 22, 29, 30, 31
Best Days for Career: 6, 13, 14, 24, 25, 26, 27

You are still in the midst of a yearly career peak until the 21st. Still on top where you belong, in your rightful place. One of the problems with this – and you're seeing it clearly – is that you become a target for those beneath you, other co-workers. Anything that goes wrong – even if it is in their personal life – tends to be blamed on the person at the top – the most visible person. However, on the 29th, Venus, your career planet, crosses the Mid-heaven and enters your 10th house. This brings more career success and opportunity.

Your health still needs attention. You are in one of your most vulnerable health periods of the year. Saturn has been in stressful aspect with you all year, but now the short-term planets join him to add to that stressful aspect. So, like last month, make sure you get enough rest. You are busy with the career and have a lot on your mind; delegate what you can and rest as much as possible. Elective activities might have to be eliminated or reduced. Health and energy will improve dramatically after the 21st.

Love doesn't seem a major concern this month. The month ahead is very social – especially after the 21st – but not necessarily romantic. This month is more about involvement with friends, groups and group activities. Friendships of the mind, friendships of kindred spirits, are more important than romance. There is a pleasure in these things too. Romantically this seems a stable kind of month. Current relationships remain intact. On the 14th and 15th Venus travels with Uranus and this will bring romantic opportunity for the unattached. It also indicates socializing with people of high status.

Finances seem good. May appears to be a prosperous month. Your financial planet is moving forward and rather quickly, and there is good financial confidence. You cover a lot of ground and make rapid progress. Mercury goes 'out of bounds' from the 12th to the 31st. This shows that you are going out of your usual sphere in pursuit of earnings – thinking outside the box, going into uncharted territory and breaking out of your limits. It seems successful, and until the 7th money is earned from your good professional reputation. A pay rise often happens under this aspect. (Sometimes the pay raise is overt and sometimes covert. It might have a different name, but the effect is 'like' a pay rise.) You have the financial favour of bosses, parents or parent figures.

From the 7th to the 29th the social dimension is important in finance. Who you know is perhaps just as important as what you know or how much you have. Friends seem supportive and provide financial opportunities. It will be good to be involved in groups and organizations, both for pleasure and from a financial perspective. Social networking seems lucrative. On the 29th, Mercury moves into your 12th house of spirituality. This is a time for following your intuition, for working on financial goals in a spiritual way, and for operating the laws of spiritual affluence.

June

Best Days Overall: 2, 3, 12, 13, 20, 21, 29, 30
Most Stressful Days Overall: 9, 10, 16, 17, 22, 23
Best Days for Love: 2, 3, 5, 6, 12, 13, 14, 15, 16, 17, 20, 21, 23, 24, 29, 30
Best Days for Money: 1, 5, 6, 9, 10, 11, 17, 18, 19, 25, 26, 27, 28
Best Days for Career: 5, 6, 14, 15, 22, 23, 24

Last month financial progress was rapid. You covered a lot of ground. Now you need to slow down a bit, get more facts, do more homework and, in general, attain financial clarity. This involves internal rather than external work. Mercury, your financial planet, goes retrograde on the 7th, but even before this he will be moving more slowly, and so should you. If you have important purchases, investments or financial decisions to make, try to do so before the 7th. Mercury's retrograde will not stop earnings, only slow things down a bit. Keep in mind that we're talking about major purchases here, not things like groceries or everyday needs.

The retrograde of your financial planet acts much like a good night's sleep. Outer activity slows down and you inwardly gather the forces needed for the next big financial push. These periodic pauses (it happens for you three times a year) are healthy and, when they are used properly, the subsequent financial expansion will be a lot healthier too.

Career is still important and the month ahead – especially until the 23rd – still seems successful. Your career planet Venus is in her own sign and house and acting powerfully on your behalf. However, the focus on your career starts to diminish after the 23rd. Short term goals are more or less attained, and while your long-term goals are probably not yet attained (we never fully attain them) progress has been made. And this too should be considered success. You are getting ready to shift gears from the 23rd onwards; getting ready to enter the sunset of your year and for the activities of night. This will actually happen next month, but you're preparing for this. You've left the office and are driving home.

Health is much improved this month. Saturn is still in a stressful aspect, but the short-term planets are either in harmony with you or leaving you alone. Enhance your health in the ways mentioned in the yearly report.

The month ahead is still very social – like last month. Romance is good and there are many romantic opportunities for singles, but the focus is more on friendships and group activities – like last month.

Venus transits an eclipse point on the 5th and 6th. This shows career changes happening and dramas with parents, parent figures or bosses. It won't hurt to drive more carefully on those days as well.

Jupiter transits an eclipse point from the 21st to the 26th. Avoid speculations during that period. Children (or children figures in your life) should be kept out of harm's way. They are apt to be more temperamental during this time.

Mars will oppose your love planet Uranus from the 22nd to the 26th. Avoid gratuitous foreign travel then and be more patient with the beloved. A current relationship will get tested.

July

Best Days Overall: 1, 9, 10, 17, 18, 27, 28
Most Stressful Days Overall: 7, 8, 13, 14, 19, 20, 21
Best Days for Love: 1, 4, 5, 6, 9, 10, 13, 14, 17, 18, 24, 27, 28
Best Days for Money: 2, 3, 5, 6, 7, 8, 13, 14, 16, 17, 24, 25, 27, 29, 30, 31
Best Days for Career: 4, 5, 6, 13, 14, 19, 20, 21, 24

Your spiritual 12th house became powerful on the 21st of last month and remains so until the 23rd of this. Spirituality has been important all year, but now it becomes even more so. You have had spiritual breakthroughs and revelations all year, but this month you will have even more. This is highly significant. A real spiritual breakthrough is a life-changing kind of event. Nothing is ever the same once it happens. The outward manifestation of this change generally happens afterwards, but the change is established.

This is a great month for spiritual studies, for meditation, prayer and the study of sacred scripture. Also, because it happens before your birthday, it is a great period to review the past year, correct any mistakes, and set goals for the year ahead which, astrologically speaking, begins on your birthday.

This month the planetary power is in the maximum Eastern position for the year ahead. You are in your period of greatest personal independence. It is not selfish to think of your own happiness and to make the changes necessary to achieve this. If you are happy you are in a position to make others happy. The Cosmos wants you to be happy. Now you can have life on your own terms. You have the power to create conditions according to your personal specifications. There's no need to adapt to things now – if conditions displease you, change them.

On the 17th Jupiter enters your own sign and you begin a multi-year cycle of prosperity. On the 23rd the Sun enters your sign and you also enter one of your yearly personal pleasure peaks. Dame fortune smiles on you now and grants her largesse. From the 24th to the 27th the Sun will travel with Jupiter – a classic signal of prosperity and good fortune. Speculations are favourable then, and it won't hurt to invest harmless sums on the lottery or some other kind of speculation.

Love and romance become excellent from the 23rd onwards. Serious love is in the air. A marriage in the year ahead would not be a surprise. But there is no rush to this. Uranus, the Love Planet, goes retrograde on the 22nd. Let love develop naturally. The retrograde of Uranus will not stop your love life, but it will slow things down a bit.

Health is excellent this month. You look good. Your self-confidence and self-esteem (which are always strong) get even stronger.

You will be leading the good life for the rest of the year ahead, and especially in this month.

August

Best Days Overall: 5, 6, 13, 14, 23, 24
Most Stressful Days Overall: 3, 4, 10, 16, 17, 30, 31
Best Days for Love: 3, 4, 5, 6, 9, 10, 12, 13, 14, 23, 24
Best Days for Money: 5, 6, 13, 14, 15, 23, 24, 25, 26, 27
Best Days for Career: 3, 4, 12, 13, 16, 17, 23, 24

Life is good. There are some bumps on the road, but bumps on the road are experienced differently in a tropical paradise than in the trenches of battle. The overall psychological climate changes the perspective. The present is good and the future looks even brighter.

You are still in the midst of one of your yearly personal pleasure peaks. In some cases it is a lifetime personal pleasure peak. You are enjoying all the pleasures of the body – good food, good wine, physical well-being and travel. Sometimes this gets overdone and there is a price to pay – you need to watch your weight this year.

The love life is even better than last month. Your personal attractiveness however could work against you. You have so many love opportunities that the current love could feel threatened. Sexual flings could erode a current relationship – even though the love is still there. Infidelity is the greatest threat to love at the moment.

You are a star in your world this month and people see you that way. You are having things your way. You are in a period where you should have things your way.

The planetary power shifts to the lower half of the Horoscope this month. Even so, happy career opportunities come to you after the 12th. Now, however, you can be more choosy. You need opportunities that don't violate your emotional comfort zone. An especially happy opportunity comes between the 17th and the 19th. A new car or communication equipment (of high quality) comes to you during this period.

The good life that you lead could upset some of the religious people in your life or could perhaps violate your own religious beliefs. There is some conflict here.

Finances are excellent this month too. Mercury, your financial planet, is in your 1st house until the 15th. This brings financial windfalls (there is a really nice payday from the 1st to the 3rd) and financial opportunity. It shows that financial opportunity is seeking you, rather than vice versa. There is nothing special that you need to do – just show up. On the 15th Mercury will enter his own sign and house, making him stronger on your behalf. On the 23rd the Sun enters the money house and you begin a yearly financial peak.

Health and energy are at a yearly high.

Not bad. Enjoy!

September

Best Days Overall: 2, 3, 10, 11, 19, 20, 29, 30
Most Stressful Days Overall: 6, 7, 12, 13, 27, 28
Best Days for Love: 2, 3, 6, 7, 10, 11, 12, 13, 19, 20, 23, 29, 30
Best Days for Money: 1, 2, 3, 4, 10, 11, 12, 13, 19, 20, 21, 22, 23, 28, 29, 30
Best Days for Career: 2, 3, 12, 13, 23

Last month, on the 1st, the planetary power began to shift from the upper half to the lower half of your Horoscope. On the 12th the lower half got even stronger, and now 70 per cent and sometimes even 80 per cent of the planets are now below the horizon. It is time to let go of the career and outer activities and to focus on the home, family and your overall emotional wellness. It's time to re-charge the batteries. This doesn't mean that you quit your job; it only means that you shift more energy and focus to the inner life – to home and family concerns. These things are as much a part of a successful career as the actual outer things that you do. They are what psychologists call 'enablers' of success. These are the psychological and emotional foundations that support outer career success. And now they need to be given more attention. From now until the end of the year you will be building up the inner forces for the next career push. Thus the next push will be healthy and natural.

Mars has been in your 4th house of home and family since July 18, and will be there until the 14th of this month. Often this indicates construction or major renovation work going on in the home. There can be conflicts with the family or in the family unit. Another reason why you need to focus more attention here.

You are still in the midst of a yearly financial peak until the 23rd – a prosperous month in a prosperous year. The Sun in your money house until that date shows that you are more personally involved in finances – you're not delegating this to others. Personal appearance – your over-all demeanour – plays a huge role in earnings and it won't hurt to invest in good clothing and accessories. It is good now to present an image of wealth, regardless of your actual bank balance. Mercury, the financial planet, enters the 3rd house of communication on the 2nd. This indicates that good sales, marketing and PR, which are always important for you, are even more so this month. Siblings and sibling figures are helpful financially. Profits can come from trading – buying and selling. On the 5th Venus enters the money house. This is a very nice transit. She is always beneficent. This transit again reinforces the importance of sales and marketing, but it also shows pay rises (either overt or covert) and the financial favour of bosses, parents or parent figures. Money can come from the government – either as direct payment or through the good graces of government.

Love is still happy this month. Jupiter's trine to Uranus from the 23rd to the 30th brings important romantic meetings and opportunity. Also happy social invitations come.

Health is excellent, and will improve further after the 14th when Mars leaves his stressful aspect to you.

October

Best Days Overall: 7, 8, 16, 17, 18, 26, 27
Most Stressful Days Overall: 3, 4, 9, 10, 24, 25, 31
Best Days for Love: 3, 4, 7, 8, 12, 13, 16, 17, 18, 22, 23, 26, 27, 31
Best Days for Money: 5, 6, 7, 8, 13, 17, 18, 19, 20, 22, 23, 26, 27, 31
Best Days for Career: 3, 9, 10, 12, 13, 22, 23

Two eclipses this month create volatility in your world and the world at large. Blockages and obstructions to progress get blasted away so that a Higher Plan can proceed. Both of these eclipses affect you strongly, so reduce your schedule during these periods.

The Lunar Eclipse of the 8th occurs in your 9th house of religion, travel and learning. Thus your religious and philosophical beliefs get tested. This testing is healthy. Our beliefs determine our life and it is good that the incorrect ones (or partially correct ones) get revealed so that adjustments can be made. Often this produces a 'crisis of faith'. Non-essential foreign travel should be avoided during this period. If you must travel, try to schedule flights around the time of the eclipse. This eclipse impacts on Uranus pretty directly, and sideswipes Pluto. Uranus is your love planet, so this signals a testing of a current relationship or marriage. This is when the dirty laundry comes out so that problems can be fixed. A good relationship will survive and get even better, but the ones that are fundamentally flawed can implode. Be more patient with the beloved this period. He or she is apt to be more temperamental than usual. Perhaps he or she is having personal dramas that impact on their mood and your relationship. The impact of the eclipse on Pluto affects the home and family, and a parent or parent figure. It tends to bring dramas – life-changing kinds of events – in the lives of these people. If there are problems in the home, now is when you find out about it. Repairs might be needed.

The Solar Eclipse of the 23rd has a much stronger impact on you. Every Solar Eclipse affects you – the Sun is the ruler of your Horoscope – but this one more so than usual. It occurs in square aspect to you. Those of you born between July 22 and July 24 are affected most of all. This eclipse again brings family dramas and challenges in the home. Whatever wasn't dealt with by the Lunar Eclipse gets dealt with now. Every Solar Eclipse brings changes – redefinitions of the image, the self-concept, and the way you want to be seen by others. If you don't define yourself for yourself, others will – and that won't be so pleasant.

Health becomes more delicate from the 23rd onwards, so be sure to get enough rest.

Overall the financial life is still excellent, but Mercury's retrograde from the 4th to the 25th complicates things. Your financial judgement is not as realistic as it could be. Try to finalize important purchases or investments before the 4th or wait until after the 25th. The period of Mercury's retrograde should be used for attaining mental clarity about finances and for seeing where improvements can be made. It is the 'pause that refreshes' – there is nothing seriously wrong with the financial life.

November

Best Days Overall: 4, 5, 13, 14, 22, 23
Most Stressful Days Overall: 6, 7, 20, 21, 27, 28
Best Days for Love: 2, 3, 4, 5, 11, 12, 13, 14, 22, 23, 27, 28
Best Days for Money: 1, 4, 5, 10, 11, 14, 15, 16, 17, 20, 21, 23
Best Days for Career: 2, 3, 6, 7, 11, 12, 22, 23

Mars was 'out of bounds' for all of last month and will be still until the 21st of this month. This indicates that in religious and philosophical matters you are exploring new worlds, new territory; you are moving outside the philosophies and world views that you were brought up in. On a physical level it signals that you are travelling to exotic, out-of-the-way kinds of places.

Health still needs watching until the 22nd. As always get more rest, and enhance your health in the ways mentioned in the yearly report. Health will improve in a big way after the 22nd. The current condition is temporary, caused by the short-term planets.

The planetary power is now firmly in the Western sector, and has been since October 23. Your cycle of personal independence is over with for a time. The Cosmos wants you to be happy, but part of your personal happiness is the happiness of other people. Others come first now. It might seem to you that you are sacrificing your personal happiness for the sake of others. But this is just how things appear superficially. Your own happiness will actually be enhanced – perhaps not immediately but in due course. Your way might not be the best way now. Others might have better ideas. Now you are in a cycle for developing the people skills. Kingly Leo likes to do things autocratically, but now is not the time for that. Modern-day kings and queens get their way as much by consensus as by decree.

With your 4th house of home and family very powerful since the 23rd of last month, you are in a period for psychological progress. This is internal progress. Your insights into moods and feelings are greatly increased. Often memories of the past come up very strongly. This is part of the psychological progress. You view these things from your present state of growth and they take on a different flavour. Much of what you once thought of as trauma and disaster is seen as actual blessing these days. Hindsight is a great cure for many psychological ills.

On the 22nd, as the Sun enters your 5th house of fun and creativity, you begin another yearly personal pleasure peak. This is a time to party, have fun and to explore the rapturous side of life. Leo heaven! This period is much stronger than in previous years. The Sun and the ruler of the 5th house, Jupiter, are in wonderful aspect with each other and also in 'mutual reception', when each is a guest in the other's house. This shows wonderful co-operation between the two planets, and a wonderful flow of energy between them. This is a fantastic aspect for either serious love or 'fun and games' love. Singles have their choice. Both seem abundant. The main challenge to serious love right now (as we have seen in other months) is infidelity. So much is being offered, it is difficult to resist.

Uranus is still activating the Lunar Eclipse point of October 8 all month. Thus there are bumps on the road to love. You and your spouse, partner or current love are basically in harmony, but there could be dramas in your lives that are complicating things.

December

Best Days Overall: 1, 2, 10, 11, 20, 21, 28, 29
Most Stressful Days Overall: 3, 4, 18, 19, 24, 25, 30, 31
Best Days for Love: 1, 2, 10, 11, 12, 13, 20, 21, 22, 24, 25, 28, 29, 30, 31
Best Days for Money: 1, 2, 10, 11, 13, 14, 20, 21, 22, 28, 29, 30, 31
Best Days for Career: 1, 2, 3, 4, 12, 13, 21, 22, 30, 31

The party continues in full force until December 22. You are still in a very strong yearly personal pleasure peak, but even Leo can't sustain this indefinitely. You will be taking a 'work break' after the 22nd. You are in the mood for work. It will be a very good time now to do those boring, detail-oriented, mundane things that you've been putting off

- your accounts, filing, etc. Job seekers have great success now. There are many, many opportunities. A job change wouldn't be a surprise. Saturn, your work planet, makes a major move out of Scorpio and into Sagittarius. You might feel that it is 'time to move on'. Many of you have been working from home these past few years and now you might find that too 'boring'. You want to be with others – in the outside world. You want work that you can enjoy. You need to enjoy the actual act of work.

Speculations are favourable until the 17th. After that, be more careful. Until the 17th money is earned in happy ways – while you're having fun or indulging in leisure. The party or sporting event can be just as lucrative as the office. You are spending more on leisure as well. The main danger here is overspending. But after the 17th your financial judgement is more down to earth, more sober, more serious. Money is earned through work and service – honest labour.

Saturn's move out of Scorpio eases much of the family pressure you've been feeling for the past few years. A parent or parent figure is less depressed, less grumpy now.

Health is good now too – happiness is a great healing force. After the 22nd you are more focused on health issues, more willing to take on serious health regimes. You can enhance the health even further by giving more attention to the heart (from the 22nd onwards), the hips and kidneys (from the 10th onwards), and the arms, shoulders, lungs, small intestines and respiratory system (from the 17th onwards).

Avoid unnecessary foreign travel from the 4th to the 7th.

Venus's transit of a previous eclipse point from the 21st to the 23rd could bring career changes.

The planetary momentum is overwhelmingly forward this month – 90 per cent of the planets are moving forward from the 21st. Since the Winter Solstice is the solar new Moon – the birth of the yearly solar cycle – this is an excellent time for launching new ventures or new products. Next month will be good for this too.

Virgo

♍

THE VIRGIN

Birthdays from
22nd August to
22nd September

Personality Profile

VIRGO AT A GLANCE

Element – Earth

  Ruling Planet – Mercury
  Career Planet – Mercury
  Love Planet – Neptune
  Money Planet – Venus
  Planet of Home and Family Life – Jupiter
  Planet of Health and Work – Uranus
  Planet of Pleasure – Saturn
  Planet of Sexuality – Mars

Colours – earth tones, ochre, orange, yellow

Colour that promotes love, romance and social harmony – aqua blue

Colour that promotes earning power – jade green

Gems – agate, hyacinth

Metal – quicksilver

Scents – lavender, lilac, lily of the valley, storax

Quality – mutable (= flexibility)

Quality most needed for balance – a broader perspective

Strongest virtues – mental agility, analytical skills, ability to pay attention to detail, healing powers

Deepest needs – to be useful and productive

Characteristic to avoid – destructive criticism

Signs of greatest overall compatibility – Taurus, Capricorn

Signs of greatest overall incompatibility – Gemini, Sagittarius, Pisces

Sign most helpful to career – Gemini

Sign most helpful for emotional support – Sagittarius

Sign most helpful financially – Libra

Sign best for marriage and/or partnerships – Pisces

Sign most helpful for creative projects – Capricorn

Best Sign to have fun with – Capricorn

Signs most helpful in spiritual matters – Taurus, Leo

Best day of the week – Wednesday

Understanding a Virgo

The virgin is a particularly fitting symbol for those born under the sign of Virgo. If you meditate on the image of the virgin you will get a good understanding of the essence of the Virgo type. The virgin is, of course, a symbol of purity and innocence – not naïve, but pure. A virginal object has not been touched. A virgin field is land that is true to itself, the way it has always been. The same is true of virgin forest: it is pristine, unaltered.

Apply the idea of purity to the thought processes, emotional life, physical body and activities and projects of the everyday world, and you can see how Virgos approach life. Virgos desire the pure expression of the ideal in their mind, body and affairs. If they find impurities they will attempt to clear them away.

Impurities are the beginning of disorder, unhappiness and uneasiness. The job of the Virgo is to eject all impurities and keep only that which the body and mind can use and assimilate.

The secrets of good health are here revealed: 90 per cent of the art of staying well is maintaining a pure mind, a pure body and pure emotions. When you introduce more impurities than your mind and body can deal with, you will have what is known as 'dis-ease'. It is no wonder that Virgos make great doctors, nurses, healers and dieticians. They have an innate understanding of good health and they realize that good health is more than just physical. In all aspects of life, if you want a project to be successful it must be kept as pure as possible. It must be protected against the adverse elements that will try to undermine it. This is the secret behind Virgo's awesome technical proficiency.

One could talk about Virgo's analytical powers – which are formidable. One could talk about their perfectionism and their almost superhuman attention to detail. But this would be to miss the point. All of these virtues are manifestations of a Virgo's desire for purity and perfection – a world without Virgos would have ruined itself long ago.

A vice is nothing more than a virtue turned inside out, misapplied or used in the wrong context. Virgos' apparent vices come from their inherent virtue. Their analytical powers, which should be used for healing, helping or perfecting a project in the world, sometimes get misapplied and turned against people. Their critical faculties, which should be used constructively to perfect a strategy or proposal, can sometimes be used destructively to harm or wound. Their urge to perfection can turn into worry and lack of confidence; their natural humility can become self-denial and self-abasement. When Virgos turn negative they are apt to turn their devastating criticism on themselves, sowing the seeds of self-destruction.

Finance

Virgos have all the attitudes that create wealth. They are hard-working, industrious, efficient, organized, thrifty, productive and eager to serve. A developed Virgo is every employer's dream. But until Virgos master some of the social graces of Libra they will not even come close to fulfilling their financial potential. Purity and perfectionism, if not handled correctly or gracefully, can be very trying to others. Friction in human relationships can be devastating not only to your pet projects but – indirectly – to your wallet as well.

Virgos are quite interested in their financial security. Being hard-working, they know the true value of money. They do not like to take risks with their money, preferring to save for their retirement or for a rainy day. Virgos usually make prudent, calculated investments that involve a minimum of risk. These investments and savings usually work out well, helping Virgos to achieve the financial security they seek. The rich or even not-so-rich Virgo also likes to help his or her friends in need.

Career and Public Image

Virgos reach their full potential when they can communicate their knowledge in such a way that others can understand it. In order to get their ideas across better, Virgos need to develop greater verbal skills and fewer judgemental ways of expressing themselves. Virgos look up to teachers and communicators; they like their bosses to be good communicators. Virgos will probably not respect a superior who is not their intellectual equal – no matter how much money or power that superior has. Virgos themselves like to be perceived by others as being educated and intellectual.

The natural humility of Virgos often inhibits them from fulfilling their great ambitions, from acquiring name and fame. Virgos should indulge in a little more self-promotion if they are going to reach their career goals. They need to push themselves with the same ardour that they would use to foster others.

At work Virgos like to stay active. They are willing to learn any type of job as long as it serves their ultimate goal of financial security. Virgos may change occupations several times during their professional lives, until they find the one they really enjoy. Virgos work well with other people, are not afraid to work hard and always fulfil their responsibilities.

Love and Relationships

If you are an analyst or a critic you must, out of necessity, narrow your scope. You have to focus on a part and not the whole; this can create a temporary narrow-mindedness. Virgos do not like this kind of person. They like their partners to be broad-minded, with depth and vision. Virgos seek to get this broad-minded quality from their partners, since they sometimes lack it themselves.

Virgos are perfectionists in love just as they are in other areas of life. They need partners who are tolerant, open-minded and easy-going. If you are in love with a Virgo do not waste time on impractical romantic gestures. Do practical and useful things for him or her – this is what will be appreciated and what will be done for you.

Virgos express their love through pragmatic and useful gestures, so do not be put off because your Virgo partner does not say 'I love you' day-in and day-out. Virgos are not that type. If they love you, they will demonstrate it in practical ways. They will always be there for you; they will show an interest in your health and finances; they will fix your sink or repair your video recorder. Virgos deem these actions to be superior to sending flowers, chocolates or Valentine cards.

In love affairs Virgos are not particularly passionate or spontaneous. If you are in love with a Virgo, do not take this personally. It does not mean that you are not alluring enough or that your Virgo partner does not love or like you. It is just the way Virgos are. What they lack in passion they make up for in dedication and loyalty.

Home and Domestic Life

It goes without saying that the home of a Virgo will be spotless, sanitized and orderly. Everything will be in its proper place – and don't you dare move anything about! For Virgos to find domestic bliss they need to ease up a bit in the home, to allow their partner and children more freedom and to be more generous and open-minded. Family members are not to be analysed under a microscope, they are individuals with their own virtues to express.

With these small difficulties resolved, Virgos like to stay in and entertain at home. They make good hosts and they like to keep their friends and families happy and entertained at family and social gatherings. Virgos love children, but they are strict with them – at times – since they want to make sure their children are brought up with the correct sense of family and values.

Horoscope for 2014

Major Trends

Both 2012 and 2013 were very strong career years. There was much success here. You were elevated, promoted and perhaps honoured for your professional achievements. Very happy career opportunities came to you. This year there is a sense of satiation here. Your major goals have been fulfilled and the focus is more on friendships, groups and organizations. On July 16 Jupiter will enter your 12th house of spirituality, initiating a cycle of spiritual growth, development and success. This will continue well into next year.

Uranus entered your 8th house of transformation and regeneration in 2011 and will be there for many more years. Whatever your age or stage in life you are in a more sexually active period. Libido is stronger than usual. This aspect also indicates that much sexual experimentation is happening. So long as it is not destructive, it will enhance pleasure and bring new knowledge.

Perhaps the main headline now – and it began back in February 2012 – is Neptune's presence in your 7th house of love and marriage. The love and social life is becoming more spiritual, more refined. You are attracting and are attracted by more refined types of people. The love life was excellent last year and this trend continues in the year ahead. The love life is also a lot more stable than it has been for many years. More on this later.

Saturn was in your 3rd house of communication last year and will be there for almost all the year ahead (only leaving on December 24). So siblings (or sibling figures in your life) and neighbours have been a challenge and difficult to handle. In most cases it is not so much because of the relationship but because of issues in their own lives. This aspect also shows a need to limit speech, to tone it down, to speak only when needed and to do your homework before you speak. Students (below college level) have more challenges in their studies and need to work harder. This will be a year for knuckling down in school. Many have changed schools in recent years and more changes are likely in the year ahead.

Your areas of greatest interest this year are communication and intellectual interests; children, fun and creativity; love and romance; sex, personal reinvention and transformation, debt, taxes, estates and occult studies; friends, groups and group activities (until July 16); and spirituality (from July 16 onwards).

Your paths of greatest fulfilment this year are communication and intellectual interests (until February 19); finance (from February 19 onwards); friends, groups and group activities (until July 16); and spirituality (from July 16 onwards).

Health

(Please note that this is an astrological perspective on health and not a medical one. In days of yore there was no difference, both of these perspectives were identical. But in these times there could be quite a difference. For a medical perspective, please consult your doctor or health practitioner.)

Health is always important to Virgo, always a focus, but this year less so than usual. The 6th house of health is not a house of power.

Health is basically good and there's no need to pay undue attention here.

This year there is only one long-term planet – Neptune – in stressful alignment with you. All the others are either making harmonious aspects or leaving you alone. So your health and energy will be good. Sure, there will be periods in the year when health is less easy than usual, thanks to temporary planetary transits, but they are not trends for the year. When the stressful transits pass, your normal health and vitality return. This year these periods will be from February 18 to March 20, May 21 to June 20, and November 22 to December 21. Be sure to get more rest during these periods.

Good though your health is you can make it even better. Give more attention to the following areas – the most vulnerable in the year ahead. First, the small intestine. This organ is always important for you, and the reflexes for it are shown on the chart.

The ankles and calves are another area that is always important for you. It is good to massage these regularly and give the ankles more

Reflexology

Try to massage the whole foot on a regular basis, but pay extra attention to the points highlighted on the chart. When you massage, be aware of 'sore spots', as these need special attention. It's also a good idea to massage the ankles and the top of the feet.

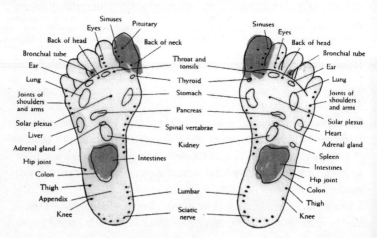

support when exercising. Weak ankles are often the hidden causes of injuries to other parts of the body.

Regular scalp and face massage will be wonderful now (and in future years). Since the face and scalp contain reflexes to the entire body, this kind of massage will strengthen the whole body and not just the face and scalp. Craniaosacral therapy will also be powerful. The bones in the skull tend to shift and need to be kept in right alignment.

The adrenals also should have some attention. Avoid anger and fear – the two emotions that stress the adrenals. Sometimes we can't prevent these emotions, but if that happens try to move out of these emotional places as quickly as possible. Meditation will be a big help.

The final vulnerable areas this year are the colon, bladder and sexual organs. Safe sex and sexual moderation are important these days. The colon needs to be kept clean and colonic irrigation might be a good idea.

Your health planet is Uranus. In the physical body he rules the ankles and calves, hence the importance of these limbs in overall health. Moreover, Uranus rules your health from the sign of Aries, which rules the head, face and scalp, and from your 8th house, which is associated with the colon, bladder and sexual organs.

The 8th house rules surgery and detoxification. It creates a tendency to see surgery as the 'quick fix' to a health problem. Sometimes it is, sometimes it isn't. Get second opinions. Detox regimes will be powerful in the year ahead as well.

Home and Family

For practically all the year ahead your 4th house of home and family is not a house of power. This will change very late in the year – during the last week – when Saturn moves into this house. This will be more of a factor for 2015 than for now.

Thus the year ahead is more or less stable on the home front. You seem basically satisfied with the present home and present arrangements and have no need to make major changes. There is nothing against a move or renovation, but nothing especially favouring it either. You have much free will in this area this year.

While the physical home and domestic arrangements are not a focus, children (and children figures in your life) most certainly are. Pluto has been in your 5th house for some years now and will be there for many years to come. Pluto in this aspect tends to complicate child birth. Often it shows abortion, miscarriage or Caesarean sections. Not always though. Perhaps the threat of these things overhangs a pregnancy, or perhaps an abortion or Caesarean is recommended. Sometimes there are medical reasons for this. However, it doesn't mean that they have to be done. Get a second opinion.

Your challenge this year will be to keep the children (or children figures in your life) out of harm's way. In the past few years they could have had near-death kinds of experiences or surgery. Pluto rules all these things. The trick will be to keep them safe without stunting or stifling their development. Some creativity will be needed. Protecting them against sexual abuse will also be an issue this year (as it has been in past years as well).

Jupiter, your family planet, spends the first part of the year in Cancer, your 11th house. Jupiter is in his sign of 'exaltation' – he reaches his highest form of expression in this sign. A good signal for family affairs. This tends to indicate that you are working to build a 'team spirit' in the family, and you seem to be successful. This team spirit can be a powerful protection for the children or children figures in your life. Everyone looks after everyone else. It also shows that you are installing high-tech gadgetry in the home.

On July 16, Jupiter moves into Leo, your 12th house. This has many readings. The first and most obvious is that the focus is on children – a reinforcement of what we said above. It shows that you are making the home more of a 'fun' place – buying toys or entertainment for the home. This too can be a protection for children. If they can have fun at home there is no need for them to be outdoors or other places, which could be less safe. It shows that your spiritual understanding will help deal with family issues. If you have issues with the family consult the Divine within. There is revelation on this subject for you.

The family planet in the 12th house would show that you are entertaining spiritual-type people or hosting spiritual kinds of events at home.

This tendency is seen with a parent or parent figure as well. Parents or parent figures could have moved last year, but if not it might happen this year. Perhaps they are renovating or buying additional properties. It seems very happy.

Siblings or sibling figures in your life have good opportunities to move – to upgrade the home – after July 16. Children or children figures can have multiple moves in the year ahead. This can either be within the present home or somewhere else. If they are young, bedrooms can be changed or renovated. If they are older it can be a move to somewhere else. They seem nomadic this year. Grandchildren (or these kinds of figures in your life) are likely to move after July 16.

Finance and Career

Your 2nd house of finance is strong for the first seven or so months of the year – until July 26. Thus there is great focus and change happening here. A Lunar Eclipse on April 15 occurs in your money house as well, reinforcing all this.

Mars spends an unusual amount of time in your money house – almost seven months, which is highly unusual. His normal transit is one and a half to two months. Mars is also part of Grand Square in the Cardinal signs. So something big is going on here. You are involved (and it seems to be with the family) in some large, major undertaking. Most likely a business, but a large-scale one. These things are always complicated. Much courage and drive is needed – much work – and Mars is supplying all this.

Mars in the money house tends to risk taking. Virgo is not generally a risk-taker. Virgo, like all the Earth signs, tends to be conservative in finance. So this is unusual too. Since Mars rules your 8th house of debt, perhaps you are taking on a lot of debt – perhaps an uncomfortable amount – and this is risky.

This is a good year to learn the difference between constructive and destructive debt. Constructive debt – when you borrow to buy things or make investments that appreciate in value – will make you rich. All the biggest businesses fund their operations with debt. But they use it wisely. The return will always vastly exceed the 'cost of the money'. Destructive debt is when you borrow to buy or invest in things that will go down in value or will be used up, such as a vacation, expensive meals or clothing. After a while such things become worthless – and you are stuck with the debt. In recent years we saw this in the property market. People borrowed huge sums to buy homes that crashed in value. This kind of debt will impoverish you. Sometimes (as in the case of the property market) it is difficult to tell whether the borrowing is constructive or destructive and this is where risk comes in.

The ruler of the 8th house in the money house often shows inheritance. Hopefully no one has to die, but you can be named in someone's will or appointed to some function that pays you. Many of you are doing extensive estate planning – this and tax issues are influencing many of your decisions. It seems to me that many of you are paying more taxes this year (a positive as this generally shows increased income) and many will be receiving large tax refunds.

Mars in the money house indicates aggressiveness in finance. Mars believes that 'we make wealth happen' – our drive and initiative make it happen. Mars wants to conquer the marketplace – to dominate it; it is not just about 'earning fair returns' or 'making a living'. The problem here is that this can be overdone and can lead to needless conflicts in business. Work hard, and use your personal initiative by all means. But needless conflict should be avoided. (Sometimes it can't, but where possible it should.)

Investors with this aspect will be 'profit takers' and 'momentum players'. More like hunters than investors.

Venus, your financial planet, is a fast-moving planet. During the year she will move through your whole chart. So money can come to you in a variety of ways and through a variety of people – all depending on where Venus is and the kinds of aspects she receives. These are the short-term trends in finances and we will discuss this in the monthly reports.

As we mentioned before, career is not a big focus this year. Some years are like that. You are coming out of a few very strong career years and it is time to shift your attention elsewhere – to friendships, groups and organizations and also to spirituality. Career should be more or less stable.

Love and Social Life

Ever since Uranus moved out of your 7th house of love and marriage in 2011 the love life has become more stable. Before that – to be blunt – it was sheer craziness. Love came and love went. Friends came into the picture and they left. Since 2003–2004 your whole social circle has changed.

Beneath all of this was a cosmic agenda. You were being liberated to follow your ideals of love – to follow the cosmic plan for your love life. And it is starting to happen. In 2012 your love planet, Neptune, moved into your 7th house. Jupiter's move into Cancer last year made fabulous aspects to your love planet – and so was Saturn. So love is in the air and this seems to me to be 'ideal' love. The dream love. Marriage could have happened last year for many of you, and it can still happen in the year ahead. Jupiter is still making nice aspects to Neptune for the first half of the year.

As our regular readers know, marriage is not meant in a 'literal' kind of way. Many of you entered relationships that were 'like' marriage or met people who were 'marriage material'.

Neptune is in his own sign and house for the long term now, for another 12 or so years. This is a positive for love. Neptune is much stronger and more effective in his own sign and house – he operates more in line with his nature. So your social magnetism is very powerful these days.

Virgos always have high standards in love. They are perfectionists in romance just as they are in all departments of life. These days the standards seem even higher than usual – nothing less than the ideal will do. And it seems attainable.

Perhaps the main challenge these days is discerning the genuine article from those who only seem like the real deal. Neptune makes you very idealistic and you might overlook many tell-tale warning signs. But as time goes on you will learn discernment. Your intuition is being trained in love matters these days. Learn to trust it.

Friends and loved ones – the worldly types – might accuse you of living in 'love cuckoo land' and of having unrealistic expectations. That's OK. Real love is a kind of 'cuckoo land' with its own rules and laws. Better the 'cuckoo land' of love than the grim, loveless prisons of the hard material world.

By the time Jupiter leaves the sign of Cancer on July 16, most of you will have achieved your social goals. It will be time to move on to other things, like spiritual growth.

The social life in general is good this year – not just romance. Jupiter in the 11th house until July 16 signals an expanded social circle. New and significant friends are coming into the picture. There is romance, but also a lot of involvement with groups and organizations. Many of you will find romantic and social opportunities online this year. But they will happen in the normal ways too – at parties, weddings and gatherings, and through family connections.

Favourable numbers for love are 1, 12 and 18.

Self-improvement

Spiritual growth is happening on two fronts this year. The first is through the love and social life, through your social interactions and what you learn about yourself through romantic involvement. The second (and this happens from July 16 onwards) is through your family relationships. Everything that is happening on these two fronts is not what it seems. There is a precise spiritual agenda behind things. Everything that is happening – pleasant or unpleasant – is for your highest good. It is hard to see this sometimes, especially when unpleasant things happen, but it is nevertheless so. The unpleasantness is really a doorway – a portal – to deeper understanding. But one must know how to enter the door. The first step is to recognize that the Cosmos intends good for you, regardless of appearances. The second step is not to judge the event – good or bad – but to just observe it and your internal reactions to it. This simple awareness will reveal the hidden purpose behind the event. Humans have their limited notions of good, but the Cosmos's notion of good is vast and far reaching. Don't judge.

In love you are being led, step by step, into the ultimate, most ideal love – the transpersonal love of the Divine. This doesn't happen overnight. The Cosmos has many roads to take you there – generally through experiencing relationships that seem ideal to you. Even your own highest concept of love on the human level pales in comparison to the Divine love. But in order to see this you have to go through the human love experiences – the highs and the lows. And this is what's happening now. When you contact the Divine love, you will always have love in your life. Whether you are in a relationship or not, you will always feel that you are on your honeymoon.

Some people think that one has to give up human relationships in order to attain the Divine love, but this is not the case. Relationships will be just one of the instruments that the Cosmos uses to love you. But it is not limited to that. It can act directly on your mind and emotions (and even your body) if it so chooses.

Everyone has a spiritual family – a soul family if you will. The soul family is generally very different from the biological family. The biological family could be called the 'karmic family'. There is a need to resolve old issues from past embodiments. The biological family is one of the laboratories where we gain knowledge and understanding. The soul family could be called the 'ideal family'. These beings love and support you unconditionally – the way a real family should be. Some of the members of this soul family could be incarnate, some not. A person can go through life and never meet one of them in the flesh. Yet, on the spiritual level, they are always there. When Jupiter moves into your 12th house on July 16, you will start meeting some of these people. Some you will meet physically, some on the inner planes. You will be made conscious of their presence.

Month-by-month Forecasts

January

Best Days Overall: 1, 2, 9, 10, 19, 20, 28, 29
Most Stressful Days Overall: 5, 6, 12, 13, 26, 27
Best Days for Love: 1, 2, 5, 6, 9, 10, 14, 19, 20, 24, 28, 29
Best Days for Money: 1, 2, 5, 6, 9, 10, 14, 15, 19, 20, 22, 23, 24, 25, 28, 29
Best Days for Career: 1, 2, 10, 11, 12, 13, 22, 23, 30, 31

You begin your year with the planetary power mostly below the horizon. You are still in the night-time of your year, in a period where the focus should be on home, family and emotional well-being. Feeling right is more important than doing right. Being in your point of emotional harmony is important now. From this place you can be powerful in your outer, external affairs.

The planetary momentum is forward this month – 80 per cent of the planets are in forward motion. This signals a good month to launch new ventures or products into the world. (There are other favourable factors operating here too.) The 1st to the 16th and the 30th to the 31st are especially favourable times for this.

The planetary power is mostly in the Western, social sector of your Horoscope. This means that you are living with the side-effects of your previous cycle of personal independence. Adapt to situations as best you can. Put others first and cultivate your social skills. As you do this your own interests will be taken care of.

The month ahead is basically happy. You are in the midst of one of your yearly personal pleasure peaks. This means it is party time – time for fun activities, for recreation. On the 20th, as the Sun enters your 6th house of health and work, you go into work mode – which for a Virgo is another form of fun.

Finances are delicate this month, but rest assured that this is a short-term issue. Your financial planet Venus is in one of her rare retrogrades (she only does this once every two years). Earnings will happen but more slowly. Delays in receiving payments or glitches with payments are quite normal under a retrograde. Deal with it as you would deal with adverse weather. Don't make things worse than they need to be. You can make this retrograde work for your benefit by reviewing your finances, isolating weak spots, and targeting corrective measures. Next month, when Venus moves forward again, you can put your plans into effect. The good news here is that your spouse, partner or current love is supportive. Job seekers have good fortune after the 20th.

Health is excellent this month. Only one long-term planet is in stressful alignment with you. The short-term planets are making harmonious aspects or leaving you alone. You can enhance your health even further in the ways mentioned in the yearly report.

Love has been good in the past year and is good in the month ahead. With Venus retrograde this is not time for a marriage, but one can enjoy love without a formal wedding.

February

Best Days Overall: 5, 6, 7, 15, 16, 17, 24, 25
Most Stressful Days Overall: 1, 2, 8, 9, 22, 23, 28
Best Days for Love: 1, 2, 5, 6, 7, 10, 16, 17, 20, 24, 25, 28
Best Days for Money: 1, 2, 5, 6, 7, 10, 11, 12, 16, 17, 18, 19, 20,
    21, 24, 25, 28
Best Days for Career: 1, 8, 9, 10, 19, 26, 27

Venus moves forward this month. You can now start implementing your financial improvements. Hopefully you have attained mental clarity around your finances now – this was the whole point of the retrograde. The financial judgement is much sounder than last month. Venus is in the sign of Capricorn, which is another positive signal for wealth. There is a healthy realism about finance and spending and a long-term perspective on it. This is a good time to set up long-term savings and investment plans. If these things are set up properly and adhered to, wealth, over the long term, is just inevitable. There is no doubt about it.

Mars, the ruler of your 8th house of regeneration is in your money house. This gives many messages. It shows, as we mentioned, good spousal support. But it also shows a need to detox the financial life – detox your possessions. Like the farmer who prunes his vines, you grow by 'cutting away' the dead wood – things, or expenses, that you don't really need. You 'plug the leaks' in your financial consciousness. This is a good time (and you have many months ahead to do this) to go through your possessions and give away or sell what you don't need or use. Reduce the clutter. If you are not actively using a thing, get rid of it now.

Job seekers still have excellent aspects until the 18th.

On the 18th the Sun enters your 7th house and you begin a yearly love and social peak. The social life gets very active. You attend more weddings and parties. There are more social invitations. The unattached meet promising prospects. Love seems especially happy from the 22nd to the 24th as the Sun activates your love planet Neptune. There is a meeting with someone spiritual – perhaps an artist, poet or musician. You are attracted to these types anyway – your love planet is in mystical Pisces for the long term.

Health becomes more delicate after the 18th. There's nothing seriously wrong with you, it is just not one of your best health periods. The stresses are being caused by short-term planets and they are temporary, not trends for the year or for your life. When these periods come pre-existing conditions can appear to worsen. Make sure you get more rest. High energy levels are the number one defence against disease.

Mercury, both the ruler of your chart and your career planet, goes retrograde on the 6th. Your personal goals and career should be under review. It is not a time for making major decisions in these areas. Clarity of mind is what's needed. By next month this should happen.

March

Best Days Overall: 5, 6, 15, 16, 24, 25
Most Stressful Days Overall: 1, 2, 7, 8, 22, 23, 28, 29
Best Days for Love: 1, 2, 7, 10, 17, 18, 19, 26, 27, 28, 29
Best Days for Money: 1, 2, 7, 10, 11, 17, 18, 19, 20, 26, 27, 28, 29
Best Days for Career: 7, 8, 19, 28, 29

Mercury starts going forward again on the 1st and career and personal issues will move forward then too. Decision-making in these areas will be much better.

The planets are shifting during this month. The lower half of the Horoscope no longer dominates; the upper and lower halves are about equal in power right now. (This will change next month.) Career and outer activities are becoming more important and home and family issues are more or less settled now, although not completely. You are more or less bouncing between the career and the home and family life this month. After the 6th, as Jupiter, your family planet, starts to move forward, is an excellent time to resolve any unsettled issues in the home. But it's time also to prepare for your upcoming career push.

You are still in the midst of a yearly love and social peak this month. Technically it ends on the 20th, but with the ruler of your Horoscope in the 7th house all month it will continue after this date. You seem more popular than ever this month – especially after the 17th. You are there for your friends and the beloved, and they know it. The new

Moon of the 1st occurs very near the Love Planet and enhances the love and social life. It should bring happy social invitations and clarity in love as the month progresses.

Mercury travels with Neptune from the 21st to the 23rd. For singles this brings a happy romantic meeting. For those who are already attached (and many of you are) it brings more closeness in the existing relationship. Love has been idealistic for some years now and this month even more so. It is much more than just 'lust of the flesh' or personal gratification. It is something spiritual and elevated.

Mercury's transit of Neptune is a spiritual period for you as well. The dream life will be more active (and you should pay attention to these visions). Social connections are helping the career.

Health still needs watching until the 20th. Like last month, make sure you get enough rest. Do your best to maintain high energy levels and your health will improve after the 20th.

Venus, the financial planet, transits a previous eclipse point from the 17th to the 19th. This will bring necessary financial changes – generally through some disturbance or problem.

Mars transits an eclipse point from the 11th to the 18th. Avoid confrontations and risky kinds of activities during this time. Your spouse, partner or current love has some short-term financial disturbance. This will lead to necessary changes.

April

Best Days Overall: 1, 2, 11, 12, 20, 21, 29, 30
Most Stressful Days Overall: 3, 4, 5, 18, 19, 24, 25
Best Days for Love: 4, 5, 6, 7, 16, 17, 24, 25
Best Days for Money: 4, 5, 6, 7, 13, 14, 15, 16, 17, 24, 25
Best Days for Career: 3, 4, 5, 7, 8, 18, 19, 29, 30

Two eclipses this month shake up the world at large, but you seem unscathed. The Lunar Eclipse of the 15th occurs in your 2nd house of finance. Thus important and dramatic financial changes are afoot. This will be a six-month process – generally it doesn't happen all at once. You will need to change your financial attitudes, thinking and strategy. Your finances get a 'reality' check. The changes you make will be good, but it can be uncomfortable while they're happening. This eclipse also affects your spouse, partner or current love's finances. What is happening with you is also happening with him or her.

Every Lunar Eclipse tests friendships. They tend to bring dramas in the lives of friends – life-changing kinds of events. This eclipse is no different. Though physically you are not much affected it won't hurt to take it easy during the period anyway.

The Solar Eclipse of the 29th also seems benign to you. It occurs in your 9th house of religion, travel and learning. Unnecessary foreign travel is best avoided during this time. It brings dramas in the lives of those you worship with – the religious people in your life. There are shake-ups in your church, synagogue or mosque. Students at college level make important changes in their educational plans – perhaps they change courses or schools. Every Solar Eclipse brings spiritual changes – changes in attitude and practice. This one seems stronger in this regard as your religious and philosophical beliefs also get tested. This can be due to spiritual-type experiences. Changes in the belief system will change every other department of life eventually – and for the better.

Though the beloved is having financial challenges due to the Lunar Eclipse, overall prosperity still seems good. He or she is in the midst of a yearly financial peak until the 20th. There is great focus on finance and this tends to success, in spite of the challenges. Your personal finances will also work out well. Friends are supportive and helpful, as is your spouse, partner or current love. The financial intuition will be especially sharp from the 6th onwards, and particularly from the 10th to the 13th. Important financial information and guidance will come in the form of dreams or through psychics, ministers or other spiritual channels. Job seekers have good fortune from the 13th to the 15th. There are career changes happening that period too.

This period – from the 10th to the 13th – also brings happy romantic opportunity. Love in general is happy this month. Venus in your house of love and marriage is always a positive sign.

Health is good this month. You can enhance it further in the ways mentioned in the yearly report.

May

Best Days Overall: 8, 9, 10, 17, 18, 26, 27
Most Stressful Days Overall: 1, 2, 15, 16, 21, 22, 28, 29
Best Days for Love: 3, 4, 6, 13, 14, 21, 22, 24, 25, 31
Best Days for Money: 3, 4, 5, 6, 11, 12, 13, 14, 21, 22, 24, 25, 31
Best Days for Career: 1, 2, 11, 12, 19, 20, 28, 29, 30

Last month on the 6th the balance of planetary power shifted to the upper half of the Horoscope. Now the upper half is dominant. Now is the time to make your career push. Now is the time to implement, in physical kinds of ways, the plans that you've been hatching for many months. You can serve your family best by being successful in your outer life. On the 21st you enter a yearly career peak, but you will feel this even before – from the 7th onwards. Mercury crosses the Mid-heaven on the 7th and enters your 10th house of career. This indicates personal success and elevation. (Sometimes elevation happens in covert ways, but it does happen.) You are honoured and respected for your achievements. Being involved in charities and good causes will also benefit the career.

Mars and Uranus are opposed to each other this month in varying degrees of exactitude. Avoid risk-taking activities, stunts, confrontations, etc. People can over-react these days. This aspect also shows that financial changes are still going on with the spouse, partner or current love. These have been in progress for some months now.

Love is still good, but there are some short-term bumps on the road this month. Be more patient with the beloved on the 11th, 28th and 29th. You're hitting a rough patch from the 21st onwards. There's nothing seriously wrong with the love life, it's just temporary stress from the short-term planets.

Though you and your spouse, partner or current love are making dramatic financial changes, you are still mutually supportive of each other. Venus and Mars (your financial planets) are in 'mutual reception', guests in each other's houses, from the 3rd to the 29th. This indicates good financial co-operation. The beloved is helping you and vice versa.

Health becomes more delicate after the 21st. Long term your health is good, this is just not one of your better months. The stress is coming from short-term planets and is temporary. As always make sure you get enough rest, and perhaps book a massage or two (or three) and more time at the health spa. Keep the batteries charged.

Mercury, the ruler of your Horoscope (and your career planet) goes 'out of bounds' from the 12th to the 31st. This shows that personally and in your career you are moving outside your normal sphere, moving outside your normal boundaries. This is probably what is needed now. Your ability to 'think outside the box' boosts your career.

June

Best Days Overall: 5, 6, 14, 15, 22, 23
Most Stressful Days Overall: 12, 13, 18, 19, 24, 25, 26
Best Days for Love: 1, 5, 6, 9, 10, 14, 15, 18, 19, 23, 24, 27, 28
Best Days for Money: 1, 5, 6, 7, 8, 10, 11, 14, 15, 18, 19, 23, 24, 27, 28
Best Days for Career: 1, 9, 10, 17, 24, 25, 26

You are still well in the midst of your yearly career peak this month. Career is successful but more complicated than last month. Mercury goes retrograde on the 7th. This will not stop your career progress but it will slow it down somewhat. Normally the retrograde of the career planet suggests a review of the career rather than overt actions. But you won't be able to avoid overt action. It's probably not possible to 'step back' from the career – there are too many demands on you. However, you can make sure that everything you do is 'perfect'. Get all the details right. This will prevent a lot of problems later on down the road. It seems the slow way of doing things, but in the end it will be faster.

Finances seem good this month. Your financial planet Venus is in her own sign and house – in Taurus. She is strong on your behalf. Earning power is stronger. Venus will be in her house until the 23rd and this tends to financial expansion. She will transit an eclipse point on the 5th and 6th, which can bring some short-term disturbance – some unexpected expense or obligation. Sometimes it reveals some flaw in your financial thinking and planning. In a way this is good – though it's not always comfortable. It forces you to make the necessary changes and adjustments.

Venus crosses the Mid-heaven and enters your 10th house on the 23rd, which is also a good financial signal. It shows action happening. It shows that earnings come from your good professional reputation and from the financial favour of bosses, parents or parent figures. Earnings can come from the government too – either as some direct payment or through policies that benefit you. Pay rises often happen under this kind of transit. Sometimes it's not an 'official' kind of thing, but more concealed – the net effect is the same, however. It's 'as if' you got a pay rise.

Mars is still in opposition to Uranus this month, so review our discussion of this last month. Be especially careful from the 22nd to the 26th when the aspect is most exact.

Love is still delicate this month. The love planet goes retrograde on the 9th, which slows things down. Your social judgement is not up to its usual standards. You're in a period of review for the love life. In spite of Neptune's retrograde, love is much improved after the 21st as the love planet receives much positive stimulation. Love is there – either serious or unserious – but there's no rush. Let love develop as it will – naturally.

Health still needs attention until the 21st. See our discussion of this last month. There is a great improvement in overall energy after the 21st.

When the Sun enters your 11th house on the 21st you are in a strong social period – both romantically (as we mentioned) and with friends and groups. This year you have made new and significant friends and there's more happening after the 21st.

July

Best Days Overall: 2, 3, 11, 12, 19, 20, 21, 29, 30, 31
Most Stressful Days Overall: 9, 10, 15, 16, 22, 23
Best Days for Love: 4, 5, 6, 7, 8, 13, 14, 15, 16, 24, 25
Best Days for Money: 2, 3, 4, 5, 6, 7, 8, 11, 12, 16, 17, 19, 20, 27, 29, 30
Best Days for Career: 5, 6, 13, 14, 22, 23, 24, 25

Last month, on the 23rd, the planetary power shifted from the social Western sector of your Horoscope to the independent East. You entered a period of personal independence. This will continue until December. People skills are great. Other people are wonderful. But now it is time to chart your own course to happiness. You have the power to do it. Enough of adapting to situations; if a condition displeases you, change it. If others don't go along with you, act independently. They will come around in due course. It is nice to coast and it is nice to have things your way. Now is a time for having things your way.

Career is still successful this month. You are honoured, respected and recognized. You're recognized for your achievements and also for who you are. But the major power this month is in your 11th house of friends and groups. The natural consequence of career success is the friendships that are made. One mixes in different and better circles.

Power in the 11th house is not only good on a social level, but it's very good for expanding your knowledge of technology, astrology, science and astronomy. Much new information will come to you. I have noted in my practice that people will often have their first Horoscope cast when the ruler of the 11th house is activated.

The natural consequence of expanded scientific knowledge is expanded spiritual knowledge. This is why the 12th house of spirituality comes after the 11th house. Science can only take us so far. Only spirituality (what is called the supernatural realm) can solve the deeper issues of science. Your house of spirituality becomes powerful from the 22nd onwards.

Jupiter's move into the 12th house on the 17th (where he will stay for the rest of the year) means that the whole year ahead – not just this month – will be more spiritual. There is much spiritual expansion, spiritual revelation, spiritual-type experiences happening. Get used to the supernatural now; it's going to be part of your everyday life for the next year or so. The dream life will start to get hyperactive and prophetic. All kinds of synchronicities will start to happen. ESP (extra-sensory perception) will get sharper. You'll be able to see into other people without needing to think about it. Intuition will be very strong and generally reliable. The invisible universe is letting you know that it is around.

The month – and year ahead – is excellent for spiritual studies, for meditation and for the study of sacred scripture. Those not yet on a spiritual path are likely to begin. Those already on the journey will have much success and satisfaction in this area.

August

    Best Days Overall: 8, 16, 17, 25, 26, 27
    Most Stressful Days Overall: 5, 6, 11, 12, 18, 19
    Best Days for Love: 3, 4, 11, 12, 13, 20, 21, 23, 24, 30, 31
    Best Days for Money: 1, 2, 3, 4, 5, 12, 13, 14, 23, 24, 28, 29
    Best Days for Career: 5, 6, 14, 15, 18, 19, 25, 26

Your 12th house of spirituality is easily the strongest in the Horoscope this month, with at least 40 per cent and sometimes 50 per cent of the planets there or moving through there. It is really the hub of your world this month – until the 23rd. Review last month's discussion of this. The battles of life are fought, and won or lost, in the chambers of the heart and mind. What happens 'out there' is purely incidental. If an interior battle was won, the result is the winning of some exterior battle. The result is not the cause. This is a month where you go deeper into these things. Until the 23rd don't try to solve a material problem by material means. Solve it spiritually and it will be solved on the material level.

This is also a good period – since it is right before your birthday – to review the past year soberly and honestly. Acknowledge what you achieved and what was not achieved. Look at the successes and the failures. If there were mistakes, resolve to correct them and form ideas of what you want for the year ahead. This way you start your personal new year (your birthday) on the right foot.

The planets are now in their maximum Eastern position. Thus personal power and personal independence are at their strongest. Use your independence in a positive way. Create happiness for yourself. Design your life to suit yourself. You don't need anyone's approval. The world will adapt to you.

You should have things your way these days. But personal independence can stress the love life or a current relationship. The beloved wants his or her way and you want yours. Neither of you is wrong. The beloved needs to understand that if you're not happy you won't be able to make him or her happy. Allow some time for adjustment.

Love is not the focal point this month anyway. Your personal happiness is. On the 23rd, as the Sun enters your sign, you begin another one of your yearly personal pleasure peaks. It's good to give the body what it craves, to pamper it and to get it in the shape that you want. You will find that if you work spiritually you will have all kinds of power over the body. You will be able to mould it and shape it to your will. The body is more responsive to these things this month.

The month ahead seems very prosperous. Venus will travel with Jupiter from the 12th onwards. The aspect will be most exact from the 17th to the 19th, but you will feel it afterwards too. This shows some nice paydays coming up. A family member – a parent or parent figure – is very generous with you. Financial intuition will be excellent from the 12th onwards as well.

September

Best Days Overall: 4, 5, 12, 13, 22, 23
Most Stressful Days Overall: 2, 3, 8, 9, 14, 15, 29, 30
Best Days for Love: 2, 3, 8, 9, 12, 13, 16, 17, 23, 26, 27
Best Days for Money: 1, 2, 3, 10, 11, 12, 13, 19, 20, 23, 24, 25, 29, 30
Best Days for Career: 4, 12, 14, 15, 20, 21, 28

Technically the best time to start new projects or launch new products is during the first half of the year, especially in the spring when the Sun is in Aries. But in your case, because you've just had, or will have, a birthday, you are now in a favourable period for starting new things. You are at the beginning of your personal solar cycle. Add to this the overwhelming forward motion of the planets – 80 per cent are moving forward from the 23rd onwards – and the favourability is increased. Moreover, add to this the power in your 1st house and the fact that you are in the strongest period of personal independence in your year and the favourability is still further increased. The best time to start new projects is from the 24th onward – as the Moon waxes.

This is a happy and prosperous month. You are still in the period for having things your way. (People generally like this, but it is a mixed blessing as this can often cause problems down the road.) You are in the midst of one of your yearly personal pleasure peaks. And, on the 23rd, you enter a yearly financial peak. Life is good. Enjoy!

Health and energy are excellent. You have all the energy you need to achieve anything you want to. The personal appearance also sparkles. There is unusual beauty and glamour in your image. The Sun in your own sign until the 23rd produces much personal magnetism or charisma. Venus in your sign (from the 8th) brings beauty, grace and a sense of style. You move in beautiful ways. The gestures of the body are elegant. This is a very good month to buy clothing and personal accessories – the purchases will be good.

Venus's move into your sign reinforces the prosperity we wrote of earlier. Venus is your financial planet. This signals financial windfalls. Financial opportunity will seek you out, there's nothing special that you need to do except to show up. You dress in expensive ways and the personal appearance and overall demeanour play a big role in earnings. Adopting the image of wealth – which you are doing this month – has a magic to it. It draws wealth and wealth opportunities to you. You are in a period of maximum financial independence for the year.

You and the beloved have been at opposite ends of the spectrum of late. You have diametrically opposite positions and perspectives. If you can bridge your differences love can be better than before. These differences will gradually ease with time.

Job seekers have wonderful opportunities from the 23rd to the 30th.

October

Best Days Overall: 1, 2, 9, 10, 19, 20, 28, 29
Most Stressful Days Overall: 5, 6, 12, 13, 26, 27
Best Days for Love: 3, 5, 6, 12, 13, 14, 22, 23, 24
Best Days for Money: 3, 7, 8, 12, 13, 17, 18, 21, 22, 23, 26, 27
Best Days for Career: 5, 6, 12, 13, 22, 23, 31

Mars has been in your 4th house of home and family – in stressful aspect to you – since September 14. It will be there until the 26th of the month ahead. Often this shows repairs, renovations or construction going on in the home. If you need to do these things, this is a good period now. Passions are high at home. There can be conflict with family members. Family members have dramatic kinds of experiences, perhaps near-death experiences or surgery (which is considered a near-death experience in astrology). Do your best to make the home safer this period. There is a tendency to accidents in the home. Emotionally, a lot of old baggage is coming up for cleansing.

The main headline this month is the two eclipses which happen. This guarantees a tumultuous kind of month.

The Lunar Eclipse of the 8th occurs in your 8th house. This shows many things. There are encounters with death (generally on a psychological level), sometimes near-death kinds of experiences and sometimes surgery is recommended. (But health is good, so get a second opinion.) Uranus, your planet of health and work, is affected by this eclipse, so there can be health scares and job changes. The conditions of the work place change. If you employ others there is instability with them, often due to dramas in their personal lives. Pluto is affected too, but not so directly. Thus cars and communication equipment get tested. It will be a good idea to drive more defensively during this eclipse period. There are dramas with siblings, sibling figures and neighbours. A nice, easy, relaxed schedule is called for, for a few days before and after the eclipse. Every Lunar Eclipse tests friendships. Often there are dramatic, life-changing kinds of events in the lives of friends.

The Solar Eclipse of the 23rd occurs in your 3rd house of communication. As with the Lunar Eclipse this will further test your car and communication equipment. Stay alert and drive safely. Students might change schools or educational plans. There are shake-ups in the schools they attend. Every Solar Eclipse also brings spiritual change – change of attitude, perspective and practice. It is good to upgrade your spiritual practice periodically and the eclipse provides the opportunity.

The other headline this month is the power in the money house. Nearly half of the planets are either there or moving through there. It's a prosperous kind of month.

In spite of possible health scares, as we've said, health is basically good.

November

Best Days Overall: 6, 7, 15, 16, 17, 25, 26
Most Stressful Days Overall: 2, 3, 8, 9, 22, 23, 29, 30
Best Days for Love: 2, 3, 10, 11, 12, 20, 22, 23, 29, 30
Best Days for Money: 2, 3, 4, 5, 11, 12, 14, 18, 19, 22, 23
Best Days for Career: 1, 8, 9, 10, 11, 20, 21

Your 3rd house of communication and intellectual interests became powerful on October 23 and is powerful until the 22nd of this month. Financial goals are more or less attained. (If the financial goals were very high, there was good progress made towards them.) Now it is time to enjoy the fruits of prosperity – free time to develop the mind, to learn, and to expand the knowledge base. Curling up with a good book has always been a personal joy for me. Yet, today, this is basically a privilege of the rich – the leisured class.

This is a very good month for students. The mind is sharper and retains more information. There should be success in studies. Whatever your age and stage in life it is good to take courses in subjects that interest you, to attend lectures, seminars and workshops. Writers, teachers and journalists also have a good month. Likewise sales and marketing people.

Health becomes more delicate after the 23rd. Overall your health is still good, but your energy is not up to its usual standard. Thus pre-existing conditions can appear (temporarily) to worsen. Also Uranus, your health planet, pretty much camps out on the Lunar Eclipse point of October 8. This can bring up health fears. But these problems are temporary. When they pass (later next month) overall health and energy will return. In the meantime, get as much rest as you can.

Uranus on the eclipse point shows dramatic changes to the health regime. Job changes are also afoot. This can be with your present company (you could be shifted to another position) or with a new company. The conditions at work are unstable right now.

Mercury on the eclipse point from the 8th to the 10th is a more serious aspect. Drive more carefully and avoid risky activities. This aspect also shows career changes – or shake-ups in your company or industry.

The planetary momentum is overwhelmingly forward this month. From the 16th onwards 90 per cent of the planets are moving forward. Thus there is quick progress to your goals, and events move faster in the world. This is still an excellent time to launch new projects or release new products. The best time is from the 22nd to the end of the month (when the Moon is waxing).

Love is becoming more harmonious now. You are much more in synch with the beloved this month. The 10th to the 12th seems particularly good. Singles will meet good prospects. Existing relationships will be happier.

December

Best Days Overall: 3, 4, 13, 14, 22, 23, 30, 31
Most Stressful Days Overall: 5, 6, 20, 21, 26, 27
Best Days for Love: 1, 2, 8, 12, 13, 18, 21, 22, 26, 27, 30, 31
Best Days for Money: 1, 2, 10, 11, 12, 13, 15, 16, 20, 21, 22, 28, 29, 30, 31
Best Days for Career: 1, 2, 5, 6, 10, 11, 21, 22, 30, 31

On the 22nd of last month, your 4th house of home and family became powerful. You are in the 'midnight hour' of your year. This is a month for making psychological progress and for coming to terms with the past. When the 4th house is strong old memories tends to come up – with no apparent rhyme or reason. But underneath, the Cosmos has its reasons. The past is being digested on a new level – in light of your present knowledge and understanding. The memories won't change. The facts are what they are, but you will interpret them in a different light. In a sense you are re-writing – re-defining – your past. It will no longer have the same kind of hold on you that it once had.

One of the problems with power in the 4th house is a tendency to live in the past – a desire to return to the 'good old days'. It is one thing to digest the past and another to 'live' there. Stay in the now – in the present – as you review your past. The past is like a movie, but you are in the present moment looking at it.

With the 4th house strong the focus is on home and family and getting into your personal point of emotional harmony. External issues – the career and outer goals – are less important now. The need is to set up the foundations – the psychological foundations – for outer success. This is internal work, the work of the midnight hour.

Health still needs watching until the 22nd, so keep in mind our discussion of this last month. Health and energy will improve after the 22nd.

The other headline this month is Saturn's move into Sagittarius on the 24th – your 4th house. Emotional and psychological issues are going to be important for the next two to three years. This move also affects overall health and energy. You will have to be more careful in these matters for the next few years.

The love life has been basically good for some years now. There has been much expansion in the social circle. Now (and for next few years) these relationships get tested. Good ones will survive and will get even better. Flawed ones will probably dissolve. You will feel this more next month and next year, but you are experiencing the beginnings of it now.

Mars will transit an eclipse point from the 4th to the 7th. Drive more carefully; avoid confrontations and risky kinds of activities during this period.

Venus will transit an eclipse point from the 21st to the 23rd. This can bring a short-term financial disturbance, but it will also bring needed changes and adjustments.

Libra

THE SCALES

Birthdays from
23rd September to
22nd October

Personality Profile

LIBRA AT A GLANCE

Element – Air

Ruling Planet – Venus
   Career Planet – Moon
   Love Planet – Mars
   Money Planet – Pluto
   Planet of Communications – Jupiter
   Planet of Health and Work – Neptune
   Planet of Home and Family Life – Saturn
   Planet of Spirituality and Good Fortune – Mercury

Colours – blue, jade green

Colours that promote love, romance and social harmony – carmine, red, scarlet

Colours that promote earning power – burgundy, red-violet, violet

Gems – carnelian, chrysolite, coral, emerald, jade, opal, quartz, white marble

Metal – copper

Scents – almond, rose, vanilla, violet

Quality – cardinal (= activity)

Qualities most needed for balance – a sense of self, self-reliance, independence

Strongest virtues – social grace, charm, tact, diplomacy

Deepest needs – love, romance, social harmony

Characteristic to avoid – violating what is right in order to be socially accepted

Signs of greatest overall compatibility – Gemini, Aquarius

Signs of greatest overall incompatibility – Aries, Cancer, Capricorn

Sign most helpful to career – Cancer

Sign most helpful for emotional support – Capricorn

Sign most helpful financially – Scorpio

Sign best for marriage and/or partnerships – Aries

Sign most helpful for creative projects – Aquarius

Best Sign to have fun with – Aquarius

Signs most helpful in spiritual matters – Gemini, Virgo

Best day of the week – Friday

Understanding a Libra

In the sign of Libra the universal mind – the soul – expresses its genius for relationships, that is, its power to harmonize diverse elements in a unified, organic way. Libra is the soul's power to express beauty in all of its forms. And where is beauty if not within relationships? Beauty does not exist in isolation. Beauty arises out of comparison – out of the just relationship between different parts. Without a fair and harmonious relationship there is no beauty, whether it in art, manners, ideas or the social or political forum.

There are two faculties humans have that exalt them above the animal kingdom: their rational faculty (expressed in the signs of Gemini and Aquarius) and their aesthetic faculty, exemplified by Libra. Without an aesthetic sense we would be little more than intelligent barbarians. Libra is the civilizing instinct or urge of the soul.

Beauty is the essence of what Librans are all about. They are here to beautify the world. One could discuss Librans' social grace, their sense of balance and fair play, their ability to see and love another person's point of view – but this would be to miss their central asset: their desire for beauty.

No one – no matter how alone he or she seems to be – exists in isolation. The universe is one vast collaboration of beings. Librans, more than most, understand this and understand the spiritual laws that make relationships bearable and enjoyable.

A Libra is always the unconscious (and in some cases conscious) civilizer, harmonizer and artist. This is a Libra's deepest urge and greatest genius. Librans love instinctively to bring people together, and they are uniquely qualified to do so. They have a knack for seeing what unites people – the things that attract and bind rather than separate individuals.

Finance

In financial matters Librans can seem frivolous and illogical to others. This is because Librans appear to be more concerned with earning money for others than for themselves. But there is a logic to this financial attitude. Librans know that everything and everyone is connected and that it is impossible to help another to prosper without also prospering yourself. Since enhancing their partner's income and position tends to strengthen their relationship, Librans choose to do so. What could be more fun than building a relationship? You will rarely find a Libra enriching him- or herself at someone else's expense.

Scorpio is the ruler of Libra's solar 2nd house of money, giving Libra unusual insight into financial matters – and the power to focus on these matters in a way that disguises a seeming indifference. In fact, many other signs come to Librans for financial advice and guidance.

Given their social grace, Librans often spend great sums of money on entertaining and organizing social events. They also like to help others when they are in need. Librans would go out of their way to help a friend in dire straits, even if they have to borrow from others to do so. However, Librans are also very careful to pay back any debts they owe, and like to make sure they never have to be reminded to do so.

Career and Public Image

Publicly, Librans like to appear as nurturers. Their friends and acquaintances are their family and they wield political power in parental ways. They also like bosses who are paternal or maternal.

The sign of Cancer is on Libra's 10th house (of career) cusp; the Moon is Libra's career planet. The Moon is by far the speediest, most changeable planet in the horoscope. It alone among all the planets travels through the entire zodiac – all 12 signs and houses – every month. This is an important key to the way in which Librans approach their careers, and also to what they need to do to maximize their career potential. The Moon is the planet of moods and feelings – Librans need a career in which their emotions can have free expression. This is why so many Librans are involved in the creative arts. Libra's ambitions wax and wane with the Moon. They tend to wield power according to their mood.

The Moon 'rules' the masses – and that is why Libra's highest goal is to achieve a mass kind of acclaim and popularity. Librans who achieve fame cultivate the public as other people cultivate a lover or friend. Librans can be very flexible – and often fickle – in their career and ambitions. On the other hand, they can achieve their ends in a great variety of ways. They are not stuck in one attitude or with one way of doing things.

Love and Relationships

Librans express their true genius in love. In love you could not find a partner more romantic, more seductive or more fair. If there is one thing that is sure to destroy a relationship – sure to block your love from flowing – it is injustice or imbalance between lover and beloved. If one party is giving too much or taking too much, resentment is sure to surface at some time or other. Librans are careful about this. If anything, Librans might err on the side of giving more, but never giving less.

If you are in love with a Libra, make sure you keep the aura of romance alive. Do all the little things – candle-lit dinners, travel to exotic locales, flowers and small gifts. Give things that are beautiful, not necessarily expensive. Send cards. Ring regularly even if you have nothing in particular to say. The niceties are very important to a Libra. Your relationship is a work of art: make it beautiful and your Libran lover will appreciate it. If you are creative about it, he or she will appreciate it even more; for this is how your Libra will behave towards you.

Librans like their partners to be aggressive and even a bit self-willed. They know that these are qualities they sometimes lack and so they like their partners to have them. In relationships, however, Librans can be very aggressive – but always in a subtle and charming way! Librans are determined in their efforts to charm the object of their desire – and this determination can be very pleasant if you are on the receiving end.

Home and Domestic Life

Since Librans are such social creatures, they do not particularly like mundane domestic duties. They like a well-organized home – clean and neat with everything needful present – but housework is a chore and a burden, one of the unpleasant tasks in life that must be done, the quicker the better. If a Libra has enough money – and sometimes even if not – he or she will prefer to pay someone else to take care of the daily household chores. However, Librans like gardening; they love to have flowers and plants in the home.

A Libra's home is modern, and furnished in excellent taste. You will find many paintings and sculptures there. Since Librans like to be with friends and family, they enjoy entertaining at home and they make great hosts.

Capricorn is on the cusp of Libra's 4th solar house of home and family. Saturn, the planet of law, order, limits and discipline, rules Libra's domestic affairs. If Librans want their home life to be supportive and happy they need to develop some of the virtues of Saturn – order, organization and discipline. Librans, being so creative and so intensely in need of harmony, can tend to be too lax in the home and too permissive with their children. Too much of this is not always good; children need freedom but they also need limits.

Horoscope for 2014

Major Trends

Coming through 2011 and 2012 with your health and sanity intact was quite an achievement. The year ahead has its challenges, but now you have the mental-emotional musculature to handle them. You should get through with flying colours.

In spite of all the challenges, there are many nice things happening this year. You will earn every last bit of them – but they will happen.

Last year on June 26 you entered a very strong and successful career period. This continues in the year ahead (until July 16). You rise in your company or profession and many happy career opportunities are coming as well. There's more on this later.

The love situation has been exciting but unstable for some years now – since 2011. However, there is romance in the year ahead. It is only the stability of it that is in question. Jupiter's move into your 11th house on July 16 shows that the social life in general is good and that you are making new and important friends. Again, there's more on this later.

Like last year, Saturn will be in your money house. There is a need to reorganize and restructure the finances. Perhaps you feel money is tight because of extra responsibilities. But if you shift things around you will have all the resources that you need.

Your health needs watching this year, but you've been through worse. Details below.

Your major areas of interest this year are the body, image and personal pleasure (until July 26); finance; home and family; health and work; love and romance; career (until July 16); and friends, groups and group activities (from July 16 onwards).

Your paths of greatest fulfilment this year are finance (until February 19); the body, image and personal pleasure (from February 19 onwards); career (until July 16); and friends, groups and group activities (after July 16).

Health

(Please note that this is an astrological perspective on health and not a medical one. In days of yore there was no difference, both of these perspectives were identical. But in these times there could be quite a difference. For a medical perspective, please consult your doctor or health practitioner.)

Health is challenging this year, although more in the first half of the year than the second. You should note a steady improvement from July 16 onwards. Happily, your 6th house of health is strong this year, so you are focused here and this is exactly what is needed. If you were ignoring things it would be more serious. Stressful health aspects don't necessarily mean sickness or disease, but it means that more effort is needed to maintain good health. If you put in the effort – and it seems that you will – health will be good.

You begin the year with four long-term planets in stressful alignment with you. This is not a joke. During the first half of the year there will be periods where the short-term planets also stress you. Those periods will be from January 1 to January 20, March 21 to April 19, and June 21 to July 16. Make sure you get a lot of rest during these times. It might be advisable to arrange more massages or to spend time in a health spa. (It won't be a bad idea to do this during the first half of the year in general, but especially during those vulnerable periods.) We will discuss this further in the monthly reports.

The good news is that there is much you can do to enhance the health and prevent problems from developing. As regular readers know, the first line of defence is to maintain high energy levels. Be ruthless about this. Refuse to waste energy on trifles, on things that don't contribute to your central purposes and goals. Avoid worry, too much thinking and too much speech. These are hidden energy wasters. Delegate tasks wherever possible. Try to plan activities in a more efficient way so that more gets done with less effort. You'll need every ounce of energy.

The next line of defence is to give more attention to the heart and the feet, which are vulnerable areas. The reflexes to the heart are shown on the chart. Avoid worry and anxiety, the spiritual root causes of heart problems. Meditation will be a help here.

Look after the feet by wearing shoes that fit and that don't upset your balance. Comfort is to be preferred over fashion (this is a bitter pill for Libra – if you can have both, all the better). Regular foot massage – see our chart – will be very powerful. Foot whirlpools and foot baths will

Reflexology

Try to massage the whole foot on a regular basis, but pay extra attention to the points highlighted on the chart. When you massage, be aware of 'sore spots', as these need special attention. It's also a good idea to massage the ankles and the top of the feet.

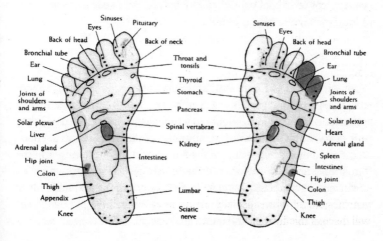

also be good. There are many foot massage and foot whirlpool gadgets on the market and it might be wise to invest in one of these and use it regularly. Make it part of your health regime.

With Neptune as your health planet you will get wonderful results from spiritual healing techniques – meditation, the laying on of hands, Reiki and the manipulation of subtle energies. If you feel under the weather a visit to a spiritual practitioner will be good.

Mars spends a lot of time in your own sign. This has some good points. It gives energy and courage and a drive to achieve. However, sometimes it can make a person push the body beyond its limits. It also makes one feel impatient. There's a tendency to rush all the time and this can lead to injuries, even if the health is good. It can make a person more confrontational and this can lead to disagreements and even violence. Watch your temper. If you feel angry, take a deep breath and count to 10 before talking. Tone down the aggressiveness.

Your health planet rules from a Water sign (Pisces). Thus you have a special connection with the healing powers of the water element. It is good to drink more water. Water purity is important for you. Tap water should be well filtered (and there are many of these gadgets out on the market), otherwise try bottled water. You will find it beneficial to hang around water if you feel under the weather – oceans, rivers, lakes and springs. Swimming and water sports are healthy exercise. Natural water is always best, but if this is impractical you can soak in your tub or whirlpool bath. Frequent showers are good at a pinch, but a long soak in the bath is better.

Home and Family

Your 4th house of home and family has been a house of power for many years now – and this will continue for many more years. It is an ultra-long-term trend. Undoubtedly this has been discussed in previous years, but it's still worth mentioning as the trend is still in effect. A cosmic detox is happening in the family circle. The impurities in the situation are being surfaced, brought into the clear light, and then cleansed and corrected. Detoxification is seldom pleasant. All kinds of unpleasant debris, unresolved issues, negative feelings and the causes for them come up. Much 'expelling' is going on. But the end result is always good. You will have renewal in the family situation and home. This won't happen overnight, but it will over time.

This is basically what is behind all the dramas happening at home and with the family. On the mundane level it brings 'crisis' in the family – a need to confront life-and-death kinds of situations. Sometimes there is actual death in the family and the aftermath, the grieving and review, is a form of detoxification. Sometimes it brings surgery and near-death experiences to family members and this too is a form of detox – deep feelings need to be confronted. Sometimes the family as a whole splits up. There are breaks in the family connection, sometimes due to divorce, sometimes due to financial conflicts, some-times due to other factors. It's 'as if' the family unit as you knew it 'died'. Always keep in mind that resurrection – renewal – always comes after death. Death and resurrection are twins; there is never one with-out the other.

Pluto's presence in the 4th house often shows major construction and renovation happening in the physical home. Pluto is working on many levels and the physical is one of them. This renovation seems more than merely 'cosmetic' – it involves breaking down walls, reshap-ing rooms, and ripping out old wiring or plumbing. It's probably expensive as well. While this is happening your home is in chaos. It's not generally pleasant but the end result is good. When the end result is understood, the chaos – physical and emotional – is much easier to handle. Most of the time we don't see the good until long afterwards, but it is enough to know that it will be revealed. The family unit will eventually reconstitute itself at a better and healthier level.

The home and family seem important on the financial level too. You are spending more on the home and family – investing there – and are most likely earning from here as well. Family financial support seems good, though turbulent.

A parent or parent figure is prospering and seems very involved and supportive of you in your financial life. You, in turn, seem financially involved with this parent.

Moves are more likely next year than now. And even a move seems to involve construction and renovation.

Siblings and sibling figures could have moved last year, but if not it could happen in the first half of 2014. I see homes near water for them.

Children or children figures in your life prosper after July 16. They are doing much travelling. A move is not out of the question here, and a parent or parent figure could have multiple moves or renovations. He or she seems 'emotionally restless'.

Finance and Career

Your money house was strong last year and will be strong in the year ahead. This is a positive for finance. It shows interest and drive focused here, a willingness to overcome all the various challenges that arise. I consider this more important than just 'easy' aspects.

There are many financial challenges to deal with this year – especially until July 26. Your financial planet, Pluto, is involved in a Grand Square aspect during the first half of the year (technically until July 16). This indicates involvement in some major project – the founding of some business or institution. These big projects are always complicated and need much juggling.

Saturn has been in your money house since last year, signalling a feeling of financial restriction. You are taking on more financial responsibility and have more burdens to carry. These seem to come from family and seem unavoidable. You probably can avoid them (human beings are powerful and can do many things) but it isn't wise to do so as there are hidden blessings there. As we mentioned earlier, you are spending more on the home and family but are earning from this as well. The family is perhaps limiting your financial freedom, but they are supportive financially – and if not in a physical, tangible way, then in emotional ways. Family connections are important in finance too.

These extra burdens are forcing important financial changes and reorganizations. Some of these changes will be dramatic, but in the end they will be good. You already know the changes that need to be made and this is a year to put them into effect.

If you make the changes, reorganize, shift things around and eliminate waste and redundancy, you will have all the resources that you need.

Your financial planet is in the sign of Capricorn and Saturn (the ruler of this sign) is in your money house. These planets are in 'mutual reception' – each is a guest in the sign and house of the other. This is something positive. It shows good co-operation between the planets. Thus the family and family connections are important financially. It shows an ability to make money from the home (or from home). It favours property investment (residential or commercial), restaurants and hotels – or industries that cater to the home. This is a nice financial aspect for psychological therapists.

The combination of the financial planet in Capricorn and Saturn in the money house suggests a business of some kind – something traditional and socially acceptable. It indicates excellent financial judgement and a long-term perspective on finance. A long-term perspective on what investments will be worth many years from now.

These are wonderful aspects for getting the financial life in 'order' – good for savings and investment programmes. Good for serious, daily financial regimens.

However, this combination of planetary aspects is not so favourable for speculations. Speculations should be avoided for the first half of the year – they don't seem fortunate. But after July 16 they become a bit more favourable. (Speculations should always be made using the inner guidance and never automatically.) The two planets involved in your financial life are not 'get rich quick' kinds of planets. Wealth is attained slowly, methodically, over time through good financial discipline and judgement.

Career, as we mentioned, was good last year and is still powerful in the year ahead – until July 16. Jupiter is in your career house until then, which is a classic indicator of career success. If you work for others there is a promotion in store. If you work for yourself, your status and prestige is increased. Jupiter will bring happy career opportunities as well. Jupiter in the sign of Cancer favours a family kind of business. It also shows that siblings and sibling figures in your life are successful this year and they seem supportive of your career goals. Good marketing and promotion – good communication skills – are very important careerwise.

Love and Social Life

Love is interesting and exciting this year – especially until July 26 – but highly unstable. The whole social circle is undergoing change and upheaval. Those of you who are married are having their marriages tested – perhaps very severely. This has been going on since 2011. Good relationships can survive this transit, but it won't be easy. It will take much effort and sheer hard work to maintain it. In a lukewarm relationship the parties are generally not willing to put in the effort, and so they go by the wayside. Divorces and separations have undoubtedly happened with Libra and they could continue to happen. These are generally not pleasant kinds of experiences. However, love can happen for you at any time and in any place. It is as if you are socially free to explore new loves.

Mars, your love planet, will spend an unusual amount of time in your own sign, from January 1 to July 26. This shows love and romance. Whatever the state of your marriage, there is love in your life. What I like here is that there's nothing much you need to do about it. This person is pursuing you, seems devoted to you, and puts your interests ahead of his or her own. However, as we said above, the stability of this is in question. Marriage is probably not advisable. Enjoy the love but keep your options open.

There is another way to read this transit. Mars in your sign could also show that your partner, aware of the challenges in the marriage, is working hard to woo you back. He or she is trying very hard to hold things together. But the question is, is it enough? With many of you, this is what's happening.

There are a lot of reasons why the love life is unstable. The first is that you and your partner seem more experimental in love. You want change. You want to shake up the routine and make it more exciting. If this is understood, this urge could be used to help the relationship. Shake up the routine. Do different and unconventional kinds of things together as a couple. As the saying goes, 'create lasting memories'. Let change happen within the relationship. With a little creativity this can be done.

There are other reasons for the crisis too. Infidelity is one of them. Perhaps there is an unwanted pregnancy; perhaps some life-changing kind of crisis in the life of your partner. It will take all your social genius (and you have plenty) to hold things together.

If you are single, working on your first marriage, it's probably not a good idea to marry these days. If you are in or working on your second marriage, the year ahead seems a stable one. If you are working on your third marriage, there is romance and a solid marriage opportunity after July 16.

On July 16 Jupiter will enter your 11th house of friends. This is not really a romantic aspect, but a good social one. You are meeting new and significant people. Your circle of friends is enlarged. You are involved with groups, group activities and organizations and it seems happy. This could also bring love affairs for singles – and the opportunity for these kinds of dalliances among those who are married. Opportunity doesn't mean that you have to indulge. It is just there. The choice is yours.

Self-improvement

Like last year, Saturn is in the money house for practically the entire year. So this is a time to gain control of the finances – especially spending – rather than let finance control you. This is the spiritual intent of the transit – to make you financially healthier and to enrich you. Prosperity can happen in two ways. The first is through increased earnings, the second through good financial management. This year (and last) your path to prosperity is via the latter. If good financial management is lacking, increased earnings will not increase your wealth. It will get frittered away in waste. However, with good financial management, when earnings increase wealth also increases.

Saturn in the money house suggests good use of a budget. Many metaphysical practitioners dislike budgets in that they see them as 'lack' thinking. But this need not be so. A good budget is really about financial control, not lack. It enables a person to allocate resources in the most effective way. A good budget should include categories for fun, leisure and the enjoyment of life – not just for necessities. A percentage of your earnings go to each important activity or expense in your life. There should be a category for savings and investment too, for building future wealth. The budget gives you guidelines on what and how much you can spend. This is its usefulness.

Neptune has been in your 6th house of health since February 2012. (It visited there briefly in 2011, but in 2012 it entered for the long haul.) We mentioned some of the purely physical effects of this transit in the health section. But there is more to health than just the physical and Neptune is going to show you this very dramatically in coming years. Many of you have already made good progress in this department, but more is coming.

Neptune in your 6th house (and as ruler of the 6th house) shows spiritual healing. You are exploring more deeply into this. This is a long-term trend. We probably wrote of this last year, but it is worth discussing again as the trend is still very much in effect. Read up all you can on this subject. Emmet Fox, Joseph Murphy and Ernest Holmes are good writers to start off with. Spiritual healing is a bit different from mind-body healing, though they are similar. Mind-body healing is mostly about making positive statements, affirmations, and using imagery to get the mind to heal the body. This is wonderful. These days this approach is mainstream. (I can remember a time when it was not.) In spiritual healing the approach is different. We use the mind and the imagination to invite the activity of a power that is essentially 'beyond' and 'above' the mind. It is the flow of this power that does the healing, not the affirmations and imagery. These are just means to an end.

This power – call it Spirit, Chi, God, Divine, Love (the labels are not important) – will often work through human instruments – doctors, therapists, health practitioners – but is not limited to doing so. It can act directly on the body as well.

This is a most exciting area of research for Libra these days. In my opinion it will, eventually, revolutionize medicine.

Month-by-month Forecasts

January

Best Days Overall: 3, 4, 12, 13, 22, 23, 30, 31
Most Stressful Days Overall: 1, 2, 7, 8, 14, 15, 28, 29
Best Days for Love: 1, 2, 3, 4, 7, 8, 9, 10, 12, 13, 19, 20, 22, 23, 28, 29, 30, 31
Best Days for Money: 1, 2, 5, 6, 9, 10, 14, 15, 19, 20, 24, 25, 28, 29
Best Days for Career: 1, 2, 9, 10, 14, 15, 21, 22, 30, 31

A very hectic and stressful month is indicated. You are involved in some major undertaking and these things are always complicated. The main thing is to watch your health. The demands on you are great, but try to find time to rest and relax more – it won't be easy, but you can do it. At least 70 per cent (and sometimes 80 per cent) of the planets (a huge, huge percentage) are in stressful aspect with you until the 11th. This is the most stressful period. But your health should be watched all month – and especially until the 20th. Never mind name, fame and glory; let's just get through the month with health and sanity intact. Enhance the health in the ways mentioned in the yearly report. It won't hurt to get regular massages and to spend free time at a health spa either.

Mars in your own sign all month gives you more energy, but sometimes it can make you 'bite off more than you can chew'. Avoid rush and haste.

You begin the year with the planetary power mostly below the horizon in the lower half of the Horoscope. You are in the midnight of your personal year. This is a time for attaining emotional harmony, for feeling right. From this place of emotional harmony your outer life will proceed in a natural and powerful way. You can safely de-emphasize the career and give your attention to the family. You won't be able to ignore the career – there are strong demands on you – but you can shift more energy to the home and family. Work on your career by inner methods, through meditation, prayer, visualization and controlled dreaming. If there is some career goal you want, imagine you are there and get into the feeling of it. Later on, when the planets shift, you can take the outer steps necessary for that goal's attainment.

The planetary power is mostly in the social Western sector this month – Libra's favourite sector. The Cosmos impels you to do what you most love to do: socialize, enhance your people skills (which are already awesome), and put others first. You get your way by consensus and the good graces of others these days.

Love is bittersweet. You have been in a cycle of social instability for some years now and this is the situation this month. Love, however, is pursuing you. You don't have to do anything except show up. Your spouse, partner or current love seems very devoted to you (a good thing this month) but the stability of this relationship is in question. He or she also seems involved in some big, complicated project.

February

   Best Days Overall: 8, 9, 18, 19, 26, 27
   Most Stressful Days Overall: 3, 4, 10, 11, 12, 24, 25
   Best Days for Love: 3, 4, 5, 6, 7, 8, 9, 16, 17, 18, 19, 24, 25, 26, 27
   Best Days for Money: 1, 2, 5, 6, 7, 10, 11, 12, 15, 16, 17, 20, 21, 24, 25, 28
   Best Days for Career: 8, 9, 10, 11, 12, 20, 28

Health is much improved over last month, but still needs attention. The percentage of stressful planets arrayed against you has dropped to around 50 to 60 per cent – still stressful, but less so. If you got through last month, you'll get through the month ahead. Happily there is more focus on health from the 18th onwards. This is a positive. The danger would be if you ignored things.

Love is still unstable. Marriage is not advisable these days. This month the beloved seems very devoted to you, but it doesn't seem enough. He or she is trying very hard, but you seem in disagreement. You will need to work harder on your relationship. Singles have ample romantic opportunities – love seeks you out. But you don't seem that thrilled with the people pursuing you. Enjoy the love life for what it is without project-ing too many hopes onto it. Love should improve next month.

Last month on the 20th you entered one of your yearly personal pleasure peaks. This continues until the 18th of this month. With all the activity and stress in your life this personal pleasure peak has not been as strong as those you've experienced in the past. Still, more rest and recreation is a positive thing these days.

You are still reorganizing your financial life these days, but this month – especially early in the month – we see increased earnings. Venus is very near Pluto, your financial planet. (This was so towards the end of last month too.) A parent or parent figure seems supportive and generous. Family and family connections are also helpful. The main thing now, as we have mentioned, is to shift things around. You don't necessarily need huge increases in earnings, just better financial management. The resources are there for what you really need.

On the 18th your 6th house of health and work becomes powerful, signalling an excellent period for job seekers. There is good fortune here. There are multiple job opportunities, not just one.

Mercury goes retrograde on the 6th. Avoid gratuitous foreign travel if possible. (Jupiter, the generic ruler of foreign travel, is also retrograde during this period.) If you must travel, allow more time to get to your destination. Don't schedule connecting flights too close together, and insure your tickets.

Continue to find and function from your point of emotional harmony. Stay in right feeling as much as possible. (It will be a challenge.)

March

Best Days Overall: 7, 8, 17, 18, 26, 27
Most Stressful Days Overall: 3, 4, 10, 11, 24, 25, 30, 31
Best Days for Love: 3, 4, 7, 8, 17, 18, 26, 27, 30, 31
Best Days for Money: 1, 2, 5, 6, 10, 11, 15, 16, 19, 20, 24, 25, 28, 29
Best Days for Career: 1, 2, 10, 11, 21, 22, 30, 31

The planets are now in their maximum Western position – Libra heaven. Your social skills are always great and now you get a chance to make them even better. On the 20th you enter a yearly social peak. More Libra heaven! Love is much improved now. Venus moves into a harmonious aspect with Mars (your love planet) after the 6th. Romance is much happier, but nevertheless still unstable. Love is close to home – right where you are. There's no need to run after it.

Some people enjoy instability in love. It is more exciting. You don't know who you're going to meet when. Love can happen at any time and in the most unexpected ways. Love strikes like lightning but can disappear just as quickly. Love is free and uncommitted.

Your love planet will be retrograde all month. Not the time to make important love decisions. Now is a time for attaining clarity in the love life. Clearly define what you want and need. See where improvements can be made. Then, when Mars start to move forward (in a few months), you can implement your plans.

The only real issue this month is your health. This needs more attention from the 20th onwards. March is not as stressful as January was, but it is still not your best health period. Make sure you get enough sleep and rest. Schedule more massages (perhaps on a weekly or even daily basis) and spend more time at the health spa. Enhance the health in the ways mentioned in the yearly report.

Mars transits an eclipse point from the 11th to the 18th. This will test love. Be more patient with the beloved this period. He or she should drive more carefully and avoid risky activities then. Venus also transits an eclipse point from the 17th to the 19th. Take it easy those days, and again avoid risky activities.

Mercury travels with Neptune from the 21st to the 23rd. This is a very spiritual kind of period. Spiritual breakthroughs can happen for those who want them. Job seekers have work opportunities in foreign lands or with foreign companies.

Now that Mercury and Jupiter are both moving forward (Mercury on the 1st and Jupiter on the 6th), foreign travel is more advisable.

April

Best Days Overall: 3, 4, 5, 13, 14, 15, 22, 23
Most Stressful Days Overall: 6, 7, 20, 21, 26, 27
Best Days for Love: 3, 4, 5, 6, 13, 14, 15, 16, 17, 22, 23, 24, 25, 26, 27
Best Days for Money: 1, 2, 6, 7, 11, 12, 16, 17, 21, 24, 25, 29, 30
Best Days for Career: 6, 7, 9, 10, 19, 20, 29, 30

A turbulent month is ahead – fasten your seat belts. Though January had more stressful aspects than now, this month could be more difficult than January, with almost as many planets in stressful alignment with you until the 20th as there were in January. There are also two eclipses this month, which increases the stress level. Keep your mind on the essentials and let lesser things go. Delegate or outsource as much work as you can. Avoid risky, stressful activities. And, of course, make sure you get enough rest.

The good news is that you seem focused on health. Venus enters your 6th house on the 6th. You seem to meet a spiritual healer – or alternative healer – from the 10th to the 13th and this is good too. You respond very well to this.

The Lunar Eclipse of the 15th seems the stronger of the two eclipses, and it occurs in your own sign. This will, over the next six months, create a redefinition of your image and self-concept. You will upgrade and refine your image. You will present a new look to the world. Generally this leads to wardrobe changes, changes of hair style, hair colouring, etc. If you haven't been careful in dietary matters it can bring a detoxification of the body. This eclipse occurs near Mars, so love is being tested as well. A current relationship can go into crisis mode. Lunar Eclipses affect the career, your industry, parents, parent figures and bosses. So there are shake-ups happening here. The rules of the game change. There can be dramas with the parents or parent figures in your life as well. Both you and the beloved should take it nice and easy during this period.

The Solar Eclipse of the 29th occurs in your 8th house of transformation and regeneration. This creates financial dramas for your spouse, partner or current love, financial shake-ups that lead to necessary changes. If you are involved in tax, insurance or estate issues there are dramatic developments. Events move forward. This eclipse, as every Solar Eclipse does, tests friendships and brings dramas to the lives of friends. It shakes up organizations or groups that you are involved with.

Personal finances are better than they have been for many months after the 20th. Pluto, your money planet, is receiving positive aspects. Pluto, however, goes retrograde on the 14th so there can be delays and glitches here. For the next few months the finances should be under review. The object is to attain mental clarity in this area.

May

Best Days Overall: 1, 2, 11, 12, 19, 20, 28, 29
Most Stressful Days Overall: 3, 4, 5, 17, 18, 24, 25, 31
Best Days for Love: 1, 2, 6, 11, 12, 13, 14, 19, 20, 24, 25, 28, 29
Best Days for Money: 3, 4, 5, 8, 9, 13, 14, 17, 18, 21, 22, 26, 27, 31
Best Days for Career: 3, 4, 8, 9, 10, 17, 18, 28, 29, 31

Though you entered the sunrise of your year on March 20, the upper half of the Horoscope doesn't really begin to dominate (and then only half heartedly) until the 3rd of this month. The Sun has risen, it is day, you are up and about, but the light of day is not as strong as usual. The night is still with you and you wouldn't mind going back to sleep for a while! So the career and outer affairs are calling to you, but a big part of you still seeks emotional harmony and wants to deal with the family. I read this as an attempt to straddle both worlds – the world of good feeling and the world of good action, the career and the home. Though you should give more attention to the career now, home and family is still very important and you have to pay attention to them too. In other words you have to do BOTH – succeed in the career and have a happy, harmonious family life. This is difficult, but if you are established in your personal point of emotional harmony, it will be much easier.

The religious and educational life is most interesting this month. Your 9th house of religion, philosophy and higher education becomes powerful on the 21st. (You will feel this even before that, when Mercury enters the 9th house on the 7th.) Not only that, the ruler of the 9th house – Mercury – is 'out of bounds' from the 12th onwards. This indicates that you are exploring new religions, new philosophies, new understandings of the meaning of life, outside the boundaries that you were brought up in. You are going into 'forbidden territory'. You will come back eventually but with new insight and understanding. In order to understand our own religious tradition it is sometimes necessary to 'step aside' – to separate from it and view it dispassionately. This 'out of bounds' phenomenon is affecting travellers and students too. Travellers will want to go to 'out of bounds' exotic kinds of places. The norms are not interesting this month. Students can go to schools and colleges that are far from home as well.

Love seems happy this month. Venus (you) and Mars (the current love) are in 'mutual reception' from the 3rd to the 29th – most of the month. Yes, you and the beloved are opposites and have opposite perspectives on things, but you seem able to bridge your differences. Mutual devotion is developing. You put the beloved's interests first and he or she puts yours first.

Health is reasonable this month but still repays watching. Enhance the health in the ways mentioned in the yearly report.

Avoid risk-taking activities on the 14th and 15th. Drive more carefully then too.

Though good financial management is still very important, earnings increase until the 21st and from the 29th onwards. Pluto, the financial planet, is still retrograde, so your finances are still under review.

June

Best Days Overall: 7, 8, 16, 17, 24, 25, 26
Most Stressful Days Overall: 1, 14, 15, 20, 21, 27, 28
Best Days for Love: 5, 6, 7, 8, 14, 15, 16, 17, 20, 21, 23, 24, 25, 26
Best Days for Money: 1, 5, 6, 9, 10, 11, 14, 15, 18, 19, 22, 23, 27, 28
Best Days for Career: 1, 7, 8, 16, 17, 27, 28

Your 9th house remains powerful until the 21st and the ruler of the 9th house, Mercury, is still 'out of bounds' until the 5th. Review last month's discussion of this.

The month ahead looks very successful. On the 21st you begin a yearly career peak. Jupiter is still in your 10th house of career, where he has been all year. Success here would be a lot greater if you were able to put your full force and attention on it, but we get a sense of 'hesitancy' about the career. You are still trying to bridge two worlds – the world of the feelings and emotions and that of the career and outer life. It is not the astrologer's place to judge. Perhaps the bridging of the two worlds is the real success, not the outer events that happen.

One again you enter into one of your vulnerable health periods on the 21st. While the stress is not as great as it was in January and April, it is still strong. Some 60 to 70 per cent of the planets come into stressful alignment with you. So do what you have to do – focus on essentials – and let lesser things go. Schedule more rest periods into your days and make sure to get enough sleep. Book more massages or reflexology treatments and try to spend more time at the health spa. Also enhance the health in the ways mentioned in the yearly report.

While you have a nice payday – financial increase – from the 8th to the 11th, finance become more problematic after the 21st. Earnings will happen but you have to work harder for them. There are more challenges happening. (The focus on the career can be a distraction here. Career success might involve some financial sacrifice.)

Love is not as good as last month, but it will improve after the 23rd. Singles have nice opportunities then. As has been the case all year, there's nothing special that you need to do to attract love. It is still pursuing you. Love is tested from the 22nd to the 26th. The current love needs to stay out of harm's way and avoid risky activities. You should also avoid risky activities on the 5th and 6th.

Jupiter's transit of an eclipse point from the 21st to the 26th shows dramas with the family and with parents or parent figures. Be more patient with them during this period. They seem under duress.

July

Best Days Overall: 4, 5, 6, 13, 14, 22, 23
Most Stressful Days Overall: 11, 12, 17, 18, 24, 25
Best Days for Love: 4, 5, 6, 13, 14, 17, 18, 24, 25
Best Days for Money: 2, 3, 7, 8, 11, 12, 16, 17, 19, 20, 27, 29, 30
Best Days for Career: 7, 8, 15, 16, 24, 25, 27

There are many changes happening in your Horoscope this month – important changes.

The planetary power shifts from the social Western to the independent Eastern sector on the 18th. This is a decisive shift. The Eastern sector starts to dominate. You are entering a period of personal independence. Libras, in general, are 'other-oriented' people. They don't much care for personal independence. Relationships are everything to them, and the ability to 'stand on one's own feet' – to stand alone if necessary – tends to be lacking in them. This is a time when you get to work on this to develop more of this quality. Now is the time to ask yourself what makes you happy. Never mind what pleases others or what the social norms are – 'what makes me happy?' What is my personal path of bliss? Once this is understood, you should pursue it now and create the conditions that make for this.

Jupiter makes a major move out of your 10th house into the 11th house of friendships on the 17th. By then the short-term career goals should have been achieved, and good progress should have been made towards your long-term goals as well. You enter a more social period now.

Mars, your love planet, has been in your own sign since the beginning of the year. Now he moves (on the 18th) into Scorpio, your money house. This is a positive signal for finance. You have the help of your spouse, partner or current love – and also of friends. A business part-nership or joint venture can happen as well. Since Mars has been in opposition to Uranus more or less all year, the love life now becomes a bit more stable too. Not completely stable, but more stable than it has been this year.

Mars's move indicates a change in the love life and love attitudes. Wealth becomes a factor in love after the 18th. You are attracted to the rich, to the good providers. Romantic opportunities happen as you pursue your financial goals or with people involved in your finances. The sexual compatibility becomes more important.

There is good news on the health front too. You still need to watch your health until the 18th – review our discussion of last month – but the planetary stress is easing up on you. On the 17th Jupiter leaves his stressful aspect and starts to make harmonious aspects with you. Mars leaving your sign on the 18th is also good for your health – there is less likelihood of accidents or injury. On the 22nd the Sun will leave his stressful aspect and start to make harmonious aspects too. By the end of the month you will feel healthier than you've felt all year.

August

Best Days Overall: 1, 2, 10, 18, 19, 28, 29
Most Stressful Days Overall: 8, 13, 14, 20, 21, 22
Best Days for Love: 3, 4, 11, 12, 13, 14, 20, 21, 23, 24, 30, 31
Best Days for Money: 3, 4, 5, 7, 8, 13, 14, 16, 17, 23, 24, 25, 26, 30, 31
Best Days for Career: 5, 6, 13, 14, 20, 21, 22, 25

Your health improved after July 23, and it improves even further after the 12th as Venus moves away from her stressful alignment. You've passed through the worst of things. If you got through January, April and July you will coast through the rest of the year ahead. Give yourself a pat on the back. If you still have your health and sanity you've done very well.

Last month was a strong career month. You were in a yearly career peak until the 23rd. On the 18th of last month Venus crossed the Mid-heaven and entered your 10th house. This showed career success and elevation. You were on top and in charge. Venus is still in your 10th house until August 12. One of the perks of career success is the people you meet at the top. And this is what's happening this month.

The main headline this month is the power in your 11th house until the 23rd. Nearly half of the planets are there or moving through there. The month ahead is very social. But the social activity of the 11th house is different than the social activity of the 7th house. In the 7th house you are involved in friendships of the heart – romantic kinds of friendships. The 11th house is about friendships of the mind – platonic kinds of friendships, friendships with people of like mind and like interests. These friendships are uncommitted. The attachments are not personal but based on the mind or self-interest. It is not a particularly romantic kind of month. (These friendships can, however, be more enduring than romantic ones.)

This is an exciting and happy area this month. You are making new and important friends. You are more involved with groups, organizations and group activities. Family connections are playing a role here.

Be more patient in love this month. It is not one of your best romantic months. You don't seem in agreement with your spouse, partner or current love. This doesn't necessarily mean you'll break up, but it will take more work and effort to keep things together.

Though there are no eclipses this period the month will feel 'as if' there were many eclipses. Many planets are re-activating previous eclipse points so there will be more turbulence and perhaps some shocking events. There'll be nothing that you can't handle though.

Avoid risk-taking activities from the 18th to the 20th. Be more patient with the beloved from the 10th to the 14th (and he or she should stay out of harm's way that period too). And be more patient with family members from the 24th to the 31st as Jupiter transits an eclipse point.

September

Best Days Overall: 6, 7, 14, 15, 24, 25
Most Stressful Days Overall: 4, 5, 10, 11, 17, 18
Best Days for Love: 1, 2, 3, 8, 9, 10, 11, 12, 13, 19, 23, 29, 30
Best Days for Money: 1, 2, 3, 4, 5, 10, 11, 12, 13, 19, 20, 22, 23, 27, 28, 29, 30
Best Days for Career: 4, 5, 12, 13, 17, 18, 23, 24

The planetary power is reaching its maximum Eastern position during this month and the next. This means that you are in your strongest period of personal independence of the year. This is a time for self-assertion (but not for riding rough shod over others), for having things your way, and for creating the conditions in your life that make you happy. It's not necessary to 'people please' these days. You can have things your way. If you make mistakes you will pay for them later on, when the planets move westward, and you will learn from them. It is time to develop more individualism. People skills are wonderful. They open doors. But in the end it is your personal abilities that matter. You have to be able to perform.

Health is getting better and better. By the 23rd, as the Sun enters your sign, you will be brimming with energy. You have all the energy you need to achieve any goal you desire. You can enhance your health further in the ways mentioned in the yearly report.

Love is complicated this month. You still need to work harder on your current relationship. Also personal independence often complicates love. Mars is still in your money house until the 14th, so wealth is still very much an attraction until then. Romantic opportunities happen as you pursue your financial goals and with people involved in your finances. On the 14th Mars enters Sagittarius, your 3rd house. This changes the love attitudes. Now you gravitate towards intellectuals – writers, teachers, journalists. Good communication with the beloved is more important now than mere money. You are attracted to those who are easy to talk to, easy to share ideas with. A good chat is as much a part of sexual foreplay as the physical actions. Love is found close to home after the 14th. It is in the neighbourhood and perhaps with neighbours. There are also romantic opportunities at lectures, workshops, at the local library or the book store. Singles should pursue their intellectual interests and love will find them.

Your 12th house of spirituality became strong on August 23 and is still strong until the 23rd of this month. So this is a period for spiritual study, for meditation and contemplation. You will also benefit from involvement with charities and good causes. The spiritual world is always close to us, but people are more receptive to it at different times. This is a period of greater receptivity on your part, so for those on the spiritual path there is success and greater understanding.

On the 23rd you enter one of your yearly personal pleasure peaks. It is a time to give the body what it needs and craves; time to fulfil the sensual fantasies; time to get the body and image in right shape and order.

October

> Best Days Overall: 3, 4, 12, 13, 21, 22, 23, 31
> Most Stressful Days Overall: 1, 2, 7, 8, 14, 15, 28, 29
> Best Days for Love: 3, 7, 8, 12, 13, 17, 18, 22, 23, 28
> Best Days for Money: 1, 2, 7, 8, 9, 10, 17, 18, 19, 20, 24, 25, 26, 27, 28, 29
> Best Days for Career: 3, 4, 12, 13, 14, 15, 22, 23

There is basically a happy and prosperous month ahead. However, with two eclipses this month there are bumps on the road. There's nothing that you can't handle, but they tend to complicate things.

The Lunar Eclipse on the 8th seems the stronger one for you. It occurs in your 7th house of love and will test a current relationship or business partnership. Be more patient with the beloved this period as he or she is apt to be more temperamental. A good relationship will survive this, but basically flawed ones might not. Reduce your schedule during this period as the eclipse makes stressful aspects to you. Overall health, though, is good – just be more careful then. Every Lunar Eclipse brings career changes, a need to redefine the career and the career path. Events will force you to do this. Often there are shake-ups in your company and industry. Often the government changes the rules of the game. There can be dramas in the lives of parents, parent figures and bosses too.

The Solar Eclipse of the 23rd occurs right on the cusp of your 2nd house and affects finances. Important financial changes will start to happen and this will be a six-month process. Your financial thinking and strategy will change and this will lead to overt physical changes. Your financial thinking has probably been unrealistic and this eclipse reveals this to you so that you can make the necessary changes. Since the Sun, the eclipsed planet, is the ruler of your 11th house, the eclipse will test friendships, computer and high-tech equipment. There are dramas and life-changing events in the lives of friends and in groups or organizations that you are involved with. This eclipse should bring prosperity to you. The financial changes will be good, as you are now in a yearly financial peak – from the 23rd onwards.

Despite the Lunar Eclipse, love is improving this month. Venus in your own sign gives beauty and grace to your self-image. You are attracting the opposite sex. It also makes harmonious aspects with the love planet Mars. The Lunar Eclipse does complicate love, but whatever happens you will have love in your life. If a current relationship breaks up, you will meet someone new. Problems in a current relationship seem easier to resolve.

The love planet spends most of the month in your 3rd house, so review our discussion of this last month. On the 26th Mars will move into Capricorn, your 4th house of home and family, and this signals yet another shift in love and love needs. You will gravitate to older, more serious people. Family values become important in love. Emotional sharing and emotional support are important.

November

Best Days Overall: 8, 9, 18, 19, 27, 28
Most Stressful Days Overall: 4, 5, 10, 11, 25, 26
Best Days for Love: 2, 3, 4, 5, 6, 7, 11, 12, 15, 16, 17, 22, 23, 25, 26
Best Days for Money: 4, 5, 6, 7, 14, 15, 16, 17, 20, 21, 23, 25, 26
Best Days for Career: 2, 3, 10, 11, 12, 21, 22

Last month Mars, your love planet, spent the entire month 'out of bounds', and this is the situation until the 21st of this month. This shows you are looking for love outside your natural boundaries. The social life in general pulls you out of your natural boundaries. You are taking new approaches to love.

The past year has not been especially prosperous. Rather it has been a year of consolidation and reorganization. But this month you are in the midst of a yearly financial peak, which began last month on the 23rd. So earnings are stronger than usual. Pluto, your financial planet, went forward in September and is moving forward this month too. Another positive. Your financial judgement is sound and realistic. Progress might be slow but it is happening. From the 8th to the 12th Mars travels with Pluto. This shows the generosity of the spouse, partner or current love. Friends are prospering and are financially supportive. Financial goals can be attained by social means.

Mars spends the entire month in your 4th house. So, as we mentioned, love opportunities happen close to home or through the family or family connections. Old romantic flames can return to the picture during this period. (Sometimes it is not the 'literal' old flame who returns, but someone who embodies their personality patterns, appearance and mannerisms – psychologically speaking it is 'as if' you are back with the old flame.) This is not something random. It has a cosmic purpose. Old issues can be resolved. The old relationship can be put in its proper perspective and you will be ready to move on from there. There is psychological healing in this.

Like last month you are attracted to people with strong family values. You might gravitate to older, more established kinds of people. Steady, solid, consistent. There is something safe and comfortable about this – especially with the instability that has been happening in love for some years now. Emotional sharing, emotional intimacy and support are the most important things these days. Emotional intimacy seems as important as physical intimacy. You show love by giving emotional support and this is how you feel loved.

Mars squares Uranus from the 12th to the 14th and this can test love. Be more patient with the beloved and with friends at this time. They are apt to be more temperamental. The beloved should also drive more carefully and avoid confrontations.

Health is good. We mean this in a 'relative' kind of way. There are still two long-term and one short-term planet stressing you, but compared to some of the months you've had this year, health is very good.

December

Best Days Overall: 5, 6, 15, 16, 24, 25
Most Stressful Days Overall: 1, 2, 8, 9, 22, 23, 28, 29
Best Days for Love: 1, 2, 3, 4, 12, 13, 15, 16, 21, 22, 24, 25, 28, 29, 30, 31
Best Days for Money: 1, 2, 3, 4, 10, 11, 13, 14, 18, 19, 20, 21, 22, 23, 28, 29, 30, 31
Best Days for Career: 1, 2, 8, 9, 10, 11, 20, 21, 30, 31

The lower half of the Horoscope has been dominant since late September. This month, the planets are at their maximum low point in the Horoscope (the nadir). On the 22nd you enter into the midnight hour of your year. Career has become less important than usual. You are in a period for building up the inner forces for the next outward career push, which will begin next spring. In the meantime the focus is on home, family and your emotional well-being. This is the time to work on your career by interior methods – through meditation, prayer, visualization, setting intentions, etc. When you are in emotional harmony these activities go better.

This is a month for psychological kinds of breakthroughs. Those of you in therapy will make good progress. Your insight into moods, feelings and the past is much greater now.

When the 4th house is strong there is a tendency to nostalgia – a tendency to want to go back to the so-called 'good old days' when things were simpler and present problems didn't exist. It is good to look back at the past, to assimilate it, digest it and extract the nutrition from past experiences, but it is not so good to live in the past or return to it. Life is always now. Now is always the best time there is.

Health is more delicate after the 22nd, but nowhere near as difficult as it was earlier in the year. If you got thorough last January and April, you will get through the month ahead.

Saturn, which has been in your money house for the past two years, leaves on the 24th and moves into your 3rd house of communication. The long, testing ordeal is over. You should see an almost immediate pick up in earnings. Long-term burdens are leaving. Hopefully, you've used the past two years to get financially healthier. Your next financial expansion will be healthier and more enduring. The month ahead will be prosperous – especially from the 24th onwards. Your financial planet, Pluto, is receiving much positive stimulation. Earnings will come easily and abundantly. Family and family connections seem the major source. This has been the case all year and will be the case for years to come.

The love planet moves into your 5th house on the 5th. This shows a new shift in love. Now you want fun. You are attracted to the person who can show you a good time. Emotional sharing was fun, but perhaps too depressing. You want someone 'up and happy'.

Scorpio

♏

THE SCORPION

Birthdays from
23rd October to
22nd November

Personality Profile

SCORPIO AT A GLANCE

Element – Water

Ruling Planet – Pluto
  Co-ruling Planet – Mars
  Career Planet – Sun
  Love Planet – Venus
  Money Planet – Jupiter
  Planet of Health and Work – Mars
  Planet of Home and Family Life – Uranus

Colour – red-violet

Colour that promotes love, romance and social harmony – green

Colour that promotes earning power – blue

Gems – bloodstone, malachite, topaz

Metals – iron, radium, steel

Scents – cherry blossom, coconut, sandalwood, watermelon

Quality - fixed (= stability)

Quality most needed for balance - a wider view of things

Strongest virtues - loyalty, concentration, determination, courage, depth

Deepest needs - to penetrate and transform

Characteristics to avoid - jealousy, vindictiveness, fanaticism

Signs of greatest overall compatibility - Cancer, Pisces

Signs of greatest overall incompatibility - Taurus, Leo, Aquarius

Sign most helpful to career - Leo

Sign most helpful for emotional support - Aquarius

Sign most helpful financially - Sagittarius

Sign best for marriage and/or partnerships - Taurus

Sign most helpful for creative projects - Pisces

Best Sign to have fun with - Pisces

Signs most helpful in spiritual matters - Cancer, Libra

Best day of the week - Tuesday

Understanding a Scorpio

One symbol of the sign of Scorpio is the phoenix. If you meditate upon the legend of the phoenix you will begin to understand the Scorpio character – his or her powers and abilities, interests and deepest urges.

The phoenix of mythology was a bird that could recreate and reproduce itself. It did so in a most intriguing way: it would seek a fire – usually in a religious temple – fly into it, consume itself in the flames and then emerge a new bird. If this is not the ultimate, most profound transformation, then what is?

Transformation is what Scorpios are all about – in their minds, bodies, affairs and relationships (Scorpios are also society's transformers). To change something in a natural, not an artificial way, involves a transformation from within. This type of change is a radical change as opposed to a mere cosmetic make-over. Some people think that change means altering just their appearance, but this is not the kind of thing that interests a Scorpio. Scorpios seek deep, fundamental change. Since real change always proceeds from within, a Scorpio is very interested in – and usually accustomed to – the inner, intimate and philosophical side of life.

Scorpios are people of depth and intellect. If you want to interest them you must present them with more than just a superficial image. You and your interests, projects or business deals must have real substance to them in order to stimulate a Scorpio. If they haven't, he or she will find you out – and that will be the end of the story.

If we observe life – the processes of growth and decay – we see the transformational powers of Scorpio at work all the time. The caterpillar changes itself into a butterfly; the infant grows into a child and then an adult. To Scorpios this definite and perpetual transformation is not something to be feared. They see it as a normal part of life. This acceptance of transformation gives Scorpios the key to understanding the true meaning of life.

Scorpios' understanding of life (including life's weaknesses) makes them powerful warriors – in all senses of the word. Add to this their depth, patience and endurance and you have a powerful personality. Scorpios have good, long memories and can at times be quite vindictive – they can wait years to get their revenge. As a friend, though, there is no one more loyal and true than a Scorpio. Few are willing to make the sacrifices that a Scorpio will make for a true friend.

The results of a transformation are quite obvious, although the process of transformation is invisible and secret. This is why Scorpios are considered secretive in nature. A seed will not grow properly if you keep digging it up and exposing it to the light of day. It must stay buried – invisible – until it starts to grow. In the same manner, Scorpios fear revealing too much about themselves or their hopes to other people. However, they will be more than happy to let you see the finished product – but only when it is completely unwrapped. On the other hand, Scorpios like knowing everyone else's secrets as much as they dislike anyone knowing theirs.

Finance

Love, birth, life as well as death are Nature's most potent transformations; Scorpios are interested in all of these. In our society, money is a transforming power, too, and a Scorpio is interested in money for that reason. To a Scorpio money is power, money causes change, money controls. It is the power of money that fascinates them. But Scorpios can be too materialistic if they are not careful. They can be overly awed by the power of money, to a point where they think that money rules the world.

Even the term 'plutocrat' comes from Pluto, the ruler of the sign of Scorpio. Scorpios will – in one way or another – achieve the financial status they strive for. When they do so they are careful in the way they handle their wealth. Part of this financial carefulness is really a kind of honesty, for Scorpios are usually involved with other people's money – as accountants, lawyers, stockbrokers or corporate managers – and when you handle other people's money you have to be more cautious than when you handle your own.

In order to fulfil their financial goals, Scorpios have important lessons to learn. They need to develop qualities that do not come naturally to them, such as breadth of vision, optimism, faith, trust and, above all, generosity. They need to see the wealth in Nature and in life, as well as in its more obvious forms of money and power. When they develop generosity their financial potential reaches great heights, for Jupiter, the Lord of Opulence and Good Fortune, is Scorpio's money planet.

Career and Public Image

Scorpio's greatest aspiration in life is to be considered by society as a source of light and life. They want to be leaders, to be stars. But they follow a very different road than do Leos, the other stars of the zodiac. A Scorpio arrives at the goal secretly, without ostentation; a Leo pursues it openly. Scorpios seek the glamour and fun of the rich and famous in a restrained, discreet way.

Scorpios are by nature introverted and tend to avoid the limelight. But if they want to attain their highest career goals they need to open up a bit and to express themselves more. They need to stop hiding their light under a bushel and let it shine. Above all, they need to let go of any vindictiveness and small-mindedness. All their gifts and insights were given to them for one important reason – to serve life and to increase the joy of living for others.

Love and Relationships

Scorpio is another zodiac sign that likes committed clearly defined, structured relationships. They are cautious about marriage, but when they do commit to a relationship they tend to be faithful – and heaven help the mate caught or even suspected of infidelity! The jealousy of the Scorpio is legendary. They can be so intense in their jealousy that even the thought or intention of infidelity will be detected and is likely to cause as much of a storm as if the deed had actually been done.

Scorpios tend to settle down with those who are wealthier than they are. They usually have enough intensity for two, so in their partners they seek someone pleasant, hard-working, amiable, stable and easy-going. They want someone they can lean on, someone loyal behind them as they fight the battles of life. To a Scorpio a partner, be it a lover or a friend, is a real partner – not an adversary. Most of all a Scorpio is looking for an ally, not a competitor.

If you are in love with a Scorpio you will need a lot of patience. It takes a long time to get to know Scorpios, because they do not reveal themselves readily. But if you persist and your motives are honourable, you will gradually be allowed into a Scorpio's inner chambers of the mind and heart.

Home and Domestic Life

Uranus is ruler of Scorpio's 4th solar house of home and family. Uranus is the planet of science, technology, changes and democracy. This tells us a lot about a Scorpio's conduct in the home and what he or she needs in order to have a happy, harmonious home life.

Scorpios can sometimes bring their passion, intensity and wilfulness into the home and family, which is not always the place for these qualities. These traits are good for the warrior and the transformer, but not so good for the nurturer and family member. Because of this (and also because of their need for change and transformation) the Scorpio may be prone to sudden changes of residence. If not carefully constrained, the sometimes inflexible Scorpio can produce turmoil and sudden upheavals within the family.

Scorpios need to develop some of the virtues of Aquarius in order to cope better with domestic matters. There is a need to build a team spirit at home, to treat family activities as truly group activities – family members should all have a say in what does and does not get done. For at times a Scorpio can be most dictatorial. When a Scorpio gets dictatorial it is much worse than if a Leo or Capricorn (the two other power signs in the zodiac) does. For the dictatorship of a Scorpio is applied with more zeal, passion, intensity and concentration than is true of either a Leo or Capricorn. Obviously this can be unbearable to family members – especially if they are sensitive types.

In order for a Scorpio to get the full benefit of the emotional support that a family can give, he or she needs to let go of conservatism and be a bit more experimental, to explore new techniques in child-rearing, be more democratic with family members and to try to manage things by consensus rather than by autocratic edict.

Horoscope for 2014

Major Trends

Saturn has been in your sign since October 2012 and will be there for practically all of the year ahead (until December 24). This is a serious time in your life. You are managing to have some fun, but you have a more serious outlook. You are thinking of your future and perhaps even old age – and this is true even for younger Scorpios. You are more ambitious than normal and have a strong work ethic. You are thinking about what you came here to do and how to go about doing it. Generally too much seriousness can lead to pessimism – a negative outlook on things and the future. But it need not be so. You can, through your work and discipline, create a happy and joyous future for yourself.

Health and energy are also affected by this transit of Saturn. There's more on this later on.

Saturn in your own sign shows a need to take a low profile. There's no need right now to flaunt yourself or your achievements. Shine, but shine silently, like the Sun.

Your serious attitudes and work ethic bode well for the career this year. On July 16, Jupiter will enter your 10th house of career, and this generally brings success, elevation, promotion and even honours. More on this later.

Pluto, the ruler of your Horoscope, has been in your 3rd house for some years now and will be there for many years to come. This shows a strong focus on communication and intellectual interests. This is a wonderful aspect for students (especially those below college level), teachers, writers and journalists. The mind will tend to be sharp and clear.

Jupiter is in your 9th house for the first half of the year. Thus there is more foreign travel in your life, until July 16.This is another wonderful aspect for students – but more for those at college or postgraduates. There is good fortune here.

Neptune has been in your 5th house of fun and creativity since February 2012. This shows that your leisure activities are becoming more spiritual and refined. A meditation seminar or spiritual lecture might be more interesting to you than a night out on the town. This aspect also shows inspired creativity, especially for those in the arts and those who have prepared themselves to receive it. Children and children figures in your life are more spiritual and sensitive.

Uranus has been in your 6th house of health and work since 2011. Thus there are many job changes happening, and dramatic changes in the health regime. More details on this later.

Your areas of greatest interest this year are the body, image and personal pleasure; communication and intellectual interests; children, fun and creativity; health and work; foreign travel, higher education, religion and philosophy (until July 16); and career (from July 16 onwards).

Your paths of greatest fulfilment this year are the body, image and personal pleasure (until February 19); spirituality (from February 19th onwards); foreign travel, higher education, religion and philosophy (until July 16); and career (after July 16).

Health

(Please note that this is an astrological perspective on health and not a medical one. In days of yore there was no difference, both of these perspectives were identical. But in these times there could be quite a difference. For a medical perspective, please consult your doctor or health practitioner.)

Your 6th house of health has been a house of power since 2011 and will be so for some more years. A good thing too; with Saturn in your own sign, your health will need watching. A strong 6th house shows that you will be on the case.

Though you need to monitor your health, it does seem basically good. For the first half of the year only Saturn is in stressful alignment with you. Later on however, from July 16 onwards, Jupiter will also be in stressful alignment. Otherwise, the other long-term planets are either in harmonious aspect or leaving you alone.

Saturn by himself is not enough to cause disease. However the energy levels are not what they should be and thus things that you always did naturally and normally might not be able to be done. This is a relative thing. Perhaps flu never bothered you, and you never needed to take precautions. Now Saturn is in the picture, the auric field is a tad weaker than usual, and so you catch it. The normal immunity that you had isn't there. Or, you always climbed a ladder and picked fruit from the top of your tree without any problem. Now Saturn is in the picture this seemingly simple procedure is more complicated. The reflexes, the judgement are just a little off, so you make a wrong move and fall.

Thus Saturn didn't actually cause the problem, but he created the internal conditions where problems could happen.

The first line of defence is to maintain high energy levels. Eliminate the time and energy wasters in your life. Observe, identify and then eliminate. Keep your focus on what is really important. Avoid useless thinking and speech. Worry and anxiety are huge energy wasters. Rest more. Plan your day so that more gets done with less effort. Delegate wherever possible.

The second line of defence is to strengthen the vulnerable areas in the body. This will generally prevent problems from happening. And

Reflexology

Try to massage the whole foot on a regular basis, but pay extra attention to the points highlighted on the chart. When you massage, be aware of 'sore spots', as these need special attention. It's also a good idea to massage the ankles and the top of the feet.

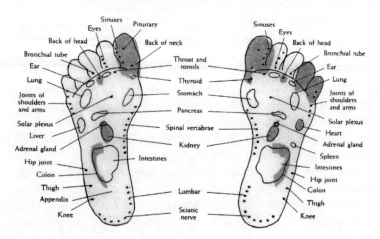

even if they can't be totally prevented, problems can be lessened to a great extent.

Using the reflexes shown on the chart, give more attention to the following areas: the heart (avoid worry and anxiety, the spiritual root causes of heart problems); the head, face and scalp (regular scalp and face massage is always powerful for you); the kidneys and hips (the hips should be regularly massaged, kidney action seems hyper during the first half of the year); the adrenals (avoid anger and fear, the two emotions that stress the adrenals); and the ankles and calves (these should be regularly massaged, and the ankles should be well supported when exercising).

With Mars as your health planet, vigorous physical exercise is always good. Good muscle tone is important.

Your health planet moves relatively quickly (though this year he spends almost seven months in the sign of Libra). This year he will move through five signs and houses of your Horoscope. Thus there are many short-term trends in health that are best covered in the monthly reports.

Your favourable numbers for health are 1, 4, 5 and 16.

Home and Family

Your 4th house is not powerful this year. It is basically empty and only short-term planets will move through there for brief periods. We do see moves happening in the year ahead. (They can happen next year too.) For the first half of the year, though, home and family life is pretty much stable.

On July 16 Jupiter moves into Leo and starts to make beautiful aspects to your family planet, Uranus. Thus moves could happen. But, as regular readers know, people don't always literally move. Sometimes they buy additional homes; sometimes they renovate or expand the home; and sometimes they buy expensive items for the home and the effect is 'as if' they had moved – the home is happier and more expansive.

These moves or renovations seem related to the career. Jupiter will be in your career house. The company you work for can move you to a different area, or perhaps a job opening happens in another city or country.

This aspect also signals that the family circle expands. Generally this happens through birth or marriage, though sometimes it does so through meeting people who are like family to you.

For the first half of the year, family support seems weak. Family obligations seem expensive and you have nothing to show for them. You seem in financial disagreement with a parent or parent figure. But all of this will change after July 16. Then the family seems supportive. Perhaps you spend on the family, but they are giving mutual support too. You can earn though them or through family connections.

Your family planet Uranus has been in your 6th house of health and work since 2011. Thus you are buying all kinds of health gadgets and exercise or sports equipment for the home, making the home into a 'health spa' or gym as much as a home. Many of you are also setting up home offices, making the home more of a workplace too. This doesn't happen overnight but is a long-term process that will continue over the next few years.

You and a parent or parent figure have been having problems for some years now – serious kinds of disagreements. This trend continues in the year ahead. You just have to work harder to make the relationship work. In the past few years there have been some separations from the family, but these seem temporary. Students might feel that the family (or a parent or parent figure) is interfering with their studies, making it more difficult to concentrate.

Parents or parent figures are not likely to move this year – nor should they. It is not advisable. Siblings or sibling figures have moved in recent years and can move again. They seem nomadic and restless. They are looking for the perfect home, and although they think they have found it, they see a newer and more perfect home yearly.

Children or children figures in your life have a stable family year. Moves are more likely next year than this year.

Finance and Career

Your money house only becomes a house of power in the final week of the year. For almost all the year it is empty, except for the temporary transits of the short-term planets. Perhaps this is the main financial weakness (especially during the first half of the year). You might not be paying enough attention here. Jupiter, your financial planet, is in opposition to Pluto, the ruler of your Horoscope, during this period, and so there are many things you'd rather be doing than making money.

We so see a lot of financial changes – sudden and dramatic ones – in the first half of the year. Your financial planet is in square aspect with Uranus. Thus family seems behind these changes. Perhaps some unexpected family expense arises, or some sudden repair for the home. (This was happening last year as well.)

Though there is much financial volatility at the beginning of the year, prosperity and earnings seem good. Jupiter is in his sign of exaltation. This shows strong earning power – 'exalted' earning power. Also Jupiter is in the 9th house, one of the most beneficent houses of the Horoscope. (Hindu astrologers consider it the most beneficent house.) Your financial planet is in basically harmonious aspect with Neptune during the first half of the year and this indicates luck in speculations. Children and children figures in your life are prospering.

Jupiter as the financial planet shows a knack for foreign investments – money from foreign countries or foreigners. Jupiter rules book publishing and for profit colleges and universities. In the sign of Cancer it indicates investments in residential property, restaurants, hotels and the food business in general.

On July 16 Jupiter moves into Leo, your 10th house of career. This should improve earnings even further. Family financial disputes will be resolved. As we mentioned, there will be better financial support from the family or family connections. Money can come from a family-type business. It shows the financial favour of parents, parent figures, bosses and authority figures. They are supportive of your financial goals.

Sometimes this aspect shows money from the government or from companies that are government contractors. Your good professional reputation becomes important then. This brings referrals and other opportunities.

Perhaps the most important thing is your focus. Jupiter in the 10th house indicates that finance becomes an important priority. You see it as your 'mission' and purpose during that period.

Uranus being in your 6th house of work since 2011 shows many job changes. You need more freedom at your workplace. You need more variety and more outlets to express your innovations and originality. The jobs that allow this are probably more satisfying for you than those that pay more but don't allow it. If you employ others there is great instability in the workforce, with high (and perhaps sudden) levels of staff turnover.

Jupiter in your 10th house is a classic indicator of career success. It shows promotion and elevation in your present company, or in your profession or business. You enjoy more status and prestige. Your professional achievements receive recognition. Often honours come your way. Always there are happy career opportunities.

The financial planet in Leo also shows luck in speculations. It shows the prosperity of children or children figures and a good feeling towards products or companies that market to children.

Your favourable financial numbers are 4, 9, 10 and 14.

Love and Social Life

Your 7th house of love and marriage is not a house of power this year. Neither is the 11th house of friendships. This year will not be a very social kind of year. Some years are like that. The Cosmos aims for well-rounded development. Thus different areas of life are accentuated at different times. Generally this aspect shows a stable kind of love year. Those of you who are married will tend to stay married; singles will tend to stay single.

Love affairs, however, are another story. These seem plentiful, but are merely for entertainment purposes. These are not likely to lead to anything serious or committed.

Saturn in your own sign (and you had this issue last year too) doesn't generally make for social popularity. It is not the kind of aspect that makes you the 'life and soul of the party'. It gives a more serious, sober demeanour. Fun activities seem frivolous. The social niceties seem frivolous. Perhaps you look askance at those who are living lives of parties and pleasure. These things are so ephemeral, so superficial.

Love and social activities have to serve some useful purpose – something more than just fun and games.

Saturn in your sign often makes a person aloof, cold and distant. There is a strong feeling of being separate from people. This could be happening unconsciously. Perhaps you don't mean to be this way, but others pick up on it and give you a lot of space. This is easily correctable. You just need to make a conscious effort to project love and warmth to others. It's good to be serious and ambitious but allow yourself to have some fun too. Allow your natural sense of humour some outlet. Serious, serious, serious all the time is unbalanced.

Those of you working towards your second marriage have strong marriage and romantic opportunities this year. Last year was also good. If nothing special happened last year, it could happen in the year ahead. Those of you working on the third marriage have a stable kind of year.

If a parent or parent figure is unattached there is good romantic opportunity after July 16. The social life in general heats up. Siblings or sibling figures are involved in romance and could marry this year. They had good romantic aspects last year too. Children or children figures in your life are attractive and alluring, but the love life is stable this year.

Your favourable numbers for love are 2, 3, 5, 7 and 12.

Self-improvement

Saturn in your own sign often creates a feeling of pessimism. This is not very good for the social life as people don't want to be 'dragged down'. The other problem is that undue pessimism can actually draw upon you the things that you fear. This is the spiritual law. There are two kinds of pessimism. One is constructive, the other destructive. Constructive pessimism is when one looks at the dark side, the worst-case scenario (which generally never happen), and figures out ways to deal with it. One then becomes an 'optimist' in the midst of the pessimism. The fear of the dark is gone. One feels free. Destructive pessimism is when one looks at the dark side and has no plan for dealing with it. One is stuck – emotionally – in the dark side. This becomes depression.

If you feel this happening to you it is good to talk about your feelings to a professional therapist or a good friend. Often this helps one to see past the dark images. If this is not feasible, there are other ways to 'out' these feelings and images in a safe way, and you need to explore them.

Don't hold these feelings in. Saturn in your sign has some positives too. It is excellent for weight loss programmes (if you need that).

Neptune has been in your 5th house since February 2012. This shows that your tastes in entertainment are becoming more spiritual, more refined. Your musical tastes will turn to the spiritual – gospel or other forms of sacred music. You could gravitate to films of a spiritual nature too. As we mentioned earlier, you might find more enjoyment at a spiritual lecture or meditation seminar than at a night on the town.

Those on the spiritual path will get good results from the path of creativity. Spirit is inspiring you on this front. Creativity is not only enjoyable for its own sake but will foster spiritual growth and understanding. The Higher Power will communicate to you through your creativity.

Mars, your health planet, spends almost seven months in your 12th house of spirituality. This shows an interest in spiritual healing. You will get results from this approach. If you feel under the weather a visit to a spiritual healer will do the trick. Regular visits will be a powerful preventive to disease. This transit also shows that you are going deeper into this area in the year ahead. Read as much as you can on the subject, and attend seminars and courses. And, most important, put these lessons into practice. You will see amazing results.

Month-by-month Forecasts

January

Best Days Overall: 5, 6, 14, 15, 24, 25
Most Stressful Days Overall: 3, 4, 9, 10, 17, 18, 30, 31
Best Days for Love: 1, 2, 9, 10, 19, 20, 28, 29
Best Days for Money: 5, 6, 14, 15, 24, 25, 26, 27
Best Days for Career: 1, 2, 9, 10, 17, 18, 21, 22, 30, 31

You begin your year with most of the planets in the Eastern sector of the chart – the sector of personal independence. But this will not last long. By the 20th the planetary power shifts to the Western, social sector. The Western sector won't dominate just yet, but becomes just as strong as the Eastern sector. You are in a cusp situation between personal independence and reliance on other people. At times you will be more personally independent and at other times more dependent. But until the 20th you have a window where conditions can be changed to your liking. Later on it will be more difficult.

The lower half of the Horoscope is much stronger than the upper half this month: 70 per cent (sometimes 80 per cent) of the planets are below the horizon. The short-term planets are heading into their nadir (the lowest point in the Horoscope). You are approaching midnight in your year. The activities of night should dominate. This is a time where the inner conditions necessary for outer success are built up and developed. Inner, emotional work is more important than outer, physical work. In order for inner work to succeed, you need emotional harmony – so strive for this now. Your career planet, the Sun, is moving through the 4th house this month (from the 20th onwards) and this reinforces this message. Your home, your family, your emotional well-being is your real career this period. Once this is in order, the outer career can proceed in a healthy way.

Life is rhythmic. One way we can define disease is as being 'out of rhythm'. Every activity of life has its natural rhythm and this shows in the Horoscope. Career is no different.

Health needs watching from the 20th onwards. There's nothing seriously wrong, but your overall energy is not up to its usual standard. So, if one is not careful, there will be greater susceptibility to microbes and other opportunistic invaders. Sometimes a pre-existing condition can seem to get worse. It's not really worse, but because your energy is lower it can feel that way. Change the energy and the symptoms weaken. When the aspects are kind to you there's no need to 'artificially' change the energy, but when they are unkind you have to do it on your own. Rest and relax more. Make sure you get enough sleep. Delegate or outsource as much work as you can.

Your love planet, Venus, is still in one of her rare (once in two years) retrogrades. So the love life is under review. Social activity slows down. There is love and love opportunities for singles, but take things nice and easy. There's no rush. The important thing now is to obtain mental and emotional clarity on a given relationship and on the love life as a whole.

Finances are also under review as the financial planet is also retrograde. This won't stop earnings, but it does slow things down a bit. Financial matters should be handled as perfectly as possible – short cuts are not really short cuts these days.

February

Best Days Overall: 1, 2, 10, 11, 12, 20, 21, 28
Most Stressful Days Overall: 5, 6, 7, 13, 14, 26, 27
Best Days for Love: 5, 6, 7, 16, 17, 24, 25
Best Days for Money: 1, 2, 10, 11, 12, 20, 21, 22, 23, 28
Best Days for Career: 8, 9, 13, 14, 20, 28

Continue to pay attention to your health until the 18th. Health can be enhanced in the ways mentioned in the yearly report. This is a great period – and year – for weight loss regimes.

Home and family issues are still paramount this month – especially until the 18th. The well-being of the family, the setting in order of the home and domestic situation, is the actual career right now. Never mind what your 'real', outer job is – spiritually it is the family, the children and children figures in your life.

Now that Venus is moving forward the love life is much better. It is progressing forward and there is more clarity about it. Venus is travelling with Pluto this month. (She is closest early in the month.) So for singles there is a romantic meeting (although it could have happened at the end of last month too). Love is close to home this month, located in your neighbourhood or with neighbours. The love planet in Capricorn shows an attraction for older, more established kinds of people. And though Venus is moving forward, love still takes time to develop. Capricorn likes slow-moving things.

The mental dimension is very important in love. You gravitate to people who are 'easy' to talk to. The sharing of ideas is a romantic turn on. You gravitate to intellectuals – writers, teachers and journalists – and people with the 'gift of the gab'. Romantic meetings can happen at the local library, at a lecture, seminar or workshop.

Health improves dramatically after the 18th.

On the 18th, as the Sun enters your 5th house you enter one of your yearly personal pleasure peaks. It is time to enjoy life, to attend parties and indulge in leisure activities. A happy kind of period.

Jupiter your financial planet is still retrograde this month. Nevertheless, you should see a boost in earnings from the 18th onwards. There could be delays and glitches involved with this, but it happens eventually. Continue to review your financial life and see where improvements can be made. Job seekers have better prospects before the 18th than afterwards.

Though this is not a very strong career period, and the focus is more on home and family, nevertheless a happy career opportunity can come on the 28th. There is also a good career opportunity for children or children figures in your life too.

March

Best Days Overall: 1, 2, 10, 11, 19, 20, 28, 29
Most Stressful Days Overall: 5, 6, 12, 13, 26, 27
Best Days for Love: 5, 6, 7, 17, 18, 26, 27
Best Days for Money: 1, 2, 10, 11, 19, 20, 22, 23, 28, 29
Best Days for Career: 1, 2, 10, 11, 12, 13, 21, 22, 30, 31

Since late January the Eastern and Western sectors of the Horoscope have been more or less in balance. You were neither independent nor dependent – you were a little bit of both. Now, on the 6th, the balance of planetary power shifts decisively to the Western, social sector of the Horoscope. This is a time for putting other people first, for taking a vacation from the self and your own concerns. This is a time for 'allowing' good to happen, rather than trying to coerce it by personal effort. As you let go of the self, miraculously you'll find that all your needs are taken care of. Too often we are in the way of our own good. This is a time where you learn this. Adapt to situations as best you can. Cultivate the social skills.

Health is still good this month, but Mars, your health planet, will make one of his rare retrogrades (lasting all month). Thus this is not a time to make drastic changes to the health regime or diet. These things need much more study. Job seekers too need more caution. There are job opportunities happening, but research them carefully. Things are not as they seem.

Mars is not only retrograde but will re-activate a previous eclipse point from the 11th to the 18th. This can bring disturbances or upheavals at the workplace. Job changes are afoot – but don't be in a rush about this. There could be health scares during this period too, but since your health is good, they will probably be just 'scares'. If you employ others there could be some instability with your employees at this time.

Finances are good this month. The financial planet, Jupiter, starts moving forward on the 6th. It still receives very nice aspects until the 20th. A prosperous month. The most important thing is that now you have more clarity about your finances, and your decision-making should be better.

Venus moves into the 4th house on the 6th. This brings changes in the love attitudes and needs. Up till then mental compatibility was important; after the 6th emotional compatibility becomes important. Emotional sex – the sharing of feelings – is as important as physical sex. Emotional intimacy is as important as physical intimacy. Two people can be in the same space but be in different universes on the emotional level. This won't do this month. Often, when the love planet is in the 4th house one meets up with old flames. Sometimes this is an actual meeting, but often it is psychological – you meet someone who embodies the same personality patterns as the old flame (and perhaps looks like him or her too). This is good, but it is not what it seems. It is really the Cosmos's way of resolving old issues in the past relationship. One re-experiences the old relationship but from a different place in oneself. Thus it gets redefined and adjusted. One is ready to move on into the future.

Venus will re-activate an eclipse point from the 17th to the 19th. This will test love. Be more patient with the beloved in this period. He or she is more flighty and temperamental.

April

Best Days Overall: 6, 7, 16, 17, 24, 25
Most Stressful Days Overall: 1, 2, 8, 9, 10, 22, 23, 29, 30
Best Days for Love: 1, 2, 4, 5, 6, 16, 17, 24, 25, 29, 30
Best Days for Money: 6, 7, 16, 17, 18, 19, 24, 25
Best Days for Career: 8, 9, 10, 19, 20, 29, 30

This is the kind of month to 'expect nothing, but be ready for everything'. Two eclipses in April shake up the world at large and your personal life. It will be a tumultuous month.

Man has free will. But the Cosmos manifests a definite plan. Often man creates things (through abuses of the free will) that are contrary to this plan. The function of the eclipse is to shatter these obstructions and allow the manifestation of a better plan to happen. This is generally not pleasant while it is happening, but the end result is good. This is normally only seen in hindsight.

The Lunar Eclipse of the 15th occurs in your 12th house and impacts on Mars. It brings spiritual changes – changes in practice, attitude and even teachings and teachers. Generally there are dramas in the lives of gurus and the spiritual people in your life. This change in spiritual attitude (generally due to some new revelation) will also impact on your overall religious and philosophical beliefs. These will get tested and fine tuned over a six-month process. Gratuitous foreign travel should be avoided during this period. Students, at the college level or beyond, will make changes to educational plans, perhaps in their colleges or subjects. There are shake-ups in your place of worship or in the lives of co-worshipers. Mars's involvement indicates job changes and instability at the workplace. If you employ others there could be instability with your staff and most likely employee changes. (This is also a six-month process.) There could be health scares and important changes to the health regime. Don't be so quick to make these changes, though; Mars is still retrograde.

The Solar Eclipse on the 29th affects all of you strongly, but especially those of you with birthdays on November 1 or 2. It occurs in your 7th house of love and marriage and will test a current relationship. Be more patient with the current love this period. A good relationship will survive the eclipse, but lacklustre ones – relationships that are fundamentally flawed or not part of the Divine Plan – will most likely dissolve. Every Solar Eclipse brings career changes and this one is no different. There are shake-ups in your company and industry. You start to redefine your career path and your public image over the next few months. You might stay in the same career but change your approach to it. Sometimes it signals a new career. There are dramas and life-changing kinds of events in the lives of parents, parent figures or bosses.

Take a nice, easy, relaxed schedule during these periods, especially over the Solar Eclipse. Since your health is more delicate after the 20th you should be getting more rest then anyway.

May

Best Days Overall: 3, 4, 5, 13, 14, 21, 22, 31
Most Stressful Days Overall: 5, 6, 19, 20, 26, 27
Best Days for Love: 6, 13, 14, 24, 25, 26, 27
Best Days for Money: 3, 4, 5, 13, 14, 15, 16, 21, 22, 31
Best Days for Career: 6, 7, 8, 9, 10, 17, 18, 28, 29

This month the upper half of your Horoscope becomes stronger than it has been all year. It doesn't dominate the Horoscope as it has in past years, but the upper half is now at its maximum strength for the year. Thus career is becoming more important. It is daytime in your year, but the night is still with you. You are a bit drowsy. It is time to be up and about, but you wouldn't mind turning over and getting some more sleep! Four long-term planets are below the horizon of your chart and will be for a good while yet. Thus you are still in a period of life where home and psychological issues are very important to you. This will be so all year, but now you should start to shift some attention to the career.

Health still needs watching until the 21st. It will improve dramatically afterwards, but in the meantime be sure to get enough rest. Do your best to maintain high energy levels.

Last month, on the 20th, you entered one of your yearly love and social peaks. This continues until the 21st. The social life sparkles.

You are attending more parties, weddings and gatherings. You are in the mood for love. You are focused here and so love tends to happen. For those planning a marriage this would be a good time to schedule it – between the 1st and the 14th is best.

Love becomes exciting, but unstable, on the 14th and 15th. There can be sudden changes of social plans, sudden romantic opportunities, and eccentric behaviour on the part of the beloved. He or she should avoid risky activities on those days.

The month ahead seems prosperous. Jupiter is moving forward and receiving basically positive aspects. Prosperity is stronger before the 21st than afterwards, but it is OK later in the month too.

Job seekers have good prospects on the 30th and 31st. If you are already employed, your good work ethic is noted by your superiors.

Children or children figures in your life have some social or romantic challenges on the 11th.

Most of the planets are still in the social, Western sector of your chart and Pluto, the ruler of your Horoscope, is still retrograde. Now is the time to obtain clarity on your personal goals and the personal conditions of your life, although not a time to make any changes yet. In this way, you will be able to make positive changes when your period of personal independence happens in a few months' time.

June

Best Days Overall: 1, 9, 10, 18, 19, 27, 28
Most Stressful Days Overall: 2, 3, 16, 17, 22, 23, 29, 30
Best Days for Love: 5, 6, 14, 15, 22, 23, 24
Best Days for Money: 1, 10, 11, 12, 13, 18, 19, 27, 28
Best Days for Career: 2, 3, 7, 8, 16, 17, 27, 28, 29, 30

Your 8th house of transformation – your favourite house – became powerful on May 21, and remains so until the 21st of this month. Scorpio heaven. It's a sexually active kind of month – and for a Scorpio this is quite something. Only Leo can compete with Scorpio sexually.

But there is more to the 8th house than just sex. It is about personal transformation and reinvention. It's about giving birth to the ideal of the self – to the person that you want to be. All these kinds of projects go well this period. You have natural abilities in these areas, but now they are greatly enhanced. The cosmic power is with you.

The 8th house is also about resurrection. When we talk about resurrection we are also talking about death – they go together. Everyone has areas in their lives in need of resurrection – for example in the love life, or some project – this is the time to resurrect these things that seemed to have died.

When the 8th house is strong people are more involved with death. They attend more funerals, wakes, memorial services and things of this nature. They tend to have more personal encounters with death too, although not necessarily literal physical death; most of the time the encounter is on the psychological level. There is a purpose here. As we confront it, we get clarity on the subject. We tend to lose our fear of death and thus we can live better while we're here. There is deep healing happening with these confrontations.

On a more mundane level, this transit indicates that the spouse, partner or current love is prospering. He or she is in the midst of a yearly financial peak and will tend to be more generous.

Personal finance seems especially good this month, particularly from the 21st onwards. This will be another yearly financial peak for you. You will need to make important financial adjustments from the 21st to the 26th, as Jupiter activates a previous eclipse point, but the changes should be good. Your overall prosperity is still very much intact.

Venus activates an eclipse point on the 5th and 6th and this can test a current relationship. More patience with the beloved over that period will prevent things from getting worse than they need to be. Good relationships survive these things.

Health is good this month but will get even better after the 21st.

July

Best Days Overall: 7, 8, 15, 16, 24, 25
Most Stressful Days Overall: 1, 13, 14, 19, 20, 21, 27, 28
Best Days for Love: 4, 5, 6, 13, 14, 19, 20, 21, 24
Best Days for Money: 7, 8, 9, 10, 16, 17, 27
Best Days for Career: 1, 7, 8, 15, 16, 27, 28

On the 21st of last month, as the Sun entered Cancer, your 9th house, you entered one of the happiest periods of your year. This period lasts until the 22nd. Health is good. Prosperity is good. You are basically optimistic about life and your future.

When energy levels are high our horizons naturally expand. Things that seemed impossible during low periods are now eminently possible and eminently do-able. This is the case right now. A strong 9th house signals foreign travel, happy educational opportunities and religious and philosophical kinds of breakthroughs. This is a very good period for college students – they are successful in their studies. Those seeking entrance to university had great aspects all year, but this month they are even better. There is good news in this area. If you are involved in legal issues, there is good news here too.

There is a lot going on in your career now. On the 17th Jupiter will cross your Mid-heaven and enter your 10th house. This brings happy career opportunities and a general elevation of your professional status. Your career is expanding greatly in the year ahead. On the 22nd the Sun enters your 10th house as well and you begin a yearly career peak. If there is a weakness in the career it is because your full attention is not focused there. Home, family and emotional issues distract you. If the focus was greater, the success would be greater. As it is, it is OK, but not what it could be.

In your chart we see a curious phenomenon. You are in a career peak but half of the planets are below the horizon. The upper half of the Horoscope is not as dominant as is usually the case at this time of year. This indicates the division in your energies mentioned above.

Your health needs more attention after the 22nd. There's nothing seriously wrong, but this is just not one of your best health periods. Do whatever you need to do, but schedule more rest periods into your life. Enhance the health in the ways mentioned in the yearly report.

This month your health planet Mars moves into your own sign on the 18th. It has been in Libra this year until now. This shows changes in your health needs and health regime. Good health is not just about 'no symptoms' but also about 'looking good'. There is a vanity component here. Your state of health is reflected in your physical appearance, so good health is better than any cosmetic or lotion from the 18th onwards. This transit also shows the power of detox regimes. These are always good for you, but now, after the 18th, they're even better.

Mars in your sign is a positive signal for health. It shows that you are on the case and paying attention, and this is needed now. But it has some dangers too. There could be a tendency to push the body beyond its limits. And this is not called for now. There is a danger of haste and rush which can lead to accidents or injury. So do what needs to be done and avoid haste.

August

Best Days Overall: 3, 4, 11, 12, 20, 21, 22, 30, 31
Most Stressful Days Overall: 10, 16, 17, 23, 24
Best Days for Love: 3, 4, 12, 13, 16, 17, 23, 24
Best Days for Money: 5, 6, 13, 14, 23, 24
Best Days for Career: 5, 6, 13, 14, 23, 24, 25

Your 10th career house was strong last month and becomes even stronger in the month ahead with 40 per cent (sometimes 50 per cent) of the planets either in that house or moving through there this month. A very successful month. In many cases this is not just a yearly career peak but one of your lifetime career peaks. We can only imagine what the success would look like if your full power and concentration were placed on it. As it is, it is very nice.

Health still needs watching until the 23rd. After that you should note big improvements. Happily, like last month, your health planet is in your own sign, so you are paying attention here. Like last month, avoid rush, haste and temper tantrums. People can over-react these days.

Your love planet, Venus, crosses the Mid-heaven and enters the 10th house on the 12th – a positive move for both the career and the love life. It shows social success as well as career success. Venus travels with Jupiter, your financial planet, from the 12th onwards, but the aspect is most exact from the 17th to the 19th. This brings happy romantic meetings and nice paydays. There are opportunities for business partnerships or joint ventures too. There are romantic opportunities with bosses and people of high status – the money people in your life. Romantic opportunities happen as you pursue your career goals and with people involved in your career. You can enhance the career by social means from the 12th onwards. It will be advantageous to attend or perhaps host the right kind of parties and gatherings. Your spouse, partner or current love also seems successful this month and seems supportive of the career as well. He or she is prospering and is very generous.

In general you mix with people of high status this month. Singles are attracted by power and position. The danger here is that you can enter relationships of convenience rather than of real love. Love seems like another career move during this period.

Finances are good, and there is a prosperous month ahead. You have the financial favour of bosses, elders, parents or parent figures. Even the government is kindly disposed to you on the financial level. Money can come from the government, directly or indirectly, or through favourable government policies or rulings. If you have issues with the authorities and need their favour, this is a good month (especially from the 17th to the 19th) to deal with this. You will get 'best case' outcomes.

The financial planet in the 10th house often indicates pay rises – either overt or covert. Sometimes it is not an 'official' pay rise, but the effect is the same.

September

Best Days Overall: 8, 9, 17, 18, 27, 28
Most Stressful Days Overall: 6, 7, 12, 13, 19, 20
Best Days for Love: 2, 3, 12, 13, 23
Best Days for Money: 1, 2, 3, 10, 11, 19, 20, 29, 30
Best Days for Career: 4, 5, 12, 13, 19, 20, 23, 24

Career is still important this month but on the 28th the lower half of your Horoscope becomes stronger than the upper half. This year, the upper half of the Horoscope has never really dominated as it should. The cycle was rather quick. It's as if you have one foot in the day and the other in the night. You're treading between two worlds. Career is important (and is still successful), but home and family issues – and your emotional well-being – are perhaps even more important. You're working to succeed at both and it's not so easy to do. There are happy career opportunities coming to you, but it's doubtful whether you will accept them if it means violating your emotional harmony or uprooting the family.

Your love planet moves speedily this month. Venus will move through three signs and houses of your Horoscope. On the one hand the transits signal social confidence. You cover a lot of territory socially. You make quick decisions. On the other hand, you're more difficult to 'figure out' lovewise. Your needs and attitudes shift very quickly. Scorpios are not generally 'fickle' people, but in love, this month at least, you seem that way.

Until the 5th Venus is in your 10th house. This shows the attraction for power and status. It shows romantic opportunities at the office, as you pursue your career goals or with people involved in your career. You want to be 'upwardly mobile' in love and in social matters. On the 5th Venus moves into your 11th house of friendships in the sign of Virgo, and will spend most of the month here. This shows a desire for a more 'egalitarian' kind of relationship – a relationship of equals. Friendship is important in love. You don't want to be an 'underling' – a hired hand – but a friend as well as a lover. Romantic opportunities come as you involve yourself in groups and group activities, in professional or trade groups and organizations. Online activities foster love. Romantic opportunities can come from the social networking sites too.

Venus in Virgo is not her strongest position. She is in her 'fall' and does not express her power to the optimum. Thus you will have to work harder to show warmth and love to others. If you're not careful you can come over as too critical and this rarely helps romance. You want perfection in love – a noble goal – and you're entitled to it. But keep in mind that perfection is a 'process' and not an established fact. Perfection is something we work towards; it rarely happens right away.

Finances are good this month. You still have the favour of the authority figures in your life – bosses, parents, parent figures and the government. Pay rises (overt or covert) can still happen. Your good professional reputation draws earnings and earning opportunities to you.

October

Best Days Overall: 5, 6, 14, 15, 24, 25
Most Stressful Days Overall: 3, 4, 9, 10, 16, 17, 18, 31
Best Days for Love: 3, 9, 10, 12, 13, 22, 23
Best Days for Money: 7, 8, 17, 18, 26, 27
Best Days for Career: 3, 4, 12, 13, 16, 17, 18, 22, 23

In August the planetary power shifted from the social Western sector to the independent East. This month the short-term planets are moving to their maximum Eastern position. So you are in your maximum cycle of personal independence now. This is the time to change conditions to your liking, to design your life according to your specifications and to have things your way. Now is the time to cultivate the virtues of personal initiative and to stand on your own two feet.

The other headline this month is the two eclipses that happen. This practically guarantees major change – both personally and for the world at large. When change happens (especially if it is major) things become tumultuous. The dust has to settle before the effects become clear.

The Lunar Eclipse on the 8th occurs in your 6th house of health and work. It affects you strongly, so take it nice and easy over this period. It signals job changes, changes in the conditions of work and instability at the place of work. It can produce health scares (but your health looks good, so they are not likely to be more than that) and changes in the health regime and diet. Both Uranus and Pluto are affected by this eclipse – Uranus, your family planet, more directly. Thus there are dramas at home and in the lives of family members. If there are flaws in your home, now is when you find out about them so that you can make the necessary repairs. Try to make the home safer this period. Parents and parent figures should avoid risky or stressful activities this period. The impact on Pluto affects your body and image. You will be redefining your image and self-concept over the next six months. You will probably dress differently and present a 'new look' to the world. You want to be perceived in a different way. Sometimes a detox of the body happens too.

The Solar Eclipse of the 23rd also impacts the body and image. Anything left undone during the Lunar Eclipse gets handled now. This eclipse will be strongest on those of you born between October the 22nd and 24th. All Scorpios should take it easy this period, but especially the ones just mentioned. Major changes will be happening in your lives in the next six months. Every Solar Eclipse brings career changes and this one is no different. Sometimes the actual career changes; sometimes people stay in the same career but approach it in a new way; and sometimes shake-ups in the company or industry force a new approach. Your career strategy and planning will need to be revised in the coming months. Venus is impacted by this eclipse too. Thus love will get tested. Good relationships will survive, but flawed ones will tend to dissolve.

November

Best Days Overall: 2, 3, 10, 11, 20, 21, 29, 30
Most Stressful Days Overall: 6, 7, 13, 14, 27, 28
Best Days for Love: 2, 3, 6, 7, 11, 12, 22, 23
Best Days for Money: 4, 5, 14, 22, 23
Best Days for Career: 2, 3, 10, 11, 12, 13, 14, 21, 22

Mars moved into your money house on September 14 and stayed there until October 26. This indicates that you were spending on health and earning through work. This month Mars will be in your 3rd house. This has health implications. Your health is basically good these days, but you can enhance it further by giving more attention to the spine, knees, teeth, bones, skin and overall skeletal alignment. Regular back and knee massage will be powerful. Good mental health is more important than usual. Avoid too much thinking or speech.

Once the dust has settled from last month's eclipses, life is basically good. You are having things your own way. Career opportunities are pursuing you and you receive interesting offers. You look successful – others see you that way. Love is also pursuing you and you are having things your way in love. If you are in a relationship, the beloved seems very devoted to you. If you are unattached, romantic opportunities are seeking you out. There's nothing much you need to do.

Both of last month's eclipses affected the body and image and indicated changes there. This is a great period to put these changes into effect, to get the body and image to where you want it to be. It is a very good time, until the 17th, to buy clothing and accessories, as your sense of style is excellent.

It's a prosperous month ahead too. On the 22nd the Sun enters the money house and you begin a yearly financial peak. Earning power is very strong. Your financial planet Jupiter receives favourable aspects from the 17th onwards. The new Moon of the 22nd seems especially prosperous: it occurs in the money house. It will not only bring a nice payday but will clarify financial issues as the month progresses.

Mars travels with Pluto from the 8th to the 12th. This brings excellent job opportunities for job seekers. This is a very dynamic aspect. It gives energy and courage, but could make you overly hasty or impatient. Slow down a little. The temper needs watching too.

Mars has been 'out of bounds' since September 30, and remains so until the 21st. Thus job seekers have been going outside their normal boundaries in the search for work. (This seems to be where the work opportunities are.) Those already employed find that their jobs take them outside the normal parameters. This can be on the physical level or in terms of the nature of the work. This same phenomenon is happening with your health too. You are exploring 'out of the box' kinds of health solutions or therapies.

December

Best Days Overall: 8, 9, 18, 19, 26, 27
Most Stressful Days Overall: 3, 4, 10, 11, 24, 25, 30, 31
Best Days for Love: 1, 2, 3, 4, 12, 13, 21, 22, 30, 31
Best Days for Money: 1, 2, 10, 11, 20, 21, 28, 29
Best Days for Career: 1, 2, 10, 11, 20, 21, 30, 31

You are still in a period of personal independence this month, but this will change later next month. So if there are personal changes – or changes of conditions – that need to be made, this is the time to do so. Later on any changes will be more difficult.

Uranus has been more or less camped out on an eclipse point since October 8, so there are continuing dramas in the home and with the family, a lot of shake-ups and changes going on. Be as patient as you can with family members; there's no need to make a challenging situation worse than it needs to be. Mars moves into the 4th house of home and family on the 5th and this can add fuel to the flames. Passions are running high in the family. There could be major repairs or construction work happening in the home. With at least 80 per cent of the planets below the horizon, the home and family need most of your attention. Career is still successful, but you're more or less treading water here now, gathering the forces for the next major career push next year.

This is still a very prosperous month. You remain in the midst of a yearly financial peak until the 22nd. But on the 8th Jupiter starts to retrograde and this could slow things down. Earnings will still be abundant, but there could be more delays and complications involved. Try to wrap up important purchases or investments before the 8th, and if you can't, try to protect yourself as best you can. Make sure the store has a good returns policy. Study the fine print of all contracts. Ask a lot of questions and resolve any doubts as best you can. After the 8th your finances are under review. You are in a period for fact-gathering, for attaining mental clarity, for exploring ways to improve the finances. It is not an especially good time actually to implement changes.

Saturn's move into your money house on the 24th reinforces what we're saying here. This also suggests a 'go slow' attitude in finance. This move, which only happens every two to three years, is significant. It shows a long-term trend in finances for the next couple of years. You enter a period for financial consolidation and reorganization. It is time to make better use of the resources that you have, to stretch them further. Sometimes this transit brings new financial responsibilities which can't be avoided. It gives the feeling of money 'being tight'. But the truth is if you shift things around here and there you will have all the resources that you need.

Your 3rd house of communication becomes powerful after the 22nd, signalling an excellent period for students. The mind is sharp and clear and there is success in their studies. When the 3rd house is strong we all become students, regardless of our age or stage in life. The mental body - a real body by the way - demands to be fed. There is a hunger and yearning for knowledge. It's a good time to take courses in subjects that interest you and to attend lectures, seminars and workshops. Good to catch up on your reading as well.

Sagittarius

THE ARCHER

Birthdays from
23rd November to
20th December

Personality Profile

SAGITTARIUS AT A GLANCE

Element – Fire

Ruling Planet – Jupiter
  Career Planet – Mercury
  Love Planet – Mercury
  Money Planet – Saturn
  Planet of Health and Work – Venus
  Planet of Home and Family Life – Neptune
  Planet of Spirituality – Pluto

Colours – blue, dark blue

Colours that promote love, romance and social harmony – yellow, yellow-orange

Colours that promote earning power – black, indigo

Gems – carbuncle, turquoise

Metal – tin

Scents – carnation, jasmine, myrrh

Quality – mutable (= flexibility)

Qualities most needed for balance – attention to detail, administrative and organizational skills

Strongest virtues – generosity, honesty, broad-mindedness, tremendous vision

Deepest need – to expand mentally

Characteristics to avoid – over-optimism, exaggeration, being too generous with other people's money

Signs of greatest overall compatibility – Aries, Leo

Signs of greatest overall incompatibility – Gemini, Virgo, Pisces

Sign most helpful to career – Virgo

Sign most helpful for emotional support – Pisces

Sign most helpful financially – Capricorn

Sign best for marriage and/or partnerships – Gemini

Sign most helpful for creative projects – Aries

Best Sign to have fun with – Aries

Signs most helpful in spiritual matters – Leo, Scorpio

Best day of the week – Thursday

Understanding a Sagittarius

If you look at the symbol of the archer you will gain a good, intuitive understanding of a person born under this astrological sign. The development of archery was humanity's first refinement of the power to hunt and wage war. The ability to shoot an arrow far beyond the ordinary range of a spear extended humanity's horizons, wealth, personal will and power.

Today, instead of using bows and arrows we project our power with fuels and mighty engines, but the essential reason for using these new powers remains the same. These powers represent our ability to extend our personal sphere of influence – and this is what Sagittarius is all about. Sagittarians are always seeking to expand their horizons, to cover more territory and increase their range and scope. This applies to all aspects of their lives: economic, social and intellectual.

Sagittarians are noted for the development of the mind – the higher intellect – which understands philosophical and spiritual concepts. This mind represents the higher part of the psychic nature and is motivated not by self-centred considerations but by the light and grace of a Higher Power. Thus, Sagittarians love higher education of all kinds. They might be bored with formal schooling but they love to study on their own and in their own way. A love of foreign travel and interest in places far away from home are also noteworthy characteristics of the Sagittarian type.

If you give some thought to all these Sagittarian attributes you will see that they spring from the inner Sagittarian desire to develop. To travel more is to know more, to know more is to be more, to cultivate the higher mind is to grow and to reach more. All these traits tend to broaden the intellectual – and indirectly, the economic and material – horizons of the Sagittarian.

The generosity of the Sagittarian is legendary. There are many reasons for this. One is that Sagittarians seem to have an inborn consciousness of wealth. They feel that they are rich, that they are lucky, that they can attain any financial goal – and so they feel that they can afford to be generous. Sagittarians do not carry the burdens of want and limitation which stop most other people from giving generously. Another reason for their generosity is their religious and philosophical idealism, derived from the higher mind. This higher mind is by nature generous because it is unaffected by material circumstances. Still another reason is that the act of giving tends to enhance their emotional nature. Every act of giving seems to be enriching, and this is reward enough for the Sagittarian.

Finance

Sagittarians generally entice wealth. They either attract it or create it. They have the ideas, energy and talent to make their vision of paradise on Earth a reality. However, mere wealth is not enough. Sagittarians want luxury – earning a comfortable living seems small and insignificant to them.

In order for Sagittarians to attain their true earning potential they must develop better managerial and organizational skills. They must learn to set limits, to arrive at their goals through a series of attainable sub-goals or objectives. It is very rare that a person goes from rags to riches overnight. But a long, drawn-out process is difficult for Sagittarians. Like Leos, they want to achieve wealth and success quickly and impressively. They must be aware, however, that this over-optimism can lead to unrealistic financial ventures and disappointing losses. Of course, no zodiac sign can bounce back as quickly as Sagittarius, but only needless heartache will be caused by this attitude. Sagittarians need to maintain their vision – never letting it go – but they must also work towards it in practical and efficient ways.

Career and Public Image

Sagittarians are big thinkers. They want it all: money, fame, glamour, prestige, public acclaim and a place in history. They often go after all these goals. Some attain them, some do not – much depends on each individual's personal horoscope. But if Sagittarians want to attain public and professional status they must understand that these things are not conferred to enhance one's ego but as rewards for the amount of service that one does for the whole of humanity. If and when they figure out ways to serve more, Sagittarians can rise to the top.

The ego of the Sagittarian is gigantic – and perhaps rightly so. They have much to be proud of. If they want public acclaim, however, they will have to learn to tone down the ego a bit, to become more humble and self-effacing, without falling into the trap of self-denial and self-abasement. They must also learn to master the details of life, which can sometimes elude them.

At their jobs Sagittarians are hard workers who like to please their bosses and co-workers. They are dependable, trustworthy and enjoy a challenge. Sagittarians are friendly to work with and helpful to their colleagues. They usually contribute intelligent ideas or new methods that improve the work environment for everyone. Sagittarians always look for challenging positions and careers that develop their intellect, even if they have to work very hard in order to succeed. They also work well under the supervision of others, although by nature they would rather be the supervisors and increase their sphere of influence. Sagittarians excel at professions that allow them to be in contact with many different people and to travel to new and exciting locations.

Love and Relationships

Sagittarians love freedom for themselves and will readily grant it to their partners. They like their relationships to be fluid and ever-changing. Sagittarians tend to be fickle in love and to change their minds about their partners quite frequently.

Sagittarians feel threatened by a clearly defined, well-structured relationship, as they feel this limits their freedom. The Sagittarian tends to marry more than once in life.

Sagittarians in love are passionate, generous, open, benevolent and very active. They demonstrate their affections very openly. However, just like an Aries they tend to be egocentric in the way they relate to their partners. Sagittarians should develop the ability to see others' points of view, not just their own. They need to develop some objectivity and cool intellectual clarity in their relationships so that they can develop better two-way communication with their partners. Sagittarians tend to be overly idealistic about their partners and about love in general. A cool and rational attitude will help them to perceive reality more clearly and enable them to avoid disappointment.

Home and Domestic Life

Sagittarians tend to grant a lot of freedom to their family. They like big homes and many children and are one of the most fertile signs of the zodiac. However, when it comes to their children Sagittarians generally err on the side of allowing them too much freedom. Sometimes their children get the idea that there are no limits. However, allowing freedom in the home is basically a positive thing – so long as some measure of balance is maintained – for it enables all family members to develop as they should.

Horoscope for 2014

Major Trends

You are just coming out of a very social period in your life. Many of you got involved in serious romances or relationships that were like marriages. Your social goals seem to have been attained and your focus now shifts to helping your spouse, partner or current love make more money. More details on this later.

Sagittarians are always great travellers, regardless of the transits and aspects of the Horoscope. This is just their nature. But this year – after July 16 – we see more travel than usual. It will be a happy kind of year. You get to do what you most love.

Jupiter's move into Leo on July 16 is also a favourable aspect for students. If you are applying to a college or university there is good news and good fortune. Those already attending colleges have success in their studies.

Your spiritual life has been undergoing much change and ferment since 2011, and the trend continues in the year ahead. You are experimenting in this area, now trying one teaching, then another, then another. On the spiritual level you are like the wandering beggar in search of wisdom. The wandering is not over yet, although pretty soon it will be and you'll settle into one path and work with it.

The year ahead – especially until July 16 – seems like a sexually active kind of year. Regardless of your age or stage in life, there is more interest here than usual. But this period is also wonderful for personal reinvention, for giving birth to your ideal self, your ideal body. Many of you have been deeply involved in these kinds of projects for many years.

Children or children figures in your life are bit difficult to handle these days. In fact, they have been a challenge since 2011. Give them as much freedom as possible as long as it isn't destructive. There's more on this later.

Your major areas of interest (and you have many) this year are finance; home and family; children, creativity and fun; sex, personal reinvention, estates, taxes and occult studies (until July 16); foreign travel, higher education, religion and philosophy (after July 16); friends, groups and group activities (until July 26); and spirituality.

Your paths of greatest fulfilment this year are sex, personal reinvention, estates, taxes and occult studies (until July 16); foreign travel, higher education, religion and philosophy (from July 16 onwards); spirituality (until February 19); and friends, groups and group activities (after February 19).

Health

(Please note that this is an astrological perspective on health and not a medical one. In days of yore there was no difference, both of these perspectives were identical. But in these times there could be quite a difference. For a medical perspective, please consult your doctor or health practitioner.)

Your 6th house of health is not a house of power this year, and this is at it should be. Health is basically good in 2014 and so there's no need to give it any major focus. You can sort of take good health for granted.

There is only one long-term planet in stressful alignment with you – Neptune. The others are either making harmonious aspects or leaving you alone. There will, of course, be periods in the year when your health and vitality are less good than usual. These things come from the short-term planetary transits. They are temporary situations and not trends for the year ahead. When they pass, normal good health and energy return. We will discuss these things in the monthly reports.

Good though your health is, you can make it even better. Give more attention to the following areas, using the reflexes shown in the chart. The neck and throat are always an issue for you. Regular neck massage is advisable. Tension tends to collect there and needs to be released; craniosacral therapy is generally powerful for you. Other important areas are the kidneys and hips (regular hip massage is advisable) and the liver and thighs (regular thigh massage is good).

Venus is your health planet. She is a fast-moving planet and over the course of the year she will move through every sign and house of your chart. Thus there are many short-term trends in health that are best discussed in the monthly reports.

There is a Solar Eclipse in your 6th house on April 29. Generally this brings health scares and dramatic changes to the health regime. The changes seem for the better this year, and the health scare will most likely be just that – scares. Your health is good.

Venus rules love and social activities, and in your chart she is the planet of friends. Thus it is very important to keep the harmony in your

Reflexology

Try to massage the whole foot on a regular basis, but pay extra attention to the points highlighted on the chart. When you massage, be aware of 'sore spots', as these need special attention. It's also a good idea to massage the ankles and the top of the feet.

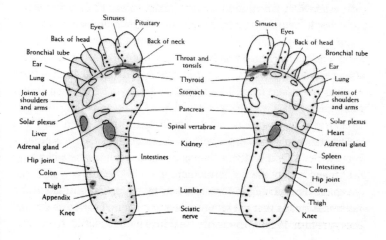

marriage, love relationships and friendships. Discord can have an impact on the physical health. If health problems do arise (God forbid), check this area and restore harmony as quickly as possible.

Towards the end of the year – on December 24 – Saturn will enter your sign. This transit can affect health and energy but this will not really be an issue for 2014 – more for 2015 and 2016. We will therefore go into it more deeply then.

Home and Family

Your 4th house of home and family is a house of power this year and for many years to come. The things that we write about here will take place over many years, as the action of a long-term planet like Neptune in a sign and house is more in the nature of a 'process' rather than an event. The events that happen are merely 'stages' in this process.

Neptune in the 4th house shows various things – and all are likely to happen over time. First off, it shows that the family circle, the family unit and family relationships are becoming more refined, spiritualized and elevated in their energy vibration and tone. In other words, things are becoming more 'ideal' – more of a reflection of the heavenly pattern of family. But the road to this can often be dramatic.

Family members are becoming more spiritual, entering a spiritual path. And while this is good, it often creates havoc in the short term. For example, sometimes a child becomes 'religious' and tries to impose his or her religious beliefs and strictures on the rest of the family, which creates discord. Sometimes the reverse happens. It is a parent who enters the path and the same kind of thing happens. It takes time and patience to sort these things out. Live and let live is the best policy, although it is not always easy to follow. The end result of this – and this is the heavenly agenda – is that the family members, through the child or parent, become acquainted with spiritual concepts and thinking and thus are forced to investigate their own notions of it. In the end everyone grows, but not always harmoniously.

Neptune is a very high and refined kind of energy. His position in the 4th house means that the family is being inundated with this energy. They will become more sensitive, more easily hurt. Little things can trigger insults, so more care and more sensitivity is needed. Voice tones and body language need to be watched.

Spirituality is the problem here and spirituality is the solution. It is only your own spiritual understanding that will help you deal with these issues.

Neptune is the planet of revelation. He shines a light on things and in the light we see the good, the bad and the ugly – hence Neptune's reputation for scandal. The light is impersonal, but what it reveals can be scandalous at times.

Sometimes this transit shows that a parent or parent figure is abusing drugs or alcohol. This is seen to be a 'short cut' out of pain, a short cut to transcendence. But with a spiritual education he or she can learn the real way to transcendence.

Moves were on the cards last year, and they are indicated for the first half of this year too. You seem attracted to homes near water, and this will be a long-term trend. It might be good to acquire fish tanks (with live fish swimming around) for your home. This is considered a healthy energy in the home and they are also decorative – like art.

Children are likely to move this year, and it seems happy. Parents or parent figures in your life could have moved last year or in 2012. This year it seems more stable. Siblings and sibling figures also have a status quo kind of family year. Grandchildren are prospering in the latter half of the year, but moves seem ill advised.

Finance and Career

Your 2nd house of finance has been a house of power for many years now, and will remain so for many more years. You are focused here and this focus is 90 per cent of your success.

The year ahead seem prosperous, although the first half of the year more so than the latter. Jupiter is making wonderful aspects to Saturn, your financial planet, until July 16. Prosperity should continue afterwards too, but you'll probably have to work harder at it.

On December 24 your financial planet will move into your own sign and will stay there until 2017. While this aspect is challenging for health and energy, it is wonderful for finance. You will enter a long-term cycle of prosperity.

Pluto has been in your money house for many years. This shows that a cosmic detox is happening in your financial life. Impurities in practice and attitude are being cut away and removed. The Cosmos has been working to make the financial life healthier, to cut costs, expenses and waste. Sometimes this happens by dramatic means. Financial 'near-death' kinds of experiences (and sometimes actual financial 'death' – bankruptcy) have been happening, and could happen in the future too. Pluto is very thorough.

With Pluto in your money house the Cosmos is calling you to prosper by removing things in the financial life that don't belong there. Perhaps you have duplicate bank or savings accounts, duplicate brokerage accounts, too many financial advisers, too many financial newsletters. This waste should be reduced.

Often people hold on to possessions that are no longer needed and which just take up space in the attic or basement. These should be got rid of as well. Functional relevance should be your guide. If a thing is not being used, sell it or give it to charity. Make room for the new and better that the Cosmos wants to come in. The financial body is a body as much as the physical body is (though it is invisible). It is subject to clogging up as much as the physical body. It needs a good detox – a spring clean.

Pluto in the money house signals an ability to attract outside money either through credit or through investment. This has been a trend for many years, but last year and this it is particularly strong. (Jupiter has been in your 8th house, which rules these things.) Thus, if you have good ideas this is a great year to attract outside investors (with the first half of the year especially good). This position often shows someone who prospers by creative kinds of financing. You have had – and will have – many opportunities to invest in troubled properties or companies and turn them around.

Pluto is also the planet of inheritance. Thus this can happen as well. Hopefully no one has to die, but you are remembered in someone's will or appointed executor for someone's estate.

With Pluto in your money house and Jupiter (the ruler of your Horoscope) in your 8th house, prosperity will happen as you seek to prosper others. The financial interest of the other (the partner or partners) should come first. As you succeed in this, your own prosperity will naturally happen.

Many of you will be called to manage other people's money. This can be the household budget, the family assets or the assets of a business or of friends. You are very good at this sort of thing these days.

It looks like a new car and new communication equipment are coming to you after July 16. Siblings and sibling figures are prospering then too and your relationship with them will improve.

Favourable numbers for money are 3, 10, 15 and 21.

This is not an especially strong career year. Your 10th house is basically empty (only short-term planets will move through there) while your 4th house of home and family is strong. You seem more or less satisfied with your career and have no need to make major changes. It will be a stable kind of career year.

Love and Social Life

As we mentioned, you are coming out of two very strong love and social years. Many of you married or got involved in very serious kinds of relationships in 2012 and 2013. Social goals seem more or less attained by now, and romance is not a major focus now. This year will be a stable romantic year. Singles will most likely stay single and those of you who are married will probably remain married.

Like last year you are still in a sexually active kind of period. Though love and sex are two different things, it does show that you are enjoying yourself.

For the as-yet-unattached, love affairs seem plentiful but they are unstable and are not likely to lead to anything serious. Love affairs with neighbours or in the neighbourhood are likely. We can also see online activities or involvement with groups and group activities providing opportunities for love affairs.

For those of you working towards your second marriage, there is romance and marriage opportunities happening after July 16. It seems happy. For those working on their third marriage we see love affairs, but the stability of these is in question.

Mercury is your love planet and he is a very fast-moving planet. Only the Moon moves faster than him. During the year Mercury moves through every sign and house of your chart. Thus there are many short-term trends in love, depending on where Mercury is and the aspects he is receiving. These are best discussed in the monthly reports.

Having a planet like Mercury as the love planet shows that love and romance can happen in a variety of venues and through a variety of people. Your tastes and needs in love change very quickly. Hence some see you as 'fickle'.

Though romance seems on the back-burner for most of you and not a major focus, friendships, groups and group activities are important and enjoyable. We see many kinds of leisure activities happening with groups or group entertainments.

Siblings and sibling figures in your life have romance this year (after July 16). If they are single there is a strong possibility of marriage. Parents or parent figures are having a status quo love year. Children and children figures in your life (of appropriate age) are very socially active this year, especially until July 26. Love is in the air. They go after what they want and seem to get it. They are unusually popular these days. Grandchildren of appropriate age (or those who play this role in your life) have a strong love year after July 16. Serious romance is in the air for them.

Favourable numbers for love are 1, 3, 6, 8 and 9.

Self-improvement

Your financial planet Saturn moved into Scorpio, your 12th house, in October 2012. Thus he has been in 'mutual reception' with Pluto (your spiritual planet) since that time and this is the situation in the year ahead. Each is a guest in the sign or house of the other. Two planets in mutual reception are considered friendly with each other – helpful and co-operative. Thus your spirituality is helping your financial life and your financial life is helping you grow spiritually. Many people find these two areas of life in conflict – each seems, on the surface, antithetical to the other. But this is not the case with you.

I read this as going deeper, into the spiritual dimensions of wealth. This is a big subject.

Many people are in bondage because of money, or because of a lack of understanding of money. Many are not fulfilling their true purposes in life because of financial blockages (or what they think are financial blockages). I have seen this so many times. The person who should paint feels that he can't afford to do so, or can't make it in that field and so chooses some lesser profession because of this. Not only is there an omnipresent sense of unease over this, but they are depriving the world of their unique gift. I see this in many other fields too. The musician becomes a cab driver or an accountant. There is nothing wrong with being an accountant or cab driver, but that is not their purpose.

Until we understand money and the source of money we will never know true financial freedom and never fully achieve our purposes in life.

Over these past few years the Cosmos has been opening doors for you in this area. It is up to you step through, though. The Cosmos will not force you.

That the Divine (or Spirit) is the source of all supply is one of the central messages of all scripture. Happily Sagittarius, more than most, understands this. Once a person learns how to access this ever-present supply, the doors of affluence will always be open. Often, the doors on the material level are closed and there's nothing much that can be done on that level. But the spiritual doors are always open for those who understand them. You can always afford to follow your true purpose – the true desire of the heart.

You already understand much about the spiritual dimensions of wealth, but this year you are going deeper into this area. Read up all you can on the subject. It will transform your whole life.

Month-by-month Forecasts

January

Best Days Overall: 7, 8, 17, 18, 26, 27
Most Stressful Days Overall: 5, 6, 12, 13, 19, 20
Best Days for Love: 1, 2, 9, 10, 11, 12, 13, 19, 20, 22, 23, 28, 29, 30, 31
Best Days for Money: 1, 2, 5, 6, 14, 15, 24, 25, 28, 29
Best Days for Career: 1, 2, 10, 11, 19, 20, 22, 23, 30, 31

You begin your year with most of the planets in the independent Eastern sector of the Horoscope. Thus you are very much in a period of personal independence. You have the power to change conditions to your will and to design your life the way you want it to be. Power is not the problem. With Jupiter retrograde, you are not sure of what you want or what you want to create. It's as if you are sitting in a high-powered sports car, with plenty of fuel in the tank but with no road map or GPS. I can go anywhere but where should I go? How do I get there? In these situations the first thing to do is to get mentally clear. Gather facts. Introspection is good. Ask for Higher Guidance. You will receive it.

Most of the planets are below the horizon of your Horoscope; the lower half of the Horoscope is dominant right now. So do whatever needs to be done careerwise but shift most of your attention to the home, family and your emotional well-being. The main thing now is to find, and function from, your personal point of emotional harmony. Once this happens the other things will fall into place. This is a time to work on your career and outer goals by the methods of night, not the methods of day. During the night, the deeper mind dreams up what it will do the next day. It visualizes all that will happen (though we are not consciously aware of this) and this is what happens during the day. Work to 'enter the state' of what you want to achieve, and to 'feel' as if you are already there. This is interior work. When the time comes for your next career push, the actions will happen naturally.

You begin your year in the midst of a yearly financial peak, so the month ahead is very prosperous. Your financial planet, Saturn, is receiving beautiful aspects until the 20th. Your financial intuition is firing on all cylinders. When your intuition comes into play, the financial life becomes more like a dance than a grind. It is rhythmic and beautiful. Money goes out, money comes in. You finish one task and another comes in. The money that comes in is earned joyfully and honourably. The past few years have been initiations into the spiritual dimension of wealth and this continues in the month ahead.

Your love planet Mercury is 'out of bounds' until the 8th. Your social life – and a current relationship – is taking you outside your normal boundaries. But no one handles this better than Sagittarius. Singles are looking for love in 'out of the way' places. Until the 11th love opportunities happen as you pursue your normal financial goals and with people involved in your finances. Wealth and material gifts are romantic turn-ons. The money people in your life could be playing Cupid. After the 11th Mercury moves into your 3rd house and this changes your love attitudes and needs. Wealth becomes less important in love. You have plenty of your own. Instead you want someone you can connect to intellectually, someone who shares your ideas, someone who is easy to talk to. The love life improves dramatically from the 11th onwards. The online world brings romantic opportunity. Lectures, seminars and workshops are enjoyable in their own right, but also lead to romantic opportunities.

February

Best Days Overall: 3, 4, 13, 14, 22, 23
Most Stressful Days Overall: 1, 2, 8, 9, 15, 16, 17, 28
Best Days for Love: 1, 5, 6, 7, 8, 9, 10, 16, 17, 19, 24, 25, 26, 27
Best Days for Money: 1, 2, 10, 11, 12, 20, 21, 24, 25, 28
Best Days for Career: 1, 10, 15, 16, 17, 19, 26, 27

Health is basically good this month, but needs watching after the 18th. There's nothing seriously wrong, just temporary stress caused by the short-term planets. The most important thing is to get enough rest. You can enhance the health this month by giving more attention to the spine, knees, teeth, bones, skin and overall skeletal alignment. Regular back and knee massages will be powerful. A visit to the chiropractor or osteopath might be a good idea too.

You are in a basically prosperous year, although earnings are less than usual before the 18th. Be patient. However, after the 18th earnings once again soar. The financial intuition becomes even stronger than last month. It might be stretching things a bit, but we could say that you are in another yearly financial peak.

The Water element in the Horoscope has been strong for some months now, but on the 18th it becomes even stronger. Water – the feeling side of things – is not your native element. You are not that at home there. People will be more sensitive and little things – perhaps even unintentional things – can set them off. You had a certain look on your face when so and so talked, or your voice tones were not right, or perhaps you rolled your eyes at an inappropriate moment. What you deemed to be 'just honesty' is taken for cruelty. Take more care now. A little awareness can save a lot of heartache later on.

Love is more complicated this month too. Mercury goes retrograde on the 6th and love can seem to go backwards. But this is only appearances. It is just time to review the love life and see where improvements can be made, although not a time for important love decisions one way or the other. You seem to lack direction (Jupiter is also in retrograde motion) and the same is true for the beloved. There is no conflict or antagonism here – just lack of direction. Love seems 'headed nowhere'. That's OK by the way. It doesn't have to 'head' anywhere right now. Allow it to develop as it will.

Mercury is also your career planet. Here the retrograde is a good thing. The power this month is in the 4th house of home and family and this is where your focus should be. Career can be de-emphasized.

The Sun makes beautiful aspects to Jupiter towards the end of the month. This brings happy travel opportunities. It is a good aspect for students too, as it indicates success in their studies.

March

Best Days Overall: 3, 4, 12, 13, 22, 23, 30, 31
Most Stressful Days Overall: 1, 2, 7, 8, 15, 16, 28, 29
Best Days for Love: 7, 8, 17, 18, 19, 26, 27, 28, 29
Best Days for Money: 1, 2, 10, 11, 19, 20, 24, 25, 28, 29
Best Days for Career: 7, 8, 15, 16, 19, 28, 29

It seems that you missed this period of personal independence. With Jupiter retrograde since the beginning of the year, it has been challenging to create conditions to your liking or to directly change conditions. The problem, as we mentioned, was lack of clarity rather than power (and certainly not money). On the 6th Jupiter will start moving forward, but the planetary power is shifting to the social, Western sector. Now the problem is lack of power, not lack of direction. Sometimes things happen this way. Your next period of independence, which will begin in September, will be different. You'll have both the power and the direction. In the meantime adapt to situations as best you can and work to cultivate your social skills.

The planetary power is now at the maximum low point of the Horoscope. This began on the 18th of last month and continues until March 20. It is the magical midnight hour of your year. Mighty things are happening beneath the surface in the interior levels of your being but are not yet manifest outwardly. Your job is to just allow the power to build up within. Don't interfere with this beautiful process by worrying or being fearful. Rest assured, the within will become the without in due course. This is nature's way.

This is a month for psychological-type breakthroughs. Your insight into mood, feeling and your personal past history is greatly enhanced. With this insight comes emotional healing. Opinions or judgements that were made about the past are now seen in a different light. History gets re-written and in a more favourable, healthier way. (The facts don't change but your interpretation of them does.)

This is a time to get the home and family life in right order. Now being a good parent is about being there for the kids and for other family members (or for those who play that role in your life).

Finances are still excellent this month. The only challenge is Saturn's retrograde on the 2nd. This won't stop your earnings but will slow things down a bit. Saturn will be retrograde for many months now. You can't just stop your financial life, but you can be more careful in your financial dealings. Study prospective purchases or investments more carefully and be as perfect as you can in your financial dealings. Work to communicate better in this area. Avoid the short cuts now (and you love short cuts); they are an illusion. Financial mistakes will only delay financial goals.

Health still needs watching until the 20th. This month you can enhance the health in the ways mentioned in the yearly report and the ways mentioned last month. After the 6th pay more attention to the ankles and calves. These should be regularly massaged. Give the ankles more support.

April

Best Days Overall: 8, 9, 10, 18, 19, 26, 27
Most Stressful Days Overall: 3, 4, 5, 11, 12, 24, 25
Best Days for Love: 3, 4, 5, 6, 7, 8, 16, 17, 18, 19, 24, 25, 29, 30
Best Days for Money: 6, 7, 16, 17, 20, 21, 24, 25
Best Days for Career: 7, 8, 11, 12, 18, 19, 29, 30

This is basically a happy month. On the 20th of last month you entered a yearly personal pleasure peak, which continues until the 20th of this month. It's party time in your year. Health is much improved as well.

Enhance the health by giving more attention to the feet from the 6th onwards. Regular foot massage will do wonders for you. Spiritual healing methods are also very powerful from after the 6th.

The month ahead would be basically idyllic were it not for the two eclipses that happen. These shake things up in the world at large and create some necessary changes in your world.

The Lunar Eclipse of the 15th occurs in your 11th house, testing friendships. There are dramas in the lives of friends. Children of the appropriate age have their love relationships tested. Computer and high-tech equipment can be temperamental during this period too, and often need replacement. Every Lunar Eclipse tends to bring psychological encounters with death, and this one is no different. It is time to evolve a healthier, less fearful attitude towards death. It's also a good idea to drive more carefully and avoid risk-taking activities. Children should be kept out of harm's way; there's no need for them to be involved in daredevil-type stunts at this time. Your spouse, partner or current love is forced to make dramatic financial changes now (this will be a six-month process). Children and children figures are affected by the eclipse too. They are making important changes to their body and image – redefining themselves for themselves and for the world.

The Solar Eclipse of the 29th occurs in your 6th house of health and work. Thus there could be job changes afoot. This could be within your present company or with another one. In general there is instability in the workplace. Those who employ others have issues with employee turnover. There can be health scares this period, but probably no more than scares. However, important changes in the health regime and diet could be initiated over the next six months. Students make important changes in their educational plans. Often this means a change of course or a change of school. Often the Solar Eclipse will bring a crisis of faith. Your belief systems get challenged by the 'facts of life'. This is a good thing when it happens – it's good to revise our belief systems periodically and to refine them – but it's not always so pleasant. Sagittarians are renowned travellers, but gratuitous foreign travel is best avoided this period.

May

Best Days Overall: 6, 7, 15, 16, 24, 25
Most Stressful Days Overall: 1, 2, 8, 9, 10, 21, 22, 28, 29
Best Days for Love: 1, 2, 6, 11, 12, 13, 14, 19, 20, 24, 25, 28, 29, 30
Best Days for Money: 3, 4, 5, 13, 14, 17, 18, 21, 22, 31
Best Days for Career: 8, 9, 10, 11, 12, 19, 20, 29, 30

The short-term planets will reach their maximum Western position this month. Personal ability always matters, but 'likeability' – the ability to get on with others – is more important now. Both qualities are basically equal in importance, but at different times one or other is paramount. The Cosmos, through the planets, ensures that we develop both sides of our nature in a balanced way. Too much focus on the self and its interest can often be a blockage to our interests. So it is good to take a vacation from ourselves and focus on other people. Interestingly, as you do this, your own needs get met in different ways.

On the 21st, as the Sun enters your 7th house, you begin one of your yearly love and social peaks. The social life in general becomes more active. Social invitations increase. There are more weddings, dinners and parties to attend. And those looking for romance are more likely to find it. Events tend to follow our interest and focus.

Your love planet, Mercury, moves speedily this month through three signs and houses of your Horoscope. Social confidence is good and you make rapid progress towards your social goals. But this also signals many changes in your love needs and attitudes. You become more difficult to 'figure out' when it comes to love. Until the 7th you are attracted to those who serve your interests. This is how you feel loved and this is how you show it. Love is practical – a form of mutual service. Love opportunities occur at the workplace or as you pursue your health goals. On the 7th Mercury enters your 7th house of romance. Now romance is more important in your love life. You like the moonlit walks on the beach, the flowers, the creative expressions of love. It is the feeling of love that matters most. Love opportunities happen in the usual places then – at parties and gatherings. On the 29th Mercury moves into your 8th house, and now sexual magnetism becomes most important. Good sex will cover many sins in a relationship.

Mercury goes 'out of bounds' from the 12th to the 31st. This is most interesting. It shows that you are going outside your normal sphere in search for love – you go into unknown territory. Sometimes this is what is necessary. You have to break out of the box.

Health needs more attention from the 21st onwards. As always – and most important – make sure you get enough rest. High energy levels are the first line of defence against disease. The health can also be enhanced through head and scalp massage from the 3rd to the 29th. Until the 3rd, give more attention to the feet. After the 29th give more attention to the neck and throat. Neck massage (and craniosacral therapy) will be powerful.

June

Best Days Overall: 2, 3, 12, 13, 20, 21, 29, 30
Most Stressful Days Overall: 5, 6, 18, 19, 24, 25, 26
Best Days for Love: 1, 5, 6, 9, 10, 14, 15, 17, 23, 24, 25, 26
Best Days for Money: 1, 9, 10, 11, 14, 15, 18, 19, 27, 28
Best Days for Career: 1, 5, 6, 9, 10, 17, 25, 26

Health still needs watching until the 21st. Review last month's discussion of this. Continue to enhance health through neck massage until the 23rd. Do your best to see that the cervical vertebrae are in right alignment. Don't allow tension to collect in the neck. For those of a more esoteric bent, chanting of mantras will be very beneficial. The body responds to sound more than usual. After the 23rd enhance the health through arm and shoulder massage. Breathing exercises will be beneficial.

You are still in a yearly love and social peak until the 21st, but this month love becomes more complicated from the 18th onwards. Mercury starts to go retrograde then. (Retrograde activity in general increases this month.) Undoubtedly you have met new people, new romantic prospects and new friends since last month. Now it is time to review things, to step back and to see if these new relationships are really what you want. It's time to slow down a bit in love and not rush things.

Last month, on the 21st, the planetary power began to shift from the lower half to the upper half of the Horoscope. This month the shift becomes even stronger. After the 23rd, 60 per cent (and sometimes 70 per cent) of the planets are in the upper half of the Horoscope – the sector of outer affairs and career. Your family planet, Neptune, starts to go retrograde on the 9th, giving a very clear message. Home and family issues need time for resolution. There's not much to be done there now. You need to focus on the career and your outer life. Mercury is also your career planet – he serves double duty in your Horoscope. So his retrograde suggests a need to study career opportunities more. Career issues should be handled with more care and attention to detail. Focus on the career now, but advance slowly and methodically.

On the 21st the Sun enters Cancer, your 8th house. This is a more sexually active kind of period. The whole year has been a sexually active one, but now even more so. Whatever your age or stage in life, the libido is stronger than usual. Prosperity increases from the 21st onwards too. Saturn, the financial planet, starts to receive very positive aspects. The only problem, financially, is that Saturn is still retrograde. Increased earnings are happening but there are more delays and glitches involved here. Patience. Patience. Patience. The deals will eventually go through. Prosperity would be greater if Saturn were moving forward, but as it is, it is OK. Your spouse, partner or current love is also prospering. He or she enters a yearly financial peak on the 21st.

Health and overall energy improve greatly from the 21st onwards.

Take a nice easy schedule from the 21st to the 26th. Be careful driving and avoid risky activities. Jupiter, the ruler of your Horoscope, transits an eclipse point over that period.

Venus transits an eclipse point on the 5th and 6th, which can bring disturbances to the job and instability at the workplace. Sometimes it brings a health scare but there's no need to panic; get a second opinion.

July

Best Days Overall: 1, 9, 10, 17, 18, 27, 28
Most Stressful Days Overall: 2, 3, 15, 16, 22, 23, 29, 30, 31
Best Days for Love: 4, 5, 6, 13, 14, 22, 23, 24, 25
Best Days for Money: 7, 8, 11, 12, 15, 16, 17, 24, 25, 27
Best Days for Career: 2, 3, 5, 6, 13, 14, 24, 25, 29, 30, 31

There are many important and positive changes happening in your Horoscope – and thus your life – this month. The ruler of your Horoscope, Jupiter, makes his once yearly move, from the sign of Cancer into that of Leo and into a very harmonious aspect with you. You are always a traveller, but now even more so. The month (and the year) ahead shows much foreign travel.

Saturn, the financial planet, starts moving forward on the 20th after many months of retrograde motion. He is still receiving very positive aspects, so the month ahead is very prosperous. Stuck deals or payments now get unstuck. Financial confidence returns. Hopefully you have used the past few months to clarify your financial goals and plans. Now you can set them into motion. The Sun's conjunction with Jupiter – from the 24th to the 27th – seems especially prosperous. There is luck in speculations and general financial good luck. The new Moon of the 26th seems particularly fortunate.

The 9th house of religion, travel and learning is your natural house. Power there, after the 23rd, is very comfortable for you. The Cosmos impels you to do what you most love to do – travel, educate yourself and explore more deeply religion and philosophy.

Health has been good this month, but you will notice an increase in well-being after the 23rd. If there have been pre-existing health problems you should hear good news about them. A doctor or therapist will get the credit, but what really happened was that the planetary power shifted in your favour. Everything else was just the 'side effect' of this. You can enhance your health even more by giving more attention to the arms, shoulders, lungs and respiratory system until the 18th. Regular arm and shoulder massage is excellent. After the 18th give more attention to the stomach, and women should pay more attention to the breasts. Diet is more of a health issue then too. Detox regimes are especially powerful after the 18th. (A kidney detox might be a good idea then.)

The love life is not as active as in previous months, but it is still good. Mercury is now moving forward again, so there is more clarity here. Social decisions should be better. Love is romantic until the 13th and love opportunities happen in the usual places – at parties and gatherings. After the 13th sexual magnetism is the most important attraction.

August

Best Days Overall: 5, 6, 13, 14, 23, 24
Most Stressful Days Overall: 11, 12, 18, 19, 25, 26, 27
Best Days for Love: 3, 4, 5, 6, 12, 13, 14, 15, 18, 19, 23, 24, 25, 26
Best Days for Money: 3, 4, 5, 7, 8, 11, 12, 13, 14, 20, 21, 22, 23, 24, 30, 31
Best Days for Career: 5, 6, 14, 15, 25, 26, 27

Your 9th house became very powerful last month. It becomes even more powerful this month – especially until the 23rd.

The 9th house (and the sign of Sagittarius) has three levels of meaning. The first and most basic level is that of the jet-setting Traveller: the person who has lunch in Paris, dinner in Vienna, and then scoots to London the next day. Nothing wrong with this, but this is only the most basic characteristic of the 9th house. The second level is that of the Academic – the Professor – the keeper and dispenser of higher learning. This is a very important function. The third level is that of the Priest. This is the person who not only teaches the Higher Knowledge, but acts as mediator between the Divine and the mundane worlds. If we analysed the charts of the Priestly class (and by this we include priests, ministers, rabbis, imams, monks and swamis) I would wager that we would see a disproportionate weighting in the sign of Sagittarius and/or power in the 9th house. Sagittarius has a natural inclination to these things.

So aside from all the travelling you'll be doing, there is going to be a keener interest in higher learning, religion and philosophy. This is a wonderful month for the study of scripture (of whatever religion you belong to). Religious and philosophical revelations and breakthroughs will happen. There will be happy educational opportunities. College students do better in their studies and college applicants receive good news.

Sagittarians enjoy their night life as much as anybody, but this month a juicy theological discussion, or the lecture of a visiting religious figure, might be more alluring. Behind every jet-setter is a closet priest or professor.

The other headline this month is your yearly career peak. This begins on the 23rd. Travel seems involved here too. In fact it is your willingness to travel and willingness to mentor those beneath you that are a major factor in your success. (Knowing the right people and attending the right parties won't hurt either – especially after the 15th.)

Finance is a bit more stressful than usual until the 23rd. There's nothing seriously wrong, but you need to work harder to achieve your financial goals. It could also be that your focus on travel, religion and education distracts you on the financial level. However, you should see much improvement here after the 23rd.

Health needs more focus after the 23rd too. Until the 12th, enhance the health by paying attention to the stomach and the diet. Women should pay more attention to the breasts. After the 12th, give more attention to the heart and overall circulation.

September

Best Days Overall: 2, 3, 10, 11, 19, 20, 29, 30
Most Stressful Days Overall: 8, 9, 14, 15, 22, 23
Best Days for Love: 2, 3, 4, 12, 13, 14, 15, 20, 21, 23, 28
Best Days for Money: 1, 2, 3, 4, 5, 8, 9, 10, 11, 17, 18, 19, 20, 27, 28, 29, 30
Best Days for Career: 4, 12, 20, 21, 22, 23, 28

July and August brought tremendous mental and philosophical expansion. The 9th house was supercharged with planetary energy. The natural consequence of this mental and philosophical expansion is career success, and this began on August 23 and continues in the month ahead. You are still very much in a yearly career peak and much success is happening. Your home and family planet, Neptune, is still retrograde. So it is safe to let go of family issues for a while and focus on your career.

Though you are enjoying much career success right now, this is nothing compared to the success you will have next year – it's only preparation.

Like last month your health needs watching, until the 23rd. Make sure to get enough rest. Sagittarius has a tendency to be overly optimistic about the body and sometimes pushes it beyond its natural limits. This is not a time for this. Until the 5th enhance the health by giving more attention to the heart, circulation and chest. Chest massage is good. After the 5th, attention should be paid to the small intestine. The good news here is that when Venus, your health planet, crosses the Mid-heaven on the 5th you will be paying more attention to your health. Problems with bosses, parents or parent figures – attacks on your professional reputation – could affect health from the 5th onwards. If problems arise, do your best to restore harmony here as quickly as possible. Happily the career looks good and this is a positive for health. Health and energy will improve after the 23rd.

Love also seems good this month. The love planet, Mercury, moves forward quickly. This indicates much forward progress in a current relationship and much social confidence. You make rapid progress towards your social goals. Mercury moves through three signs and houses this month but will spend the bulk of it, from the 2nd to the 28th, in the sign of Libra, your 11th house. For singles this shows love and romantic opportunities occurring in the online world, on social networking or dating sites. It also shows opportunities as you get involved with groups, group activities and professional organizations. A current friend wants to be more than that. Friendship this month should precede romance. Get to know the other as a friend before you jump in.

This month on the 5th the planetary power begins to move into the Eastern, independent sector of your chart. You are entering a period of enhanced personal independence. Jupiter, the ruler of your Horoscope, is moving forward as well. Thus now, for the first time this year, you have both the power and the direction to change uncomfortable conditions. You know what needs to be changed and you can set about doing it. You don't have to adapt to situations now. Create your life according to your personal specifications. The cosmic teacher now wants you to develop your independence, your personal initiative and personal abilities. It's time to stand on your own two feet.

October

Best Days Overall: 7, 8, 16, 17, 18, 26, 27
Most Stressful Days Overall: 5, 6, 12, 13, 19, 20
Best Days for Love: 3, 5, 6, 12, 13, 22, 23, 31
Best Days for Money: 1, 2, 5, 6, 7, 8, 14, 15, 17, 18, 24, 25, 26, 27, 28, 29
Best Days for Career: 5, 6, 13, 19, 20, 22, 23, 31

Your 11th house of friendship became powerful on the 23rd of last month and is powerful until the 23rd of this. So you are in a strong social period. The natural consequence of career success is an enhanced social life. You meet new people at the top, people of like mind and like interests. You learn the value of friendships and networking. The friends that you meet now are people who support your fondest hopes and wishes. This is the definition of friendship from the astrological perspective. A person who smiles and seems friendly but doesn't wish those things for you is not a real friend.

On the 23rd, as the Sun enters your 12th house, you enter one of the most spiritual periods of your year. Nearly half of the planets will be in this house or moving through there this month.

But the main headline for this month is the two eclipses that happen in it. These always produce dramas in the world.

The Lunar Eclipse of the 8th occurs in your 5th house of fun and creativity and affects the children or children figures in your life. They will be making important personal changes over the next six months. They are redefining themselves, their personalities and self-concept. They will eventually present a whole new image to the world. In the meantime, do your best to keep them out of harm's way during this period. They should avoid risky kinds of activities. This eclipse impacts on both Uranus and Pluto, but more directly on Uranus. Thus cars and communication equipment get tested and often there is a need for replacements. It will be a good idea to drive more carefully this period, more mindfully and more defensively.

The impact on Pluto affects the spiritual life – your attitudes, approach, practice and teachings. These get 'reality checked'. Important changes will happen here in the coming months. Every Lunar Eclipse brings psychological encounters with death. Sometimes people have dreams about it. Sometimes they have 'close calls' – near-death kinds of experiences. People in your life who are teetering on the verge between life and death will often choose to depart on a Lunar Eclipse. The eclipse sort of 'pushes them over the edge'. Your spouse, partner or current love has a temporary financial crisis and is forced to make important changes.

The Solar Eclipse of the 23rd occurs in your 12th house of spirituality and reinforces the spiritual changes brought on by the Lunar Eclipse. This can also bring dramas, shake-ups and upheavals in spiritual organizations that you are involved with, and in the lives of gurus or spiritual mentors. Every Solar Eclipse tests your religious and philosophical beliefs. It is good that twice a year you get a chance to upgrade and refine this area. The true beliefs – those that are congruent to reality – will hold up, but the other ones – the ones that are sometimes true, partially true or untrue – get revised or discarded. College students make important changes to their educational plans.

Gratuitous foreign travel should be avoided during this eclipse period.

November

Best Days Overall: 4, 5, 13, 14, 22, 23
Most Stressful Days Overall: 2, 3, 8, 9, 15, 16, 17, 29, 30
Best Days for Love: 1, 2, 3, 8, 9, 10, 11, 12, 20, 21, 22, 23
Best Days for Money: 3, 4, 5, 11, 12, 14, 21, 23, 25, 26, 30
Best Days for Career: 1, 10, 11, 15, 16, 17, 20, 21

Your 12th house of spirituality is still very powerful this month. This is a month for spiritual-type breakthroughs, for direct, personal experiences with the invisible world. It is a very good month for meditation, spiritual study, attending spiritual lectures and for developing the spiritual faculties – the intuition, ESP, dowsing, clairvoyance (nowadays called 'remote viewing') and clairaudience. It is normal at such times to want more solitude. Spiritual work always goes better in solitude. Don't worry; there is nothing wrong with you. You are not anti-social. This is a short-term phase.

Spirituality has been important in finance for some years now and is especially important right now. Pay attention to your intuition, to dreams and to the inner leadings of the spirit. On the 8th your love planet enters the 12th house, so spirituality becomes important in love too. You need someone who is on your spiritual wavelength right now, someone who shares your spiritual ideals. Mere sexual magnetism will not be enough. From the 8th to the 23rd, as the love planet moves through the 12th house, romantic opportunities happen in spiritual-type settings – at the yoga studio, the prayer meeting or meditation seminar. Psychics, astrologers, spiritual channels and ministers have important information regarding love and finances these days.

The natural consequence of a spiritual breakthrough is a 'new beginning' – it's as if you start over fresh. And this happens as the Sun enters your own sign on the 22nd. Many of you will have birthdays in November, others in December. The birthday, astrologically speaking, is a new beginning – your personal new year.

The month ahead seems very happy. On the 22nd you enter one of your yearly personal pleasure peaks. The planetary power will also be in its maximum Eastern position for the year, making it a great time to make the changes that you need to make and to create conditions according to your liking – a time for having things your way. You should see fast progress towards your goals.

On the 23rd Mercury crosses the Ascendant and enters your 1st house. Love sparkles then. Love is pursuing you. Your spouse, partner or current love is very devoted to you. You are number one in his or her life. Singles don't have to do much to find love, it comes to them. Just go about your normal business – just show up.

This is a month, especially until the 17th, for going deeper into spiritual healing. Health is basically good this month, but if you feel under the weather you might want to see a spiritual healer. You respond very well to this.

Job seekers have good fortune after the 17th. Job opportunities come to you and there's nothing special that you need to do.

December

Best Days Overall: 1, 2, 10, 11, 20, 21, 28, 29
Most Stressful Days Overall: 5, 6, 13, 14, 26, 27
Best Days for Love: 1, 2, 5, 6, 10, 11, 12, 13, 21, 22, 30, 31
Best Days for Money: 1, 2, 8, 9, 10, 11, 19, 20, 21, 22, 23, 28, 29
Best Days for Career: 1, 2, 10, 11, 13, 14, 21, 22, 30, 31

Though there are some bumps on the road – some excitement and change – the month ahead is basically happy and prosperous. You are still in a yearly personal pleasure peak, and this is a time to enjoy all the sensual delights and the pleasures of the body. Health and energy are good. Many planets in your 1st house indicates much personal magnetism and charisma. You look good. The opposite sex takes notice. You are still having love (and life in general) on your terms. If there are conditions that you still need to change, try to do this before the 8th when Jupiter starts to retrograde.

Prosperity is also very strong this month. There are two important developments here. You enter a yearly financial peak on the 22nd. This should bring peak earnings for the year. With 60 and sometimes 70 per cent of the planets in or moving through the money house this month, there is a lot of financial power. On the 24th, your financial planet Saturn enters your own sign. This will bring financial windfalls to you – especially to those of your born early in the sign. You are seen by others as a 'money person'. You dress expensively. You project the image of wealth. The next few years should be prosperous as well. Finance is important to you and you are focused here. The problem might be too much focus.

Health is excellent right now (though for the next two years you will need to be more watchful here). You can enhance the health further by giving more attention to the liver and thighs (always important for you) until the 10th, and to the spine, knees, teeth, bones, skin and overall skeletal alignment subsequently. Regular back and knee massages will be powerful.

Sagittarians enjoy the good life so your weight is often a problem. But now, from the 24th onwards (and for the next two to three years) weight-loss regimes will go well. Those of you who need to will start shedding the pounds.

Uranus has been more or less camping out on an eclipse point since October. This is the case in the month ahead too. Communications have been a bit patchy. Siblings or sibling figures in your life are having crises and dramas. There could be dramas with your neighbours as well. Continue to drive carefully and defensively.

Mars will transit an eclipse point from the 4th to the 7th. Children or children figures need to avoid taking risks and should also drive more carefully.

Venus transits an eclipse point from the 21st to the 23rd. This can bring job changes or disturbances at work and perhaps a heath scare too. However, your health is good overall and any scare is not likely to be more than that. Get a second opinion.

Capricorn

♑

THE GOAT

Birthdays from
21st December to
19th January

Personality Profile

CAPRICORN AT A GLANCE

Element – Earth

Ruling Planet – Saturn
   Career Planet – Venus
   Love Planet – Moon
   Money Planet – Uranus
   Planet of Communications – Neptune
   Planet of Health and Work – Mercury
   Planet of Home and Family Life – Mars
   Planet of Spirituality – Jupiter

Colours – black, indigo

Colours that promote love, romance and social harmony – puce, silver

Colour that promotes earning power – ultramarine blue

Gem – black onyx

Metal – lead

Scents – magnolia, pine, sweet pea, wintergreen

Quality – cardinal (= activity)

Qualities most needed for balance – warmth, spontaneity, a sense of fun

Strongest virtues – sense of duty, organization, perseverance, patience, ability to take the long-term view

Deepest needs – to manage, take charge and administrate

Characteristics to avoid – pessimism, depression, undue materialism and undue conservatism

Signs of greatest overall compatibility – Taurus, Virgo

Signs of greatest overall incompatibility – Aries, Cancer, Libra

Sign most helpful to career – Libra

Sign most helpful for emotional support – Aries

Sign most helpful financially – Aquarius

Sign best for marriage and/or partnerships – Cancer

Sign most helpful for creative projects – Taurus

Best Sign to have fun with – Taurus

Signs most helpful in spiritual matters – Virgo, Sagittarius

Best day of the week – Saturday

Understanding a Capricorn

The virtues of Capricorns are such that there will always be people for and against them. Many admire them, many dislike them. Why? It seems to be because of Capricorn's power urges. A well-developed Capricorn has his or her eyes set on the heights of power, prestige and authority. In the sign of Capricorn, ambition is not a fatal flaw, but rather the highest virtue.

Capricorns are not frightened by the resentment their authority may sometimes breed. In Capricorn's cool, calculated, organized mind all the dangers are already factored into the equation – the unpopularity, the animosity, the misunderstandings, even the outright slander – and a plan is always in place for dealing with these things in the most efficient way. To the Capricorn, situations that would terrify an ordinary mind are merely problems to be managed, bumps on the road to ever-growing power, effectiveness and prestige.

Some people attribute pessimism to the Capricorn sign, but this is a bit deceptive. It is true that Capricorns like to take into account the negative side of things. It is also true that they love to imagine the worst possible scenario in every undertaking. Other people might find such analyses depressing, but Capricorns only do these things so that they can formulate a way out – an escape route.

Capricorns will argue with success. They will show you that you are not doing as well as you think you are. Capricorns do this to themselves as well as to others. They do not mean to discourage you but rather to root out any impediments to your greater success. A Capricorn boss or supervisor feels that no matter how good the performance there is always room for improvement. This explains why Capricorn supervisors are difficult to handle and even infuriating at times. Their actions are, however, quite often effective – they can get their subordinates to improve and become better at their jobs.

Capricorn is a born manager and administrator. Leo is better at being king or queen, but Capricorn is better at being prime minister – the person actually wielding power.

Capricorn is interested in the virtues that last, in the things that will stand the test of time and trials of circumstance. Temporary fads and fashions mean little to a Capricorn – except as things to be used for profit or power. Capricorns apply this attitude to business, love, to their thinking and even to their philosophy and religion.

Finance

Capricorns generally attain wealth and they usually earn it. They are willing to work long and hard for what they want. They are quite amenable to foregoing a short-term gain in favour of long-term benefits. Financially, they come into their own later in life.

However, if Capricorns are to attain their financial goals they must shed some of their strong conservatism. Perhaps this is the least desirable trait of the Capricorn. They can resist anything new merely because it is new and untried. They are afraid of experimentation. Capricorns need to be willing to take a few risks. They should be more eager to market new products or explore different managerial techniques. Otherwise, progress will leave them behind. If necessary, Capricorns must be ready to change with the times, to discard old methods that no longer work.

Very often this experimentation will mean that Capricorns have to break with existing authority. They might even consider changing their present position or starting their own ventures. If so, they should be willing to accept all the risks and just get on with it. Only then will a Capricorn be on the road to highest financial gains.

Career and Public Image

A Capricorn's ambition and quest for power are evident. It is perhaps the most ambitious sign of the zodiac – and usually the most successful in a worldly sense. However, there are lessons Capricorns need to learn in order to fulfil their highest aspirations.

Intelligence, hard work, cool efficiency and organization will take them a certain distance, but will not carry them to the very top. Capricorns need to cultivate their social graces, to develop a social style, along with charm and an ability to get along with people. They need to bring beauty into their lives and to cultivate the right social contacts. They must learn to wield power gracefully, so that people love them for it – a very delicate art. They also need to learn how to bring people together in order to fulfil certain objectives. In short, Capricorns require some of the gifts – the social graces – of Libra to get to the top.

Once they have learned this, Capricorns will be successful in their careers. They are ambitious hard workers who are not afraid of putting in the required time and effort. Capricorns take their time in getting the job done – in order to do it well – and they like moving up the corporate ladder slowly but surely. Being so driven by success, Capricorns are generally liked by their bosses, who respect and trust them.

Love and Relationships

Like Scorpio and Pisces, Capricorn is a difficult sign to get to know. They are deep, introverted and like to keep their own counsel. Capricorns do not like to reveal their innermost thoughts. If you are in love with a Capricorn, be patient and take your time. Little by little you will get to understand him or her.

Capricorns have a deep romantic nature, but they do not show it straightaway. They are cool, matter of fact and not especially emotional. They will often show their love in practical ways.

It takes time for a Capricorn – male or female – to fall in love. They are not the love-at-first-sight kind. If a Capricorn is involved with a Leo or Aries, these Fire types will be totally mystified – to them the Capricorn will seem cold, unfeeling, unaffectionate and not very spontaneous. Of course none of this is true; it is just that Capricorn likes to take things slowly. They like to be sure of their ground before making any demonstrations of love or commitment.

Even in love affairs Capricorns are deliberate. They need more time to make decisions than is true of the other signs of the zodiac, but given this time they become just as passionate. Capricorns like a relationship to be structured, committed, well regulated, well defined, predictable and even routine. They prefer partners who are nurturers, and they in turn like to nurture their partners. This is their basic psychology. Whether such a relationship is good for them is another issue altogether. Capricorns have enough routine in their lives as it is. They might be better off in relationships that are a bit more stimulating, changeable and fluctuating.

Home and Domestic Life

The home of a Capricorn – as with a Virgo – is going to be tidy and well organized. Capricorns tend to manage their families in the same way they manage their businesses. Capricorns are often so career-driven that they find little time for the home and family. They should try to get more actively involved in their family and domestic life. Capricorns do, however, take their children very seriously and are very proud parents – particularly should their children grow up to become respected members of society.

Horoscope for 2014

Major Trends

Last year was a strong love and social year and the trend continues in the year ahead. Not only is love in the air, but there is more friendship happening too. More on this later.

You have been involved in personal transformation and personal reinvention for many years now, and the trend continues this year. Friends are helping, new technology is helping, but still it is hard work. Things will go much easier here – and there is success – from July 16 onwards.

Finance is so-so during the first half of the year. There are no disasters, but nothing special on the positive side either. This will change after July 16 and the year will turn out to be prosperous. More details later.

Career is active but very hectic, especially in the first half of the year. Success will happen but through much hard work, much effort. The main challenge is to integrate the career with home and family obligations. Again, there's more on this later.

Neptune has been in your 3rd house of communication since February 2012. This shows that your thinking and speech are becoming more refined. For students this is a mixed blessing. On the one hand your intuition is strengthened; on the other, there can be a tendency to ignore basic facts. There is a need to learn to integrate logic and intuition. Each has its place.

The family situation has been volatile and unstable for some years now and the trend continues in the year ahead. As in past years, your challenge is to maintain your emotional equilibrium.

Your areas of greatest interest this year are the body, image and personal pleasure; communication and intellectual interests; home and family; love and romance (until July 16); sex, personal reinvention, estates, taxes, debt and occult studies (after July 16); and friends, groups and group activities.

Your paths of greatest fulfilment this year are love and romance (until July 16); sex, personal reinvention, estates, taxes, debt and occult studies (after July 16); friends, groups and group activities (until February 19); and career (after February 19).

Health

(Please note that this is an astrological perspective on health and not a medical one. In days of yore there was no difference, both of these perspectives were identical. But in these times there could be quite a difference. For a medical perspective, please consult your doctor or health practitioner.)

Health needs watching this year, especially during the first half of the year. While the aspects are nowhere near as severe as they were in 2011 and 2012, they still strongly affect you. Three long-term planets are in stressful alignment with you until July 16. Part of the problem is that your 6th house of health is basically empty (only short-term planets will move through there). Thus you might not be paying attention even though you should. It will take conscious effort on your part to stay on the case healthwise.

Having three long-term planets stressing you is difficult enough, but there will be times in the year when the short-term planets will join the party and these will be particularly vulnerable times. This year these periods will be from March 21 to April 19 and from June 21 to July 16. Be sure to get as much rest as possible at those times. It might be good to book regular massages, reflexology or acupuncture treatments then, or to perhaps spend some free time at a health spa in your area. This is a good idea for the first half of the year, but especially during those periods.

Adequate rest and maintaining high energy levels is your first line of defence. But it will also be good to give more attention to the following areas – the vulnerable areas of your Horoscope. (The reflexes for these areas are shown in the chart.)

Pay attention to the heart. Avoid worry and anxiety as much as possible, as these are two emotions that are the spiritual root causes of heart problems. If there is something positive to be done about a situation by all means do it. If not, pray, and let go. The worry does nothing to help the situation.

The spine, knees, teeth, bones, skin and overall skeletal alignment are also vulnerable areas. Regular back and knee massages will be powerful, and give the knees more support when exercising. Regular visits to a chiropractor or osteopath will be a good idea – the vertebrae need to be kept in right alignment. If you're out in the sun use a good sun screen. Yoga, Pilates, the Alexander Technique and Feldenkrais are excellent therapies for the spine.

Reflexology

Try to massage the whole foot on a regular basis, but pay extra attention to the points highlighted on the chart. When you massage, be aware of 'sore spots', as these need special attention. It's also a good idea to massage the ankles and the top of the feet.

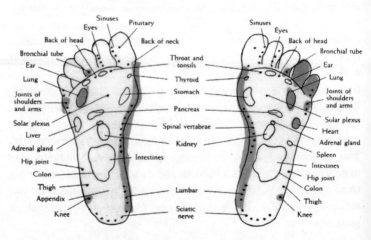

Other vulnerable areas are the lungs, small intestine, arms, shoulders and respiratory system. Regular arm and shoulder massages will be beneficial here. Tension tends to collect in the shoulders and needs to be released regularly.

Mercury, your health planet, is a fast-moving planet. Except for the Moon he is the fastest in the zodiac. Every year he will visit – at some time or another – every sign and house in your chart. Thus there are many short-term trends in health, depending on where Mercury is and the aspects he receives. These are best discussed in the monthly reports.

Mercury will go retrograde three times this year – from February 6 to the 28th, from June 7 to July 2 and from October 4 to the 25th. These are times to review your health goals and see where improvements can be made. They are not times for making drastic health decisions or changes. (Often we are sorely tempted to do this, but it is best avoided.)

Pluto has been in your sign for many years now, which indicates a tendency to surgery, especially of the cosmetic type. It doesn't mean that you have to do it, but that you would be more inclined.

Home and Family

Your 4th house of home and family has been a house of power since 2011 and this is the case in the year ahead and for some more years to come. It's a very volatile area of life.

The family unit has been unstable for some years. Passions are running high. More freedom in the family, for you and for the family as a whole, is needed. Often Uranus in the 4th house shows break ups in the family unit – sometimes divorces, sometimes general fallings out. It will take much work and effort to keep things together, although it can be done if the work is put in.

Uranus in the 4th house also signals unstable moods and emotions. This can be both personal and with family members. Moods can shift instantaneously from positive to negative and back, which makes life challenging. You never know what to expect from the family from one moment to the next. This is especially true with one of the parents or parent figures.

You seem to be working to create a team spirit in the family but it is rough going. The intentions are good, but they're not so easy to implement.

Uranus is your financial planet. His position in the 4th house shows that you are spending more on the home and family, and are investing here. But you can also earn here too. This aspect shows that you are working more from home. The financial life is centred in the home and not so much the office.

Uranus rules technology, inventions and innovations. Thus you are installing all kinds of high-tech gadgetry in the home. Perhaps things that relate to finance: financial software or financial hook-ups.

With Uranus in the 4th house, moves could have already happened and more can happen in the future. It is an aspect for 'multiple' or 'serial' moves. Sometimes what is indicated is not actual moves but serial renovations, serial redesigns. When you think you have the home exactly as you want it, you discover a new home or a new design or layout that is even more ideal.

This aspect often indicates people living in different places for long periods of time. Though you haven't actually moved (in a legal sense) it is 'as if' you have moved a few times.

A parent or parent figure could have moved in 2013, and if they haven't, they might move this year instead. The move seems happy. Siblings and sibling figures are having a stable kind of year on the home front. They are likely to stay where they are. Children or children figures in your life are likely to move from July 16 onwards. Grandchildren of appropriate age are having the home renovated or repaired. This seems to happen suddenly and unexpectedly.

Finance and Career

Your money house is not a house of power this year and this is perhaps the biggest financial weakness in the Horoscope. You might have your eye off the ball. You might not be giving finance the attention it needs. A glittering social life could be one reason; another could be family disturbances. Capricorns are generally interested in finance – and good at it too – but this year you need to force yourself a bit.

Though family relationships are unstable, there does seem to be good financial support from the family, and from you to the family. Your chart shows a family business. This could be with your own family (and this could be part of the tension here) or businesses run like a family. Family connections are important financially too.

The financial planet in the 4th house favours investment in residential property (although commercial real estate is naturally good for you as well), restaurants, the food business (wholesale or retail), hotels and any industry that caters to the home or family. The field of psychological therapy is good too. Those of you in the health professions would do well in family practice.

Jupiter, your spiritual planet, spends most of the year in square aspect to the Uranus. Thus your financial intuition will need verification. Real intuition should always be trusted, but sometimes one can misinterpret the meaning. Perhaps you are giving too much to charitable institutions (a good thing) and it makes you feel stressed. Giving should always be 'proportional'.

Jupiter in square aspect to the financial planet generally creates problems of 'excess' – generally overspending. But Capricorn is less susceptible to this than most.

Jupiter will move into Leo, your 8th house, on July 16. This will radically change the whole financial life. He will start to make beautiful aspects to Uranus from this date. This shows prosperity and an intuition that can be trusted – a clear, unambiguous intuition. You will spend more under this aspect too, but you will earn more.

Jupiter in the 8th house signals the prosperity of your spouse, partner or current love – and of friends in general. They are likely to be more generous with you. It also shows inheritance, though no one need actually, literally, die. You can be named in someone's will or appointed executor to someone's estate. If you have good ideas for new projects this will be a good period to attract outside investors. The period will be good for either borrowing or paying down debt – according to your need.

The career is highly active – and hectic – until July 26. Mars spends almost seven months in your 10th house of career. You are fending off competitors (this can be personal competitors or competitors to the company you work for). You seem aggressive in the career. The family as a whole – though things are turbulent – seems more successful too. (Perhaps their strong ambitions are part of the cause of the turmoil.)

Mars is your family planet. His position in your career house gives many messages. Whatever your job or profession, whatever your outer work is, your family is your real career, your real mission for the first seven months of the year. The family does seem supportive of your career goals and actively helping. You are working to integrate your home and your office. The home will become more like an office and the office will become more 'homelike'. Family connections are helpful for finance and the career.

Love and Social Life

When Jupiter moved into your 7th house on last year, you entered a very powerful and happy romantic cycle. And this continues until July 16. The whole social life sparkles. Sure there are some bumps on the road. The Moon, your love planet, is the fastest of all the planets. Every month she moves through all the signs and houses of your Horoscope. Every month, she waxes and wanes and will receive some positive or negative aspects. But these are short-term events, not trends for the year ahead, and are best dealt with in the monthly reports.

Jupiter in the 7th house is a classic signal for love, romance or marriage. He indicates a serious kind of relationship. Perhaps it is not legally a marriage, but it would be something that is 'like' a marriage. If you are already married (and this could have happened last year) this aspect would show opportunities for business partnerships or joint ventures.

Jupiter in this house increases and expands the social circle. New friends come into the picture – and good ones. There are more parties and gatherings. People attend more weddings too.

As we mentioned earlier, the social life could be distracting you from finance. And it does seem difficult to balance the two interests. But this too is short term. After July 16 it will be easier to integrate these areas.

Jupiter is your spiritual planet. His position in your house of romance gives us many messages. It shows that you are attracting more refined and spiritual people on the social level. Spiritual and philosophical compatibility is important both in love and in your choice of friends.

The physical aspects of love are always important, but if there is no philosophical and spiritual compatibility it is doubtful whether the relationship can last.

Love and romantic opportunities come in various ways: in spiritual settings, perhaps at the yoga class, spiritual retreat, prayer circle, meditation seminar or charitable function. They can also happen in educational settings, at college or university or at some college function.

You have the kind of aspects of someone who falls in love with the guru, minister or professor. You gravitate to 'mentor' types – people you can learn from.

It is said that we grow through our relationships (Libra especially holds this as an article of faith), and this year it is certainly the case for you. Your relationships will bring new spiritual understanding and growth.

Those of you working on attaining their second marriage will have an active and happy social year, but will probably not marry. If you are already married, you will most likely stay married. Those working on their third or fourth marriages have excellent marriage opportunities.

Parents or parent figures are having their relationships tested. Things are highly unstable here. If they are unattached, marriage is not advisable. Single or unattached siblings or sibling figures will find serious love next year, but this year is a more or less status quo kind of year.

Self-improvement

Personal transformation – the giving birth to the ideal you – has been a major interest for some years now, as we have mentioned. The interest becomes even more intense after July 16 as Jupiter moves into your 8th house. Personal reinvention involves mental, emotional and often physical detoxification. You are already the self that you dream of being; it has just been buried by wrong thinking, feeling and the negative experiences and memories that these produce. Graffiti has been painted on what is essentially a divine masterpiece. The removal of the graffiti can be messy, and it is seldom a pleasant experience. The end result is always good, but while it is happening, one needs a strong stomach. It is helpful to understand that the more intense the emotional or mental pain is, the more is being cleansed from the system. And the better the eventual outcome will be. The unpleasantness is temporary; the outcome is for ever (as long as you don't fall back into old patterns).

This is an excellent Horoscope for students. (Last year was also good.) There is success in studies. The mind is sharp but also intuitive. It absorbs knowledge by osmosis. You just need to expose yourself to the right books and the right teachers and the knowledge will be absorbed.

Even if you are not a full-time student, this is an excellent year to expand the mind and your knowledge base. There will be great satisfaction in taking courses in subjects that interest you.

Maintaining your emotional equilibrium has been a challenge for some years now. With Uranus in the 4th house the emotional life tends to extremes – ultra high or ultra low. Some people treat this chemically, through medication. But this is not a permanent cure. The best way is through meditation. This will give permanent and lasting results. There are many forms of meditation, many schools, and this should be explored in the year ahead.

Month-by-month Forecasts

January

Best Days Overall: 1, 2, 9, 10, 19, 20, 28, 29
Most Stressful Days Overall: 7, 8, 14, 15, 22, 23
Best Days for Love: 1, 2, 9, 10, 14, 15, 19, 20, 21, 22, 28, 29, 30, 31
Best Days for Money: 3, 4, 5, 6, 7, 8, 14, 15, 17, 18, 24, 25, 26, 27, 30, 31
Best Days for Career: 1, 2, 9, 10, 19, 20, 22, 23, 28, 29

You begin your year in the midst of a yearly personal pleasure peak, with 40 per cent (and sometimes 50 per cent) of the planets in or moving through your 1st house. A happy month. The pleasures of the body's five senses offer themselves to you. Health and energy are good.

Self-esteem and self-confidence are strong. You look good and you feel good.

The planetary power is now in its maximum Eastern position. Thus you are in a period of maximum independence. You can and should have things your way, and this is an excellent time to create conditions as you desire them to be. There's no need to 'people please' these days (though others should always be respected). Take the actions you need to that will create personal happiness and harmony.

Last month the planetary power shifted from the upper to the lower half of the Horoscope. It's a new year (because of your birthday) but it's also night-time in your year. Career demands are strong and you seem very active there, but start paying attention to your emotional needs and to the home and family. It's time to build up your inner forces for your next career push in six months time. Work on your career by interior means: set goals, visualize, enter the feeling-state of what you want to achieve. Then when the next career period comes, your actions will be natural, powerful and effortless.

With Mars in your 10th house you will still be active – in a physical way – in your career. Do the things that must be done physically, but work primarily through inner methods. The retrograde of Venus, the career planet, reinforces what we are saying here.

The month ahead is prosperous. On the 20th you enter a yearly financial peak. Money comes from work, from your spouse, partner or current love and from insurance, estates or creative kinds of financing. Tax issues and estate planning (for those of you of the appropriate age) are influencing many financial decisions now.

Love has been wonderful for many months now and is still good this month. Many a marriage happened last year and marriage could be on the cards in the year ahead too. This would not be a good month for it though. Venus is retrograde and the occupant of your 7th house of romance, Jupiter, is also retrograde.

The planetary momentum is overwhelmingly forward this month; 80 per cent of the planets are moving forward. Not only that, but your personal and the universal solar cycles are both waxing. (Your personal cycle starts to wax on your birthday.) This is an excellent time to launch new ventures or release new products into the world. For those of you who had birthdays last month, the 1st to the 16th and the 30th and

31st are the best times to do this. For those of you with birthdays this month, from your birthday to the 16th and from the 30th to the 31st are best.

February

Best Days Overall: 5, 6, 7, 15, 16, 17, 24, 25
Most Stressful Days Overall: 3, 4, 10, 11, 12, 18, 19
Best Days for Love: 1, 2, 5, 6, 7, 8, 9, 10, 11, 12, 16, 17, 20, 24, 25, 28
Best Days for Money: 1, 2, 3, 4, 10, 11, 12, 13, 14, 20, 21, 22, 23, 26, 27, 28
Best Days for Career: 5, 6, 7, 16, 17, 18, 19, 24, 25

Last month was favourable for starting new projects or launching new products, and this month is even more favourable. Until the 6th, 90 per cent of the planets are moving forward. The period from the 1st to the 6th (as the Moon waxes) is most favourable. After that, Mercury starts to retrograde and the percentage of planets in forward motion drops a little. It will still be a good to launch new projects, just not as good.

Love is still wonderful this month – even better than last month. Venus, the universal love planet, moves forward all month, and Jupiter in your 7th house starts to receive beautiful aspects from the 18th onwards. Though love is good all month it will be better from the 1st to the 14th, as the Moon (your own love planet) waxes. Love is spiritual these days. Romantic opportunities happen in spiritual settings, in meditation seminars, prayer meetings and spiritual retreats or at charitable events.

The Eastern sector of the Horoscope is still dominant and most of the planets are moving forward. So make those changes that need to be made. Create your life as you desire it to be. You will see fast progress here.

Prosperity is still strong this month, especially until the 18th. You are still in the midst of a yearly financial peak. Venus in your sign shows that happy career opportunities are coming to you – and you can be choosy now. Choose the opportunities that don't violate your emotional harmony. Venus in your sign shows that you look success-ful; others see you that way. You dress the part.

Mercury's retrograde from the 6th onwards shows a need to avoid major changes to the health regime or diet. Health issues are under review. The retrograde is a good period for study and fact gathering, but not so good for making final decisions. Job seekers too need more caution. Job opportunities are not what they seem – get more facts. Ask questions. Resolve doubts. Unnecessary foreign travel is best avoided as well. If you must travel, protect yourself as best you can. Insure your tickets. Allow more time for getting to and from your destination and try not to schedule connecting flights too closely together. (The two planets that rule foreign travel in your Horoscope – Mercury and Jupiter – are both retrograde from the 6th onwards.)

Health and energy are basically good. You can enhance it further this month until the 13th by giving more attention to the feet. Foot massage and spiritual techniques are very potent. After the 13th, give more attention to the ankles and calves. These should be massaged regu-larly, and give the ankles more support when exercising.

March

Best Days Overall: 5, 6, 15, 16, 24, 25
Most Stressful Days Overall: 3, 4, 10, 11, 17, 18, 30, 31
Best Days for Love: 1, 2, 7, 10, 11, 17, 18, 21, 22, 26, 27, 30, 31
Best Days for Money: 1, 2, 3, 4, 10, 11, 12, 13, 19, 20, 22, 23, 26, 27, 28, 29, 30, 31
Best Days for Career: 7, 17, 18, 26, 27

Mercury and Jupiter, the two planets that rule foreign travel in your Horoscope, move forward this month. Mercury goes forward on the 1st and Jupiter on the 6th. Thus foreign travel is best undertaken after the 6th.

The element of Water has been strong all year, and this continues in the month ahead. It is basically a happy time. An era of good feeling. But there are things that need to be understood. People are more emotionally sensitive now. Every little nuance of feeling is magnified and exalted – for good or bad. Feelings that would be ignored under different aspects take on a new importance. People will tend to over-react to seemingly minor things such as body language, posture and voice tones. Be more mindful about this as it can save a lot of heart ache (and endless explanations) down the road.

Though you are not in a yearly spiritual peak, the month ahead is a very spiritual-type month. Those of you on the path will make great progress and have spiritual breakthroughs and revelations (this was the case last month too), while those not on the path will be experiencing non-rational kinds of events, coincidences that can't be explained logically. The invisible world is letting you know that it is around and active.

With 80 per cent of the planets still in forward motion, on the 20th you enter the best starting energy of the zodiac, as the Sun goes into Aries. This is an exceptionally good time to start new ventures or launch new products into the world. The time of the new Moon on the 30th seems especially good for this.

Family life has been unstable for some years now. This is the case in the month ahead. It is both unstable and very complicated. It is good that you are paying attention here. Your 4th house of home and family becomes powerful from the 20th onwards. It would be tempting to make dramatic changes or decisions then, but Mars, your family planet, is retrograde all month. Things are not what they seem; get more facts. Do your best to maintain your emotional equilibrium.

Health needs more attention from the 20th onwards too. As always the most important thing is to get enough rest to maintain high energy levels. Health can be enhanced in the ways mentioned in the yearly report, but there are other ways too. Until the 17th continue to pay attention to the ankles and calves. Massage them regularly. After the 17th give more attention to the feet. Spiritual healing methods will be powerful then too. And spiritual healing will be especially powerful from the 21st to the 23rd.

April

Best Days Overall: 1, 2, 11, 12, 20, 21, 29, 30
Most Stressful Days Overall: 6, 7, 13, 14, 15, 26, 27
Best Days for Love: 4, 5, 6, 7, 9, 10, 16, 17, 19, 20, 24, 25, 29, 30
Best Days for Money: 6, 7, 9, 10, 16, 17, 18, 19, 22, 23, 24, 25, 26, 27
Best Days for Career: 4, 5, 6, 13, 14, 15, 16, 17, 24, 25

Health still needs watching until the 20th of this month. Review our discussion of last month. Until the 7th enhance the health by giving more attention to the feet. Foot massage and spiritual healing techniques are still powerful. After then, give more attention to the head, face and scalp. Regular scalp massage will be effective. It will also be good to get more physical exercise. The muscles need to be toned.

The main headlines this month are the two eclipses that happen.

The Lunar Eclipse of the 15th has a very strong effect on you, so take a nice, relaxed, easy schedule for a few days before and after it. This eclipse occurs in your 10th house of career, signalling career changes. You might not change the actual career (though this often happens) but the way you approach things. Your career thinking has most likely not been realistic and the eclipse reveals this to you. There are shake-ups in your company or industry and dramas in the lives of bosses, parents or parent figures. Since this eclipse affects Mars there are shake-ups in the family too, and dramas in the lives of family members. Sometimes there are unexpected repairs needed in the home. Every Lunar Eclipse tests love – the Moon is your love planet. In this case it is most likely showing that a love relationship moves dramatically forward. Marriages often happen under the impact of eclipses. Good things can often be as stressful (and time consuming) as bad things.

The Solar Eclipse of 29th is a bit kinder to you, but it won't hurt to reduce your schedule a bit anyway. The good news here is that your overall health and energy are much stronger than with the previous eclipse. This eclipse occurs in your 5th house of fun, creativity and children, so there are dramas in the lives of children and children figures. They should avoid risky kinds of activities this period. Those of you in the creative arts will be making important changes in your field of creativity. Friends have been stressed all year, but now their marriages or love relationships get tested.

Because the Sun is ruler of your 8th house of transformation every Solar Eclipse tends to bring encounters (generally psychological encounters) with death. There is a need to reach a deeper understanding of this. Sometimes an eclipse brings 'close calls', or near-death kinds of experiences – experiences where you say, 'Wow! A second either way and I'd have been gone.' These are love letters from the Cosmos: 'Life on earth is short and fragile. Get to work on the really important things.'

Your spouse, partner or current love is making dramatic financial changes, generally because of some crisis or disturbance.

May

Best Days Overall: 8, 9, 10, 17, 18, 26, 27
Most Stressful Days Overall: 3, 4, 5, 11, 12, 24, 25, 31
Best Days for Love: 3, 4, 5, 6, 8, 9, 10, 13, 14, 17, 18, 24, 25, 28, 29, 31
Best Days for Money: 3, 4, 5, 6, 7, 13, 14, 15, 16, 19, 20, 21, 22, 24, 25, 31
Best Days for Career: 6, 11, 12, 13, 14, 24, 25

The Western sector of your Horoscope has become stronger and stronger since March 20, but it is only now, as Venus crosses from East to West on the 3rd, does it become dominant. The era of personal independence is over for a while. Conditions can still be changed, but with much more difficulty than usual. It's best now to adapt to situations as best you can. If you have created well during this past period of independence, life is comfortable and enjoyable. If there have been mistakes, you are experiencing the consequences, the discomfort, and will make the corrections necessary during the next period of independence. Now it is time to develop the social skills and to allow things to happen rather than trying to 'make' them happen by personal effort. Good comes to you through others. Success depends on the 'likeability' factor more than personal abilities or skills (important though they are).

Last month on the 20th you entered another one of your yearly personal pleasure peaks. You've been working very hard this year and now it's time for some recreation and fun. This doesn't mean that you let go of your legitimate responsibilities. (Capricorns are unlikely to do that anyway.) You handle them, but schedule more time for fun and for enjoying life. Even work can be enjoyed if you approach it in the right way.

Party time ends (or rather, it slows down a bit) after the 21st as you once again have a zest for work. You are in the mood for work. This is very good for job seekers as prospective employers pick up on this energy. It's also a good period to do the boring but necessary detail-oriented tasks that you've been putting off, such as accounts, filing, cleaning the home and office, etc. If you employ others this is a good period in which to interview and hire new employees.

Health is basically good, but you can enhance it further by giving more attention to the neck and throat until the 17th, and to the lungs, arms and shoulders, afterwards. Neck and shoulder massage is powerful until the 17th. Cranioacral therapy would also be good. Arm and shoulder massage is always good for you, and especially after the 17th. If you feel under the weather, get out in the fresh air and do some deep breathing.

Finances are good this month but you're dealing with many challenges. This has been the case all year. You have to work harder to achieve your financial goals. Venus travels with Uranus, your financial planet, on the 14th and 15th and this signals a nice payday. There is luck in speculations too.

Love is still happy and will get even better next month. Serious romance is happening or has already happened. The love life goes better from the 1st to the 14th and from the 28th onwards as the Moon waxes. The social magnetism is much stronger then.

June

Best Days Overall: 5, 6, 14, 15, 22, 23
Most Stressful Days Overall: 1, 7, 8, 20, 21, 27, 28
Best Days for Love: 1, 5, 6, 7, 8, 14, 15, 16, 17, 23, 24, 25, 26, 27, 28
Best Days for Money: 1, 2, 3, 10, 11, 12, 13, 16, 17, 18, 19, 20, 21, 27, 28, 29, 30
Best Days for Career: 5, 6, 7, 8, 14, 15, 23, 24

Your work planet Mercury has been 'out of bounds' since May 12 and remains so until the 5th of this month. This shows that job seekers are going outside their normal boundaries in search of work. Those already employed are being asked to do things outside the norm too. The same holds true for travel. It is the 'out of the way' – the places less travelled – that attract you now. We see this same phenomenon in your health regime. You are trying things outside your normal routine. Probably this is what is necessary now.

During this month and the next, the planetary power is at its maximum Western position for the year. The social life is becoming more active. There is something to be said about letting go of personal interests and personal concerns. It is like taking a vacation. There's no need to look after number one, or worry too much about number one. Keep the focus on others and their interests and number one will do very well – sometimes in strange and unexpected kinds of ways.

On the 21st you enter a yearly love and social peak. Marriage, or relationships that are 'like' marriages, has been signalled in your chart since last year. Many will tie the knot this coming month. Those still unattached will not remain unattached for long. There is abundant – and happy – romantic opportunity. Your social magnetism is strong all month but will be stronger from the 1st to the 13th and from the 27th to the 30th. The new Moon of the 27th is especially good for love. It will also clarify the love life well into next month. Whatever information is needed to make good love and social decisions will come naturally.

Health needs more attention after the 21st. Enhance the health in the ways mentioned in the yearly report, but during this period pay special attention to the stomach and diet (until the 18th) and to the arms, shoulders, lungs and respiratory system after that date. The good news is that your health house is still powerful after the 21st and you are on the case.

Mercury goes retrograde on the 7th. Thus job seekers need to be more cautious after then. There are many job opportunities this month, but things might not be as they seem. Get more facts. If you are travelling to foreign destinations, it's best to do so before the 7th if you can. If this is not possible, protect yourself as best you can. Allow more time getting to and from your destination, and insure your tickets. Changes in the health regime need more research after the 7th and diagnoses and tests done after the 7th need verification. They could be inaccurate.

July

Best Days Overall: 2, 3, 11, 12, 19, 20, 21, 29, 30, 31
Most Stressful Days Overall: 4, 5, 6, 17, 18, 24, 25
Best Days for Love: 4, 5, 6, 7, 8, 13, 14, 15, 16, 24, 25, 27
Best Days for Money: 1, 7, 8, 9, 10, 13, 14, 16, 17, 18, 27, 28
Best Days for Career: 4, 5, 6, 13, 14, 24

Continue to monitor the health until the 22nd. Enhance it in the ways mentioned in the yearly report but also through arm and shoulder massage (until the 13th), and by dietary means afterwards. The stomach and breasts (for women) need more attention after the 13th. Good mental health is important before the 13th. Intellectual purity will not only enhance the outer affairs but the health as well. After the 13th, emotional harmony becomes more important. Health will improve greatly after the 22nd. On the 17th Jupiter will move away from his stressful aspect to you, and on the 18th Mars will do likewise. Both of these planets have been in stressful aspect to you since the beginning of the year. In addition, on the 23rd the Sun moves away from his stressful aspect. If there have been health problems you should start hearing good news now.

You are still in the midst of a yearly love and social peak. For some of you this is a lifetime love and social peak as well. You couldn't ask for better romantic aspects right now. Love and social activities will be happy and active all month, but will start to taper off after the 22nd. Your love and social goals are more or less attained and now you can move on to other things.

By the 18th the planetary power will have shifted to the upper half of the Horoscope. Family is still important (and will be important for years to come) but now it is time to focus on the outer life – on the career and outer objectives. You are in the summer time of your year and the Sun has risen. It is time to be up and about and focusing on the activities of the day. Night is over. Pursue your goals by objective, outer methods. If you have used the night-time of your year properly, the actions you take now will be natural and powerful. They will be like arrows winging their way directly to the target.

Jupiter makes his annual move this month, from Cancer into Leo – from your 7th house to your 8th. Your spouse, partner or current love seems well fixed this year. He or she is in a prosperity period and on the 23rd, he or she enters a yearly financial peak as well. The year, and month, ahead is more sexually active. This is a period for dealing with estate and tax issues. If you have insurance claims there is good fortune after the 17th, and especially after the 23rd.

Much of the stress in the career vanishes after the 18th. It seems less hectic and conflict is reduced. Your good work ethic boosts the career until the 18th – superiors take notice. After then the career is enhanced by social means, by attending or perhaps hosting the right kind of parties. Your spouse, partner or current love is supportive of the career, friends in general too.

August

Best Days Overall: 8, 16, 17, 25, 26, 27
Most Stressful Days Overall: 1, 2, 13, 14, 20, 21, 22, 28, 29
Best Days for Love: 3, 4, 5, 6, 12, 13, 14, 20, 21, 22, 23, 24, 25
Best Days for Money: 5, 6, 9, 10, 13, 14, 23, 24
Best Days for Career: 1, 2, 3, 4, 12, 13, 23, 24, 28, 29

Pluto, the planet of transformation and personal reinvention, has been in your sign for many years now, so many of you are involved in these kinds of projects. You are in the midst of giving birth to yourself – to your own ideal of self. These things don't happen overnight but tend to be long term, multi-year (and sometimes multi-lifetime) processes. With your 8th house of transformation unusually strong this month, these projects are ever more interesting – and very successful. There is great progress happening. Some of you are transforming yourselves through mechanical means – plastic surgery, eye tucks, stomach tucks and the like. Others are doing this through meditation and diet – the spiritual methods.

With the 8th house strong, detoxification regimes of all sorts are powerful, especially until the 15th. This is a good month for liver and kidney detoxes specifically. The aspect is not only good for physical detoxifications but for mental and emotional detoxes as well.

Health is good this month, and you can enhance it further in the ways mentioned above, but also by giving more attention to the heart and chest until the 15th (chest massage is good) and to the small intestine afterwards.

Uranus, your financial planet, went retrograde on the 22nd of last month, and will remain so for many more months. This won't stop earnings but it will slow things down a bit. Perhaps you should be slower and more methodical about your finances now. You won't be able to stop your financial life for all of the Uranus retrograde, but you can aim to be more careful in your financial dealings, investments and purchases. 'Dot the i's and cross the t's' – pay attention to detail. Avoid financial short cuts. In other words, be your true Capricorn self in financial matters. The Sun's trine aspect to Uranus from the 7th to the 10th looks like this could be a nice pay period. Debts are easily paid or made. There is credit available if you need it. Venus's conjunction with Jupiter from the 17th to the 19th brings luck in speculations. Children or children figures in your life seem more prosperous that period.

Take a nice easy schedule on the 1st and 2nd and from the 10th to the 14th. The Sun and Mars transit eclipse points. Your spouse, partner or current love prospers this month (and in the year ahead) but he or she can have some financial drama on the 1st and 2nd.

Your dreams and intuition need to be verified more acting on them from the 24th to the 31st. The message can be accurate but your take on it could be amiss.

Love is more or less stable this month, and is not such a big issue as it was over the past two months. I read this as contentment in love. There's no need to make major changes or moves.

September

Best Days Overall: 4, 5, 12, 13, 22, 23
Most Stressful Days Overall: 10, 11, 17, 18, 24, 25
Best Days for Love: 2, 3, 4, 5, 12, 13, 17, 18, 23, 24
Best Days for Money: 1, 2, 3, 6, 7, 10, 11, 19, 20, 29, 30
Best Days for Career: 2, 3, 12, 13, 23, 24, 25

The planetary power shifts this month and the Eastern, independent sector of the Horoscope becomes dominant. You will start to feel this from the 23rd onwards and it becomes more pronounced towards the end of the month – on the 30th. You are entering another cycle of personal independence. The planetary power moves towards you rather than away from you. There's nothing wrong with relationships or with pleasing others, but now the Cosmos calls you to develop your personal skills and personal initiative. It's about learning to stand on your own two feet and accepting personal responsibility for your happiness. By now, after almost six months of Western sector dominance, you more or less know what conditions are comfortable or uncomfortable. You are entering a period where it is easier to make any necessary changes.

Your 9th house is very powerful this month, until the 23rd. Thus foreign lands call to you. Travel opportunities will come and you might want to take them. This is a wonderful period for students and they have success in their studies. It is also a good month to pursue your religious and philosophical interests.

The main headline this month is the career. Sixty per cent (and sometimes 70 per cent) of the planets are above the horizon, and your career house becomes very powerful on the 23rd. You enter a yearly career peak. A highly successful period. Home and family issues can safely be de-emphasized. A willingness to travel and to mentor others enhances the career. You are a disciple to those above you and a mentor to those below you. Your good work ethic also helps – it is noted by your superiors.

Health becomes more delicate after the 23rd. As always, make sure you get enough rest. Your health planet Mercury moves speedily this month but spends the bulk of September in Libra, your 10th house (from the 2nd to the 28th). Aside from the ways mentioned in the yearly report, your health can be enhanced by giving more attention to the kidneys and hips. A kidney detox might be a good idea. Regular hip massage is also good. The good news here is that the health planet in the 10th house shows you are focused here. Good health is high on your priorities and you're paying attention. Love problems can impact on the physical health during this period. So if, God forbid, problems arise, restore the harmony here as quickly as you can.

Finances are a mixed picture this month. On the one hand, Jupiter makes fabulous aspects to your financial planet all month (and especially from the 23rd to the 30th), but the short-term planets are stressing Uranus from the 23rd onwards. I read this as prosperity, but that you need to work harder for it. Not such a smooth ride.

October

Best Days Overall: 1, 2, 9, 10, 19, 20, 28, 29
Most Stressful Days Overall: 7, 8, 14, 15, 21, 22, 23
Best Days for Love: 3, 4, 12, 13, 14, 15, 22, 23
Best Days for Money: 3, 4, 7, 8, 16, 17, 18, 26, 27, 31
Best Days for Career: 3, 12, 13, 21, 22, 23

There are two main headlines this month. The first is your yearly career peak, which is still in full swing until the 23rd. This is a successful month in the worldly sense. The other headline is the eclipses that happen this month. One in particular, the Lunar Eclipse of the 8th, affects you very strongly.

It will be good to reduce your schedule until the 23rd anyway as this is one of your vulnerable health periods – but especially around the eclipse period. Avoid risky, stressful kinds of activities. If you can, re-schedule them for another time. This eclipse occurs in your 4th house of home and family and impacts on both Uranus and Pluto (more directly on Uranus; with Pluto it is a 'sideswipe'). This indicates family dramas, perhaps repairs in the home. It shows dramas with parents or parent figures. The eclipsed planet, the Moon, generically rules these areas so these are issues now. Family members are more temperamental this period. Since the Moon is your love planet, love is also being tested. This is when the dirty laundry comes out, when long-suppressed issues, irritations and problems start to surface so that they can be dealt with. It doesn't mean a relationship break up – though this sometimes happens – but a testing of love. Love needs testing every now and then.

The impact on Uranus signals dramatic financial changes, usually through a disturbance or crisis. Perhaps you are hit with some unexpected and unforeseen expense. Perhaps (more likely) your financial thinking and planning haven't been realistic. Now you find out about it and are forced to make changes. Ultimately, these changes will be good, but while they are happening it is not that pleasant. The impact on Pluto shows dramas in the lives of friends and the testing of friendship. Good friendships survive, but flawed ones tend to dissolve. Often the problem is not the relationship itself, but dramas that happen in your friends' personal lives test the friendship. All Capricorns are affected, but those of you born between January 4 and January 7 are most affected.

The Solar Eclipse of the 23rd is easier on you but it won't hurt to reduce your schedule anyway. This eclipse occurs in your 11th house of friends and once again tests friendships. Computers and high-tech equipment will get tested as well. Technology is a wonderful thing when it works properly but when glitches arise, oh my, what a nightmare! It might be a good idea to have important files backed up before the eclipse hits. Also make sure that your anti-virus, anti-spam and anti-hacking software is up-to-date and running well. Since the Sun is the ruler of your 8th house, every Solar Eclipse brings encounters (generally psychological encounters) with death. There's no need to tempt the dark angel by doing risky kinds of things. This also shows that your spouse, partner or current love is making dramatic financial changes.

November

Best Days Overall: 6, 7, 15, 16, 17, 25, 26
Most Stressful Days Overall: 4, 5, 10, 11, 18, 19
Best Days for Love: 2, 3, 10, 11, 12, 21, 22, 23
Best Days for Money: 4, 5, 13, 14, 22, 23, 27, 28
Best Days for Career: 2, 3, 11, 12, 18, 19, 22, 23

Though technically the Lunar and Solar Eclipses happened last month, you (and the world at large) will be feeling some 'after shocks' in the month ahead. This is because some of the planets are re-activating these eclipse points.

Uranus is basically camping out on an eclipse point all month (and this will be the case for the rest of the year). So the finances are undergoing dramatic change. There is instability here. Nevertheless, prosperity is still intact (especially from the 22nd onwards); there are just many bumps and surprises along the road. Expect the unexpected. You have to be nimble and alert here. (Computers and high-tech equipment can also be temperamental these days.)

Mars re-activates an eclipse point from the 14th to the 17th, which brings dramas in the family and home with family members, parents and parent figures. Be more careful driving that period too. The planet has been 'out of bounds' since September 30 and is still 'out of bounds' until the 21st. Family members are moving outside their usual borders these days, perhaps into forbidden territory. Solutions to family problems lie 'outside the box'.

Mercury re-activates an eclipse point from the 8th to the 10th. Avoid needless foreign travel during that period. This transit can bring disturbances or dramas at the workplace and changes in the health regime as well.

Health is much improved this month. Mercury moves speedily this month, but spends the bulk of it in Scorpio, from the 8th to the 28th. Detox regimes are powerful (especially from the 17th to the 19th). Safe sex and sexual moderation become important. Before the 8th, enhance the health through hip massage and by giving more attention to the kidneys. After the 28th, spiritual healing techniques will be powerful.

Love remains more or less stable this month. Those who are married will most likely stay married and current relationships seem intact; singles will most likely stay single. The social magnetism will be strongest from the 1st to the 6th and from the 22nd onwards, as the Moon waxes.

Drive more carefully and be more patient with family members from the 8th to the 14th. Family members too need to avoid risky activities then.

December

Best Days Overall: 3, 4, 13, 14, 22, 23, 30, 31
Most Stressful Days Overall: 1, 2, 8, 9, 15, 16, 28, 29
Best Days for Love: 1, 2, 8, 9, 10, 11, 12, 13, 20, 21, 22, 30, 31
Best Days for Money: 1, 2, 10, 11, 20, 21, 24, 25, 28, 29
Best Days for Career: 1, 2, 12, 13, 15, 16, 21, 22, 30, 31

December will be basically a happy month, but big changes are afoot under the surface.

Saturn, the ruler of your Horoscope, makes a major (once in every two and a half years) move from Scorpio into Sagittarius – from your 11th house to your 12th. He will be there for the next two and a half years. This signals that spirituality is going to become a major focus in the coming years. Your 12th house of spirituality became powerful towards the end of last month and is still powerful until the 22nd of this month. So you are in a strong spiritual period and will be experiencing all kinds of spiritual phenomena these days (and this will continue for some years). The dream life is more active and prophetic than usual, and there are more unexplained coincidences happening. Those on a spiritual path are having breakthroughs and enjoying success in this area. Those of you not on the path are very likely to enter it in the coming years.

Capricorns are very down-to-earth people. They are natural 'empiricists': if I can see it, feel it, touch it or measure it, it exists. If not, it doesn't exist. The spiritual attitude and approach is diametrically opposite to this. Here the attitude is that the empirical world is only a fraction of what reality is and is fundamentally an illusion. Capricorns will generally attain their ends in the normal material ways. The spiritual approach is to work in the invisible world and 'allow' phenomena to happen. So Capricorns have to make more adjustments than most when embarking on a spiritual path. The methods are alien to them. Once they set their minds to it though, they tend to be successful. There were many great gurus who were Capricorns.

Health is good this month, especially after the 22nd. Many planets are in or moving through your sign. The cosmic power is moving towards you, supporting you. You look good. You have more self-confidence and self-esteem. You have charisma. You get your way in life. Health can be enhanced even further by giving more attention the liver and thighs (until the 17th) and to the spine, knees, teeth, bones, skin and overall skeletal alignment (always important to you) afterwards.

Uranus is still camping out on an eclipse point this month, so many financial changes are happening and there is much instability here. Earnings seem stronger (and come more easily) up to the 22nd. After that, more effort – a lot more effort – is needed to attain your financial goals. Uranus goes retrograde on the 21st, so try to do your holiday shopping before then. Financial confidence is not what it should be and this can be a blessing in disguise. It forces you to do more homework, get more facts, and to attain mental clarity. Earnings temporarily slow down from the 22nd onwards.

On the 22nd you enter a yearly personal pleasure peak. This is a time to enjoy all the pleasures of the senses, a time to pamper the body and give it what it needs. It's a time to get the body and image into the shape you want.

Aquarius

~~~

THE WATER-BEARER

Birthdays from
20th January to
18th February

Personality Profile

AQUARIUS AT A GLANCE

Element – Air

Ruling Planet – Uranus
  Career Planet – Pluto
  Love Planet – The Sun
  Money Planet – Neptune
  Planet of Health and Work – Moon
  Planet of Home and Family Life – Venus
  Planet of Spirituality – Saturn

Colours – electric blue, grey, ultramarine blue

Colours that promote love, romance and social harmony – gold, orange

Colour that promotes earning power – aqua

Gems – black pearl, obsidian, opal, sapphire

Metal – lead

Scents – azalea, gardenia

Quality – fixed (= stability)

Qualities most needed for balance – warmth, feeling and emotion

Strongest virtues – great intellectual power, the ability to communicate and to form and understand abstract concepts, love for the new and avant-garde

Deepest needs – to know and to bring in the new

Characteristics to avoid – coldness, rebelliousness for its own sake, fixed ideas

Signs of greatest overall compatibility – Gemini, Libra

Signs of greatest overall incompatibility – Taurus, Leo, Scorpio

Sign most helpful to career – Scorpio

Sign most helpful for emotional support – Taurus

Sign most helpful financially – Pisces

Sign best for marriage and/or partnerships – Leo

Sign most helpful for creative projects – Gemini

Best Sign to have fun with – Gemini

Signs most helpful in spiritual matters – Libra, Capricorn

Best day of the week – Saturday

Understanding an Aquarius

In the Aquarius-born, intellectual faculties are perhaps the most highly developed of any sign in the zodiac. Aquarians are clear, scientific thinkers. They have the ability to think abstractly and to formulate laws, theories and clear concepts from masses of observed facts. Geminis might be very good at gathering information, but Aquarians take this a step further, excelling at interpreting the information gathered.

Practical people – men and women of the world – mistakenly consider abstract thinking as impractical. It is true that the realm of abstract thought takes us out of the physical world, but the discoveries made in this realm generally end up having tremendous practical consequences. All real scientific inventions and breakthroughs come from this abstract realm.

Aquarians, more so than most, are ideally suited to explore these abstract dimensions. Those who have explored these regions know that there is little feeling or emotion there. In fact, emotions are a hindrance to functioning in these dimensions; thus Aquarians seem – at times – cold and emotionless to others. It is not that Aquarians haven't got feelings and deep emotions, it is just that too much feeling clouds their ability to think and invent. The concept of 'too much feeling' cannot be tolerated or even understood by some of the other signs. Nevertheless, this Aquarian objectivity is ideal for science, communication and friendship.

Aquarians are very friendly people, but they do not make a big show about it. They do the right thing by their friends, even if sometimes they do it without passion or excitement.

Aquarians have a deep passion for clear thinking. Second in importance, but related, is their passion for breaking with the establishment and traditional authority. Aquarians delight in this, because for them rebellion is like a great game or challenge. Very often they will rebel strictly for the fun of rebelling, regardless of whether the authority they defy is right or wrong. Right or wrong has little to do with the rebellious actions of an Aquarian, because to a true Aquarian authority and power must be challenged as a matter of principle.

Where Capricorn or Taurus will err on the side of tradition and the status quo, an Aquarian will err on the side of the new. Without this virtue it is doubtful whether any progress would be made in the world. The conservative-minded would obstruct progress. Originality and invention imply an ability to break barriers; every new discovery represents the toppling of an impediment to thought. Aquarians are very interested in breaking barriers and making walls tumble – scientifically, socially and politically. Other zodiac signs, such as Capricorn, also have scientific talents. But Aquarians are particularly excellent in the social sciences and humanities.

Finance

In financial matters Aquarians tend to be idealistic and humanitarian – to the point of self-sacrifice. They are usually generous contributors to social and political causes. When they contribute it differs from when a Capricorn or Taurus contributes. A Capricorn or Taurus may expect some favour or return for a gift; an Aquarian contributes selflessly.

Aquarians tend to be as cool and rational about money as they are about most things in life. Money is something they need and they set about acquiring it scientifically. No need for fuss; they get on with it in the most rational and scientific ways available.

Money to the Aquarian is especially nice for what it can do, not for the status it may bring (as is the case for other signs). Aquarians are neither big spenders nor penny-pinchers and use their finances in practical ways, for example to facilitate progress for themselves, their families, or even for strangers.

However, if Aquarians want to reach their fullest financial potential they will have to explore their intuitive nature. If they follow only their financial theories – or what they believe to be theoretically correct – they may suffer some losses and disappointments. Instead, Aquarians should call on their intuition, which knows without thinking. For Aquarians, intuition is the short-cut to financial success.

Career and Public Image

Aquarians like to be perceived not only as the breakers of barriers but also as the transformers of society and the world. They long to be seen in this light and to play this role. They also look up to and respect other people in this position and even expect their superiors to act this way.

Aquarians prefer jobs that have a bit of idealism attached to them – careers with a philosophical basis. Aquarians need to be creative at work, to have access to new techniques and methods. They like to keep busy and enjoy getting down to business straightaway, without wasting any time. They are often the quickest workers and usually have suggestions for improvements that will benefit their employers. Aquarians are also very helpful with their co-workers and welcome responsibility, preferring this to having to take orders from others.

If Aquarians want to reach their highest career goals they have to develop more emotional sensitivity, depth of feeling and passion. They need to learn to narrow their focus on the essentials and concentrate more on the job in hand. Aquarians need 'a fire in the belly' – a consuming passion and desire – in order to rise to the very top. Once this passion exists they will succeed easily in whatever they attempt.

Love and Relationships

Aquarians are good at friendships, but a bit weak when it comes to love. Of course they fall in love, but their lovers always get the impression that they are more best friends than paramours.

Like Capricorns, they are cool customers. They are not prone to displays of passion or to outward demonstrations of their affections. In fact, they feel uncomfortable when their other half hugs and touches them too much. This does not mean that they do not love their partners. They do, only they show it in other ways. Curiously enough, in relationships they tend to attract the very things that they feel uncomfortable with. They seem to attract hot, passionate, romantic, demonstrative people. Perhaps they know instinctively that these people have qualities they lack and so seek them out. In any event, these relationships do seem to work, Aquarian coolness calming the more passionate partner while the fires of passion warm the cold-blooded Aquarius.

The qualities Aquarians need to develop in their love life are warmth, generosity, passion and fun. Aquarians love relationships of the mind. Here they excel. If the intellectual factor is missing in a relationship an Aquarian will soon become bored or feel unfulfilled.

Home and Domestic Life

In family and domestic matters Aquarians can have a tendency to be too non-conformist, changeable and unstable. They are as willing to break the barriers of family constraints as they are those of other areas of life.

Even so, Aquarians are very sociable people. They like to have a nice home where they can entertain family and friends. Their house is usually decorated in a modern style and full of state-of-the-art appliances and gadgets – an environment Aquarians find absolutely necessary.

If their home life is to be healthy and fulfilling Aquarians need to inject it with a quality of stability – yes, even some conservatism. They need at least one area of life to be enduring and steady; this area is usually their home and family life.

Venus, the planet of love, rules the Aquarian's 4th solar house of home and family as well, which means that when it comes to the family and child-rearing, theories, cool thinking and intellect are not always enough. Aquarians need to bring love into the equation in order to have a great domestic life.

Horoscope for 2014

Major Trends

Saturn has been in your 10th house of career since October 2012 and will be there for almost all the year ahead (he leaves on December 24). This is challenging for the career, but if handled properly will bring lasting success. More details on this later.

When Jupiter entered Cancer in June 2013 you entered a prosperity cycle which continues well into the year ahead. Many of you landed good jobs – dream jobs – and this can still happen under this aspect in the year ahead.

Neptune has been in your money house since February 2012 and will be there for many years to come. Your financial intuition is superb these days. You are going deeper into the spiritual dimensions of wealth – the very essence and source of it. This is a long-term trend that will continue for many years to come. More on this later.

On July 16 Jupiter will enter your 7th house of love, marriage and social activities. This will initiate a happy and expanded love life which should continue well into next year. Love is in the air and you're being prepared for it. Again, there is more on this later.

Health is basically good this year. However, after July 16 you will have two long-term planets in stressful alignment with you so it will need more watching. See later for more details.

Uranus, your ruling planet, is involved in a long-term Grand Square until July 26, which is highly unusual. You are involved in a large project or undertaking – very large. You seem personally involved here; it's something that you are doing for yourself.

Your areas of greatest interest this year are finance; communication and intellectual interests; health and work (until July 16); love and romance (after July 16); career; and spirituality.

Your paths of greatest fulfilment this year are health and work (until July 16); love and romance (after July 16); career (until February 19); and religion, philosophy, higher education and foreign travel (after February 19).

Health

(Please note that this is an astrological perspective on health and not a medical one. In days of yore there was no difference, both of these perspectives were identical. But in these times there could be quite a difference. For a medical perspective, please consult your doctor or health practitioner.)

Health and energy become more complicated later on in the year, after July 16. But overall, your health looks good. Your 6th house of health is strong until July, and this shows that you're paying attention to this area. The extra focus on health during the first half of the year will serve you well later on.

As regular readers know, there is much you can do to enhance your health and prevent problems from developing. This year give more attention to the following areas (using the reflex points shown in the chart): the heart (all year but especially after July 16). Avoid worry and anxiety, the states that are the spiritual root causes of heart problems. Things can be handled without worry with a little bit of practice. Worry is merely a mental habit we have fallen into. The world considers it 'normal', but spiritually it is considered pathology.

Also pay attention to the ankles and calves. These are always important for you. Massage them regularly and give the ankles more support when exercising. The stomach and breasts are also always important. Right diet is a health issue for you in general, and how you eat is perhaps as important as what you eat. Take meals in a calm, relaxed way. Give thanks for your food and elevate the energy vibration of eating to a higher level. This will raise the energy vibrations of the food and also your own vibration. Food should digest better.

The liver and thighs are another important area until July 16. Massage the thighs regularly. A herbal liver cleanse would be a good idea this year. Parsley and beets are good for cleaning the liver, but there are other methods too.

Maintaining healthy emotional states – peaceful, joyous feelings – is always important for you healthwise, and this year is no different. This is easier said than done, but with practice – especially if you meditate – you can get better and better at it. Emotional discord is the first symptom of a physical health problem (in your case). Be aware of what is happening in your feelings and if they are not right bring them into harmony as quickly as possible.

Good family relations and general domestic harmony are also always important for you. Problems here can impact, rather quickly, on the physical health. If problems arise, strive to bring things into harmony as quickly as possible.

With the Moon as your health planet, health problems often come from the 'memory body', from past records that have been re-stimulated. Though I'm not generally a fan of past-life regression, if your health is affected, it might be a good idea.

The Moon is the fastest moving of all the planets. In any given month she will move through every sign and house of your Horoscope.

She will wax and wane, and will receive and give positive and negative aspects. Thus there are many short-term health trends (in your Horoscope these trends fluctuate almost daily) and these are best discussed in the monthly reports.

Favourable numbers for health are 2, 4, 7 and 9.

Home and Family

Your 4th house of home and family is not a house of power this year. It is basically empty and only short-term planets will move through there – and for very brief periods. This shows a stable kind of year. I read this as a good thing. You seem basically satisfied with the present arrangement and have no need to make major changes. You can if you like, the Cosmos gives you free will, but the need isn't there. Moves or renovations most likely happened in 2011 and 2012. Now things seem quiet.

A Solar Eclipse on April 29 occurs in your 4th house and this will shake things up a bit. If there are flaws in the home or in family rela-

Reflexology

Try to massage the whole foot on a regular basis, but pay extra attention to the points highlighted on the chart. When you massage, be aware of 'sore spots', as these need special attention. It's also a good idea to massage the ankles and the top of the feet.

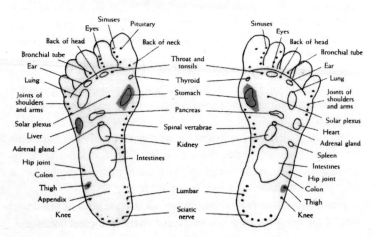

tionships the eclipse will reveal them so that they can be corrected. Probably though, this eclipse will not bring long-term family changes, just short-term drama and excitement. There are no other planetary powers supporting it.

Venus is your family planet. She moves very quickly and during the year she will move through your entire chart. Thus there are many short-term trends at home that will depend on where Venus is at a given time and the kinds of aspects she receives. These are best dealt with in the monthly reports.

Venus will be retrograde throughout January. This, therefore, will not be a time for making important decisions about the home and family. Instead it will be a time for fact gathering, reviewing information and attaining mental clarity. Once this is attained (and it will be) you will be in a position to make good decisions when Venus starts moving forward on February 1.

The marriage of a parent or parent figure (and business partnerships too) are being severely tested this year. This was the case last year too. These can survive but only with a lot of work and commitment. A parent or parent figure is likely to move after July 16. This seems a happy move. Sometimes it is not an actual move in the literal sense but the effect is the same. Sometimes the individual buys a second home or renovates and expands the present one. The health of a parent or parent figure will be helped by exploring alternative therapies.

Siblings and sibling figures in your life are restless and rebellious. A move is likely this year. (It could have happened last year too.) Marriage is not advisable for them, as they are too much into personal freedom these days.

Children and children figures in your life seem very prosperous these days, but on the home front, the year is a stable one. Their love relationships will get tested next year. They are making very dramatic changes to the health regime.

Finance and Career

You money house has been powerful for some years now and will be powerful for many more years to come. There is a great focus on finance and this focus is 90 per cent of success. I consider interest and focus more important than mere 'easy aspects'. The interest is the drive – the urge – and when this is present, people will prosper even in the midst of adversity. They are willing to confront and deal with all the challenges that arise.

Last year you had the best of both worlds. You had the drive AND the easy aspects. So prosperity is happening. This is the case until July 16 this year too. You are spending more, for sure, but also earning a lot more.

Neptune, the most spiritual of the planets, is your financial planet. So the spiritual dimensions of wealth have always been important to you. But now, ever since Neptune moved into his own sign of Pisces in February 2012, this interest is intensified. And you are probably getting good results with spiritual methods of finance: meditation, visualization, charitable giving and accessing the supernatural (rather than the natural) sources of supply. Your financial intuition is always good – Neptune is the planet of intuition – but this year it will be superb. Saturn, your spiritual planet, has been making nice aspects to Neptune since October 2012.

In finance you most definitely march to a different tune. But it works. Friends and colleagues are most likely astounded. You don't do the 'normal' kinds of things. Yet, you prosper. Intuition will achieve more in one moment than many years of standard, intensive labour and planning.

On a mundane level, Neptune rules oil, gas and water utilities, shipping, ship builders, fishing and all industries that involve water. He also rules for-profit hospitals, nursing homes, hospices, anaesthetics, pain killers and mood-enhancing drugs. These industries are interesting as investments, businesses or jobs. People in these industries are likely to be important in your financial life.

Jupiter has been in your 6th house of health and work since June last year, and will remain there until July. This shows happy – and lucrative – job opportunities. Many of you landed good jobs last year, but if not, it can still happen in the year ahead. Those of you who employ others are expanding your workforce.

Friends and social connections seem important on the financial level too. They seem very supportive.

Aquarians are natural computer and online people. They take to it like a fish to water. These skills are important financially too, regardless of the actual business or job that you do. Online businesses and activities are profitable these days.

Saturn has been in your 10th house of career since October 2012. This makes the career more challenging. Sometimes this transit shows a demanding or overbearing boss. It indicates that one advances career-wise through merit and sheer performance, not because of social connections or family pull. Social connections can open doors for you, but in the end, you have to perform. Merit will prevail, especially this year.

Saturn is your spiritual planet and he is involved in your career. Neptune, the generic spiritual planet, rules your finances. So, the spiritual dimension is important in the career as well as in finance. If you are involved in a worldly type of career, get more involved in charities and causes you believe in. Volunteer your time. Donate. This will enhance the outer career in very subtle ways.

Favourable financial numbers are 1, 12 and 18.

Love and Social Life

The year starts off slowly in this department. No disasters, but nothing special on the positive side either. The love life is stable. This is basically a preparation period. On July 16, Jupiter will enter your 7th house of love and romance and stays there for the rest of the year. The fun begins. Jupiter will not only be in your 7th house but he will be making very beautiful aspects to Uranus, the ruler of your Horoscope. So love is in the air. Marriages or relationships that are 'like' marriage are happening. If you are already married, your relationship becomes more romantic, more honeymoonish.

Jupiter is your planet of friends. His move into your 7th house gives us many messages. It shows that romance can happen through friends – friends are playing Cupid. Sometimes it shows than an existing friendship starts to become more than that. Sometimes it shows online virtual meetings or love relationships that are conducted online or through skyping or texting.

Romantic opportunities come to you through involvement with groups, group activities or organizations (one of your favourite activities anyway). The message I get here is that you need to just be yourself, do the things that you love to do, follow your passion, and romance will just happen with very little planning or manipulation on your part.

Jupiter in your 7th house also shows your needs in love – your love attitudes. In this case, Jupiter is reinforcing your native attitudes. You want friendship in love. You want romance, but you also want to be friends with the beloved. You want to feel that you and the beloved are 'team mates' as well as lovers – a relationship of peers and equals.

You are always innovative and experimental in all things, not just love. And now you meet someone who is also innovative and experimental. You will probably be doing all kinds of unconventional things as a couple.

Jupiter involved in your love life shows that you are attracted to foreigners, highly educated types and perhaps even religious types. You are attracted to refined kinds of people, people you can learn from. A foreign trip will bolster romance; it will bolster an existing relationship or lead to a new one.

Serious romance is in the air whether you are working towards your first, third or fourth marriage. Those in or working towards their second marriage are having their relationships tested until July 26. Marriage is more 'iffy' here. It can happen, but there is nothing special supporting it. However there will be dating, parties and new friends coming into the picture. The social life will be active and happy.

Your love planet is the Sun. He is a fast moving planet and during the year he will visit every sign and house of your Horoscope. So there are many, many short-term trends in love, depending on where the Sun happens to be and the aspects he receives. These are best dealt with in the monthly reports.

Favourable numbers for love are 5, 6, 8 and 19.

Self-improvement

Your intuition is being trained in two ways this year, in finance and the career. The two spiritual planets of your chart are involved in both these areas.

When intuition – guidance from on high – is involved in anything, all the facts and rules of the material plane don't matter. Intuition will often guide you in ways that counter the so-called facts or existing conditions. You will not do anything dishonourable or hurtful but will ignore 'market conditions', the unemployment situation, share prices and 'conventional wisdom'. This is the hard part. It takes faith to follow intuition. Often we have to go against the 'appearance' of things and often against our own material assessment of a situation. You receive an intuition and a big part of you is screaming in protest. It's impossible. It can't be. Yet, time and events will show that your intuition was correct – and, in hindsight, eminently logical.

Most people look askance at idealism in worldly, practical matters. Idealism is respected, but 'it doesn't pay'. In your case this is not so. With you the 'ideal' is the practical way to go. This is not a time for compromising on these things.

Saturn in the 10th house of career shows that you are taking on more career responsibilities. More burdens. Generally we shy away from new burdens or responsibilities and try to avoid them. But this is not a time for this. Accept them (the ones that are legitimate) and carry them. As you do you find that you grow as a person and in your career. You will find that you can do more than you thought you could. You get 'stretched' as a person. This is part of the Divine Agenda happening in the career. If career matters get overwhelming at times (and this is likely these days), surrender everything to the Divine and let it handle things. If you do this sincerely, from the heart, with no reservation, you will achieve peace and the career problems will straighten themselves out in magical and beautiful ways. This applies to financial matters too. Invite the Higher Power into the situation and allow it to operate the way it wants without interference. Things will straighten right out.

Month-by-month Forecasts

January

Best Days Overall: 3, 4, 12, 13, 22, 23, 30, 31
Most Stressful Days Overall: 9, 10, 17, 18, 24, 25
Best Days for Love: 1, 2, 9, 10, 17, 18, 19, 20, 28, 29
Best Days for Money: 5, 6, 14, 15, 24, 25
Best Days for Career: 1, 2, 9, 10, 19, 20, 24, 25, 28, 29

You begin your year with the planetary power in its maximum Eastern position. This will be the case next month too. You are in your period of maximum personal independence. You have the power to change conditions to your liking and to design your life according to your personal specifications. With the planetary momentum mostly forward this month you should see fast progress to your goals. You are in a cycle where you are less in need of other people. Personal initiative matters. Who you are and what you can do are more important than who you know. People skills are always good, but your personal skills are more important now.

The planets make an important shift from the upper half to the lower half of the Horoscope this month, on the 20th. The outer career is becoming less of a focus. You are ending a yearly career push. Now it is time to build up the inner forces needed for the next career push which will begin in about six months' time. It will be good to focus on the home, family and your emotional well-being from the 20th onwards. Your family planet, Venus, is retrograde all month, so you can focus on the family but need not make important decisions or changes. Be there for your family, cement family relationships and alliances, but avoid major decisions.

This is basically a happy month. On the 20th you enter one of your yearly personal pleasure peaks. This is where you give the body (your most loyal servant) its due. You take care of it and get it into right shape.

Love is excellent this month. Love is pursuing you and will find you after the 20th. There's nothing much you need to do. With both the ruler of your 7th house of love and romance and the ruler of your 5th house of fun and creativity in your own sign, singles have the option of either serious love or just fun-and-games love. Both are there if you want it. You are having love on your terms from the 20th onwards. A current love is very devoted to you and puts your interests ahead of his or her own. Happy social opportunities come to you as well.

Once your birthday happens, you are in a great cycle for starting new projects or releasing new products into the world. The 30th and 31st are exceptionally good starting periods.

Health is excellent right now. Most of the planets are either in harmonious aspect to you or leaving you alone. You have plenty of energy – especially after the 20th – to achieve anything you desire. Health regimes (and health in general) go better from the 1st to the 16th and on the 30th and 31st.

Finances are reasonable this month. There are no disasters but equally no especially great things happening either. It's a kind of status quo financial month.

February

Best Days Overall: 8, 9, 18, 19, 26, 27
Most Stressful Days Overall: 5, 6, 7, 13, 14, 20, 21
Best Days for Love: 5, 6, 7, 8, 9, 13, 14, 16, 17, 20, 24, 25, 28
Best Days for Money: 1, 2, 10, 11, 12, 20, 21, 28
Best Days for Career: 5, 6, 7, 15, 16, 20, 21, 24, 25

This is another happy, prosperous month. You are still in the midst of a yearly personal pleasure peak, until the 18th, although personal pleasures – the delights of the five senses – will be strong even after then. The ruler of your 5th house of fun will be in your sign from the 13th onwards.

On the 18th, as the Sun enters your 2nd money house, you begin a yearly financial peak. Prosperity has been strong for some months, and although last month was a little slow on the financial front, much financial progress is happening now. The 22nd to the 24th seem especially prosperous as the Sun travels with your financial planet Neptune, indicating the financial favour of your spouse, partner or current love and of friends in general. Social contacts are important financially from the 18th onwards, and especially those days. A business partnership or joint venture is likely. Friends are prospering too and seem supportive; you have their financial favour. The financial intuition is firing on all cylinders. Pay attention to dreams and spiritual messages from psychics, astrologers, spiritual channels and ministers – there is important financial information to be found there.

Until the 18th singles need not do much to attract love. Love is seeking them out. All they have to do is go about their normal routine and it will happen. After the 18th love and romantic opportunities come as you pursue your financial goals or with people involved in the finances. The money people in your life (and in general) are very alluring then. Love is expressed in physical, material ways – through financial support or material gifts. This is how you feel loved and this is how you show it.

However, there is a strong spiritual component to love as well and this complicates things. Money is important, but you want someone on your spiritual wavelength as well, someone who supports your spiritual practice and agrees with your ideals. A poet who is also a millionaire would fit the bill, but these kinds of people are not so easy to find!

Mercury goes retrograde on the 6th, so avoid speculation then. Children or children figures lack direction in life and the spouse, partner or current love needs to review his or her financial life. Important financial decisions should be made before the 6th or postponed to next month, when Mercury starts to move forward again.

Health is basically good. You can enhance it further in the ways mentioned in the yearly report. Health and energy should be better from the 1st to the 14th as the Moon waxes. Job seekers have better luck that period too.

March

Best Days Overall: 7, 8, 17, 18, 26, 27
Most Stressful Days Overall: 5, 6, 12, 13, 19, 20
Best Days for Love: 1, 2, 7, 10, 11, 12, 13, 17, 18, 21, 22, 26, 27, 30, 31
Best Days for Money: 1, 2, 10, 11, 19, 20, 28, 29
Best Days for Career: 5, 6, 15, 16, 19, 20, 24, 25

The planetary power below the horizon becomes even stronger, as Venus moves from the upper to the lower half of your Horoscope on the 6th. Keep in mind our previous discussions of this. Career is important, but your point of emotional harmony is even more important. Right state is more important than outer success. Right state will lead to outer success, but not the other way around.

Venus moving into your sign on the 6th is a positive sign for love. You look good. You have a great sense of style and there is more grace to the personality and physical image now. It would be better to shop for clothing and personal accessories after the 6th than before, as your choices will be good.

This transit shows foreign travel and happy educational opportunities. There's nothing much you need to do; the opportunities will find you.

Prosperity is still strong this month as you are still in the midst of a yearly financial peak until the 20th. You have a lot of financial support from friends, from the beloved and from the spiritual people in your life. The financial intuition is still very good.

Mercury travels with the financial planet from the 21st to the 23rd. This shows luck in speculations and important financial ideas and information coming to you. Children and children figures in your life are supportive or provide ideas and inspiration.

The love planet remains in your money house until the 20th, so review our discussion of this last month. It then moves into your 3rd house of communication, signalling a shift in the love needs and in the venues of love. Now good communication is important in love. Mental sex is just as important as physical sex and good conversation could be considered an important part of foreplay. You are attracted to people who are easy to talk to. You are attracted to intellectual-type people – writers, journalists and teachers. Love opportunities occur in the neighbourhood and perhaps with neighbours. Love opportunities also happen in educational settings, at lectures, seminars, workshops, bookshops or the local library. It is always good to learn and to expand the knowledge base, but this month there is the added joy of romantic opportunity.

Health is still good this month. Health and energy should be strongest from the 1st to the 16th and on the 30th and 31st. Job seekers should have better luck during those periods too.

The new Moon of the 30th occurs in your 3rd house but also very close to Uranus, the ruler of your Horoscope. So aside from bringing clarity to educational issues, it will also be a mini personal pleasure peak. It also brings a happy romantic meeting.

April

Best Days Overall: 3, 4, 5, 13, 14, 15, 22, 23
Most Stressful Days Overall: 1, 2, 8, 9, 10, 16, 17, 29, 30
Best Days for Love: 4, 5, 6, 8, 9, 10, 16, 17, 19, 20, 24, 25, 29, 30
Best Days for Money: 6, 7, 16, 17, 24, 25
Best Days for Career: 1, 2, 11, 12, 16, 17, 20, 21, 29, 30

Your 4th house of home and family becomes very powerful from April 20 onwards. This is a period for psychological progress and insight, and a Solar Eclipse in your 4th house on the 29th will accelerate this process. It tends to flush out old traumas and memories of the past so that they can be dealt with.

There are two eclipses this month. The Lunar Eclipse of the 15th is relatively benign. It occurs in your 9th house and thus your religious and philosophical beliefs will be tested as the months go by. Life facts challenge them and often there is a crisis of faith. Sometimes the beliefs are valid and the challenges only show you more nuance. But sometimes the beliefs need modification, and sometimes they need to be thrown out; which is which will become evident in the coming months. Changes in the belief system have a more profound effect than mere psychological changes. The whole life is affected. The interpretation of events gets changed.

Mars is affected by this eclipse, so cars and communication equipment will get tested. Often they will need replacement. It is a good idea to drive more carefully during this period. There will be dramas in the lives of siblings, sibling figures and neighbours. Perhaps there is some major construction work or other sorts of change in your neighbourhood. Lunar Eclipses tend to disturb the workplace and sometimes bring health scares. They also bring changes to the overall health regime and diet.

The Solar Eclipse of the 29th has a much stronger affect on you. A more relaxed schedule is called for from the 20th onwards anyway, but especially during the eclipse period. This eclipse, as we mentioned, occurs in your 4th house and thus affects the home and family. Often there is a need for repairs in the home as hidden flaws get revealed. There are dramas in the lives of family members, and especially in the lives of parents and parent figures. These are life-changing kinds of events. Family members are apt to be more temperamental this period, so be patient. There's no need to make things worse than they need to be. The dream life will be very active then, and often the dreams will be disturbing. But don't put too much stock in them right now. Much of it is just psychic flotsam and jetsam stirred up by the eclipse. Every Solar Eclipse tests love. This doesn't mean that a current love relationship will break up – good ones survive. But much repressed material comes out that needs to be dealt with. Be more patient with the beloved at this time.

Make sure to get plenty of rest from the 20th onwards. Enhance the health in the ways mentioned in the yearly report. Health and energy will tend to be better from the 1st to the 15th.

The Sun travels with Uranus on the 1st and 2nd and this brings happy love opportunities and significant romantic meetings.

Venus travels with Neptune from the 10th to the 13th. This shows a nice payday – personally and for a parent or parent figure. There is good family support those days (better than usual).

May

Best Days Overall: 1, 2, 11, 12, 19, 20, 28, 29
Most Stressful Days Overall: 5, 6, 13, 14, 26, 27
Best Days for Love: 6, 7, 8, 9, 10, 13, 14, 17, 18, 24, 25, 28, 29
Best Days for Money: 3, 4, 5, 13, 14, 21, 22, 31
Best Days for Career: 8, 9, 13, 14, 17, 18, 26, 27

The planetary power shifts this month from the independent Eastern sector to the social Western one. Your period of personal independence is over with (for now), and it will be more difficult to take arbitrary actions to change conditions and to have your own way. Others have to be considered. Your good comes from the good graces of others. You've had time to develop your personal skills and have things your way, now it's time to cultivate the social skills – your people skills. Though you have awesome talent, a lack of 'likeability' will hamper progress these days. Without the ability to get on with others, personal talent is almost meaningless – it can't be put to use.

In any theatrical production the audience sees only a fraction of what is really happening. There is more going on behind the scenes – with the stagehands, director, make-up artists and props manager – than what is actually happening on stage. The 'behind the scenes' activity is what makes the actual show – what is visible – possible. Astrologically speaking you are in the 'behind the scenes' phase of your year. Don't discount this. The stage is being set for your outer career push. Without this interior work, your goals can't be achieved. By focusing your attention and imagery on what you want to achieve, the 'stagehands' receive their directions and things, internally, get set up. Nothing seems to be happening overtly, but important things are occurring.

The planets are now at their maximum low point of the year. Your state of emotional harmony will help the stagehands behind the scenes do their work properly. This should be your main thrust now.

Health needs watching until the 21st. You will see vast improvement in it afterwards, but in the meantime make sure to get enough rest. Enhance the health in the ways discussed in the yearly report. The 12th to the 14th seems a particularly vulnerable period, so be sure to get enough rest on those days.

Love is a bit more delicate this month but will improve after the 21st. Perhaps you or the beloved are bit too moody in love. In a bad mood the relationship seems 'absolutely horrible', with no redeeming features whatsoever. In a good mood, everything is hunky-dory and has always been that way. The truth, of course, is somewhere in between. The other problem in love is that you or the beloved could be living in the past. You could be reacting in the light of past experiences instead of the situation in the here-and-now. Once you see this, the situation will improve.

Singles will find love opportunities close to home, through the family or family connections. Family members are playing Cupid these days.

June

Best Days Overall: 7, 8, 16, 17, 24, 25, 26
Most Stressful Days Overall: 2, 3, 9, 10, 22, 23, 29, 30
Best Days for Love: 2, 3, 5, 6, 7, 8, 14, 15, 16, 17, 23, 24, 27, 28, 29, 30
Best Days for Money: 1, 9, 10, 11, 18, 19, 27, 28
Best Days for Career: 1, 9, 10, 18, 19, 27, 28

Retrograde activity increases this month; 40 per cent of the planets are retrograde after the 9th – the maximum for the year. This should also be considered a time for 'behind the scenes' activity. A preparation period. Without this period the show won't go on. Action in the world is slowing down, so you might as well have fun and enjoy the leisurely pace of life. Last month on the 21st you entered one of your yearly personal pleasure peaks, and this continues until the 21st of the month ahead. This is a time for leisure activities, for exploring the 'rapture' side of life.

Love is much happier this month. It doesn't seem too serious though. It's more about fun and entertainment, especially until the 21st. Love affairs seem as satisfying as serious committed love, and you don't want to get too serious these days. You are attracted to people who can show you a good time. Singles have plenty of these kinds of fun-and-games opportunities. Love opportunities happen in the usual sorts of places, at night spots, places of entertainment, parties, etc.

After the 21st, love attitudes shift. Love is now not just about fun – which is ephemeral – but about practical service to the beloved. This is real love. When someone acts this way towards you, you feel loved. This is the way that you show love too. 'Service,' say the gurus, 'is love in action.' Romantic opportunities happen at the workplace or with co-workers. They also happen as you pursue your health goals or with people involved in your health.

You are in a prosperous year overall, but even in a basically prosperous year there are high periods and low periods. You are coming out of a low period into a higher period. The 27th to the 30th seems a particularly good period with a nice payday, only there could be delays involved. Your financial planet Neptune goes retrograde on the 9th. Prosperity will still happen, but it will be a little slower than usual.

Job seekers have had excellent aspects all year, and on the 21st the aspects get even better. It is doubtful that we will find any unemployed Aquarians these days (unless they choose this state).

Mars is basically opposite Uranus all month, but the aspect is very exact from the 22nd to the 26th. Be more careful driving. Communication equipment and cars can be more temperamental in this period. Be more patient with siblings, sibling figures and neighbours as well. They seem opposed to you and there is some disagreement here.

Venus transits an eclipse point on the 5th and 6th. Avoid gratuitous foreign travel on those days, and be more patient with family members.

Jupiter transits an eclipse point from the 21st to the 26th. Be more patient with friends. High-tech equipment can be more temperamental then too.

July

Best Days Overall: 4, 5, 6, 13, 14, 22, 23
Most Stressful Days Overall: 1, 7, 8, 19, 20, 21, 27, 28
Best Days for Love: 1, 4, 5, 6, 7, 8, 13, 14, 15, 16, 24, 27, 28
Best Days for Money: 7, 8, 15, 16, 17, 24, 25, 27
Best Days for Career: 2, 3, 7, 8, 11, 12, 19, 20, 29, 30

Though your overall health and energy could be better, there are never-theless many happy things going on – many happy changes.

The planets move into their maximum Western position this month. Your 7th house of love becomes powerful on the 22nd and you begin a yearly love and social peak. Jupiter also moves into your 7th house, on the 17th and will remain there for the rest of the year and well into 2015. For many of you this is not a yearly love peak but a lifetime love peak. Love is in the air. It is happening. Marriage could happen this month or in the year ahead. You are in a marrying mood and you meet people who feel the same way. (Sometimes it is not literal marriage that happens, but relationships occur that are 'like' a marriage.)

The symbolism of the Horoscope shows various scenarios in love. Someone who was 'just a friend' now becomes more than that – a romantic interest. Friends play Cupid and introduce you to Mr or Miss Right. You meet Mr or Miss Right at some group activity or organiza-tion, or perhaps online, on a social networking or dating site. Or some-one you worked with in the past or met at work now becomes a romantic interest.

Romantic meetings can happen all month (and all year), but from the 24th to the 27th seems a very likely time. It is good few days for the social life in general, not only romance. It is also an excellent financial period.

Health (as we said) could be better. The good news is that your atten-tion is focused here this month. You are on the case, so health will tend to be good. You are giving it the attention it deserves. Pay particular attention to your health on the 1st, 6th, 7th, 18th, 19th, 24th and 27th. These are the more vulnerable days of the month. Enhance the health in the ways mentioned in the yearly report.

This is still a great month (especially until the 17th) for job seekers.

Uranus starts to go retrograde on the 22nd. This signals that personal goals, goals involving the body, image and personal appear-ance, are under review. Perhaps it is good that personal self-confidence is not as strong as usual – you are on holiday from your self. The focus is on others. Their way is probably better than your way these days.

August

Best Days Overall: 1, 2, 10, 18, 19, 28, 29
Most Stressful Days Overall: 3, 4, 16, 17, 23, 24, 30, 31
Best Days for Love: 3, 4, 5, 6, 12, 13, 14, 23, 24, 25
Best Days for Money: 3, 4, 5, 11, 12, 13, 14, 20, 21, 23, 24, 30, 31
Best Days for Career: 3, 4, 7, 8, 16, 17, 25, 26, 30, 31

Mars crossed your Mid-heaven on the 18th of last month and is now in the 10th house of career for the entire month. Not only that, but the planetary power shifts this month from the lower half to the upper half of the Horoscope. You are ready for your yearly career push. Home and family issues, though important, can be de-emphasized. Now is the time to succeed in the outer world and you will do it by objective, physical methods. If you have allowed the cosmic 'stagehands' to do their work properly over the last few months your actions will be natural, powerful and well choreographed.

Mars in the 10th house indicates that the career is hectic and active. There might be much conflict and competition happening, or at least more than usual. You can enhance the career with good PR, advertising and good use of the media. Siblings and sibling figures seem successful this month and seem helpful to you. As mentioned in the yearly report, it is good to enhance your career and public image through involvement with charities and good causes.

Career is complicated this month, however, due to the wonderful love and social life you're having. It seems to distract you from your career focus. You are still in the midst of a yearly (and sometimes lifetime) love and social peak. Your 7th house of love is even stronger than it was last month, with up to 50 per cent of the planets either camped there or moving through there this month. Half of the Cosmos is conspiring to bring love to you.

A hectic social life and hectic career can be a drain on energy. Thus health needs watching, at least to the 23rd. Be sure to get enough rest, especially on the 2nd, 3rd, 9th, 10th and 14th (and on your most stressful days, as shown above). The problem this month is that you might be ignoring health issues. You have to force yourself to pay attention.

Finance takes a back seat to love and career this month. Neptune, your financial planet, is still retrograde, so earnings can be happening more slowly. Lack of focus is also an issue. You might not be paying enough attention here. You are in a period of financial review, so see where improvements can be made. Get as much information as you can. Make plans. When Neptune moves forward you will be able to implement these plans.

The retrograde of your financial planet doesn't mean that you stop all financial activity. This would be impossible as Neptune is retrograde for many months in the year. But do your best to avoid major purchases or important financial decisions until he moves forward again. If something has to be done, make sure it is considered thoroughly.

September

Best Days Overall: 6, 7, 14, 15, 24, 25
Most Stressful Days Overall: 12, 13, 19, 20, 27, 28
Best Days for Love: 2, 3, 4, 5, 12, 13, 19, 20, 23, 24
Best Days for Money: 1, 2, 3, 8, 9, 10, 11, 16, 17, 19, 20, 26, 27, 29, 30
Best Days for Career: 4, 5, 12, 13, 22, 23, 27, 28

Even in the best of love periods there are times when the cycle is higher or lower than usual. The love situation is still wonderful, but it does taper off a bit this month. A good thing too. No one can take that much intensity for too long. On the 23rd of last month your 8th house of transformation became powerful, and it is even more powerful this month – until the 23rd. This signals a sexually active kind of month. When your 7th house was strong, romance – the feeling of love – was important. Now love is more about sexual magnetism. Regardless of your age or stage in life, the libido will be stronger than usual.

Power in the 8th house also shows that your spouse, partner or current love is prospering. He or she is in a yearly career peak and will be more generous with you now. A good thing too – your personal earnings are not that strong right now (although this will improve after the 23rd). If you have insurance, estate or tax issues there is good fortune this month. (Next year will be even more fortunate in that department.)

Power in the 8th house is good for detoxification regimes of every variety – physical, emotional, mental and financial. This is a good month to take stock of your possessions and get rid of what you don't use or don't need. This will clear the decks for the new good that wants to come in. It's a good time too to clear the mind of ideas, opinions and 'isms' that are not valid or true. Perhaps they are harmless, but they do clutter things up.

As we mentioned, personal finance improves after the 23rd. Jupiter, the planet of abundance, makes beautiful aspects to the ruler of your Horoscope from the 23rd to the 30th. Friends seem helpful and supportive on the financial level.

The Sun makes wonderful aspects to Pluto, your career planet, from the 2nd to the 4th. This indicates mixing socially with influential people. Career is enhanced through social means. Moreover, your spouse, partner or current love is very supportive of your career.

On the 28th the planetary power will begin to shift from the social Western sector to the independent Eastern one. (The shift will become even stronger next month.) Your period of dependence is about over. It was great to put others first, but now it's getting time to look after number one.

Health is good this month and will get even better after the 23rd. In fact, you will start to feel better after the 14th, when Mars moves away from his stressful aspect to you. By the 23rd you will have all the energy you need to achieve anything you set your mind to. Give more attention to the health (rest and relax more) on the stressful days listed above, and also on the 5th, 11th, 12th, 18th, 19th and 26th.

October

Best Days Overall: 3, 4, 12, 13, 21, 22, 23, 31
Most Stressful Days Overall: 9, 10, 16, 17, 18, 24, 25
Best Days for Love: 3, 4, 12, 13, 16, 17, 18, 22, 23
Best Days for Money: 5, 6, 7, 8, 14, 17, 18, 23, 24, 26, 27
Best Days for Career: 1, 2, 9, 10, 19, 20, 24, 25, 28, 29

You are entering one of the most successful periods of your year. On the 23rd you enter a yearly career peak that will continue well into next month. Continue to focus on the career and let family and home issues go for a while.

Success is happening but there are bumps on the road. There are two eclipses this month. Both have an impact on you. The good news is that many obstacles to your future success will get blasted away. However, it is not that pleasant while it is happening.

The Lunar Eclipse of the 8th seems, on the surface, to be quite benign to you, but it is a pretty direct hit on the ruler of your Horoscope, Uranus. Thus you should reduce your schedule and avoid risky activities over this period. There is no need right now to test the limits of your body. This eclipse occurs in your 3rd house and will test cars and communication equipment. These will tend to be more temperamental. Computer and high-tech equipment will also get tested. If there are inherent flaws in these things, now is when you find out and can make the necessary repairs and corrections. It will be a good idea to drive more carefully at this time and to see that important files and photos on your computer are backed up.

The impact on Uranus shows that you are redefining your personality, self-concept, body and image. Over the next six months you will present a new image to the world. If you haven't been careful in dietary matters (and you should be) this eclipse can bring a detox of the body. A new you is emerging from this chaos.

The Solar Eclipse of the 23rd also affects you strongly, especially those of you with birthdays from January 19 to 22. Take it nice and easy over this period. Stressful, risky activities should be re-scheduled. Spend more quiet time at home, watch a good movie or read a good book. This eclipse occurs right on the Mid-heaven of the Horoscope and thus affects the career. Sometimes it brings an actual change in the career, but most often the career remains the same although you approach it in a different way. These kinds of eclipses tend to bring shake-ups in your company or industry – management shake-ups or dramatic changes of policy. The rules of the game get changed. (This is also a six-month process.) There are dramas in the lives of bosses, parents or parent figures.

Every Solar Eclipse tests love and this one is no different. You've expanded your social circle greatly recently and a good testing is very much in order. The sheep and the goats need to be separated. Repressed feelings come out for cleansing. In many cases (and this could be one of them) an eclipse of the love planet signals marriage or a furthering of the commitment to one another. The current relationship must go further or dissolve.

Aside from the eclipse phenomena, health needs more attention from the 23rd onwards. You are busy with your career, but try to schedule more rest periods. Try to schedule massages or more time at the health spa on your stressful days listed above.

November

Best Days Overall: 8, 9, 18, 19, 27, 28
Most Stressful Days Overall: 6, 7, 13, 14, 20, 21
Best Days for Love: 2, 3, 10, 11, 12, 13, 14, 21, 22, 23
Best Days for Money: 2, 3, 4, 5, 10, 11, 14, 20, 23, 29, 30
Best Days for Career: 6, 7, 15, 16, 17, 20, 21, 25, 26

In August the love life was a distraction to your career, but it is not so now. You seem to have integrated these two areas very well. The love life shines and so does the career. The beloved also seems successful and is supportive of your career. His or her success is helping yours. This has been the case since the 23rd of last month.

If there are still any of you out there who are as yet unattached (unlikely though this is), there are romantic opportunities as you pursue your normal career goals and with people involved in your career. You have the aspects for an office romance – romance with bosses or superiors. This is especially so from the 17th to the 19th. Power and position are romantic allurements now. You want someone you can look up to, someone you can respect and who can help you attain your career goals.

The social dimension plays a big role in your success these days. Knowing the right people, socializing with them and being liked by them opens many doors. It is a good idea to attend or host the right parties and gatherings this month. The two love planets in your Horoscope, Venus (the generic love planet) and the Sun (the actual love planet), are both moving through your 10th career house. Even the family seems supportive of the career.

Continue to watch the health until the 22nd. As always, make sure you get enough rest – especially on your stressful days (listed above) and on the 4th, 5th, 6th, 11th, 12th, 19th and 20th.

Finances have been much improved since the end of last month, and they remain so until the 22nd of the coming month. After that you will have to work harder to attain your financial goals. The good news though is that Neptune, your financial planet, will start moving forward again on the 16th. By then you should have more mental clarity on your financial picture and your decision-making will be better.

Technically there are no eclipses this month, but we have some 'after shocks' from last month's eclipses. Uranus is camping out on the eclipse point of October 8, so avoid risky kinds of activities. You are still very much into re-defining yourself.

Mars activates this same point from the 14th to the 17th. Drive more carefully over these days. Cars and communication equipment will be temperamental then, and communications can be problematic.

Mercury activates the Solar Eclipse point of October 23 from the 8th to the 10th. This too affects cars and communication equipment. Children or children figures in your life should avoid daredevil-type stunts. Your spouse, partner or current love could have some temporary financial crisis.

December

Best Days Overall: 5, 6, 15, 16, 24, 25
Most Stressful Days Overall: 3, 4, 10, 11, 18, 19, 30, 31
Best Days for Love: 1, 2, 10, 11, 12, 13, 20, 21, 22, 30, 31
Best Days for Money: 1, 2, 8, 10, 11, 18, 20, 21, 26, 27, 28, 29
Best Days for Career: 3, 4, 13, 14, 18, 19, 22, 23, 30, 31

Stern Saturn has been in your 10th house of career for more than two years, but on the 24th he finally makes a move into your 11th house of friends. Up to now you have been earning success the hard way, through sheer merit and by outperforming all your competitors. Merit is still important, but now the career is easier. Many of you have had demanding bosses these past few years. The bosses will change now.

If the same bosses remain they will be less strict with you. Or, you will have new bosses who go easier on you.

Saturn's move from Scorpio into Sagittarius is also a positive one for your health and energy. It is much improved now. If there have been pre-existing conditions, you should start hearing good news about them. After the 24th there is only one long-term planet – Jupiter – in stressful alignment with you. The others are either in harmonious aspect or leaving you alone.

Mars moves into your sign on the 5th. This gives more energy. You are more personally dynamic and active. You excel in sports and exercise regimes. A new car and/or communication equipment is coming to you. Mars activates an eclipse point from the 4th to the 7th so drive more carefully over that period, watch the temper and don't be in a rush. Make haste slowly.

With up to 90 per cent of the planets in the independent Eastern sector, and with Mars in your own sign, personal independence is very strong. This is the time to take personal responsibility for your own happiness and to stand on your own two feet. You have all the power you need to create conditions as you desire them to be. You can and should have things your way (so long as it isn't destructive). Choose happiness. The planetary momentum is forward this month too, and you should see fast progress towards your goals.

Your 11th house of friends became powerful on November 22and it remains powerful until the 22nd of this month. Aquarius heaven. The Cosmos impels you to do what you most love doing do – to network, be involved with friends and groups, and go deeper into science, astrology and technology.

Love is happy this month – especially until the 22nd. A current relationship becomes more harmonious. Singles have happy romantic meetings. Singles are meeting people who are 'marriage material' this period. Marriage or relationships that are like marriages wouldn't be a surprise.

The ruler of your Horoscope, Uranus, is still near an eclipse point, so continue to avoid risky activities, daredevil-type stunts or unmindful testing of your physical limits. You are still very much in a period of self redefinition. A new you is being born.

Pisces

THE FISH

Birthdays from
19th February to
20th March

Personality Profile

PISCES AT A GLANCE

Element – Water

Ruling Planet – Neptune
  Career Planet – Jupiter
  Love Planet – Mercury
  Money Planet – Mars
  Planet of Health and Work – Sun
  Planet of Home and Family Life – Mercury
  Planet of Love Affairs, Creativity and Children – Moon

Colours – aqua, blue-green

Colours that promote love, romance and social harmony – earth tones,
  yellow, yellow-orange

Colours that promote earning power – red, scarlet

Gem – white diamond

Metal – tin

Scent – lotus

Quality – mutable (= flexibility)

Qualities most needed for balance – structure and the ability to handle form

Strongest virtues – psychic power, sensitivity, self-sacrifice, altruism

Deepest needs – spiritual illumination, liberation

Characteristics to avoid – escapism, keeping bad company, negative moods

Signs of greatest overall compatibility – Cancer, Scorpio

Signs of greatest overall incompatibility – Gemini, Virgo, Sagittarius

Sign most helpful to career – Sagittarius

Sign most helpful for emotional support – Gemini

Sign most helpful financially – Aries

Sign best for marriage and/or partnerships – Virgo

Sign most helpful for creative projects – Cancer

Best Sign to have fun with – Cancer

Signs most helpful in spiritual matters – Scorpio, Aquarius

Best day of the week – Thursday

Understanding a Pisces

If Pisces have one outstanding quality it is their belief in the invisible, spiritual and psychic side of things. This side of things is as real to them as the hard earth beneath their feet – so real, in fact, that they will often ignore the visible, tangible aspects of reality in order to focus on the invisible and so-called intangible ones.

Of all the signs of the zodiac, the intuitive and emotional faculties of the Pisces are the most highly developed. They are committed to living by their intuition and this can at times be infuriating to other people – especially those who are materially, scientifically or technically orientated. If you think that money, status and worldly success are the only goals in life, then you will never understand a Pisces.

Pisces have intellect, but to them intellect is only a means by which they can rationalize what they know intuitively. To an Aquarius or a Gemini the intellect is a tool with which to gain knowledge. To a well-developed Pisces it is a tool by which to express knowledge.

Pisces feel like fish in an infinite ocean of thought and feeling. This ocean has many depths, currents and undercurrents. They long for purer waters where the denizens are good, true and beautiful, but they are sometimes pulled to the lower, murkier depths. Pisces know that they do not generate thoughts but only tune in to thoughts that already exist; this is why they seek the purer waters. This ability to tune in to higher thoughts inspires them artistically and musically.

Since Pisces is so spiritually orientated – though many Pisces in the corporate world may hide this fact – we will deal with this aspect in greater detail, for otherwise it is difficult to understand the true Pisces personality.

There are four basic attitudes of the spirit. One is outright scepticism – the attitude of secular humanists. The second is an intellectual or emotional belief, where one worships a far-distant God-figure – the attitude of most modern church-going people. The third is not only belief but direct personal spiritual experience – this is the attitude of some 'born-again' religious people. The fourth is actual unity with the divinity, an intermingling with the spiritual world – this is the attitude of yoga. This fourth attitude is the deepest urge of a

Pisces, and a Pisces is uniquely qualified to pursue and perform this work.

Consciously or unconsciously, Pisces seek this union with the spiritual world. The belief in a greater reality makes Pisces very tolerant and understanding of others – perhaps even too tolerant. There are instances in their lives when they should say 'enough is enough' and be ready to defend their position and put up a fight. However, because of their qualities it takes a good deal to get them into that frame of mind.

Pisces basically want and aspire to be 'saints'. They do so in their own way and according to their own rules. Others should not try to impose their concept of saintliness on a Pisces, because he or she always tries to find it for him- or herself.

Finance

Money is generally not that important to Pisces. Of course they need it as much as anyone else, and many of them attain great wealth. But money is not generally a primary objective. Doing good, feeling good about oneself, peace of mind, the relief of pain and suffering – these are the things that matter most to a Pisces.

Pisces earn money intuitively and instinctively. They follow their hunches rather than their logic. They tend to be generous and perhaps overly charitable. Almost any kind of misfortune is enough to move a Pisces to give. Although this is one of their greatest virtues, Pisces should be more careful with their finances. They should try to be more choosy about the people to whom they lend money, so that they are not being taken advantage of. If they give money to charities they should follow it up to see that their contributions are put to good use. Even when Pisces are not rich, they still like to spend money on helping others. In this case they should really be careful, however: they must learn to say no sometimes and help themselves first.

Perhaps the biggest financial stumbling block for the Pisces is general passivity – a *laissez faire* attitude. In general Pisces like to go with the flow of events. When it comes to financial matters, especially, they need to be more aggressive. They need to make things happen, to create their own wealth. A passive attitude will only cause loss and missed opportunity. Worrying about financial security will not provide that security. Pisces need to go after what they want tenaciously.

Career and Public Image

Pisces like to be perceived by the public as people of spiritual or material wealth, of generosity and philanthropy. They look up to big-hearted, philanthropic types. They admire people engaged in large-scale undertakings and eventually would like to head up these big enterprises themselves. In short, they like to be connected with big organizations that are doing things in a big way.

If Pisces are to realize their full career and professional potential they need to travel more, educate themselves more and learn more about the actual world. In other words, they need some of the unflagging optimism of Sagittarius in order to reach the top.

Because of all their caring and generous characteristics, Pisces often choose professions through which they can help and touch the lives of other people. That is why many Pisces become doctors, nurses, social workers or teachers. Sometimes it takes a while before Pisces realize what they really want to do in their professional lives, but once they find a career that lets them manifest their interests and virtues they will excel at it.

Love and Relationships

It is not surprising that someone as 'otherworldly' as the Pisces would like a partner who is practical and down to earth. Pisces prefer a partner who is on top of all the details of life, because they dislike details. Pisces seek this quality in both their romantic and professional partners. More than anything else this gives Pisces a feeling of being grounded, of being in touch with reality.

As expected, these kinds of relationships – though necessary – are sure to have many ups and downs. Misunderstandings will take place because the two attitudes are poles apart. If you are in love with a Pisces you will experience these fluctuations and will need a lot of patience to see things stabilize. Pisces are moody, intuitive, affectionate and difficult to get to know. Only time and the right attitude will yield Pisces' deepest secrets. However, when in love with a Pisces you will find that riding the waves is worth it because they are good, sensitive people who need and like to give love and affection.

When in love, Pisces like to fantasize. For them fantasy is 90 per cent of the fun of a relationship. They tend to idealize their partner, which can be good and bad at the same time. It is bad in that it is difficult for anyone to live up to the high ideals their Pisces lover sets.

Home and Domestic Life

In their family and domestic life Pisces have to resist the tendency to relate only by feelings and moods. It is unrealistic to expect that your partner and other family members will be as intuitive as you are. There is a need for more verbal communication between a Pisces and his or her family. A cool, unemotional exchange of ideas and opinions will benefit everyone.

Some Pisces tend to like mobility and moving around. For them too much stability feels like a restriction on their freedom. They hate to be locked in one location for ever.

The sign of Gemini sits on Pisces' 4th solar house (of home and family) cusp. This shows that Pisces likes and needs a home environment that promotes intellectual and mental interests. They tend to treat their neighbours as family – or extended family. Some Pisces can have a dual attitude towards the home and family – on the one hand they like the emotional support of the family, but on the other they dislike the obligations, restrictions and duties involved with it. For Pisces, finding a balance is the key to a happy family life.

Horoscope for 2014

Major Trends

In general Pisceans live more in the invisible, spiritual world than they do on earth. This is their nature. But with Neptune, the ruler of your Horoscope, in Pisces this year this tendency is even stronger. While this is comfortable for you, it will be necessary to force yourself to deal with everyday practical reality too. Yes, your home is in heaven, but for now you're acting here on earth and you should keep more focus here.

Last year was prosperous and happy, and the trend continues in the year ahead. There are more details on this later.

Jupiter entered your 5th house of fun and creativity in June last year and will be there until July this year, signalling a happy period, a holiday kind of period. You are into fun and creativity. On July 16 Jupiter will enter your 6th house of work, and you will become more serious and work oriented. This is a very nice aspect for job seekers.

Pisceans of the appropriate age have been more fertile than usual in the past year and the trend continues in the year ahead.

Many Pisceans are in the creative fields, and this is an excellent year for this. (Last year was good too.) Personal creativity is very much enhanced.

Students have been making major changes to their educational plans over the past few years and the trend continues in the year ahead. Thus there are changes of schools, changes of courses and changes in the rules of the school. These seem dramatic.

Last year was not a year for serious romance; it was more about love affairs – entertainment-type relationships. This trend continues in the year ahead. More on this later.

Your areas of greatest interest in the year ahead are the body, image and personal pleasure; finance; children, fun and creativity (until July 16); health and work (after July 16); religion, philosophy, higher education and foreign travel; and friends, groups and group activities.

Your paths of greatest fulfilment are children, fun and creativity (until July 16); health and work (after July 16); religion, philosophy, higher education and foreign travel (until February 19); and sex, estates, taxes, other people's money, and occult studies (from February 19 onwards).

Health

(Please note that this is an astrological perspective on health and not a medical one. In days of yore there was no difference, both of these perspectives were identical. But in these times there could be quite a difference.

For a medical perspective, please consult your doctor or health practitioner.)

Health is basically good this year. All the long-term planets are either in harmonious aspect or are leaving you alone. Of course there will be periods in the year when your health and energy are less easy than usual. These periods come because of short-term planetary transits – they are temporary things and not trends for the year. When they pass, your normal health and vitality returns.

Your 6th house of health is not a house of power until July 16. This shows that there's no need to give too much attention to health as it is basically good. You can take good health for granted. But after July 16 you start to focus more on this area. I read this as the Cosmos preparing you for next year. On December 24, Saturn will move into stressful alignment with you and this will impact on health. It is more of an issue for next year rather than this, however the extra attention you pay to health, the regimes that you undertake, will stand you in good stead in 2015.

Reflexology

Try to massage the whole foot on a regular basis, but pay extra attention to the points highlighted on the chart. When you massage, be aware of 'sore spots', as these need special attention. It's also a good idea to massage the ankles and the top of the feet.

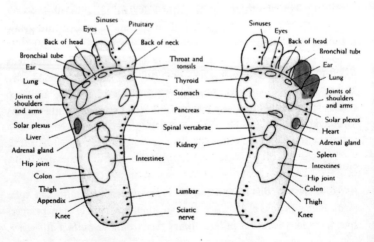

Good though your health is you can make it even better. Pay attention to the heart (this is always important for you and the reflex to the heart is shown in the chart). Avoid worry and anxiety, the two emotions that are considered the spiritual root causes of heart problems. Worry is considered normal in the secular world – everyone does it. Spiritually, however, it is considered pathology. It achieves absolutely nothing and actually makes matters worse (it puts out negative vibrations into the environment and wastes precious life energy). If there is something positive that can be done about a troubling situation, of course you should do it. If there isn't anything that you can do, pray or make some positive affirmation about the situation and enjoy your life. Time will show the next actions to take.

The feet are also always important for you. You, more than most, benefit from foot reflexology and foot massage. Foot hydrotherapy and foot whirlpools are also good for you. (There are many such massagers and foot baths out on the market and it might be advisable to invest in one of these things.) Wear shoes that fit correctly and that don't unbalance you – it's best to sacrifice fashion for comfort although if you can have both, all the better.

The liver and thighs become important after July 16 when Jupiter enters your 6th house of health. The thighs should be regularly massaged, and a Liver detox might be a good idea. (There are all kinds of herbal methods for this.) The reflex to the liver is shown.

Neptune has been in your sign since February 2012 and will be there for many more years. Thus the body is being refined and spiritualized. It is becoming a more sensitive kind of instrument. Thus it is good to avoid alcohol and drugs. The body can over-react to these things.

Refined, spiritual-type exercises are good these days – things like yoga or tai chi. You will get more out of these than vigorous contact sports. These suit your body type much better.

Your health planet is the Sun – a fast-moving planet. Every month he will change signs and houses, and so there are many short-term trends in health, depending on where the Sun is and the aspects he receives. These are best discussed in the monthly reports.

Favourable numbers for health are 5, 6, 8 and 19.

Home and Family

Your 4th house of home and family is not a house of power this year, Pisces. Generally this shows a state of contentment with the status quo. There is no need to make major changes in the home or with the family. You can if you want to – the Cosmos gives you free will – but the overwhelming urge for change is not there. Many of you moved or renovated your home during the past two years, and this reinforces the sense of contentment here.

Though your 4th house is basically empty (only short-term planets will move through there for brief periods), your 5th house of children is very strong. So the focus is more on the children (or the children figures in your life) and not so much on the family as a whole.

Pisceans of the appropriate age have been unusually fertile since 2012, and the trend continues in the first half of the year ahead. There is a strong desire for children these days. Some of you might even consider adoption or undertaking fertility treatments.

Jupiter is your career planet. His position in your 5th house until July 16 shows that you consider the children your career, your mission, your highest priority. Whatever your outer, worldly career is, the children are the real career. This will change after July 16. More on this later.

The children seem prosperous this year, although much depends on their age and stage. However, whatever their age, expensive items are coming to them. They live a more prosperous kind of lifestyle. They are travelling too, and if they are of appropriate age there are very happy job opportunities coming to them. Moves are not seen here.

Parents and parent figures in your life could have moved last year and, if they did not, this can still happen in the year ahead. Sometimes they don't literally move but the effect is 'as if' they have moved. Sometimes they buy an additional home, renovate the existing home, or buy expensive items for the home. Homes near water are indicated for them. Also, they need to check any home for potential water damage.

The parents or parent figures are prospering this year – they prospered last year too. They are also more generous with you.

Siblings or sibling figures in your life are likely to move or renovate their homes this year. If they are of appropriate age they too seem more fertile than usual.

Finance and Career

Your money house has been powerful since 2011 and will be powerful for years to come. There is great focus here – and also much change and excitement.

Last year – especially the latter half – was prosperous, and this trend continues in the year ahead and especially until July 16. Jupiter is making beautiful aspects to the Sun.

Uranus in your money house indicates new inventions and new technology. There are various ways to read this. This can show that you are earning from technology, or it can show that whatever field or business you're involved with technology is important. Good to invest in the latest technology, as it's important to stay up to date.

Uranus in the money house shows online kinds of ventures too. This aspect favours start-ups, new industries, new ideas and innovations. Uranus doesn't care that something is new and has never been done before. This is all the more reason to do it. You are happy to experiment and to take big risks these days.

Jupiter has been in your 5th house since June 2013 and will be there until July 16. This shows luck in speculations – a person who catches the lucky financial breaks. Until July it might be advisable to invest harmless sums on the lottery or some other kind of speculation. Of course this should only be done by intuition and not automatically. The Cosmos has many ways to supply you.

Last year was a good career year and the trend continues this year. Jupiter, your career planet, is in harmonious aspect with Neptune, the ruler of your Horoscope. So, there have been (and there can be in the year ahead) pay rises, promotions and honours in the career. Happy career opportunities will continue to happen in the year ahead. What I like here is that the career path seems enjoyable. You are managing to have fun. After July 16, however, you will earn your career success though hard work. Your good work ethic will be noted by your superiors.

For those just starting out, I like the entertainment field careerwise until July 16. Afterwards, the health field is interesting. And whatever field you're in, people in these professions can be important in your career. Perhaps you are involved with these kinds of people as clients.

Your financial planet, Mars, spends an unusual amount of time in Libra, your 8th house of transformation, this year. He is there from January 1 to July 26. (A normal Mars transit is one and a half to two months – here he is spending almost seven months in Libra!) There are various ways to read this. This often indicates inheritance or involvement with estates and tax issue. It generally signals that estate planning and taxes are greatly influencing the financial decision-making. It shows a need to prosper others – partners or investors, to put their financial interest ahead of your own. Often this transit indicates someone who is managing the wealth of others (the family, the household or investors). Debts are easily made or easily paid off, depending on your need. There is good access to outside capital. The line of credit is increased. There are opportunities to invest in troubled companies or properties and to turn them around. This will be a good period to cut costs and eliminate waste and redundancy in the financial life – to detox it.

As we mentioned earlier, Jupiter's move into your 6th house of health and work on July 16 shows very happy job opportunities happening for the rest of the year ahead.

Favourable financial numbers are 1, 4, 5 and 16.

Love and Social Life

Your 7th house of love and romance is not a house of power this year. You are more involved with friendships, groups and group activities than with romance. Some years are like that. This tends towards the status quo; those who are married will tend to stay married, and singles will tend to stay single. There is a basic contentment with the status quo and you don't feel a need to make major, dramatic changes.

(Next year will be a very different story. Your 7th house will become powerful and the love life will get much more active. For singles there will be marriage or marriage opportunities happening. This year however, you are in preparation for it.)

Though marriage is not indicated this year, we do see love affairs. Jupiter is in your 5th house of fun and love affairs until July 16. Perhaps you need to experience 'entertainment' kind of love in order to be ready for the more serious love that will happen next year (and perhaps in 2016 as well).

Mercury is your love planet. Except for the Moon he is the fastest moving of all the planets. In a given year he will move through all the signs and houses of your Horoscope – and sometimes more than once (he goes retrograde three times in a year). Thus there will be many short-term trends in love, depending on where Mercury is and the aspects he receives. These are best discussed in the monthly reports.

Having such a fast-moving planet ruling love shows someone whose love needs change frequently. Hence you might have a reputation for being 'fickle' in love, or flighty. It is normal for you to be this way – it is the way you're wired up. However, not everyone can handle this. The best relationship is with someone who can meet (and cope with) all these changing needs.

Marriage doesn't seem in the stars for those working towards their second, third or fourth marriages either. For those working on their second or third it doesn't even seem advisable this year.

Parents and parent figures are also having a stable kind of love year. If they are married they will most likely stay married; if they are unattached, they will stay that way. Siblings and sibling figures, however, are having their relationships severely tested. If they are unattached marriage is not advisable this year. Children or children figures have love this year, and marriages or relationships that are 'like' marriages are seen. They had love last year too. Grandchildren of the appropriate age are having stable love years.

Favourable numbers for love are 1, 6, 8 and 9.

Self-improvement

You have been under the influence of intense spiritual energy since 1998, and from 2012 this energy became even more intense. You are on a spiritual path either formally or informally and it is important to understand some of the adventures that happen on this path. There is not much literature on this subject. Thus experiences happen that seem strange and undocumented.

First, as we mentioned, the physical body itself is becoming more refined – it's being elevated in energy vibration. Diets that were OK even a few years ago are probably not all right now. The diet needs to be more refined too. This should be checked with a professional, but the important thing is to monitor how you feel under different diets.

The refinement of the physical body will make it more sensitive to psychic vibrations. You will feel vibrations in a tangible, physical kind of way. It will not necessarily be in a dream or vision or feeling. You will experience them in your body – good or bad. If you are around negative kinds of people, this can be quite painful. The solution is to be around positive, uplifting kinds of people. Solitude is to be preferred to negative people.

The refinement of the physical body will enable the power of spirit to act directly on the body, without human intervention. Thus you will find that many maladies or physical discomforts can be dispersed by a word, image or a simple meditation session.

Spirituality is all about 'letting go'. It is a constant process of 'letting go' of the lesser in order to embrace the greater (see Guy Finley's *The Secret of Letting Go* for a more detailed explanation of this). This doesn't happen all at once – no human could take it – but as a process over time. Eating chocolate is not evil, but if one wants a svelte figure – a greater good – one might let go of it. Often in life things happen that irritate or anger us, and often the anger is very justified. But if one wants a higher state of consciousness – more spiritual good – one will let go of these things. This goes on and on and on. Learning to let go in a joyful kind of way is one of the greatest arts one can learn.

Spirituality is also marked by constant 'leaps into the unknown'. Now, the so-called 'unknown' is very well known to spirit but to us it is unknown. The fear of the unknown must be overcome. Once this happens new vistas of joy and good will be revealed.

This influx of spiritual energy and revelation is testing your old tried and true religious and philosophical beliefs. Saturn has been in your 9th house since October 2012. Perhaps your beliefs were based on certain experiences. Perhaps they were inherited from the family. Perhaps they were taught in school. Now, however, the influx of light and life, dynamic life, is upsetting the apple cart. What you thought was once true is now seen in a different light. Perhaps now you see that your old beliefs are only partially true, or sometimes true. Perhaps you see that you had misinterpreted what was taught to you. And now you have to restructure your belief system in the light of your new revelations. This can be hard work. And this is happening to you now.

Month-by-month Forecasts

January

> Best Days Overall: 5, 6, 14, 15, 24, 25
> Most Stressful Days Overall: 12, 13, 19, 20, 26, 27
> Best Days for Love: 1, 2, 9, 10, 11, 19, 20, 22, 23, 28, 29, 30, 31
> Best Days for Money: 3, 4, 5, 6, 7, 8, 12, 13, 14, 15, 22, 23, 24, 25, 30, 31
> Best Days for Career: 5, 6, 14, 15, 24, 25, 26, 27

The universal solar cycle is waxing (the days are getting longer) and there is much forward momentum to the planets (80 per cent of them are going forward). The Eastern, independent sector of the Horoscope is dominant. Normally this would be an excellent time to start new projects or release new products into the world. But your personal solar cycle is in its waning phase (until your birthday), so it might be better to wait until then.

Though your yearly career peak recently ended (your next one will be in November) career is still important. You are finishing up career projects now. With the upper half of your Horoscope still very dominant, keep your focus on the career. You can safely de-emphasize home and family issues for the moment.

Health and energy are excellent. There are no planets in stressful aspect with you (only the Moon will temporarily make stressful aspects – see your most stressful days above). You have all the energy you need to achieve anything you want to achieve. If you like you can enhance your good health by giving more attention to the spine, knees, teeth, bones, skin and overall skeletal alignment until the 20th. Back and knee massages will be very good. After the 20th, give more attention to the ankles and calves (massage them regularly).

Your love planet, Mercury, is 'out of bounds' until the 8th. This shows that you are going outside your usual limits in search for love. Or perhaps your social life, or beloved, pulls you outside your limits. Sometimes people go into 'forbidden territory' in search of love. Until the 11th there are love opportunities online in the social networking or dating sites. There are also opportunities as you get involved with groups, group activities and organizations. After the 11th, love opportunities happen in spiritual-type settings such as at meditation seminars, spiritual lectures, prayer meetings or charity events.

Finances are a bit stressful until the 20th. Earnings come but you have to work harder for them. Happily you have the energy to do this. You should see major improvements after the 20th as the short-term planets start making harmonious aspects to Mars, your financial planet. Be patient until then. Help is on the way.

There are no eclipses this month, but there are some 'after shocks' from previous eclipses. The Sun activates an eclipse point from the 14th to the 19th. This can bring disturbances at the job and instability at the workplace. Venus activates an eclipse point from the 1st to the 7th. Be more careful driving during that period, as cars and communication equipment can be more temperamental. Mercury also transits an eclipse point from the 8th to the 10th and on the 18th and 19th. Be more patient with the beloved at these times; he or she is apt to be more temperamental.

February

Best Days Overall: 1, 2, 10, 11, 12, 20, 21, 28
Most Stressful Days Overall: 8, 9, 15, 16, 17, 22, 23
Best Days for Love: 1, 5, 6, 7, 10, 15, 16, 17, 19, 24, 25, 26, 27
Best Days for Money: 1, 2, 3, 4, 8, 9, 10, 11, 12, 18, 19, 20, 21, 26, 27, 28
Best Days for Career: 1, 2, 10, 11, 12, 20, 21, 28

This month the planetary power shifts from the upper (objective) half of the Horoscope to the lower (subjective) half. Your career planet is in retrograde mode to boot. It is time to shift psychological gears. Career issues need more clarity before taking action. Only time will resolve things. From the 18th onwards you should start giving more attention to the home, family and your emotional well-being.

The interesting thing here is that many happy career developments are taking place behind the scenes after the 18th but they will unfold later on. Career opportunities will come but you can afford to be more choosy about them. If they violate your 'emotional wellness' or uproot your family you might want to decline or negotiate better terms.

Pisceans, in general, are spiritual people – natural-born mystics and visionaries. With Neptune in your own sign for many years to come, these tendencies are even stronger. And with your 12th house of spirituality very powerful since the 20th of last month, they are more powerful still. Your challenge will be stay in your body and not drift off. It's OK to have your head in the clouds, but, as the saying goes, keep your feet firmly on the ground. The dream life is so beautiful, so interesting, that awakening from that and getting up in the morning will be the challenge. Nothing in the mundane world can compare to it. If you remember that you incarnated for a purpose – to do a job here on earth in this mundane world – it will be easier.

Spirituality, supernatural experiences and spiritual breakthroughs pervade the entire month ahead. Even after the Sun leaves your 12th house on the 18th, it will enter your own sign of Pisces, which also enhances spirituality.

This is a very happy month ahead. Until the 18th you are engaged in the activities that you most enjoy (spiritual-type activities), and after the 18th you enter one of your yearly personal pleasure peaks. The natural consequence of a spiritual breakthrough is enhanced physical well-being.

Job seekers have good fortune this month from the 18th onwards. Jobs are seeking you and they look like good ones. There's nothing special that you need to do. Love too seeks you out, but love is more complicated as your love planet is retrograde from the 6th onwards. It pursues you and then it sort of 'pulls back' as if the potential amour is indecisive. This will clarify next month.

Health is still excellent.

March

Best Days Overall: 1, 2, 10, 11, 19, 20, 28, 29
Most Stressful Days Overall: 7, 8, 15, 16, 22, 23
Best Days for Love: 7, 8, 15, 16, 17, 18, 19, 26, 27, 28, 29
Best Days for Money: 1, 2, 3, 4, 7, 8, 10, 11, 17, 18, 19, 20, 26,
    27, 28, 29, 30, 31
Best Days for Career: 1, 2, 10, 11, 19, 20, 22, 23, 28, 29

Last month and this month, the planetary power is in its maximum Eastern position for the year. This is your period of maximum personal independence. The planetary power is moving towards you. You can and should have things your way. Your way is the best way these days. This is the time to change conditions that irk you – to improve them and design them according to your specifications. It is also an excellent time to launch new ventures or release new products into the world – especially from your birthday onwards. The planetary momentum is forward, the universal solar cycle is waxing, and from your birthday onwards your personal solar cycle will wax as well. Go boldly towards your goals. You will see fast progress towards them.

Now that Mercury, your love planet, is moving forward, the love life is much improved. With your 1st house strong until the 20th, you look good and have much personal charisma. You have 'star quality' this month. You have faith and confidence in your self and the opposite sex takes notice. Until the 17th love opportunities occur in spiritual settings such as meditation seminars, yoga classes, prayer meetings or charity events. After the 17th, as Mercury crosses your Ascendant and enters your 1st house, love pursues you. Just show up. Nothing more is required. Singles have a very happy and significant meeting between the 21st and the 23rd. Those involved in a relationship will have happy social experiences or invitations. The current relationship seems more romantic than usual.

March is a prosperous month too. Job seekers still have good fortune. On the 20th you enter a yearly financial peak – a period of peak earnings. The new Moon of the 30th seems particularly prosperous – a nice payday. There is luck in speculations. You catch the lucky financial breaks. This new Moon will have other positive effects. It will clarify the financial life, and with your financial planet retrograde all month, clarity is much needed now. There are a few bumps on the road. Mars will transit an eclipse point from the 11th to the 18th. There is some financial disturbance – perhaps an unexpected expense. You will be tempted to make dramatic financial changes because of this. Be cautious about this, however. Mars is retrograde, so do more homework before making any changes.

Health is still excellent. You have all the energy you need to achieve whatever you want to achieve.

April

Best Days Overall: 6, 7, 16, 17, 24, 25

Most Stressful Days Overall: 3, 4, 5, 11, 12, 18, 19

Best Days for Love: 4, 5, 6, 7, 8, 11, 12, 16, 17, 18, 19, 24, 25, 29, 30

Best Days for Money: 3, 4, 5, 6, 7, 13, 14, 15, 16, 17, 22, 23, 24, 25, 26, 27

Best Days for Career: 6, 7, 16, 17, 18, 19, 24, 25

The main headline this month is the two eclipses which happen. Eclipses affect everyone. They affect the world at large and every person in some unique kind of way. The issue is not whether you are affected, but to what degree. In your case, these eclipses are relatively benign.

The Lunar Eclipse of the 15th occurs in your 8th house of transformation. Thus there can be encounters with death, although generally this is on the psychological level. However, if a person is teetering between life and death – a borderline case – this kind of eclipse can push them over the edge. The Dark Angel comes calling. He lets you know he is around. He has messages for you and his own unique way of delivering them. It won't hurt to reduce your schedule during this period – there's no need to tempt the Dark Angel more than necessary.

This eclipse indicates financial dramas and perhaps crises in the life of the spouse, partner or current love. Financial changes need to be made. Thinking and strategy have most likely been unrealistic and the eclipse reveals this. This eclipse brings such dramas and crises to you as well, for Mars, the financial planet, is affected. Every Lunar Eclipse affects the children in your life. They should be kept out of harm's way. Dramatic events are probably happening in their lives as well. Avoid speculations this period.

The Solar Eclipse of the 29th occurs in your 3rd house of communication. Thus cars and communication equipment get tested. There can be major communication failures during this eclipse and for a few days before and after too. People often ask me, 'How can a material object be affected by an eclipse? How can a planetary energy affect a solid object?' Yet they are. There is no such thing as 'solidity'; it is an illusion of the five senses. Even the most solid of objects is in reality a pattern of energy at a certain vibration. If the energy pattern is disrupted, you will have malfunctions in the so-called solid object. The more delicate and refined the object is, the greater the disruption will be.

This eclipse impacts on the siblings and sibling figures in your life, and neighbours too. There are dramas and life-changing events in their lives. (This will happen as a six-month process.) It won't hurt to drive more carefully this period. Every Solar Eclipse also affects the health and the health regime. Often such eclipses produce health scares – a terrifying diagnosis from a doctor or some test shows something seriously wrong. But health is good these days, so these will most likely be only scares. Second opinions will bring relief. The overall health regime gets refined and updated too.

May

Best Days Overall: 3, 4, 5, 13, 14, 21, 22, 31
Most Stressful Days Overall: 1, 2, 8, 9, 10, 15, 16, 28, 29
Best Days for Love: 6, 8, 9, 10, 11, 12, 13, 14, 19, 20, 24, 25, 29, 30
Best Days for Money: 1, 2, 3, 4, 5, 11, 12, 13, 14, 19, 20, 21, 22, 24, 25, 28, 29, 31
Best Days for Career: 3, 4, 5, 13, 14, 15, 16, 21, 22, 31

The planetary power is approaching the maximum low point in your chart. You are approaching the springtime of your year (on the 21st) but it is night. Growth is happening but is not yet visible. Continue to focus on the home, the family and your emotional well-being. These are the behind-the-scenes actions that make a successful career possible. If these activities are done properly – if there is stability in the home and family and good emotional harmony – the career will naturally be successful almost as a side effect.

Well-being is the alignment of the personal rhythm with the rhythms of life. The pauses between the beats are as important as the beats themselves.

You are still in a period of personal independence but this will soon be over. If there are changes that need to be made, now is the time to make them. Later on it will be more difficult.

Health will need more attention after the 21st. Overall, the health is still wonderful, but this is not one of your better periods. Be sure to get more rest after the 21st – high energy levels are always the first line of defence against disease. You can enhance the health by giving more attention to the neck and throat (until the 21st) and to the arms, shoulders, lungs and respiratory system afterwards. Neck massage is powerful until the 21st. Afterwards, arm and shoulder massage is powerful. Good mental health is important all month. Strive for intellectual purity. Give the mental body what it needs – good nutrition and exercise. Keep your thinking positive and constructive.

Prosperity is still strong this month. On the 3rd, Venus enters your money house and stays there until the 29th, indicating that earnings come from sales, marketing, advertising and good PR. It's important to get the word out about your product or service. The social dimension (Venus's natural domain) is also important financially. Who you know is perhaps as important as how much you have.

Your love planet goes 'out of bounds' once again, from the 12th to the 31st. This is the second time this year. There are many scenarios here. You are going outside your normal boundaries in search for love. You are attracted to 'forbidden love'. Perhaps the beloved or friends pull you outside your normal boundaries. You are exposed to all kinds of 'outside the box' love. Love has many forms of expression and this is a month where you learn about it.

The love planet will spend the bulk of the month – from the 7th to the 29th – in your 4th house of home and family. Thus you are socializing more from home. Emotional intimacy is very important in love – that and good communication. They go hand in hand. Old flames from the past can reappear in your life. Moodiness in love can be a problem.

June

Best Days Overall: 1, 9, 10, 18, 19, 27, 28
Most Stressful Days Overall: 5, 6, 12, 13, 24, 25, 26
Best Days for Love: 1, 5, 6, 9, 10, 14, 15, 17, 23, 24, 25, 26
Best Days for Money: 1, 7, 8, 10, 11, 16, 17, 18, 19, 20, 21, 25, 26, 27, 28
Best Days for Career: 1, 10, 11, 12, 13, 18, 19, 27, 28

Continue to watch the health more until the 21st. You should see a big improvement afterwards. Until the 21st enhance the health in the ways mentioned last month. Arm and shoulder massage is good, as is plain old fresh air. If you feel under the weather, get out in the fresh air and do some deep breathing. After the 21st enhance the health by dietary means and by giving more attention to the stomach. Women should give more attention to the breasts too. Work to keep your mood positive and constructive. (This is important all month.) Joy itself is a powerful healing force and you discover this in the month ahead. If you feel under the weather (and especially after the 21st), do something fun. A night out on the town or a creative hobby will be therapeutic. Laughter, this period, is the best medicine.

This month the planetary power shifts from the independent East to the social West – an important shift. You've had your way since the beginning of the year. Now it is time to take a holiday from your self and your personal concerns. Often it is the excessive focus on the self that blocks good from happening. It is time to put others first. There's nothing wrong with looking after number one, it just depends on the stage of your cycle. As you put others first now, you'll discover that your own good, your own needs, are taken care of naturally.

With the planetary power shifting to the social West, creating conditions to suit you and making changes are now more difficult. Now is the time for experiencing the consequences (good or bad) of what you created over the past six months. If you created well, life is pleasant. If there have been errors – well, you have to live with them for a while until your next period of independence comes. You are in a cycle of paying karma.

After the 21st you enter another one of your yearly personal pleasure peaks. A time for fun and leisure. The timing for this is good too. The planets are at their maximum retrograde activity for the year with almost half of them retrograde. Things in the world are slowing down so you might as well enjoy your life.

Mercury remains 'out of bounds' until the 5th. After that he 'comes back into the fold'. You've had your fill of avant-garde love and now want to return to the normal boundaries. The main complication this month is your love planet's retrograde from the 6th onwards. This doesn't stop love, but it slows things down a bit. It is a good opportunity to review your current relationship, and the love life in general, and see where improvements can be made. Later, when Mercury goes forward again next month, you can put these plans into practice.

Mercury retrogrades back into your 4th house on the 18th. Moodiness in love can be a problem. Singles find romantic opportunities close to home, through the family or family connections. Old flames – or people who resemble them – come into the picture, and there is a desire to go back to old love experiences that were pleasant. But this is really an illusion. Those experiences were unique in time and can never be totally replicated. The Now is always new and unique.

July

Best Days Overall: 7, 8, 15, 16, 24, 25
Most Stressful Days Overall: 2, 3, 9, 10, 22, 23, 29, 30, 31
Best Days for Love: 2, 3, 4, 5, 6, 13, 14, 24, 25, 29, 30, 31
Best Days for Money: 4, 5, 6, 7, 8, 13, 14, 16, 17, 18, 24, 25, 27
Best Days for Career: 7, 8, 9, 10, 16, 17, 27

This is a happy kind of month. A party kind of month. You are still in one of your yearly personal pleasure peaks until 22nd. After then you are more or less 'partied out' and are ready for some serious work.

Interestingly, your career blossoms through fun ways, perhaps through networking at the theatre, resort or at a party. As you pursue your happiness, career advancement just naturally happens. To the world this can seem 'irresponsible', but the end results speak for themselves. But this is short lived. Your career planet Jupiter moves out of Cancer into Leo on the 17th – from your 5th house of fun to your 6th house of work. So the work ethic does start to matter. And this is the trend in the year ahead. Good connections will open doors for you, but ultimately you have to perform.

Job seekers have fabulous opportunities from the 24th to the 27th. The job aspects are good after that as well (in fact, the entire year ahead is good for this). It is unlikely that there'll be any unemployed Pisceans by the end of the year, except by choice. The 24th to the 27th also brings happy career opportunities, and especially on the new Moon of the 26th.

Health is good this month. By the 18th there are no stressful aspects on you. Only the Moon will make temporary short-term stressful aspects. A recipe for good health. Health does become more important from the 17th onwards. Your problem could be too much emphasis – hypochondria – rather than any real health concerns.

Love is happy this month, especially from the 13th onwards. There are happy romantic meetings from the 17th to the 20th as the love planet makes a trine to the ruler of your Horoscope. Love is about fun from the 13th onwards. You are attracted to people who can show you a good time. The responsibilities that come with love are not interesting – and this perhaps is the problem. Are you ready to face the tough times with this person?

The financial planet has been in the sign of Libra all year. However, this month, on the 18th, Mars finally moves into Scorpio. This is a positive for finance. Mars is in harmonious aspect with you and earnings should increase after the 18th. Overspending, however, could be a problem.

August

Best Days Overall: 3, 4, 11, 12, 20, 21, 22, 30, 31
Most Stressful Days Overall: 5, 6, 18, 19, 25, 26, 27
Best Days for Love: 3, 4, 5, 6, 12, 13, 14, 15, 23, 24, 25, 26, 27
Best Days for Money: 3, 4, 5, 11, 12, 13, 14, 20, 21, 23, 24, 30, 31
Best Days for Career: 5, 6, 13, 14, 23, 24

During this month and the next, the planets will be in their maximum Western position. Moreover, your 7th house of love becomes very strong on the 23rd of this month and you enter a yearly love and social peak. Personal merit and personal initiative matter, but these days it's not about that. It's about developing 'likeability', the people skills, the ability to get others to co-operate with you. This ability extends and multiplies the personal skills. More gets done with less personal effort. When you put others first, which is what the Cosmos is calling you to do, it's as if you have access to all the limitless resources of the Cosmos. Not just your own. Your own needs will be amply taken care of. The planetary power is moving away from you, and it seems, at the moment, far from you. It flows towards others – and so should you.

Health needs more watching after the 23rd. There's nothing seriously wrong. It is just that the short-term planets are in temporary stressful alignment with you. The pace you were maintaining easily over the past few months could now be problematic. Make sure to get more rest. You can enhance the health by giving more attention to the heart (always important for you) and to the small intestine (from the 23rd onwards). Discords in love – with friends or your current love relationship – can impact on your health. If problems arise, restore harmony as quickly as you can. Beauty is a powerful healing force. If you feel under the weather go to some scenic spot and just sit there and absorb the beauty. Listening to beautiful music or viewing beautiful art will also be good.

There is an important and happy love meeting between the 1st to the 3rd. This is a good career period too. A new car or communication equipment comes to you from the 17th to the 19th. There is also happy career opportunity then.

The Sun transits a previous eclipse point on the 1st and 2nd, which can bring disturbance at the job, while Mercury transits an eclipse point on the 5th and 6th. Be more patient with the beloved and family members over those days.

Mars transits an eclipse point from the 10th to the 14th, bringing financial dramas and changes, and you should be more careful driving between the 18th and the 20th, as Venus transits an eclipse point. Finally, Jupiter transits an eclipse point from the 24th to the 31st, bringing dramas in the career and in the lives of bosses, parents, parent figures and elders.

September

Best Days Overall: 8, 9, 17, 18, 27, 28
Most Stressful Days Overall: 2, 3, 14, 15, 22, 23, 29, 30
Best Days for Love: 2, 3, 4, 12, 13, 20, 21, 22, 23, 28
Best Days for Money: 1, 2, 3, 8, 9, 10, 11, 19, 20, 29, 30
Best Days for Career: 1, 2, 3, 10, 11, 19, 20, 29, 30

The planetary power shifts this month. From the 5th, the upper (objective) half of the Horoscope starts to dominate. It is mid-summer in your year but the Sun has just risen. It is time to begin to gather the harvest. Let go of home and family issues and focus on your outer objectives – your career. On a spiritual level this shift in power means you should focus on the work that you and you alone came here to do. Emotional wellness is always important, but now it will happen by doing right, by succeeding. Success will bring emotional harmony.

Love is still active and happy. You are still in your yearly love and social peak. The only challenge now is bridging your interests with those of the beloved. With Neptune retrograde and many planets in the Western, social sector of the Horoscope, it's probably good to give in to the beloved. Let others have their way. Your way is probably not the best way now and you seem outnumbered.

Overall the health is excellent, but it still needs watching until the 23rd. Make sure you get enough rest. When these vulnerable cycles hit it is difficult to maintain the same pace as usual. The energy is not there and thus mishaps can occur. You can enhance the health by giving more attention to the small intestine until the 23rd, and to the kidneys and hips after that. Maintaining harmony in love and in your friendships is important all month. Discord can be a root cause of problems.

Finances look good this month. Mars is in your expansive 9th house until the 14th and this tends to prosperity. (Be careful of overspending though – sometimes optimism can be unrealistic.) There is travel related to business, foreign travel. On the 14th Mars crosses your Mid-heaven and enters your 10th house of career, bringing financial opportunity. The financial planet in the 10th house often indicates pay rises (either overt or covert). You have the financial favour of bosses, parents and parent figures. Your good professional reputation enhances earnings or leads to earning opportunities. Finance is very high on your agenda from the 14th onwards, and this tends to success. You look up to the money people and aspire to be like them.

Your 8th house of transformation becomes powerful from the 23rd onwards, signalling a sexually active kind of period. Your spouse, partner or current love is now in a yearly financial peak and is likely to be generous with you.

The period from the 23rd to the 30th brings spiritual revelations and breakthroughs, and these seem helpful in the career. This is an excellent time to enhance the career by getting involved in charities and voluntary work.

October

Best Days Overall: 5, 6, 14, 15, 24, 25
Most Stressful Days Overall: 12, 13, 19, 20, 26, 27
Best Days for Love: 3, 5, 6, 12, 13, 19, 20, 22, 23, 31
Best Days for Money: 7, 8, 17, 18, 26, 27, 28
Best Days for Career: 7, 8, 17, 18, 26, 27

Mars, your financial planet, is still in your 10th house for most of the month ahead, until the 26th. Review our discussion of last month as much still applies now. However, on September 30th Mars went 'out of bounds' and remains so for all of this month. There are many scenarios as to exactly what will happen. Basically you are going into unknown territory in the pursuit of earnings, into new markets and areas outside your normal boundaries. Sometimes this is necessary. It could be that your bosses, parents or parent figures are instigating this. In finance you are taking the 'road less travelled'. (Once you travel it however, you find that many others have also gone down this road.) You seem personally uncomfortable with this – which would be natural.

There are two eclipses this month. The world at large is shaken up, but you seem relatively unscathed. You are certainly affected by them, but not as badly as you could be.

The Lunar Eclipse of the 8th occurs in your money house. This brings financial changes: changes of direction, changes of strategy, and changes of thinking. (Keep in mind that your financial planet is 'out of bounds' as this eclipse occurs.) Often these involve changing investments, banks, brokers or financial planners. There are dramas in the lives of the money people in your world. Uranus is directly affected and thus there are important spiritual changes happening, in practices, teachers, teachings and attitudes. There are dramas in the lives of gurus and in spiritual organizations you belong to. Every Lunar Eclipse affects children and children figures in your life. They should reduce their schedules over this period. Speculations are best avoided as well. Those of you in the creative arts (and many Pisceans are) will make important changes too. Your creativity will start to take a new turn.

The Solar Eclipse of the 23rd occurs right on the cusp of your 9th house. Gratuitous foreign travel is best avoided for the few days before and after the eclipse. With your 9th house strong this month, many of you will be travelling, but try to schedule your trips around this period. This eclipse ties in with the spiritual changes that we see. It will test your religious and philosophical beliefs. It will force you to re-evaluate and modify these things over the next six months. And, as you do so, your whole life changes. Ultimately, philosophy and religion trump psychology.

Every Solar Eclipse affects the health, the job and the workplace. This is because the Sun, the eclipsed planet, rules these things in your chart. Health is basically good right now, so any health scares are likely to be no more than that – scares. However, there is instability in the workplace and with employees (if you have them). Job changes often happen as well.

November

Best Days Overall: 2, 3, 10, 11, 20, 21, 29, 30
Most Stressful Days Overall: 8, 9, 15, 16, 17, 22, 23
Best Days for Love: 1, 2, 3, 10, 11, 12, 15, 16, 17, 20, 21, 22, 23
Best Days for Money: 4, 5, 6, 7, 14, 15, 16, 17, 23, 25, 26
Best Days for Career: 4, 5, 14, 22, 23

Health is basically good this month. Until the 17th there are no planets making stressful aspects to you (only the Moon will do so occasion-ally), so you have all the energy you need to achieve whatever you set your mind on. You can enhance health further if you wish by giving more attention to the colon, bladder and sexual organs. After the 22nd, though, you need to pay more attention to your health. As has been the case all year, there is nothing seriously wrong. It is just that the short-term planets are temporarily stressing you. You probably won't be able to keep up the pace of early in the month. If you try, problems can arise. Make sure to get enough rest. Be mindful of the body and alert to its messages. After the 22nd enhance the health by giving more attention to the liver and thighs. Liver detoxification might be a good idea. Regular thigh massage will also be good.

Having said this, the month ahead is very successful. On the 22nd you enter a yearly career peak. You have a good work ethic and your superiors take note. There is honour and recognition of your achieve-ments. You are appreciated. Promotions (overt or covert) are likely. Happy career opportunities come, and job seekers have good fortune after this date.

Your financial planet is still 'out of bounds' until the 21st, and you should review our discussion of this last month. Being in unknown territory does have its drawbacks, as you learn from the 14th to the 17th when Mars transits a previous eclipse point. Things are not as they appeared, and some financial adjustments have to be made. However, you do have the financial favour of friends.

Love seems good this month. Mercury moves very speedily this month but spends the bulk of the month – from the 8th to the 28th – in your 9th house and in harmonious aspect to you. Your love planet's speedy motion indicates much social confidence. You cover a lot of territory and you make rapid progress towards your goals. The love planet in the 9th house indicates that you are attracted to foreigners. Foreign travel can lead to romance during this period. Existing relationships can be improved through travel too. Romantic opportunities also occur in religious or educational settings – at your place of worship or school, (or at religious or educational functions). There is a good harmonious connection between you and the beloved. Singles are likely to meet good prospects this period.

On the 28th Mercury crosses the Mid-heaven and enters your 10th house, which is also a very good aspect for love. Your spouse, partner or current love seems successful and supports your own career ambitions. Singles will meet people that they can 'look up to'. You start to mix – socially – with successful and socially prestigious people. The career is enhanced by your social connections.

December

Best Days Overall: 8, 9, 18, 19, 26, 27
Most Stressful Days Overall: 5, 6, 13, 14, 20, 21
Best Days for Love: 1, 2, 10, 11, 12, 13, 14, 21, 22, 30, 31
Best Days for Money: 1, 2, 3, 4, 10, 11, 15, 16, 20, 21, 24, 25, 28, 29
Best Days for Career: 1, 2, 10, 11, 20, 21, 28, 29

On November 16th Neptune, the ruler of your Horoscope, started to move forward. He has been retrograde for many months, since June. Moreover, on November 28 the planetary power shifted from the social Western sector to the independent East. This is beautiful synchronicity. Your personal goals are more or less clarified. You are ready to move forward. And now the planetary power supports this. The planets are now moving towards you. You've had six months to work with others and to develop your people skills. Now the rhythm of life demands that you start thinking of number one again. Your personal happiness is important in the scheme of things – make no mistake about this. But now it is up to you. You've been adapting to situations for six months and by now you know what's comfortable and what's not. Now you have the power to change things and to create new conditions more to your liking. This power will only increase over the next few months.

You are still in your yearly career peak until the 22nd, signalling a successful month ahead. Career goals are being achieved. If your goals are large they may not be completely achieved, but good progress is made towards them. This should also be considered success. Career, in most cases, is a long-term journey. If we have completed a few legs of the journey, even though we are still far from our destination, we should rejoice. Progress has been made. We've done our part for the present cycle.

Saturn is making a major move out of Scorpio and into Sagittarius on the 24th. You won't feel it too much this month (unless you were born between February 18 to the 20th – early Pisces) but you will feel it in coming years. Career will now be more demanding. You will have to perform. You will have to succeed by sheer merit and by no other means. You need to be truly the best at what you do. Bosses and authority figures will be stricter with you.

Saturn's move will also impact on your health. This year has been relatively plain sailing healthwise. For much of the time there were no stressful aspects to you. But now Saturn is moving into a stressful alignment and will be there for the next two to three years. Those of you with birthdays early in Pisces will feel this shift this month – and strongly. Those born later in the sign will feel it in the coming years. Your previous pace of life probably can't be maintained. Some things – the extraneous things – will have to be dropped. It will force tough decisions about your priorities, and this is Saturn's purpose.

In general health needs watching until the 22nd. (This applies to all Pisceans.) Health can be enhanced through paying more attention to the liver and thighs. Like last month, liver detoxes and thigh massage will be powerful.